Marketing

An Analytical Perspective

Peter Mudie

Napier University

Prentice Hall

London New York Toronto Sydney Tokyo Singapore
Madrid Mexico City Munich Paris

First published 1997 by
Prentice Hall Europe
Campus 400, Maylands Avenue
Hemel Hempstead
Hertfordshire, HP2 7EZ
A division of
Simon & Schuster International Group

Typeset in 10/12pt Times Roman
by MHL Typesetting Ltd, Coventry

Printed and bound in Great Britain by
Biddles Ltd, Guildford and King's Lynn

Library of Congress Cataloging-in-Publication Data

Mudie, Peter.
Marketing : an analytical perspective / Peter Mudie.
p. cm.
Includes bibliographical references and index.
ISBN 0-13-357757-0
1. Marketing. I. Title.
HF5415.M753 1997
658.8–dc21 96-40334
CIP

British Library Cataloguing in Publication Data

A catalogue record for this book is available from the British Library

ISBN: 0-13-357757-0

1 2 3 4 5 01 00 99 98 97

To Beatrice, Paul and

my sister Maureen

Contents

Preface

For all those concerned with the study of Marketing there should be on-going debate over two essential ingredients, namely, what should be taught (width and depth of coverage) and how it should be taught (descriptive, analytical, theoretical, practical).

As with other business subjects, there will be a range of options from which one can select. At one end is the descriptive treatment of, *inter alia*, essential frameworks, e.g. product lifecycle, market segmentation, channels of distribution. At the other end are substantive theories which will be subjected to hypothesis testing and experimentation. Clearly, there is a great deal of life in between, as evidenced by the rise in the number of textbooks on marketing specialisms, e.g. international, services, marketing research, marketing communication. Another variant spanning the range has been one of level, namely strategic versus tactical approaches to the subject.

It was with these thoughts in mind that I decided to write this book. Marketing, by its very nature, is a creative activity, and much of the decision-making judgemental. The depth and range of analysis does, of course, vary depending on type of organization, background of management, availability of resources and so on. What this book sets out to do is to highlight a certain level of analysis that should facilitate decision-making.

The emphasis throughout the book is both operational and eclectic. Operational in the sense of confronting the more short-term, everyday issues of marketing, e.g. calculating a price, evaluating the salesforce, managing a retail outlet and planning a media schedule. After graduation, students will enter the operational side of marketing, and perhaps remain there for many years. A small percentage will reach the dizzy heights of strategic decision-making.

The emphasis of the book is eclectic in terms of drawing upon concepts and techniques from other disciplines such as economics, accounting and statistics. We are continually being reminded by the business community of the need for marketing graduates to be skilled in these other disciplines and how these disciplines can be of value. There is, I believe, an overriding need to discourage the student response in a marketing class which says, 'Oh, that's accounting. We've done that.'

The book is designed to encourage students to feel comfortable with, and interested in analysis and calculations, and report presentation. In addition, it aims to assist with project and case study work. As for who should use this book and at what level, I am reticent about being too prescriptive. I believe that the book is relevant at both undergraduate and postgraduate levels. For those developing modules covering 'analytical aspects' I would hope that the book merits consideration. It could play a supporting role on courses covering the principles of marketing.

An Instructor's Manual accompanies the book and contains a range of practical exercises suitable for tutorial sessions. For each exercise, a solution is provided, and there is also a set of transparency masters.

Acknowledgements

I am indebted to a number of people who have contributed to the appearance of this book. Julia Helmsley of Prentice Hall encouraged me to write the book. Judy Goldfinch, senior lecturer in mathematics at Napier University, wrote Chapter 9, and Val Finch, senior lecturer in law, wrote Chapter 10. Heather Owen, lecturer in accounting at Napier University, reviewed Chapter 3. David Windle, lecturer in mathematics at Napier University gave advice and support. Dr Jannie Hofmeyr of Research Surveys (Pty) Ltd, Cape Town, gave me generous access to the conversion model and permission to use the model in the book. Alison Pinnock, formerly senior project leader at the Institute of Grocery Distribution, now senior trade marketing manager at Bristol–Myers Consumer Products, provided the material on direct product profitability, a subject upon which she has written extensively. Fiona Leitch, media manager, Morgan CIA, Edinburgh, reviewed the section on media planning.

Fiona Muirhead, business development manager, Television Sales Scotland provided the sample airtime proposal. Les Mitchell, senior lecturer, Edinburgh College of Art, made significant contributions to the section on design. Karam Ram, British Motor Industry Heritage Trust, gave permission to reproduce the Issigonis sketch of the Mini, and Seema Merchant the Benetton advertisements.

I am also grateful to Karen Fisher at Napier University for typing the manuscript, to Napier University library staff for their excellent service and to the anonymous reviewers for their kind comments and suggestions.

Peter Mudie
Edinburgh, March 1997

CHAPTER 1

Customer focus

WHAT IS IT ABOUT?

A question that consumers, and people in general, are entitled to ask is, 'Why are certain organizations good at making them feel satisfied whilst others make them feel dissatisfied?' This chapter begins by summarizing research carried out in the hope of providing answers to this vexed question.

One guide to whether or not customers are satisfied is an analysis of compliments and complaints. By drawing on some findings from the hospitality industry, a framework of value to managers trying to provide a desirable service has been developed. For those wishing explicitly to measure **customer satisfaction**, a model of how to proceed, including a range of scales, is specified for consideration.

However, nowadays it is not simply a matter of achieving customer satisfaction. Organizations want to retain customers not only because of the costs involved in continually acquiring new ones but also in the hope that loyal customers will become more profitable customers. What this means in practice is discussed together with a model of how we should understand **commitment** to any product or service.

Finally, the question of **image**. Organizations are becoming increasingly concerned with how they are perceived by the public in general. Evidence is provided of factors that can affect image along with suggestions as to how image may be measured.

Organizations must satisfy their customers if they are to survive and have any hope of success. In one study of companies deemed to be winners in both customer satisfaction and long-term financial performance, six characteristics were found that helped to explain those companies' success in implementing the marketing concept[1] (see Figure 1.1).

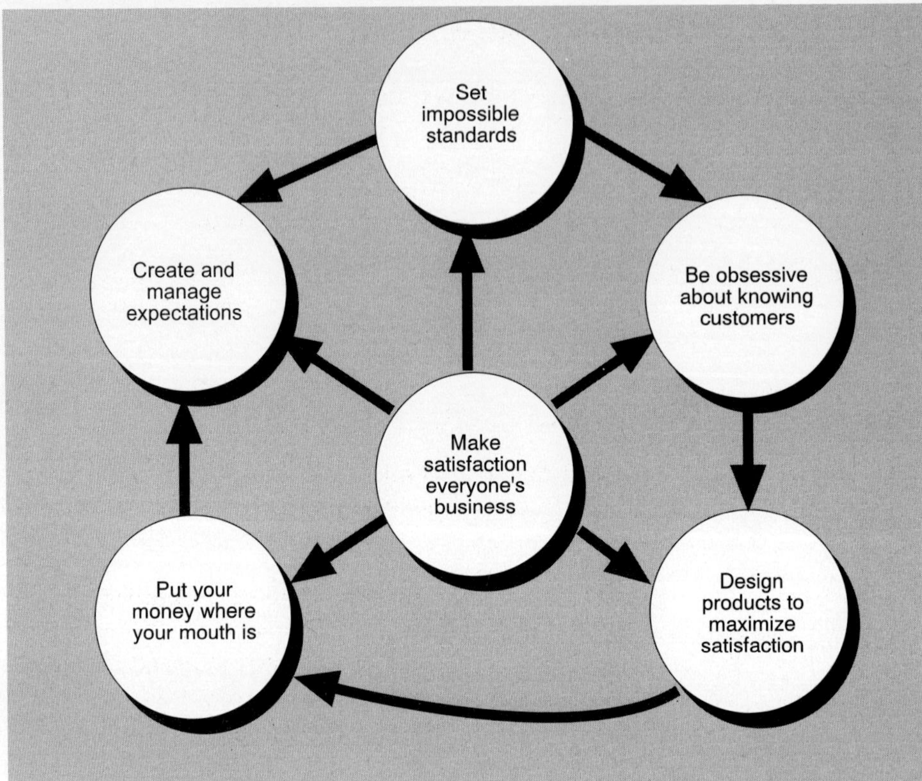

FIGURE 1.1 Six key characteristics of customer satisfaction. Source: Lele, M.M. and Sheth, J.D., *The Customer is Key*, Wiley, 1991.

Lele and Sheth show how each of these characteristics in turn, and in combination, lead to success (Lele and Sheth, 1991). Running through this prescriptive framework is an overriding desire and commitment to deliver what the customer expects. Marketing is no longer to be viewed as a business function but rather a philosophy in which every employee is intensely and personally interested in keeping the customer happy. In interview after interview the researchers asked, 'What's the secret to your company's success?' Repeatedly the answer came back, 'There's no secret you can identify. It's many things, but at the heart of it is dedication to quality throughout the company ... We try to get all of our employees involved.'

The findings point to 'making customer satisfaction everybody's business' as the key to the winners' success. This raises questions about marketing as a philosophy, not merely a function, along with a corporate culture in which people are trained, motivated and rewarded 'properly'. According to a group of leading marketers, the traditional model of the marketing mix needs to be superseded by a new set of 'Ps': people, participation, perceptions, personality and passion.[2] How things are done, and why, should be as prominent in studying customer satisfaction as a price cut or a packaging redesign.

Fundamentals of customer satisfaction

The research cited above[3] found four distinct factors affecting customer satisfaction (Figure 1.2). The major aspects of each are:

- **Product**. Basic design, how familiar designers are with customer needs, what incentives drive the designers, manufacturing and quality control.
- **Sales activity**. What messages the company sends out in its advertising and promotion programmes, how it chooses and monitors its salesforce/intermediaries, and the attitudes that it projects to the customer.
- **After-sales**. Guarantees, parts and service, feedback, complaints handling, and overall responsiveness to a customer with a problem.
- **Culture**. Intrinsic values and beliefs of the firm as well as the tangible and intangible symbols and systems it uses to instil these values into employee behaviour at all levels.

Much needs to be made of what drives customer satisfaction. A recurring view that merits further examination is that, in studying satisfaction, a distinction has to be made between one's 'core' product offering and one's 'supplemental' (or sometimes, value-added) services.[4] Examples of core products are: safe transport from one city to another via airplane, a doctor's proper diagnosis and treatment, a lawyer's sound legal advice, a hotel room with a comfortable bed and clean bath, the car to be purchased from a dealer. Examples of supplementals are: a movie and meal on board the airplane, the doctor's friendly bedside manner, the trustworthiness of the lawyer, bathroom amenities and mini bars in the hotel room, and the car dealership's financing. In studies of customer

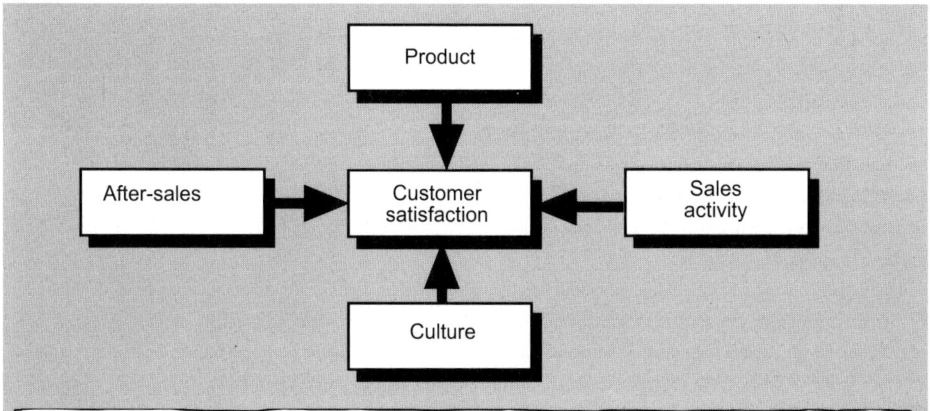

FIGURE 1.2 Factors affecting customer satisfaction. Source: Lele, M.M. and Sheth, J.D., *The Customer is Key*, Wiley, 1991.

satisfaction across a range of industries, managers are evidently often surprised to find their customers are judging them 'on the little things', (i.e. on the supplementals). Reasons cited for this phenomenon are:

- Customers assume that the core offering will be of high quality – it is a given. Further, while a poor core will result in customer dissatisfaction, a good core execution alone is not sufficient for customer satisfaction.
- Within and across competitors, there is typically little variability in the core product offerings: planes usually do arrive safely, medical treatment is fairly accurate, hotel rooms usually do have decent bedding, etc.
- Most consumers find the core of some services hard to judge, e.g. legal advice. What varies more, and is easier to evaluate, are the supplementals. Interpersonal social skills differ greatly from doctor to doctor and lawyer to lawyer, and hotel rooms and lobby accoutrements also vary widely; all these things are easy to judge.

All of this is very interesting, particularly in view of the fact that a cursory examination of any issue of *Which?* magazine will testify to significant variations or differences across a wide range of competing products and services, in terms of the core. For example, in a *Which?* survey of solicitors, quality of service (in terms of advice) and charges (for the same work) were found to vary substantially.[5]

Factors most likely to earn compliments or complaints

Compliments and complaints can highlight the aspects of a product or service about which customers really care. They may not give a truly accurate picture of overall satisfaction as, unlike a scientific survey, feedback is initiated by customers who may not be representative of the whole customer base. Nevertheless, such customers serve as a useful guide. Whatever the product or service, some attributes, it is argued, have a greater potential to cause dissatisfaction (indicated by complaints), while others are more likely to be cited when a customer is highly satisfied (indicated by compliments). Some attributes cause dissatisfaction when they are not right or not provided, but not high satisfaction when they are done well. On the other hand, some attributes can lead to high satisfaction while their absence or poor performance does not necessarily cause dissatisfaction. Many will recognize this analysis as stemming from Herzberg's two-factor theory of motivation.

A survey of hotel and restaurant management sought to determine the frequency of complaints and compliments in the hospitality industry.[6] Findings in respect of the hotels are presented in Exhibits 1.1 and 1.2.

Compared with compliments, guests were more likely to complain about such service areas as the price of rooms, speed of service, availability of parking and accommodations, checkout times and adequacy of credit. According to Cadotte and Turgeon, high performance in these areas will not enhance the hotel's image in the guest's eyes, but weak performance will seriously detract from the guest's evaluation of

Exhibit 1.1 Frequent complaints and compliments in hotels

Complaints

1. Price of rooms, meals and other services
2. Speed of service
3. Quality of service
4. Availability of parking
5. Employee knowledge and service
6. Quietness of surroundings
7. Availability of accommodations requested
8. Checkout time
9. Cleanliness of establishment
10. Adequacy of credit

Compliments

1. Helpful attitude of employees
2. Cleanliness of establishment
3. Neatness of establishment
4. Quality of service
5. Employee knowledge and service
6. Convenience of location
7. Management's knowledge of service
8. Quantity of service
9. Spaciousness of establishment
10. Quietness of surroundings

Source: Cadotte, E.R. and Turgeon, N., 'Key factors in guest satisfaction', *Cornell HRA Quarterly*, February 1988.

Exhibit 1.2 Comparative rankings of hotel attribute compliments and complaints

Attribute	**Complaint rank**	**Compliment rank**
Price of rooms, meals and services	1	15
Speed of service	2	11
Availability of parking	4	17
Availability of accommodations	7	18
Checkout time	8	23
Adequacy of credit	10	21
Accuracy of bill	11	25
Helpful attitude of employees	12	1
Neatness of establishment	15	3
Convenience of location	23	6
Management's knowledge of service	21	7
Quantity of service	13	8
Spaciousness of establishment	20	9
Cleanliness of establishment	9	2
Quality of service	3	4
Employee knowledge of service	5	5
Quietness of surroundings	6	10
Responsiveness to complaints	16	12
Variety of service	17	13
Uniformity of establishment appearance	25	14
Employee appearance	22	16
Hours of operation	19	19
Quality of advertising	24	20
Overbooking	18	22
Traffic congestion in establishment	14	24

Source: Cadotte, E.R. and Turgeon, N., 'Key factors in guest satisfaction', *Cornell HRA Quarterly*, February 1988.

the hotel. On the other hand, attributes that drew many compliments compared with complaints were the helpful attitude of employees, neatness and spaciousness of the property, convenience of location, management's knowledge of service, and quantity of service. In other words, these attributes can lead to high satisfaction if present, while few complain if they are absent or performance is only indifferent.

From their findings, the authors develop a framework which can be of value to managers who are trying to provide a desirable service (Exhibit 1.3). A brief description of each will shed light on what they mean:

- **Dissatisfiers**. Low performance or absence of the desired feature is more likely to earn a complaint. Exceeding the threshold performance standard will not, however, generate compliments. For example, parking – if a place can be found, customers think nothing of it; if not, they are quick to complain.
- **Satisfiers**. Unusual performance apparently elicits compliments but average performance or even absence will probably not cause dissatisfaction or complaints, e.g. large portions in a restaurant.
- **Criticals**. Capable of eliciting both positive and negative feelings, e.g. quality of service ranks high in compliments and complaints, as does employee knowledge of service.
- **Neutrals**. Those attributes that received few compliments or complaints are probably not important nor easily raised to customers' standards.

Exhibit 1.3 Typology of potential for compliments and complaints

		Potential for compliments: Low	Potential for compliments: High
Potential for complaints	High	Dissatisfiers	Criticals
	Low	Neutrals	Satisfiers

Source: Cadotte, E.R. and Turgeon, N., 'Key factors in guest satisfaction', *Cornell HRA Quarterly*, February 1988.

Monitoring and measuring customer satisfaction

Organizations can be proactive by obtaining feedback on how effective they are in providing value to the customer. Are they doing the right things from the customer's perspective and are they measuring what is important to them? Surveys, group discussions and mystery shopping are just some of the ways in which organizations can obtain measures of how well they are doing. A more reactive posture is in evidence when complaints are in the ascendancy and customers are seen to be lost through failure to address the problems to the customers' satisfaction.

While everyone knows what satisfaction means, it clearly does not always mean the same thing to everyone. Researchers have defined it in a variety of ways, including the following:

- A level of happiness resulting from a consumption experience.
- A cognitive state resulting from a process of evaluation of performance relative to previously established standards.
- A subjective evaluation of the various experiences and outcomes associated with acquiring and consuming a product relative to a set of subjectively determined expectations.
- A two-factor process of evaluating a set of 'satisfiers' and a set of 'dissatisfiers' associated with the product.
- One step in a complex process involving prior attitude towards a product or service, a consumption experience resulting in positive or negative disconfirmation (see below) of expectancies followed by feelings of satisfaction or dissatisfaction which mediate post-consumption attitude which subsequently influences future purchase behaviour.

Definitions such as these simply serve to reinforce the difficulties involved in operationalizing this concept and subsequently measuring it. A model that has received increasing attention and interest is that of disconfirmation[7] (Figure 1.3).

Researchers generally agree that consumer satisfaction (goods or services) results from a subjective comparison of expected and perceived attribute level. This model holds that where perceived performance meets or exceeds expectations, the customer is satisfied, even perhaps delighted; where performance falls short of expectations the customer is dissatisfied. Before any measurement occurs it is important to be aware of a number of issues.

Issues relating to expectations

- **Knowledge and experience of consumer**. Just how much credence we attach to prior expectations must be subject to an assessment of how well informed consumers are. Those with little or no prior knowledge or experience may, if they are willing, communicate expectations which are unreasonable, impractical, unattainable, unclear and even transitory.

- **Level of expectations**. How are we to interpret levels of expectation – minimum tolerable, adequate, desired, ideal in terms of customer satisfaction? For example, if a patient expects to wait one hour in a hospital and in fact does so, are we to conclude he is satisfied? (Assumption: one hour is an unreasonable time to wait).

- **Customer satisfaction**. Developing the previous point, should those whose expectations are at a high level and are met or exceeded be regarded as more satisfied than those whose expectations are more modest?

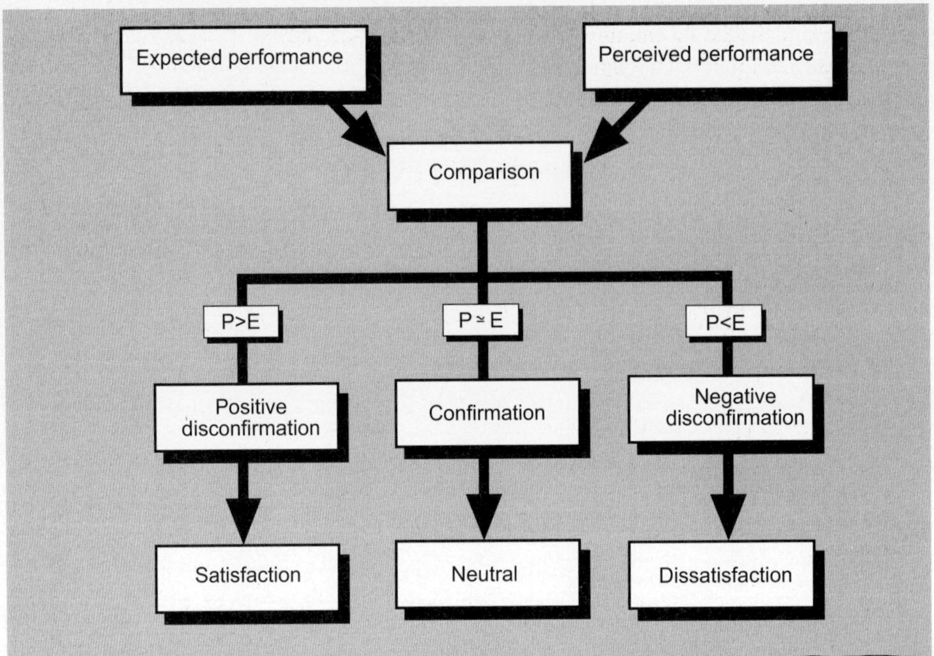

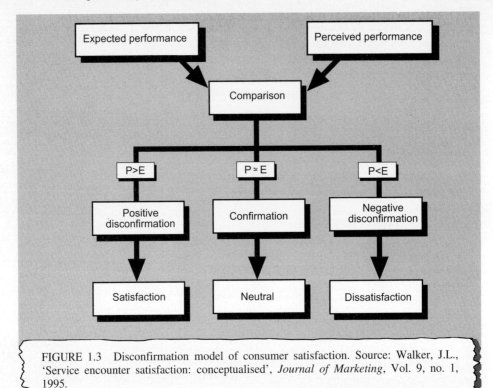

FIGURE 1.3 Disconfirmation model of consumer satisfaction. Source: Walker, J.L., 'Service encounter satisfaction: conceptualised', *Journal of Marketing*, Vol. 9, no. 1, 1995.

- **Performance significantly below expectations**. How likely are consumers to think, 'maybe I expected too much' or 'perhaps I judged too harshly'?

- **Exceeding expectations**. How often do we hear such statements as, 'We don't want to just meet our customers' expectations, we want to exceed them' or, 'We don't want simply to satisfy our customers (by meeting expectations), we want to "delight" them (or "amaze" them) by exceeding their expectations'? The problem with this approach to expectations management is that customers will adapt to this better-than-expected experience – then what must the organization do to continue to surprise the customer?

- **Components of expectations**. From a theoretical perspective, expectations are said to involve three aspects:[8]
  - an anticipated performance level, e.g. 'I will be served in 15 minutes';
  - a probability estimate of the likelihood of the levels occurring, e.g. 'I am fairly sure that I will be served in 15 minutes';
  - an evaluation of the anticipated attribute level, e.g. '15 minute service is fairly good'.

Normally, the first of the above three would form the basis of research where the statement would simply read, 'I expect to be served in a little less than 15 minutes'. However, there are occasions where obtaining an evaluative measure assists our understanding of customer satisfaction, e.g. the extent to which the attentiveness of a retail assistant is desirable or undesirable, good or bad.

The pioneering work on the measurement of service quality by Zeithaml and colleagues[9] put the whole subject into context by developing a set of statements for expectations and perceptions on which respondents were asked to indicate their degree of agreement from strongly agree to strongly disagree. For example:

- Excellent companies will provide their services at the time they promise to do so. (*Expectation*)
- The XYZ company provides its services at the time it promises to do so. (*Perception*)
- Employees of excellent companies will have the knowledge to answer customer questions. (*Expectation*)
- Employees of the XYZ company have the knowledge to answer your questions. (*Perception*)

Although the scale refers to service quality it can be relevant for determining customer satisfaction as it draws a comparison between what is desired and what is received. In addition to the expectations/perceptions model, a range of scales has been developed to measure satisfaction[10] (see Exhibit 1.4 for examples).

Anyone looking to measure consumer satisfaction need look no further than the types of example in Exhibit 1.4. Which one to use is the question at issue. Scale type 4, for example, is not regarded as a good discriminator of satisfaction. Much more potential for representing the construct of satisfaction is offered by scale type 8 as it allows a much clearer distinction to be made by consumers, which in turn communicates more clearly to organizations how they are perceived. The graphic measures probe for essentially the same information as the verbal measures but they are better able to communicate the concept of quantities of satisfaction or dissatisfaction thus removing some of the ambiguities of the verbal measures.

Customer loyalty

The traditional role of marketing has been to win customers. Little attention or effort was devoted to keeping them. This preoccupation with customer acquisition rather than customer retention has been criticized as a 'leaky bucket' approach to business. So long as enough new customers are acquired to replace those existing customers lost through the hole in the bucket, success in the form of sales is achieved.

It has been estimated that most organizations lose significantly more than 30 per cent of their customers before, or at the time of a repurchase decision, mainly through poor service; and the only reason market shares do not drop is because competitors are usually in the same position and are losing customers to their rivals.[11] What all this means is that

Exhibit 1.4 Measurement scales in consumer satisfaction/dissatisfaction

(a) EVALUATIVE/COGNITIVE MEASURES

Verbal

Disconfirmation measures

1. My expectations were:

Too high: It was poorer than I thought	Accurate: It was just as I had expected	Too low: It was better than I thought
____	____	____

2.

Much more than I expected	Somewhat more than I expected	About what I expected	Somewhat less than I expected	Much less than I expected
____	____	____	____	____

Degree of satisfaction measures

3. Overall, how satisfied have you been with this ——?

100% Completely satisfied	90	80	70	60	50 Half-and-half	40	30	20	10	0% Not at all satisfied

4. How satisfied were you with this ——?

Very dissatisfied	Somewhat dissatisfied	Neither satisfied nor dissatisfied	Somewhat satisfied	Very satisfied

Graphic

5. Imagine that the following circles represent the satisfaction of different people with ——.

Circle 0 has all minuses in it, to represent a person who is completely dissatisfied with ——.

Circle 8 has all plusses in it, to represent a person who is completely satisfied with ——. Other circles are in between.

0 1 2 3 4 5 6 7 8

Which circle do you think comes closest to matching your satisfaction with ——?

6. On the next page is a picture of a ladder. At the bottom of the ladder is the worst —— you might reasonably expect to have. At the top is the best —— you might expect to have. On which rung would you put ——?

Exhibit 1.4 continued

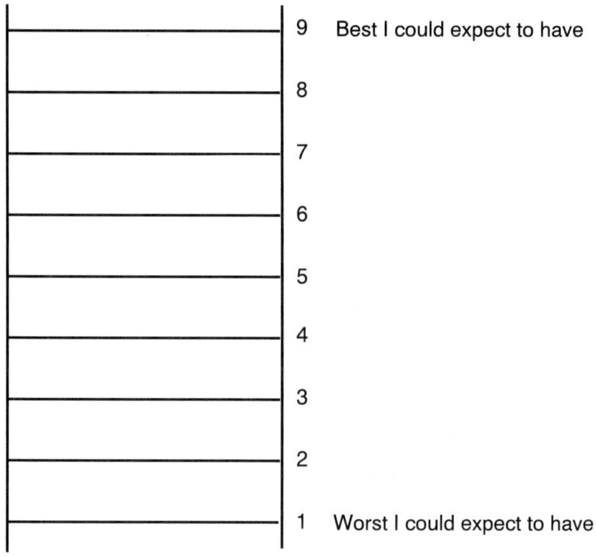

(b) EMOTIONAL/AFFECTIVE MEASURES

Verbal

7. Likert scales

Strongly agree	Agree	Neither agree nor disagree	Disagree	Strongly disagree

I am satisfied with ——.
My choice to —— was a good one.
I feel bad about my decision concerning ——.

Graphic

8. How do you feel about ——?
I feel:

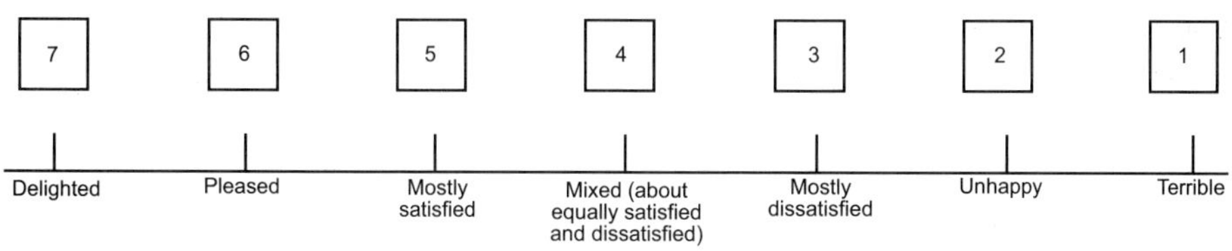

[A] Neutral (neither satisfied nor dissatisfied)
[B] I never thought about it.

Exhibit 1.4 continued

9. Faces scale
Here are some faces expressing various feelings. Below each is a letter

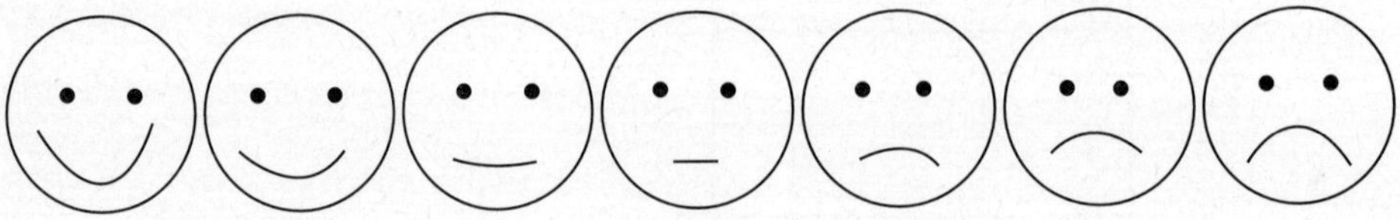

Which face comes closest to expressing how you feel about——?

(c) BEHAVIOURAL MEASURES

Verbal

10. How likely are you to use/visit/shop here again?

Very unlikely	Unlikely	Likely	Very likely
−2	−1	+1	+2
___	___	___	___

Source: Hausknecht, D.R., 'Measurement scales in consumer satisfaction/dissatisfaction', *Consumer Satisfaction, Dissatisfaction and Complaining Behaviour*, Vol. 3, 1990.

there is a high turnover of dissatisfied customers searching for a company that they can trust and have faith in. As one observer points out:

> It has always been incredible to me how insensitive companies can be to their customers. Most of them don't seem to understand that their future business depends on having the same customer come back again and again.[12]

Ladder of loyalty

Customer loyalty has been defined as a commitment to do business with a company on an on-going basis.[13] A simple way of displaying the idea of loyalty is with a ladder (Figure 1.4). Through the development of appropriate marketing strategies the aim is to convert suspects into committed, loyal advocates for the organization.

Another way of viewing the 'loyalty concept' is with a set of scales[14] (Figure 1.5). What an organization needs to avoid more than anything is a growing number of disaffected ex-customers who will be critical and advise other customers or prospects not to buy from the organization.

An illustration of loyalty can be seen from a survey of the UK motoring market (Exhibit 1.5).[15] Respondents were asked about the likelihood, if their cars were to be replaced today, of buying a car of the same make. At the two extremes, 91 per cent of Volvo owners would consider another Volvo as against 61 per cent of Fiat owners.

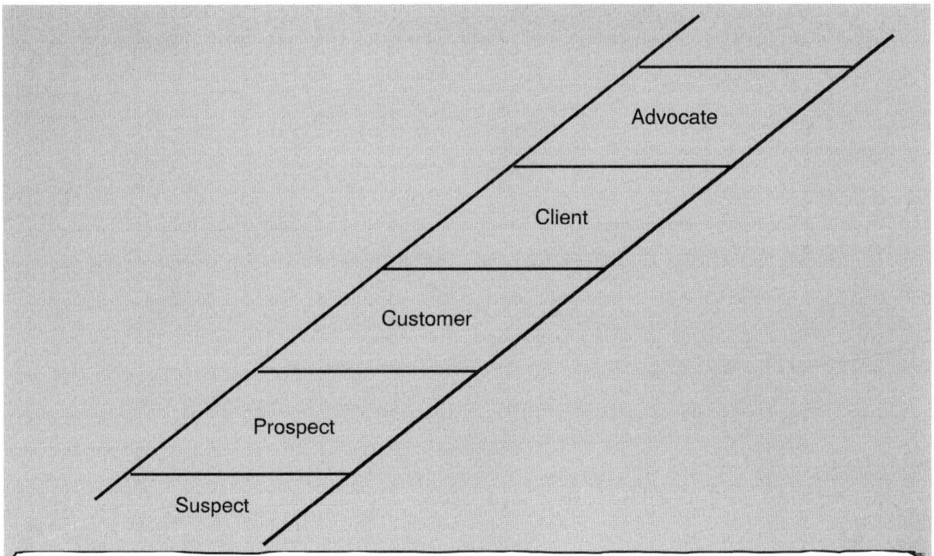

FIGURE 1.4 The ladder of loyalty.

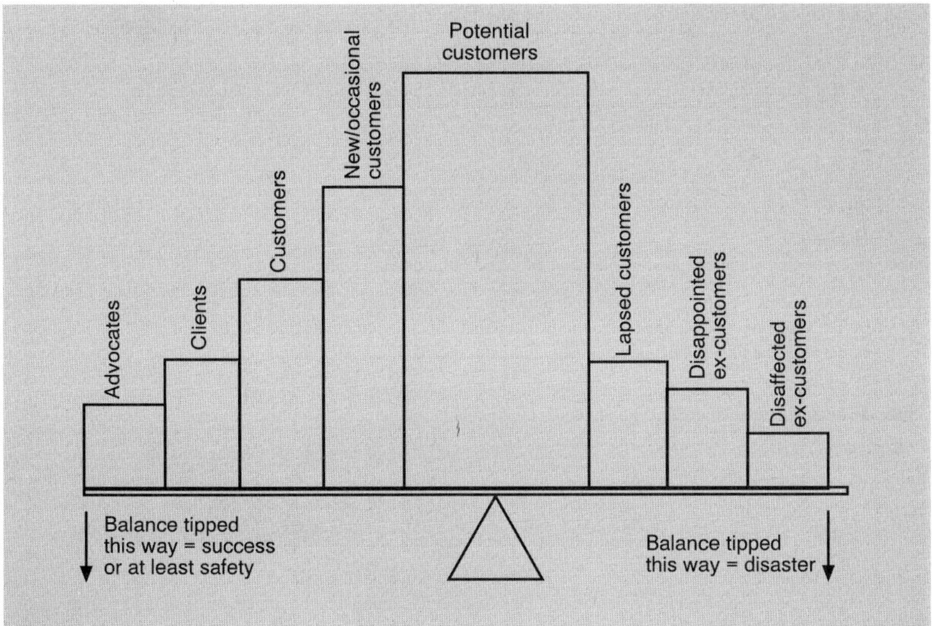

FIGURE 1.5 The scales of customer power. Source: Smith, I., *Meeting Customer Needs*, Butterworth/Heinemann, 1994.

Exhibit 1.5 Satisfaction with current make of car

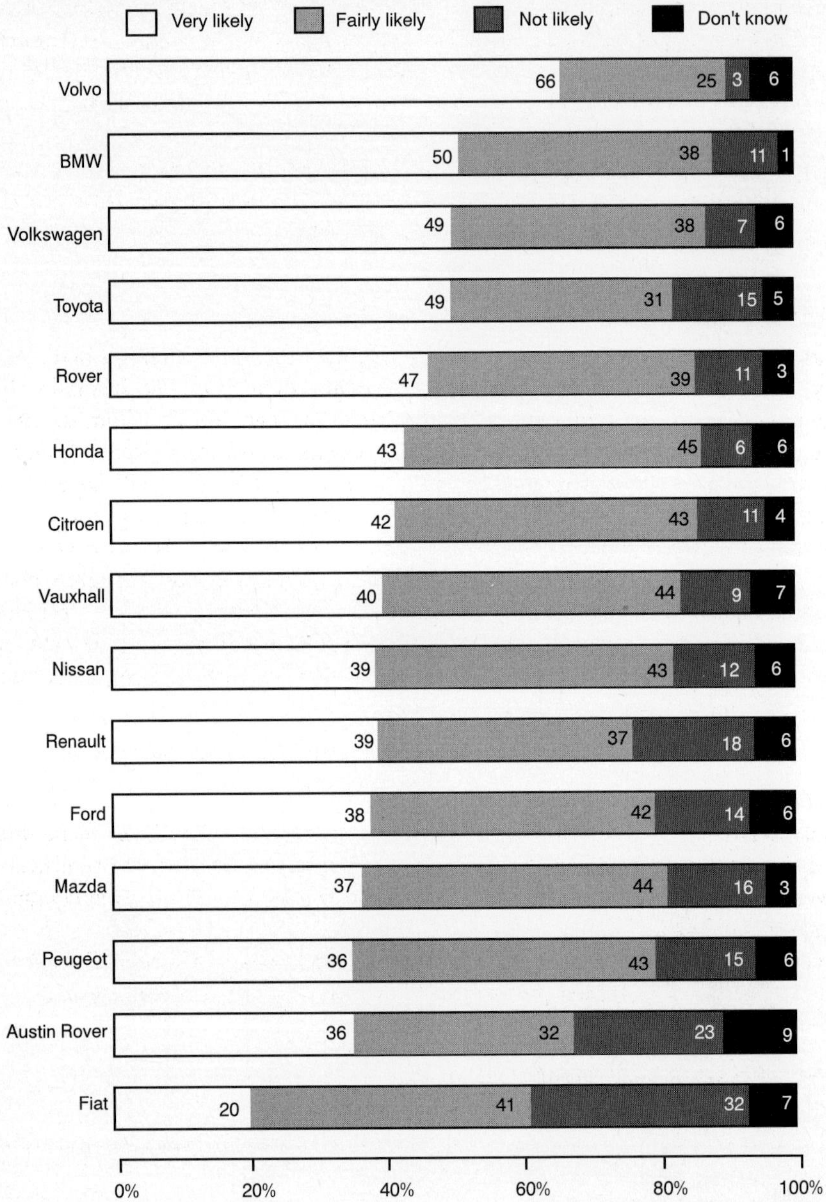

Source: IPC Motoring Survey 1993, IPC Magazines.

Customer retention

To appreciate further the implications of the IPC motoring survey, consider the following situation. Volvo and Fiat each start with 100 car owners with an average replacement period of three years. Using the sum of 'very likely' and 'fairly likely' from Exhibit 1.5, after nine years (three purchases) how many customers would Volvo and Fiat have? Look at Table 1.1.

Although Table 1.1 is a highly simplified analysis – it ignores such things as Fiat owners switching back or Fiat gaining sales from owners of other makes of car – it still offers some help in explaining movements in market share.

Retention rate and average customer lifetime

The measurement of customer loyalty is known as the 'customer retention rate'. As a company's retention rate improves, the average 'life' of a customer increases. For example, if a company can find a way of increasing its average retention from an annual 80 per cent to 90 per cent it will actually double the average customer lifetime from five to ten years (Figure 1.6). If it retains 80 per cent of its customers it will have had to replace all of them over a five year period (5 × 20 per cent). If it retains 90 per cent it will lose just half of them over the same time period (5 × 10 per cent = 50 per cent).

Bain & Co. also found across a range of industries in the UK and USA (particularly the financial services sector) that increased customer retention brought increased customer lifetime value. According to Bain, a 5 per cent increase in the retention rate generates increases in profits ranging from 25 to 85 per cent. In general terms, lifetime value of a customer can be calculated as follows:

$$\text{Lifetime value} = \text{Average transaction value} \times \text{Frequency of purchase} \times \text{Customer life expectancy}$$

For a more detailed discussion of lifetime value, see chapter 6, under 'direct marketing'. To take a simple example, just one loyal pizza customer buying on average one pizza per week over a ten year period would be worth £1560 (£3 × 52 × 10) to the company, leaving aside inflation.

Of course financial worth is not just a matter of total sales revenue. As Bain & Co. noted, it is a matter of increased profitability, for which seven reasons are given:

- Costs of acquiring new customers can be substantial.
- Loyal customers tend to spend more.

TABLE 1.1 Customer retention and loss

	Number of customers at the end of			Number of customers lost after 3 purchases
	Year 3	Year 6	Year 9	
Volvo	91 (100 × 0.91)	83 (91 × 0.91)	75 (83 × 0.91)	25
Fiat	61 (100 × 0.61)	37 (61 × 0.61)	23 (37 × 0.61)	77

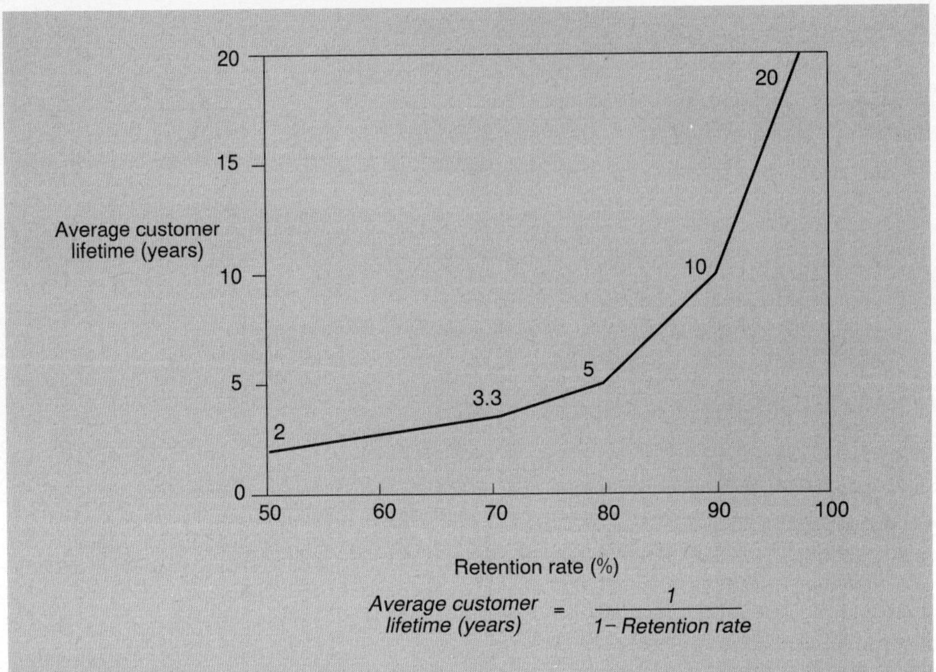

FIGURE 1.6 Customer retention model: impact on customer lifetime. Source: Bain & Co.

- Regular customers tend to place frequent, consistent orders and, therefore, usually cost less to serve.
- Satisfied customers are more likely to introduce new customers to the company through word of mouth recommendation.
- Satisfied customers are often willing to pay premium prices to a supplier they know and trust.
- Retaining customers makes gaining market entry or share gain difficult for competitors.
- The information gathered on loyal customers through database management allows the company to communicate regularly with them, and enable them to encourage customers to buy more through special offers, etc. Figure 1.7 illustrates the root causes of, and their respective contribution to increased profitability over time.

A key criticism made of the customer retention concept is that customer longevity does not always result in significant profitability improvements.[16] Bain & Co.'s response has been that 'our position has never been that simply increasing retention rates will magically produce profits. For example, foolish investments to retain hopelessly unprofitable customers would destroy profits. Our point is that substantially high profits require high retention. Therefore, understanding the link between retention and profits is

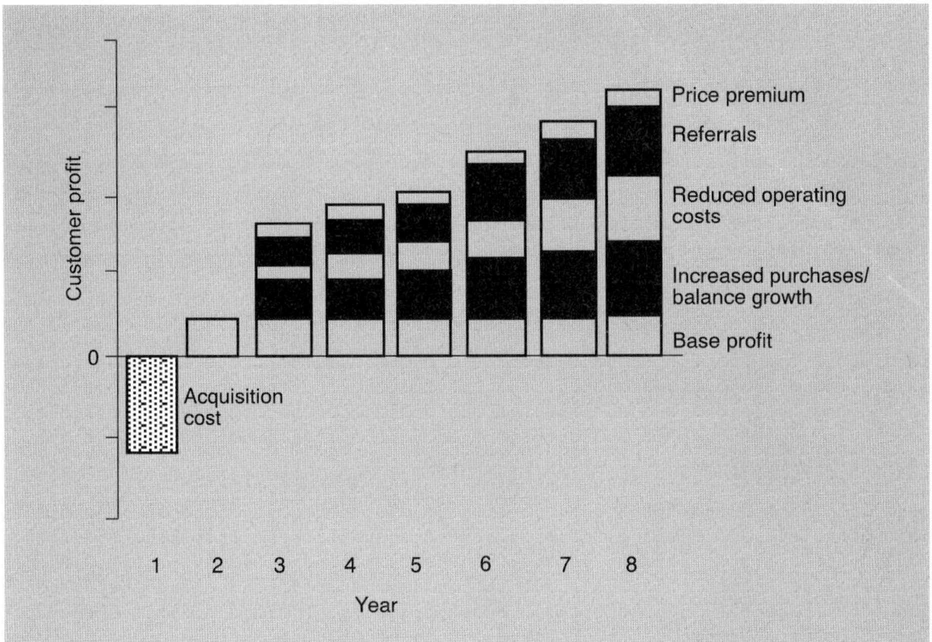

FIGURE 1.7 Customer retention model. Source: Bain & Co.

essential'.[17] The argument revolves around the types of customer retained. One critic gave the following example to illustrate the point.[18]

Three types of retail banking customer

A customers: Acceptable annual contribution
B customers: Unacceptable but positive annual contribution
C customers: Negative annual contribution

In the first quarter of year 1: 1000 new customers
In the second year of year 1: 500 lost money (type C)
200 made a little but not much (type B)
300 were strong contributors (type A)

By the end of year 3, there are 500 customers left:
Of the 500 initially unprofitable, 150 remain
Of the 200 who made a little, 100 remain
Of the 300 who made strong contributions, 250 remain

Type A customers now made up 50 per cent of that total, as against 30 per cent at the beginning.

The resulting improvement in profitability has been caused by the departure of Cs, *not* by the change of status of Cs to Bs and Bs to As.

If an A customer is worth £250 per year, a B customer is worth £50 per year and a C customer is worth −£150 per year, what change has there been in the average annual contribution between early in year 1 and the end of year 3? Table 1.2 tells us that the average annual contribution has gone from £10 to £90 owing to the rise in the proportion of A customers, the most profitable type.

TABLE 1.2 Customer retention and profitability: comparison of average annual contributions

	Customer	Number of customers	Profit per customer (£)	Total profit (£)
Year 1, quarter 2	A	300	250	75 000
	B	200	50	10 000
	C	500	(150)	(75 000)
		1000		10 000
£10 000 ÷ 1000 = £10 per customer				
End of year 3	A	250	250	62 500
	B	100	50	5 000
	C	150	150	(22 500)
		500		45 000
£45 000 ÷ 500 = £90 per customer				

The conversion model

The major aim of marketing is to satisfy customer needs. However, will satisfied customers be more loyal customers? As we have seen, increases in customer loyalty can bring dividends in terms of higher sales and profits; so it is not surprising that organizations are seeking to retain their customers by whatever means possible (witness the rise of loyalty schemes). Research by Dr Jannie Hofmeyr, however, a South African religious psychologist turned market researcher has thrown doubt on the many schemes designed to encourage loyalty.[19] Customers who are '100 per cent satisfied' will switch allegiance at the drop of a hat, and dissatisfied, disgruntled customers stay, loath to defect to another brand. British Airways has found a defection rate of 13 per cent among its satisfied customers – exactly the same figure as among customers who were dissatisfied. Why is this?

According to Hofmeyr and his colleagues, at any one time a certain proportion of a brand's followers (be it a consumer product, service, political party, religion) will be on what he calls a conversion trajectory. Effective customer retention – and the successful poaching of rivals' customers – depends on understanding the factors that drive individuals along that trajectory.

The conversion model developed by Hofmeyr is an approach to measuring commitment of customers which goes beyond the measurement of satisfaction. (In over four hundred studies across eighty product categories around the world, satisfaction was seen to be a poor predictor of behaviour.)

Overview of the conversion model

The basic idea behind the model is very simple:

- Users of a product or brand are segmented in terms of how strongly committed they are to continuing to use the product or brand.
- Non-users are segmented in terms of how close to or far from becoming users they are. An example from the laundry detergents market illustrates the segmentation within the model (Exhibit 1.6).

Users of Persil

- The *entrenched* segment tells us what proportion of all consumers are strongly committed to Persil.
- The *average* are less committed.
- The *shallow* still less committed.
- The *convertible* are users who are most likely to defect.

Non-users of Persil

- The *available* are those who do not use Persil but who are most likely to become users.
- The *ambivalent* are close to becoming users, but are in two minds as to whether or not to switch.
- The *weak unavailable* and *strong unavailable* are two grades of unavailability.
- The *category in trouble* quantifies the proportion in the market who are shallow or controvertible users of some other brand and who, in addition, are unavailable to all brands. In other words, they are consumers who do not like any of the brands on offer. A large 'category in trouble' segment indicates that there may be new product opportunities. In a full conversion model analysis every brand is profiled uniquely in the above way.

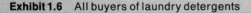

Exhibit 1.6 All buyers of laundry detergents

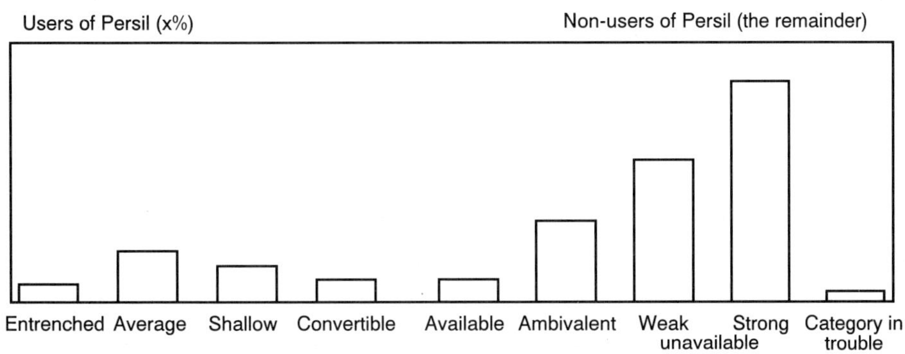

Source: Research Surveys (Pty) Ltd, Cape Town, South Africa.

Commitment

As commitment is central to the model the question must be asked, 'What makes a customer committed?' Hofmeyr points to four crucial factors:

- **Needs/values fit**. The extent to which the current choice satisfies all the needs and values that the customer brings to the marketplace. If we want to know how committed people are to their choices, then we must at least find out how well they rate the performance of their choice in terms of their expectations. If people do not get what they expect, dissatisfaction results.
- **Involvement**. The more involved people are in a choice, whether it is banks or toothpaste, the more carefully they will choose. Once having chosen, they tend to stay with their choice. If dissatisfaction sets in, people tend to tolerate it rather than change, at least for a while. They often try to fix the relationship. To understand involvement we must measure the importance that consumers attach to a particular decision.
- **Attraction of alternatives**. The level of dissatisfaction at which conversion will take place is affected by the extent to which alternatives attract. Conversion can even take place at relatively high levels of satisfaction if there are strongly attractive alternatives.
- **Extent of ambivalence**. Few choices involve a straightforward comparison of a thoroughly bad option with a thoroughly good one. The advantages and disadvantages of each have to be compared and assessed, and this exercise puts the customer in a state of ambivalence. Ambivalence makes them less committed. Yet, conversion is delayed because neither option has a clear-cut advantage.

Just how committed are people?

By choosing seven product categories from his research, Hofmeyr illustrates the strength of commitment that people were found to have towards brands (Exhibit 1.7).

Commitment was shown to vary considerably across product categories. Notice that the variation is independent of the size of the competitive set. Beer, with a large competitive set, evokes higher commitment than cat litter. Pasta, with a small competitive set, evokes lower commitment than beer.

In the mayonnaise and pasta markets, the average repertoire is just more than one brand per consumer. In the beer market, the average repertoire is well over three brands per consumer. The commitment of people to their main brand is therefore independent of repertoire size for the category.

You may care to reflect a little more on the findings illustrated in Exhibit 1.7. Just why is commitment so poor in the cat litter and car markets and so strong in, for example, the mayonnaise market?

The unquestionable attractiveness of the conversion model is its complete generalizability – across product categories, contexts and cultures.

Exhibit 1.7 Commitment across product categories

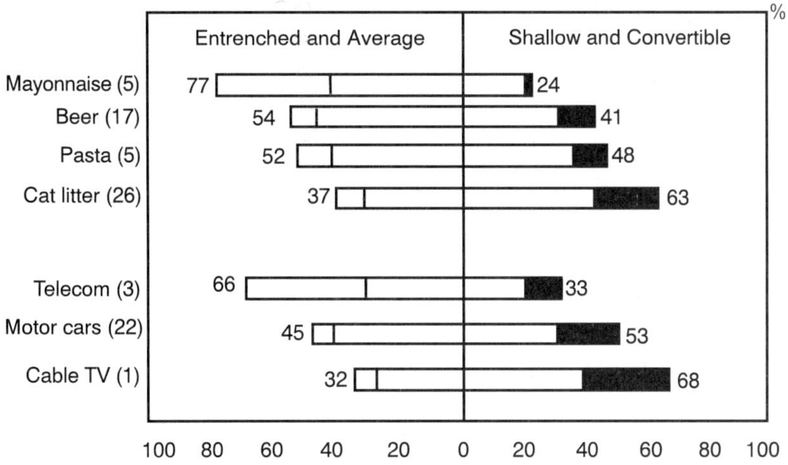

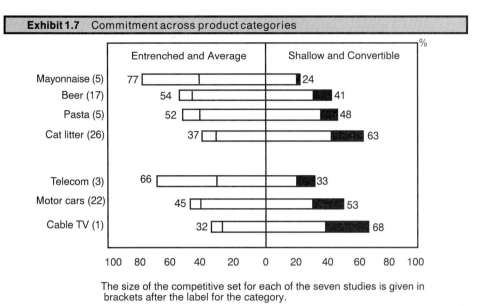

The size of the competitive set for each of the seven studies is given in brackets after the label for the category.

Corporate image

The traditional approach in marketing has been the development of product and brand images. Little notice was taken of who made the product or where it came from. That is now changing: the focus is on the image of companies and organizations. According to Michael Peters, 'in a world where products and services are rapidly imitated, emotional attachment will be the only competitive advantage and corporations will become more powerful than brands in generating such associations'.[20] There is more to this, however, than simply the discovery of a new outlet for competitive advantage. Peters gets to the heart of the issue in a later comment when he states that, 'consumers have become cynical and vigilant, their confidence is growing and purchases are made on the basis of quality and value for money'. The implication for managers is that 'they will have to find a way of overriding an innate suspicion of corporate power and demonstrate to the consumer that they have a corporate soul'.

In another article similar sentiments were expressed by Alan Mitchell who stated:

> Consumers' attitudes are changing too. Concerns about the environment and corporate ethics have created, among some, an active decision to choose only 'kosher' companies. Among the rest, there is growing doubt.[21]

Trust in the product or service provided, and not just the brand, is becoming crucial, suggests Wally Olins, co-founder of corporate identity experts Wolff Olins. He states that 'Consumers are no longer prepared to accept brands at face value. They want to know where they come from.'

Traditionally, marketers argued that associating a brand with a company is gambling with the company. Company marketers now discount these fears: consumers are more sophisticated nowadays, they say. Indeed the stated reason for not doing it is actually a reason for doing it: if the company's reputation is on the line, everyone will make sure nothing goes wrong. In Japan, where company brands are the norm, 'if a company is not prepared to put its stamp on a product, consumers think there must be something wrong with it', says Chris Macrae, a Coopers and Lybrand adviser on brand strategies.

Corporate branding is now top of the agenda. It is particularly apt for the global-type companies for whom individual branding is becoming less of an option. We can point to Kellogg's, IBM, Kodak, Sony and others as successful ambassadors in this area.

What is image?

It is generally agreed that the term 'image' represents the sum of beliefs, attitudes and impressions that a person or group has of an object. We can have an image of a politician, product, country, company, etc. It describes not individual traits or qualities but the total impression that an object makes on the minds of others.

There is sometimes confusion between 'corporate image' and 'corporate identity'. There is, however, a clear distinction:

- **Image** is the picture of an organization as perceived by target groups.
- **Identity** is associated with the way in which a company presents itself to its target groups.

Corporate identity was originally synonymous with logo, but the concept has gradually broadened and is generally agreed to embrace four major areas of activity:[22]

- Products/services – what you make or sell.
- Environments – where you make or sell it (the place or physical context).
- Information – how you describe and publicize what you do.
- Behaviour – how people within an organization behave towards each other and to outsiders.

Corporate identity can be thought as a bundle of characteristics which enables one organization to be distinguished from another. Organizations give out cues or signals through their behaviour, communication and symbols. Signals can be concrete, e.g. logo, delivery period; or abstract, e.g. donations to charity demonstrating its sense of social responsibility. It is these signals or cues which form the basis for the formation of image.

Images are powerful. Above all, an organization is what people feel it is and believe it is. Organizations should be aware of how they are perceived. Perceptions can be incorrect, imagined and subjective. Consequently, corporate identities and personalities will require re-examination and adjustment. Images can only be changed through serious questioning of what a company is doing and believes in. To attempt a change of image through tinkering with advertising, packaging and logos may simply bring about distrust and cynicism.

There are different types of image, namely:

- The **current** image – the way that a company is seen by different groups.
- The **mirror** image – the way that a company thinks it is seen by different groups.
- The **wish** image – the way that it would like to be seen by the different groups.

Clearly, the wish image is the ideal that organizations strive to achieve. As for the other two, a gap is often present between how companies think they are perceived and how they are actually perceived.

Some findings on corporate image

Mintel and BMRB have conducted research on the subject of corporate image. Three issues, in particular, are interesting – see Exhibits 1.8–1.10 below.

Why do companies promote an image?

In 1993 and 1995 Mintel asked over one thousand adults,

> Which of these reasons do you think companies generally have for promoting themselves?

The reasons and level of responses are shown in Exhibit 1.8.

It is difficult not to agree with Mintel's conclusion that, 'it is understandable that 83 per cent of respondents believe "to improve sales" to be the chief reason for corporate promotions. Companies are essentially in business to encourage sales and make profit, and anything they do will inevitably be interpreted by the public with that in mind. What is significant is the sharp increase in "to give a caring image". Companies and public alike are recognising, and are party to, a desire for more caring in contrast to the harshness of the 1980s.'

Exhibit 1.8 Public perception of reasons for corporate promotions

	1993 %	1995 %	1993–95 % change
To improve their sales	80	83	+3
To tell people they are better than the competition	46	50	+4
To give a caring image	37	50	+13
To appeal to a new set of customers	42	46	+4
To tell people they have new products	37	45	+8
To improve people's feelings towards them	34	37	+3
To look more modern and fashionable	25	25	–
To counteract bad press	20	21	+1
To appear more international	17	20	+3
To encourage you to buy shares in the company	31	19	–12
To make their shares more attractive to the City	–	13	–

Base: 1017 adults.
Source: BMRB/Mintel.

Factors in corporate image

A special question was put to the general public in 1995 (not asked in 1993) to provide a perspective on various identity, reputation and image issues for companies. Mintel asked:

> Which, if any, of these things would you say are most important to a company's overall reputation or image?

The items and response levels are listed in Exhibit 1.9. According to Mintel,

> the general public is taking a very down-to-earth viewpoint on companies and their reputations. Good products or services at fair prices are essentials, and the next three are all basically connected with treatment of customers – service, complaints handling, attitude of staff. Giving to charities and ethics are less prominent.

Mintel states that,

> they [the public] do not insist on a company they deal with being charitable, prestigious or ethically aware, but they react favourably to these characteristics. As long as a company provides good products, services and value for money, unsavoury or unworthy practices would seem to have little impact. The public may feel it has little choice or power to influence the prevalence of sleaze, corporate greed and 'fat cat' salaries that blight corporate image.

Exhibit 1.9 Factors in corporate image: the general public's view

	%
Quality of products	85
Fair pricing	65
Customer service	51
Response to customer complaints	46
Behaviour/attitude of staff	44
Customer advice or information (e.g. store magazines, leaflets, recipes)	29
Its advertising	26
Policy on environmental or ethical issues	19
Treatment of staff/industrial relations	18
How long established	16
Involvement in local charities	13
Logo or company symbol	9
International trading reputation	7
Directors' pay	6
Profits/share price	5
Celebrity endorsements	5
Level of giving to national charities	4
Political affiliations	1

Base: 1017 adults.
Source: BMRB/Mintel.

The logo (traditional hallmark of corporate identity) received a derisory 9 per cent. Its value lies in being a vehicle for recognition and differentiation from competitors rather than an integral component of image.

Companies that offer value for money

Value for money, though difficult to be objective about, is now regarded as a 'fundamental' in marketing. The public was asked their views on twenty-five of the biggest companies selling consumer goods and services. The question asked was,

> Which, if any, of these companies would you say provide goods or services that are good value for money?

Exhibit 1.10 lists the companies involved and the public's response.

Exhibit 1.10 Companies perceived to provide value for money

	1993 %	1995 %	% point change 1993–95
Boots	56	64	+8
Tesco	26	40	+14
Sainsbury	36	39	+3
BBC	27	29	+2
Safeway	na	26	na
Virgin	na	26	na
The Body Shop	na	23	na
Cadbury's	na	20	na
BT	21	19	−2
McDonald's	na	16	na
Thomson Holidays	na	15	na
British Gas	37	14	−23
British Airways	9	13	+4
Lever Brothers	na	11	na
Procter & Gamble	na	10	na
Coca-Cola	na	10	na
Mars	na	9	na
Mercury Communications	10	9	−1
Hoover	na	9	na
Nestlé–Rowntree	na	7	na
ICI	5	6	+1
Esso	5	6	+1
Shell	5	5	–
Whirlpool	na	4	na
BP	5	4	−1
InterCity	na	5	na

Base: 1993: 938 adults; 1995: 1107 adults.
Source: BMRB/Mintel.

Boots the Chemist evidently has the best corporate image of the top twenty-five UK companies as it was rated top not only on value for money but also for being in touch with its customers, being trustworthy and clear in what it stands for. Only in concern for social and environmental issues was Boots topped by rival The Body Shop. What is worthy of further research is how value for money is not related directly to success or even popularity: the highly successful Coca-Cola and McDonald's empires have low-value ratings. Although the products are enjoyed, is there a deeper antagonism towards large, powerful corporations over whom consumers exercise little control?

Measurement of corporate image

According to Zimmer and Golden[23] there are two difficulties surrounding the identification of image. They are:

- **conceptualization** – what the image is or what the components of image are;
- **measurement** – the way that the consumer's perception is elicited.

Their comments provide the backdrop to what are, in essence, contrasting approaches to image identification. Should we attempt to reflect consumers' own image definitions (unstructured approaches) rather than their responses to definitional components provided by the researcher (structured approaches)?

Structured approach

The structured approach is the traditional and still frequently used method of image measurement. The boundaries of image perception are predetermined through dimensions or language imposed on the consumer.

One of the most popular techniques is the semantic differential. This is a scaling procedure in which respondents are asked to indicate how accurately, in their opinion, each attribute describes or fits the object under study. It can be used to compare two or more objects or an old image with a new image. An example is given in Figure 1.8.

The profile of each supermarket (sometimes referred to as a snake diagram because of its shape) is obtained by computing an average score on each attribute. In exceptional circumstances computing an average score would be inappropriate, for example where half the sample ticked 1 on a particular attribute and the other half ticked 5 – computing an average of 3 would be meaningless.

The final column in Figure 1.8 invites respondents to say how important each attribute is to them, on, say, a four-point scale of very important through to quite unimportant. It is advisable to include this as it will give a more complete picture of image. It is argued that when ticking a scale point on a semantic differential, respondents are expressing the strength of their feelings. The fact is that they very often indicate only the magnitude of the attribute in relation to the object. Highly rating a store on 'wide variety of merchandise' will often mean that respondents believe that the store has a wide variety rather than they feel very strongly about this. The total score would be found by multiplying the scale average score by the importance average score for each attribute

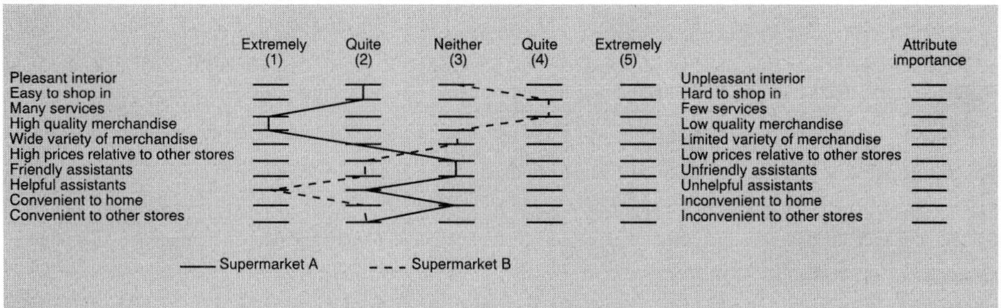

FIGURE 1.8 Image comparison of two supermarkets.

and adding them. The semantic differential can have a seven-point scale and be bipolar rather than monopolar, e.g. modern versus old-fashioned instead of pleasant versus unpleasant atmosphere.

Likert scale

This is in essence a variant of the responses obtained by the semantic differential. The format is very straightforward. A series of statements are developed and respondents are required to state their degree of agreement from strongly agree through to strongly disagree, for example:

	Strongly agree	Agree	Neither	Disagree	Strongly disagree
Tesco sells quality products	—	—	—	—	—
Tesco staff are friendly	—	—	—	—	—
Tesco is cheap	—	—	—	—	—

Portraying and scoring the results is the same as for the semantic differential. The Mintel study referred to early used a Likert-type approach as it simply invited respondents to say whether they agreed with a number of statements.

Scaling instruments: a caveat

For anyone wanting to 'measure' image using some scaling procedure, care must be taken over aims and what they are asking respondents to do. There are different types of attribute:[24]

- Those which confront the consumer with a *judgement task* (experience can play a role), e.g. store A is a dirty shop.
- Those which confront the consumer with a *reaction task* (judgement on the basis of experience is difficult or clearly impossible), e.g. store A makes inordinate profit at the expense of the consumer.

Measurement is complicated not only by the different nature of the attributes normally used but also by the different levels of experience that consumers have. The experience of a particular consumer may be slight or even none at all. In such cases only reactions, not judgements, are possible. Reaction tasks are akin to what is termed 'associative knowledge' which may be more or less remote from reality. These images resemble stereotypes, e.g. Germans are industrious.

The KS-technique developed by van Westendorp and van der Herberg avoids much of the 'measurement problem' by using a simply structured association technique. Basically, respondents are presented by a deck of cards on which are the image attributes and invited to indicate whether an attribute fits the image object, does not fit or a third reply, 'no impression' which is a valid answer. Figure 1.9 portrays the findings using the KS-technique for the association 'a pleasant shop' with two supermarkets.

Confronted with the statistics from the survey, management may with ease, according to the authors, set targets or norms for image policies – much more easily than when the data are presented as averages. Such norms can be set either in terms of Profile (basically my image is sound – relative value – but knowledge needs to be improved), in terms of Balance (enough people have an impression about me, but the quality of the image needs improvement), or in terms of both, such norms can be simply set in percentage terms.

The authors claim the following advantages for the technique:

- People are not forced into choices.
- It is better suited to the all-or-nothing character of genuine images than the usual rating techniques.

Unstructured approach

The key feature of the unstructured approach is that the respondent is not constrained by predetermined scales or statements. Respondents may be asked to:

- report the first word or thing that comes to mind when a company is mentioned
- list attributes, characteristics or terms that come to mind when a company is mentioned
- list factors important in selecting a company
- indicate what is liked most or least about a company

Zimmer and Golden focused on consumer descriptions of image without any direction or prompting.[25] Their study of retail stores simply asked, 'Please describe your image of . . .'. Their research investigated whether people viewed store image in terms of attributes, global perceptions or some other way, and without asking for individual attributes or an overall impression, the possibility of either or both responses was allowed. Making sense of the responses can be more difficult, though content analysis offers a solution.

Bernstein describes a simple technique for reaching a management consensus on how the company is viewed.[26] The participants are asked to name those attributes which, in their opinion, have played a decisive role in the development of the company, and which

Basic data

	Association 'a pleasant shop' with two supermarkets	
	Coldmart	Warmmart
Attribution	%	%
(a) quite so	23	40
(b) quite not so	41	14
no impression	36	45
Total	100%	100%

Statistics

Name	Nature	Computation	Meaning
Profile (P)	Subset of people associating	a + b	Importance of attribute in relation to store
Image balance (IB)	Number of reactions in one direction less number of reactions in other direction	a - b	Indication of unanimity in directionality (limited by profile)
Relative value of image (RVI)	Number of desirable reactions, based upon profile	a / (a + b)	Relative image position of the store (based upon profile)

Graphical presentation

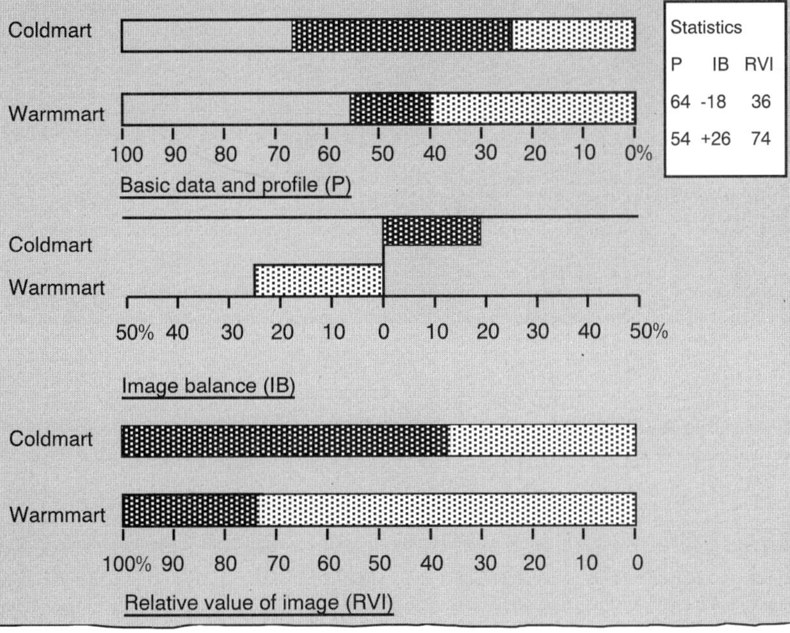

FIGURE 1.9 The KS-technique: data, statistics and graphical representation. Source: van Westendorp, P.H. and van der Herberg, L.J., 'The KS technique: more value from image research for less money', *ESOMAR Congress Proceedings, Amsterdam*, 1984.

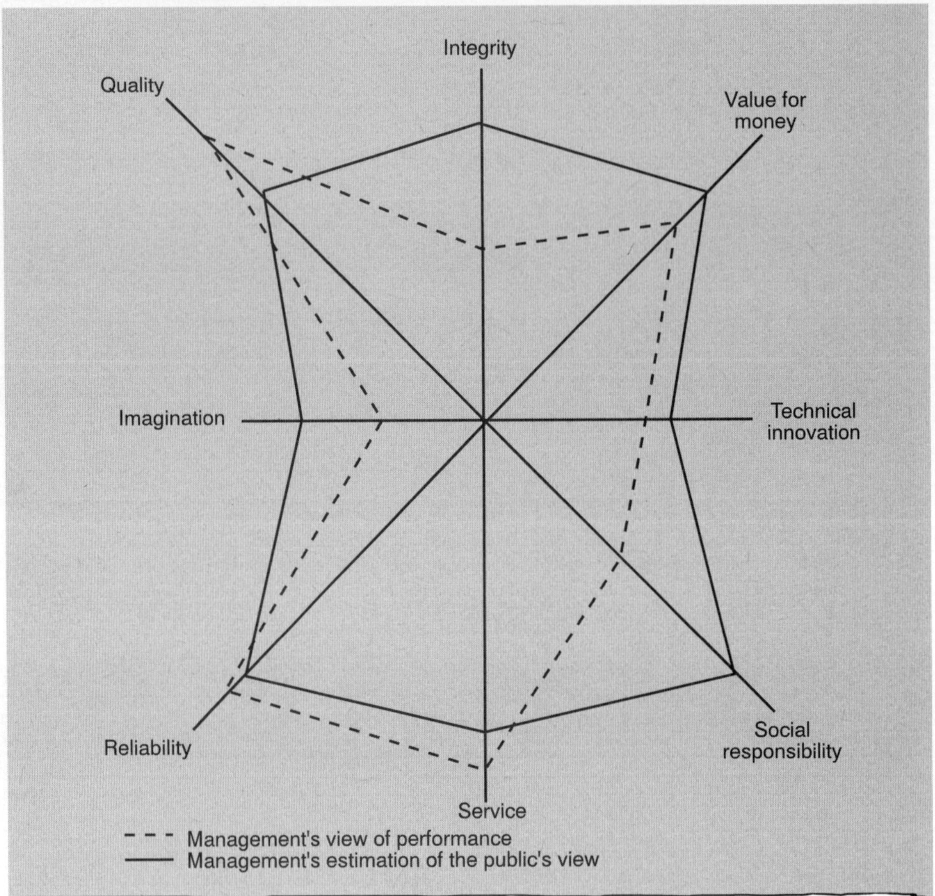

FIGURE 1.10 Management perspective on image – cobweb method. Source: adapted from Bernstein, D., *Company Image and Reality*, Holt, Rinehart & Winston, 1986.

may also be important for its future development. The list must include all company values which seem relevant, even if some of them have perhaps fallen out of favour. After discussions, participants have to choose eight attributes considered to be relevant.

These eight attributes are then charted on a wheel (or cobweb or radar plot) with each spoke being a nine-point scale – zero at the centre, nine at the end. Basically, management is asked to give its collective view of performance on each dimension as well as its estimation of the public's view (Figure 1.10).

Although in this illustration there is a discrepancy, it is a marked one in a minority of cases, e.g. management perceives itself to be much more honest and socially responsible than it thinks the public rates the company on these dimensions. At least management exhibits awareness of the public's view on these matters. If an independent view regards these low ratings as reflecting the truth, the only conclusion to be drawn is that management is deluding itself. On the other hand, if management is correct, why are consumers' views perceived as so low?

The main aim of this type of exercise is to stimulate discussion. The exercise does, however, focus on the picture that the managers have of their company, which is not necessarily the same as the view of the company held by other employees or members of target groups.

References

1. Lele, M.M. and Sheth, J.D., *The Customer is Key*, Wiley, 1991, p. 57.
2. Mitchell, A., 'Hard facts and soft options', *Marketing*, 21 November 1991, pp. 24, 25.
3. Lele and Sheth (1991) *op. cit.*
4. Iacobucci, D., Grayson, K. and Ostrom, A., 'Customer satisfaction fables', *Sloan Management Review*, Summer 1994, p. 95.
5. 'Rough justice', *Which?*, October 1995, p. 8.
6. Cadotte, E.R. and Turgeon, N., 'Key factors in guest satisfaction', *Cornell HRA Quarterley*, February 1988.
7. Walker, J.L., 'Service encounter satisfaction: conceptualised', *Journal of Services Marketing*, Vol. 9, no. 1, 1995.
8. Oliver, R.L., 'Conceptualisation and measurement of disconfirmation perceptions in the prediction of customer satisfaction' in *Refining Concepts and Measures of Consumer Satisfaction and Complaining Behaviour*, Hunt, H.K. and Day, R.L. (eds), 1980.
9. Zeithaml, V.A., Parasuraman, A. and Berry, L.L., *Delivering Service Quality: Balancing Customer Perceptions and Expectations*, Free Press, 1990.
10. Hausknecht, D.R., 'Measurement scales in consumer satisfaction/dissatisfaction', *Consumer Satisfaction, Dissatisfaction and Complaining Behaviour*, Vol. 3, 1990.
11. Smith, S., 'Building loyalty through communication', *Marketing Business*, November 1994, p. 26.
12. Davidow, W.H., *Marketing High Technology*, Free Press, 1986, p. 172.
13. Christopher, M. and McDonald, M., *Marketing: An Introductory Text*, Macmillan, 1995, p. 271.
14. Smith, I., *Meeting Customer Needs*, Butterworth/Heinemann, 1994.
15. *IPC Motoring Survey*, IPC Magazines, 1993.
16. Carroll, P., 'The fallacy of customer retention', *Journal of Retail Banking*, Vol. XIII, no. 4, 1991/92, p. 25.
17. Reichheld, F.F., 'The truth of customer retention', *Journal of Retail Banking*, Vol. XIII, no. 4, 1991/92, p. 22.
18. Carroll, P. (1991/92) *op. cit.*
19. Research Surveys (Pty) Ltd, Cape Town, South Africa.
20. Peters, M., 'Corporate unity and the search for new identity', *Marketing*, 17 November 1994, p. 16.
21. Mitchell, A., 'In good company', *Marketing*, 3 March 1994.
22. Olins, W., *Corporate Identity*, Thames & Hudson, 1994, p. 29.
23. Zimmer, M.R. and Golden, L.L., 'Impressions of retail stores: a content analysis of consumer images', *Journal of Retailing*, Vol. 64, no. 3, 1988.
24. van Westendorp, P.H. and van der Herberg, L.J., 'The KS technique: more value from image research for less money', *Esomar Congress Proceedings, Amsterdam*, 1984.
25. Zimmer and Golden (1988) *op. cit.*
26. Bernstein, D., *Company Image and Reality*, Holt, Rinehart & Winston, 1986.

CHAPTER 2

Market analysis

WHAT IS IT ABOUT?

An essential first step to practising marketing is a comprehensive analysis of the market that you are interested in. A **general framework** is set out that will help you to achieve this. Two markets are described: arts and vegetarianism. It is hoped that their selection will encourage discussion of the challenges inherent in market analysis, in particular the marketing action required to develop and sustain markets regarded as somewhat removed from everyday commercial activity.

Success in many markets is achieved by securing a **competitive advantage**. An example of how it can be achieved is discussed.

One market analysis technique growing in importance is **geodemographics**. Geodemographics invariably receives only a brief mention in textbooks, but here an explanation of how it works is provided.

Finally, as there is often a need to get some indication of demand 'beyond today' a number of **forecasting techniques** are applied and commented upon.

A logical place to begin a study of marketing is the market, as this is the focus for all activity aimed at identifying and securing customers. Although there is a tremendous variety of markets, our understanding of them should be advanced by applying a common set of questions. We probably tend to think of markets in a very traditional sense, namely the market for cars, washing machines, etc. However, there are other markets which are attracting increasing attention from marketers, for example vegetarianism, the arts and religion.

Markets vary in many other respects, for example there are global markets, neighbourhood markets, business-to-business markets. Some of these possess characteristics peculiar to them, but overall we must try to approach the study of markets by applying a general framework (the common set of questions mentioned earlier).

General framework

- **Where do customers come from?** Generally we can say that all customers or prospects for any type of product, brand or service can be located in one of three market groups (Figure 2.1). Note that people move from one group to another based on their needs, their experiences, or as they are influenced by marketing activity.

- **Who are our customers?** Knowing the characteristics of customers facilitates targeting and positioning:
  - For consumer markets – age, sex, family size, marital status, life style, place of residence, etc.
  - For business-to-business markets – types of industry, size and location of company, nature of company in terms of innovativeness, buying criteria (price, quality, service), etc.

- **What is the size of the total market?** This is usually stated in terms of value (how much is spent) and volume (how many units are bought).

- **What is the market trend?** Is it growing, declining, static?
  Consider market growth – care must be exercised over what we mean. There may be growth in value (owing to price rises and/or consumers trading up to the higher price end of the market) but not in volume. Growth in volume can be explained in terms of:
  - non-users coming into the market (group N in Figure 2.1);
  - existing users buying more frequently or buying more on each occasion (applies to fast-moving consumer goods).

Figures 2.2 and 2.3 illustrate volume and value trends in the footwear and dishwasher markets.

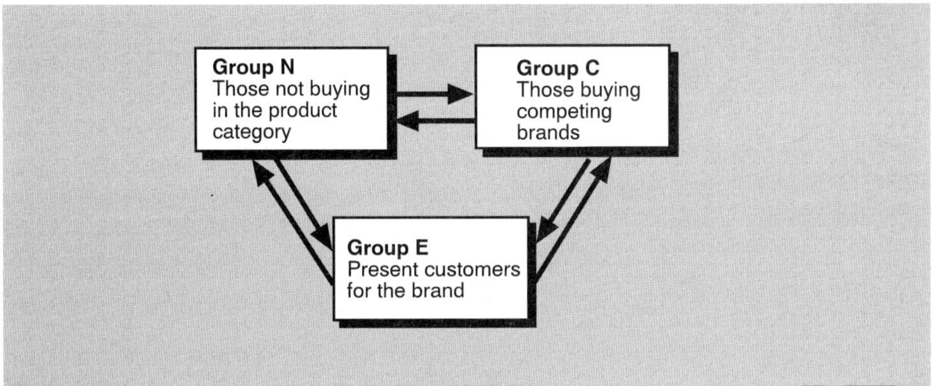

FIGURE 2.1 Where do customers come from?

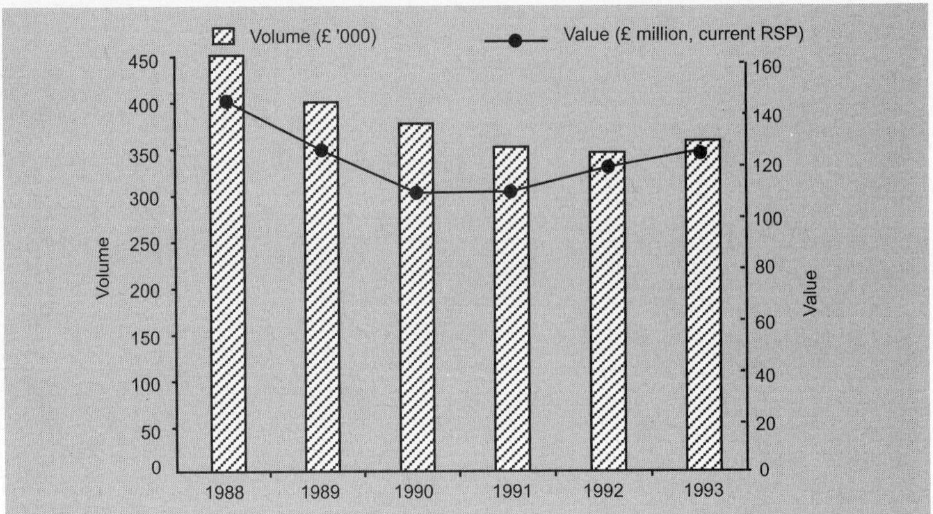

FIGURE 2.2 UK dishwasher market 1988–93. Source: *Euromonitor: Market Research (GB)*, May 1995.

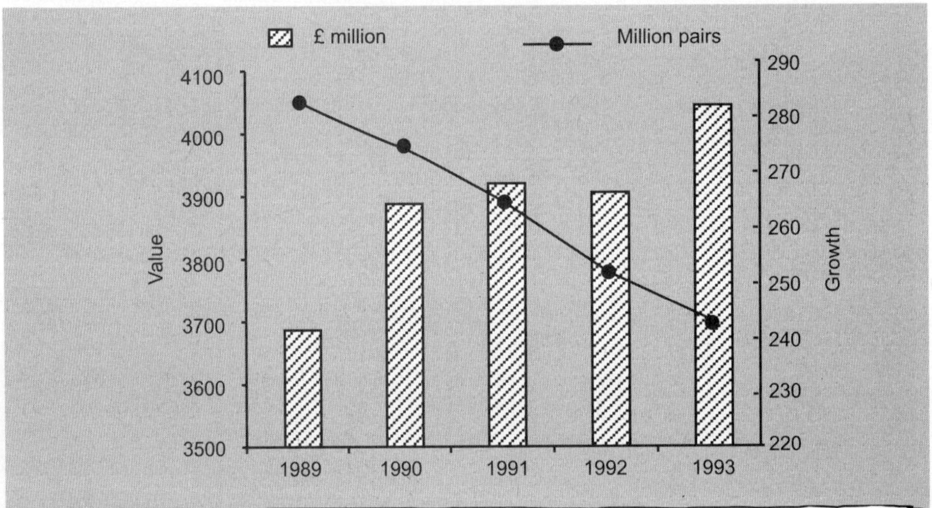

FIGURE 2.3 UK footwear market 1989–93. Source: *Euromonitor: Market Research (GB)*, February 1995.

The dishwasher market exhibited a downward trend in both value and volume followed by growth. The improvement in value sales was due to consumers trading upmarket. For many consumers, product quality and durability have become more important than price.

A number of factors explain the poorer performance in volume sales:

- Economic recession.
- Stagnation of the property market.
- Size of the average British kitchen.
- Consumers' lack of knowledge and acceptance of product benefits.

This last point is interesting as it is believed that growth prospects rest, to a great extent, on consumers being educated about the basic advantages of the product, namely time-saving qualities, cleaner and more hygienic results and greater annual savings of water and energy compared with hand-washing.

As for the shoe market, apart from an upsurge in the late 1980s, growth in value terms has been sluggish. This can be explained by the keep-fit, aerobics crazes and the fashion for wearing fitness clothing for leisure having plateaued. In addition there has been a tendency among consumers to trade down, in contrast to the dishwasher market.

In volume terms, the market has been in steady decline for the past twenty years, due mainly to general changes in lifestyles. For example, modern consumers do much less walking, in favour of travelling by car, and tend to have more sedentary lifestyles, which means that shoes now last much longer. It goes without saying that the economic recession had a part to play in falling sales.

Market potential and saturation

Market potential

Market size and growth patterns clearly vary over time owing, in part, to the introduction of new products and modification of existing ones. Meanwhile, organizations are continually searching for ways to increase demand for their existing products and services.

There are in essence two components of market potential: the number of possible users and the frequency of purchase that can reasonably be expected.

The frequency of purchase is largely conditioned by the nature of the product, e.g. newspapers can be purchased daily, washing machines every 8–10 years. Evidence from the cinema-going market shows Londoners to be much more frequent visitors to the cinema than the Welsh (Table 2.1).

Market analysis seeks to identify factors that may account for the difference between the two regions:

- Cultural factors, e.g. attitude to going out.
- Economic factors, e.g. income levels, unemployment, car ownership.
- Demographic factors, e.g. profile of age groups, family sizes.
- Geographical factors, e.g. ease of access (to cinemas).

Some of these factors may make it difficult for cinema marketers to increase the number of cinema-goers and/or the frequency of attendance. A programme of price incentives,

TABLE 2.1 Frequency of cinema-going (percentage of respondents aged over 15 years)

	London (%)	Wales (%)
Heavy (once a month or more)	17	8
Medium (less than once a month – at least twice a year)	28	22
Light (less often)	12	12
Never go to the cinema	56	42

Source: CAA/NRS, 1994.

extensive advertising and attractive films may simply not be enough to make inroads into the non-cinema-going market.

The lesson to be learnt from the cinema is that markets have boundaries. The expansion or contraction of these boundaries is a function not only of marketing activity but also of environmental conditions. In the question of boundaries, and as a practical approach to the matter of gathering together and building an audience, think of the broad mass of people in terms of their attitudes and behaviour towards the arts (Figure 2.4).

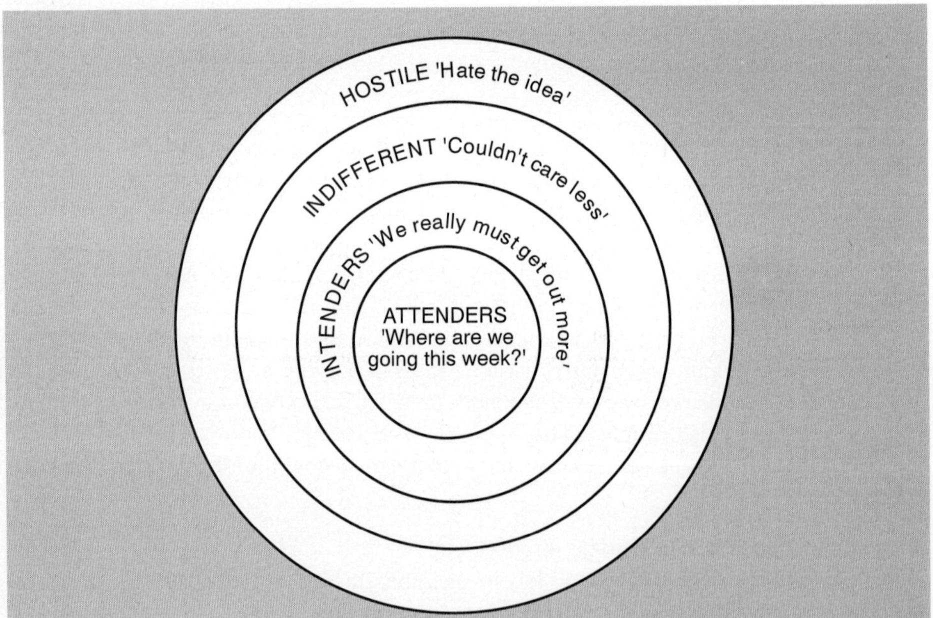

FIGURE 2.4 The Arts 'audience'.

Underlying this useful way of analyzing a market is the classification of beliefs that people with favourable attitudes towards the arts can fairly easily become customers, that people who hold no strong opinions either way may one day have their attitudes changed, and people who hate the whole idea are best ignored.

Market saturation

From the previous discussion, market potential taught us that organizations strive to reach the maximum number of customers for their product or service. There comes a point, however, where prospects for any further extension of the market simply run out. For fast-moving consumer goods (foodstuffs, toiletries, alcohol), the measure for considering the matter of market saturation is per capita consumption. Table 2.2 shows a hypothetical example of per capita consumption for six geographical areas.

The first observation should remind us of the dangers of over-reliance on absolute numbers. Based on the raw data, area 6 appears to be the best area to promote the product. However, the per capita consumption indicates that area 3 is best. Alternatively, looking at the index of consumption, the consumption per person is 41 per cent above the national average. Over a period of years, little movement in the per capita figure might indicate saturation.

What per capita does not reveal, as it is an average measure, is how consumption is distributed throughout the population. It may well be that in some of the geographical areas a minority of the population is responsible for a majority of the consumption. Another way of illustrating the data in Table 2.2 is distribution of consumption over a year (Table 2.3).

A limited amount of seasonality is in evidence in Table 2.3, as over half the yearly consumption (55 per cent) occurs between April and September.

For consumer durables, a high proportion of replacement buyers means that a product is approaching its 'upper limit' (Table 2.4).

In this case TVs and fridges are near the upper limit, whereas for dishwashers and

TABLE 2.2 Per capita consumption

Geographical area	Population '000	Consumption '000	Per capita consumption[a] '000	Index of consumption[b]
1	36	420	11.6	56
2	111	2010	18.1	87
3	120	3510	29.2	141
4	99	2640	26.6	128
5	90	1050	11.6	56
6	204	4050	19.8	95
Total	660	13680	20.7	100

[a] Per capita consumption is calculated by dividing consumption by population.
[b] The index of consumption is calculated by dividing the per capita consumption for each geographical area by the total per capita consumption.

TABLE 2.3 Seasonal pattern of per capita consumption

Month	Consumption '000	Percentage of total	Index of consumption[a]
January	984.96	7.2	86
February	998.64	7.3	88
March	1 012.32	7.4	89
April	1 231.20	9.0	108
May	1 231.20	9.0	108
June	1 258.60	9.2	110
July	1 450.08	10.6	127
August	1 272.24	9.3	112
September	1 190.16	8.7	104
October	1 039.68	7.6	91
November	1 026.00	7.5	90
December	984.96	7.2	86
Total	13 680.04	100.0	100

[a] The index of consumption is computed by dividing the percentage consumed by average monthly consumption (100 ÷ 12 = 8.3), so for January, 86 is found by dividing 7.2 by 8.3.

TABLE 2.4 Replacement versus new purchases

Product	Replacement purchases %	New purchases %
Colour TV	76	24
Dishwashers	20	80
Microwaves	30	70
Fridges	85	15

microwaves there is room for growth. Microwave ownership grew by one-third in the short space of four years between 1988 and 1992. Progress towards the saturation point will be driven by the attractions of microwaveable frozen goods and the demographic patterns (ownership is greatest amongst large adult households and least in the over-65 age group).

We can see from Exhibit 2.1 how and why a market evolves.

Structure and profitability in markets

It is generally recognized that many markets are made up of four distinct sections each with its own combination of price and quality (Figure 2.5).

Whatever the market that an organization competes in, attention is continually drawn towards action aimed at increasing profitability. Figure 2.6 summarizes the range of options open to organizations intent on improving profitability.

The market is the focus of the left-hand side of Figure 2.6. To the right, profitability gains are sought through looking inwards on operations. Appreciating structure and

Exhibit 2.1 The vegetarian market

The Realeat Survey into attitudes to meat-eating has been commissioned and released regularly since 1984. A summary of its findings for 1984–1995 is set out below.

OVERALL MARKET

An all-time high of 4.5 per cent of the population is now (1995) vegetarian, an increase of 114 per cent on the figure of 2.1 per cent in the 1984 survey. The most staggering advances have come in the figures for 'non-meat-eaters', those who are vegetarian, vegan or no longer eat red or white meat, who now number 12 per cent of the population.

The principal reason for these changes continues to be 'health reasons' and cited by 45 per cent of vegetarians as their primary motivation. The traditional moral, taste or finance reasons do not figure prominently. In fact, finance as a motivation for eating less meat remains at an all-time low of 1.8 per cent.

WOMEN AND MEN

Women have been in the vanguard in the moves towards vegetarianism and non-meat consumption. There are now twice as many vegetarian women than men.

One-quarter of all women aged 16–24 no longer eat meat but there has been dramatic increases in women aged 35–44, 45–64, and 65+, with rises of 25, 20 and 37 per cent, respectively.

Some major changes have also occurred in the figure for men aged 45–64, up more than six times the original 1984 level.

SOCIO-ECONOMIC GROUP

Although significant advances were made by the lower social grades in the 1993 survey, the 1995 survey returns the higher social grades to their traditional role of leading the trend towards declining meat consumption and vegetarianism: 6.2 per cent of ABs nationally are now vegetarian, an increase of 15.8 per cent over the 1984 survey. ABs also lead the way in removing meat from their diet, with a figure of 15 per cent compared with the national average of 12 per cent.

Significant increases have also come from the C1 social grade. As may be expected, 32 per cent of DEs give finance as their main reason for eating less red meat, against a national average of 18 per cent citing that reason.

REGION

The region which traditionally led the way in reducing meat consumption is the South, in particular the South-east. In the 1995 survey, the Midlands and Wales have featured, with huge declines in meat consumption. There are now more non-meat-eaters in the Midlands and Wales than in the South, North or Scotland. As has been the case in every Realeat Survey to date, there are more vegetarians in the South than in any other region, with 5.2 per cent against a national average of 4.5 per cent. The number of non-red-meat-eaters in Scotland is now three times that of the first 1984 survey.

Source: The Vegetarian Society UK, 1996.

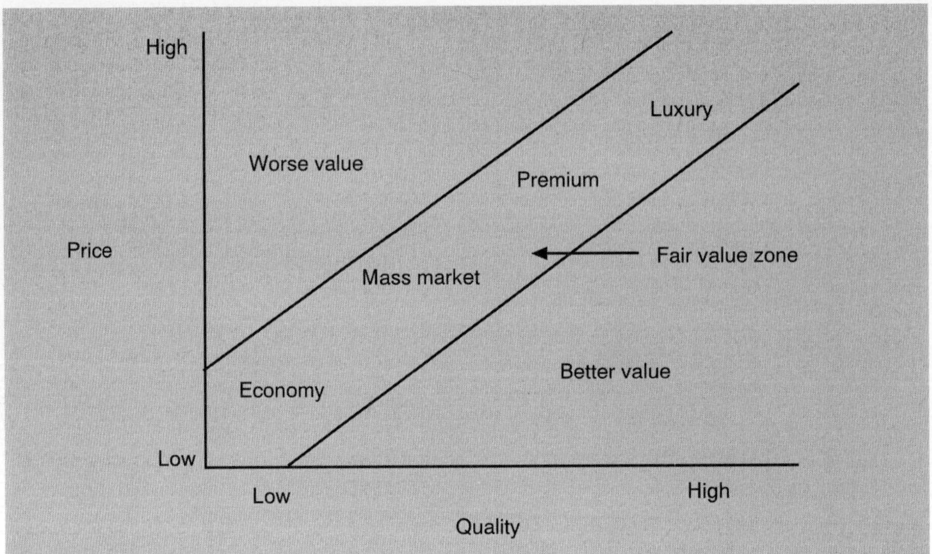

FIGURE 2.5 Structure of markets.

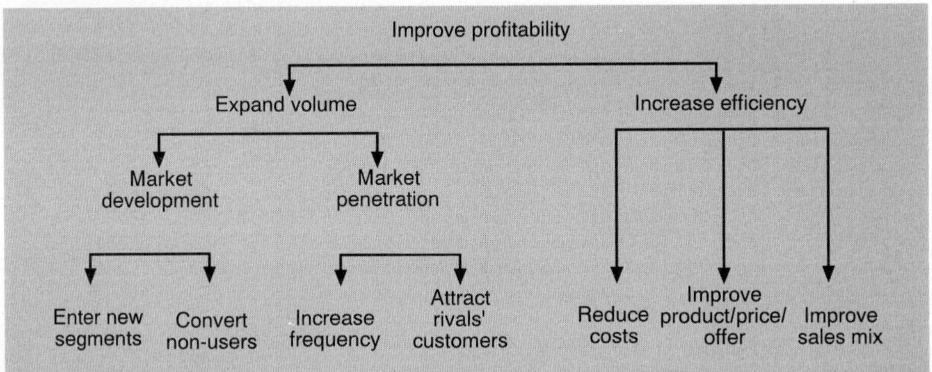

FIGURE 2.6 Options for improving profitability.

profitability is important when it comes to positioning a product or service and developing marketing plans.

Product/market grid

A simple yet effective way of portraying a market is through a product/market grid. Consider how this may appear for, say, the floor covering market (Figure 2.7).

		Markets (customer groups)		
		Residential	Institutional	Commercial
Products (customer needs)	Ceramic tile	1	2	3
	Brick/ stone	4	5	6
	Sheet vinyl	7	8	9

FIGURE 2.7 Product market grid for floor coverings.

Before selecting one or more of the nine segments in which to do business, a potential entrant must consider a number of issues (several of these you should remember from earlier in the chapter):

- How attractive is any market segment in terms of:
  - market size
  - market growth rate
  - strength of competition
  - profit potential
- What are the critical success factors (CSFs)? For example:
  - innovative products
  - help in design and application
  - timely response to enquiries
  - delivery reliability
  - price and payment conditions
  - service and maintenance
  - salesperson skill
  - distribution network

Any potential entrant must assess its capacity to perform on these critical success factors by using a strength and weaknesses analysis.

Targeting and positioning

Assume that a large manufacturer of vinyl products used by the construction industry is considering entering this market. Success in such a venture will hinge on doing a better job of serving the chosen market than competitors do. To achieve this, the company must focus primarily on identifying its competitors' weaknesses and capitalizing on its own strengths to differentiate an offer. Setting up a matrix should assist the company in

Compet-itors / CSF	Importance of the CSF	Potential Entrant	Competitor A	Competitor B	Competitor C
Innovative products					
Design and application					
Delivery reliability					
Price					
Distribution network					

FIGURE 2.8 Market opportunity evaluation matrix.

reaching a decision.[1] The matrix must contain the critical success factors, their respective importance, and how well the potential entrant is likely to perform, together with the perceived performance of the major competitors (Figure 2.8).

Each CSF along with the performance of the four companies can be scored. For example, each CSF weighted out of 100, say CSF 1 = 20, CSF 2 = 30, CSF 3 = 25, CSF 4 = 15, CSF 5 = 10; each company rated out of 10 on each CSF; multiply the weighted CSF scores by the company score to obtain an overall measure. This will give the potential entrant a picture of how it compares with potential competitors.

Suppose the potential entrant decides to target the residential/sheet vinyl segment (box 7 in Figure 2.7). Within that segment a further subdivision is possible, namely new and replacement floor covering by residential contractors and DIY replacement. The company decides to focus on the latter. A differentiating and positioning strategy now needs to be developed for that market. To assist in this process the present position of competitors should be determined. The company turns to some initial research of how the four competitors are perceived in terms of price and quality. The research is portrayed on what is known as a product positioning map (Figure 2.9).

The company feels that there is an opportunity to position itself as high price/high quality (top right of Figure 2.9). It feels equipped in terms of skills and resources to meet the demand that research indicates exists for a high priced, high quality product.

Further research shows that price and quality are not the only concerns of what is a potentially growing market. Easier upkeep and installation, not well provided for by existing companies, are viewed as attractive benefits by potential customers. The entrant feels that it has what it takes to differentiate a product in this area. This is further evidence of where its position in this market ought to be.

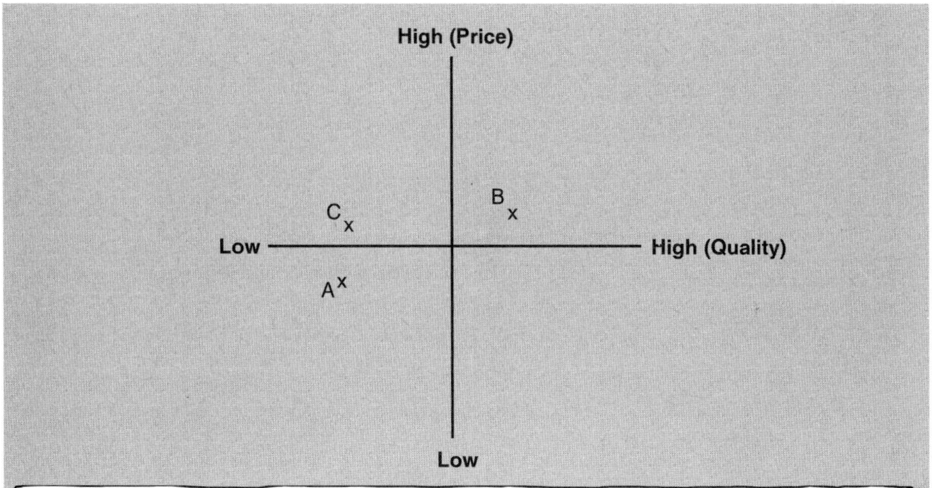

FIGURE 2.9 Product positioning map.

Competitive advantage

What the above example illustrates is the essential competitiveness that characterizes marketing activity and the behaviour of markets in general. Companies are constantly in search of an edge in the marketplace and the 'buzz' phrases are:

- Being competitive.
- Offering differential advantage.
- Positioning.

What is competitive advantage?

Competitive advantage is largely about being different and/or better than the opposition in a way that is important to target customers. Companies might deliver more customer value by offering consumers lower prices for products and services similar to those of competitors or by providing more benefits that justify higher prices. Obviously, competitive advantage results from differentiation among competitors – but not just any differentiation. For a producer to enjoy a competitive advantage in a product/market segment, the difference or differences between him and his competitors must be felt in the marketplace: that is, they must be reflected in some attribute that is a key buying criterion for the market. Furthermore, the differentiation must be enough to win the loyalty of a significant set of buyers; it must have a footprint in the market.

The basis for securing a competitive advantage are many and varied, for example:

- Product performance – sound and picture clarity of a television.

- Distribution – speed and reliability of deliveries.
- Salesforce – quality of problem-solving.
- Price – value for money.
- Service personnel – courtesy, responsiveness, competence.

Seeking a competitive advantage gives rise to companies positioning themselves against each other in the marketplace. We saw an example of this earlier in respect of the floor-covering market. One way to assess the current position of a product or service relative to competitors' is to compare the various offerings on some set of objective physical characteristics. This type of assessment is carried out by *Which?* magazine, the UK's most comprehensive source of independent information on products and services. Exhibit 2.2 shows a typical extract from the magazine.

From Exhibit 2.2 we can see that the top two sections – specification and performance – fit the objective, physical characteristics assessment. When we come to the third section – ratings – the characteristics may still be susceptible to objective measurement. However, consumer perceptions now take over as the measuring rod. While the physical properties definitely influence the benefits provided, consumers typically evaluate a product more on the basis of what it does than what it is, for example an analgesic is judged on how quickly it brings relief, a toothpaste on the freshness of breath provided, a beer on its taste, and a car how comfortably it rides.

The evaluation of many products and services is subjective because it is influenced by factors other than physical properties. Marketing, it is claimed, is not a battle of products, it is a battle of perceptions.[2]

Example of competitive advantage analysis

A restaurant (referred to as MG) was experiencing a steady decline in business. In order to discover reasons for this decline, the owner decided to engage in an extensive analysis of how customers judged MG's value relative to that of competitors. The study involved the following steps:[3]

- Identify relevant competitors by defining the primary market segments.
- Identify the primary benefits sought.
- Measure benefit importance and competitor performance.

Findings from the research can be seen in Table 2.5.

Competitive advantage is determined by the extent to which the benefit spread outweighs the price spread. Clearly, the most attractive competitive position is one where a greater level of benefits are provided at a lower price than competitors. Such a position can be difficult to achieve and sustain. The question thus becomes: Is a favourable or unfavourable price spread justified by the benefit spread?

Panel D in Table 2.5 shows that MG is at a disadvantage relative to all three primary competitors. That is, price spreads either outweigh benefit spreads, or favourable price spreads do not offset unfavourable benefit spreads. To focus attention on action needed to improve competitive position an importance/performance matrix may be constructed

Exhibit 2.2 Extract from *Which?* survey

Car facts

		Fiat Punto 75 ELX	Nissan Micra 1.3 LX	Peugeot 106 1.4 XR	Rover 114 SLi	Vauxhall Corsa 1.4i LS	VW Polo 1.3 CL[1]
Specification	Price (£) 1▷	9,580	9,525	9,615	9,046	9,135	9,774
	Engine capacity (cc)	1242	1275	1360	1396	1389	1296
	Engine power (bhp)	75	75	75	75	60	55
	Number of doors	5	5	5	5	5	5
	Length (mm)	3780	3705	3570	3560	3730	3730
	Width (mm) 2▷	1880	1780	1890	1805	1760	1830
	Luggage capacity (litres) 3▷	285/615	215/480	215/465	240/550	245/550	255/560
	Fuel tank capacity (litres)	47	42	45	33	46	45
Performance	¼ mile (seconds) 4▷	19.5	18.5	18.9	18.6	19.8	20.5
	0 to 60mph (seconds) 5▷	13.5	11.7	12.7	11.8	14.6	15.9
	30 to 50mph in fourth gear 6▷	11.0	10.5	9.8	9.3	11.6	9.6
	60 to 70mph in fifth gear 6▷	9.8	10.1	8.8	7.8	11.9	9.1
	Top speed (mph)	103	99	104	103	97	97
	Braking from 60mph (m) 7▷	44	49	45	51	43	49
	Overall mpg 8▷	40	44	43	40	38	39
	Motorway mpg 9▷	43	42	45	40	42	42
	Oil consumption (mpp)	None	None	None	1,915	None	None
Ratings	Engine and gears	○	○	★	○	●	★
	Brakes	○	○	○	●	○	○
	Steering	○	○	○	○	●	★
	Roadholding and grip	○	○	★	○	○	★
	Controls	★	★	○	●	○	○
	Visibility	●	○	○	○	○	○
	Seats	★	○	○	●	★	★
	Space for people	○	○	●	●	○	○
	Ride	○	○	★	○	○	★
	Noise	●	○	○	○	○	○
	Heating	●	★	○	○	○	★
	Ventilation	●	●	○	○	○	★
	Luggage	★	○	○	●	○	○
	Security 10▷	2[6]	1	5	7	2	2
	Secondary safety 11▷	6.5[2]	5[3]	4.5	6[4]	6	7
Information	General guarantee (years/miles)	1	3/60,000	1	1	1	1
	Perforation rust (years) 12▷	8	6	6	6	6	6
	Service (miles/months)	9,000/12	9,000/12	9,000/12	12,000/12	10,000/12	10,000/12
	Insurance group 13▷	6	5	6	5	4	4[5]

1 Model no longer available 2 Punto scores 8 with driver's airbag now fitted as standard 3 Micra scores 6 with driver's airbag now fitted as standard 4 Rover scores 5 without airbag 5 Polo 1.4 version is group 5 insurance 6 Punto now scores 5 as an immobiliser is standard

Key

★ good overall
○ adequate or a mixture of good and bad
● poor overall or some serious shortcomings

Notes

The models highlighted in **red** are recommended in the Best Buy Guide, p17.

Specification

1 This is the list price, including delivery charge but excluding road fund licence and insurance. But see p 16 and p17, for the discount we got on the cars we bought.
2 This figure includes both door mirrors.
3 The first figure is with the seats in place. The second figure is with the rear seat folded and the luggage loaded to window level.

Performance

All our performance tests take place at a test track. Tests are done with the cars loaded with a driver and two passengers, so our results may differ from manufacturers' figures.
4 The time to cover ¼ mile from a standing start.
5 Acceleration from rest to 60mph through the gears.
6 These acceleration tests simulate overtaking times.
7 The average minimum distance in metres needed to bring the car to a halt from 60mph.
8 The average fuel consumption while the car was on test – over 6,000 miles of normal motoring.
9 The fuel consumption at a steady 70mph.

Ratings

The ratings are based on scores awarded by our driver panel, combined, where appropriate, with measurements taken by our technical testers.
10 These ratings are calculated using the times from our break-in tests, and awarding points for proven security features – the higher the better.
11 This tells you how well the car should protect you in the most common types of crash. See the summaries, starting on p18, for more details.

Information

12 This is rusting that starts from the inside of a panel and then rusts through.
13 Groups recommended by the Association of British Insurers – individual companies may vary.

Changes since our tests

The VW Polo 1.3 engine has been replaced by a 1.4. litre version. The Vauxhall Corsa is now supplied with different tyres.

Source: *Which?*, October 1995, published by Consumers' Association, 2 Marylebone Road, London, tel. 0800 252-1000.

TABLE 2.5 Computation of degree of competitive advantage

Panel A: Weighted benefit scores
Market segment: Adults

Benefit	Importance[a]	Average performance ratings[b]			
		MG	Competitor A	Competitor B	Competitor C
Cleanliness	5.8	5.8	5.3	6.0	6.1
Menu selection	6.4	4.5	5.1	6.5	5.1
Quality of food	6.6	5.7	4.8	6.1	5.0
Presentation of food	5.8	6.3	4.5	4.9	5.3
Courtesy of waiting Staff	4.9	6.0	5.1	5.0	6.0
Knowledge of waiting Staff	5.1	5.5	5.3	5.4	5.1
Spaciousness	6.1	5.0	4.9	6.6	5.8
Noise level	5.8	5.3	4.8	5.4	6.0
Availability of parking	6.0	4.4	6.1	6.5	6.5
Convenience of location	5.5	5.3	5.8	5.0	6.1
Weighted benefit scores		310.84	299.41	349.73	329.90

[a] Importance ratings were measured on a 7-point scale where 1 = Not important and 7 = Very important.
[b] Performance ratings were measured on a 7-point scale where 1 = Poor performance and 7 = Excellent performance.

Panel B: Benefit spreads
Weighted benefit score of MG = 310.84

Competitor	Weighted benefit score	Spread	% Spread
Competitor A	299.41	+11.43	+3.68
Competitor B	349.73	−38.89	−12.51
Competitor C	329.90	−19.06	−6.13

Panel C: Price spreads
Perceived price of MG = 5.5[a]

Competitor	Price	Spread	% Spread
Competitor A	4.40	+1.10	+20.00
Competitor B	5.90	−0.40	−7.23
Competitor C	4.10	+1.40	+25.45

[a] Where 1 = Very inexpensive and 7 = Very expensive.

Panel D: Degree of competitive advantage

	Benefit spread	−	Price spread	=	Competitive advantage
Versus Competitor A	+3.68%	−	+20.00%	=	−16.32%
Versus Competitor B	−12.51%	−	−7.23%	=	−5.28%
Versus Competitor C	−6.13%	−	−25.45%	=	−31.58%

Source: Smith, D.C., Andrews, J. and Blevins, T.R., 'The role of competitive analysis in implementing a market orientation', *Journal of Services Marketing*, Vol. 6, no. 1, 1992.

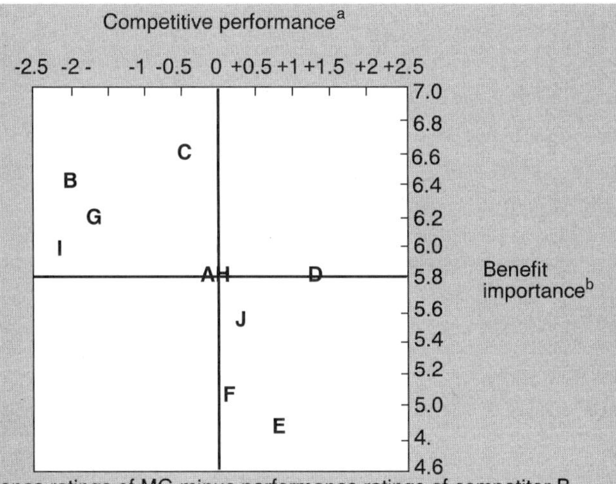

[a]Performance ratings of MG minus performance ratings of competitor B
[b]Importance is based around the median weight of 5.8

Benefits
A = Cleanliness
B = Menu selection
C = Quality of food
D = Presentation of food
E = Courtesy of waiting staff
F = Knowledge of waiting staff
G = Spaciousness
H = Noise level
I = Availability of parking
J = Convenience of location

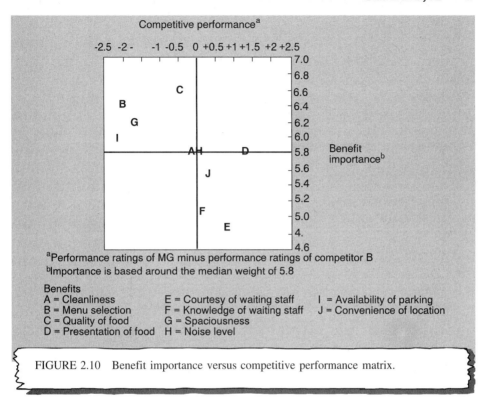

FIGURE 2.10 Benefit importance versus competitive performance matrix.

(Figure 2.10). This shows how MG is viewed relative to a competitors (in this case B) over the range of benefits.

The first and most obvious action for MG is to improve performance on benefits that are highly important to consumers and on which performance is below that of competitors (i.e. benefits B, G and I). A second tactic is to elevate the importance of the benefits on which MG performs well but which are not seen by consumers as being that important.

Geodemographics

For anyone undertaking a market analysis, geodemographics is likely to be encountered in one form or another. Launched by CACI in 1979, ACORN – A Classification of Residential Neighbourhoods – became a byword for geodemographics. Other similar systems have developed since then. The underlying principle of geodemographics could hardly be more simple: 'You are where you live'. The wider interpretation of this is equally straightforward: that the things people buy, what they do – their habits, hobbies and attitudes – are in some fundamental way influenced by where they live. Alternatively, people who tend to do, buy and think the same sorts of things tend to live in the same areas.

The ACORN classification is built using national census data because it is the only data source which provides a complete picture of people across the country. ACORN geographies are updated every year so that the areas profiled for analysis of customers continue to provide a highly accurate picture of the people living there.

Applications of ACORN

Acorn classifications can help to identify more profitable sites and achieve better addresses for mailings and door-to-door distributions by profiling existing customers and targeting new prospects more accurately. The classifications can be especially useful in the following exercises:

- **Site location analysis**. Using ACORN profiles of the purchasing behaviour and socio-economic status of people living in the catchments of a retailer's most successful outlets, ACORN can identify sites with similar profiles for new stores or branches.
- **Sales planning**. Defining a sales territory by ACORN type shows immediately which areas are best suited to a particular range of products and services.
- **Media planning**. An ACORN analysis of various media gives the tool for understanding which media to use to target consumers.
- **Market research sample frames**. ACORN can help generate the most representative sample frames for market research, identifying areas with the right consumer mix.
- **Planning for public services**. Health care and government services can be focused more effectually with an ACORN analysis of a local area revealing the likely needs of the population.
- **Database analysis**. ACORN can be used to profile both in-house customer files or bought-in lists by ACORN type.
- **Direct mail**. By selecting from CACI's Electoral Roll database of 40 million names and addresses (the ACORN list) according to the ACORN types relevant to particular products, new prospect lists can be identified for direct mailings.
- **Door-to-door leaflet campaigns**. ACORN can segment and define a target market by postal sector for effective and customized distribution planning in door-to-door promotions.
- **Coding**. Once an in-house list has been coded by ACORN type, existing customers can be approached for cross-selling into other products.

The ACORN family

In addition to the standard ACORN, CACI has created a family of specialist ACORN classifications including:

- Change ACORN to track the differening levels of consumer confidence.
- Household ACORN to target households for direct mail.
- Investor ACORN to identify the people most likely to buy high value products.
- Scottish ACORN to define distinctive demographics of people in Scotland.
- Northern Ireland ACORN to define the distinctive demographics of people in Northern Ireland.
- Financial ACORN to isolate areas in terms of their financial activity.
- Custom ACORN to define your own classification using your customer purchasing data.

The ACORN classification

ACORN classifies people into any one of 6 categories, 17 groups or 54 types. These are set out in Exhibit 2.3.

To gain some idea of what an area profile involves, consider the following summary of Type 18 from the ACORN classification.

TYPE 18 Funished flats and bedsits, younger, single people

Demographics: Extremely high concentrations of 15–24 year olds and very strong in the 25–44 age group. The type has 3.7 times the national proportion of single, non-pensioner households.

Socio-economic profile: Unemployment is nearly twice the national average. 75 per cent are employed in services – 24 per cent higher than average. High concentration of students. Almost 14 per cent have a degree, compared with only 6 per cent nationally. Above-average numbers of both professional and managerial workers. The proportion driving to work is 40 per cent less than the average, but proportion travelling by rail is almost 3 times greater than the average.

Housing: Mainly rented flats and very high concentration of bedsits (31 per cent) – this is 27 times higher than the national rate.

Food and Drink: 44 per cent of grocery trips are made on foot – this is 2.8 times more than the national average. Freezer ownership slow but consumption of frozen ready meals is high. Other popular food – ground coffee, fresh and dried pasta and fruit juice. 64 per cent more people than average are heavy drinkers of draught lager. Vodka and table wine are also popular.

Durables: Car ownership well below average. Almost 60 per cent of households have no car. But there are above-average proportions of large and expensive cars in these neighbourhoods. Purchase of video cameras is 5 times the average and expenditure on computer games systems and compact discs is much higher than average.

Financial: The income profile peaks in 3 distinct areas – very low incomes of less than £5000, medium incomes of £20 000–£25 000 and very high incomes of £40 000+ per annum.

Exhibit 2.3 ACORN categories, groups and types

CATEGORY A – THRIVING

GROUP 1
Wealthy Achievers, Suburban Areas
TYPE 1 Wealthy Suburbs, Large Detached Houses
TYPE 2 Villages with Wealthy Commuters
TYPE 3 Mature Affluent Home-owning Areas
TYPE 4 Affluent Suburbs, Older Families
TYPE 5 Mature, Well-off Suburbs

GROUP 2
Affluent Greys, Rural Communities
TYPE 6 Agricultural Villages, Home-based Workers
TYPE 7 Holiday Retreats, Older People, Home-based Workers

GROUP 3
Prosperous Pensioners, Retirement Areas
TYPE 8 Home-owning Areas, Well-off Older Residents
TYPE 9 Private Flats, Elderly People

CATEGORY B – EXPANDING

GROUP 4
Affluent Executives, Family Areas
TYPE 10 Affluent Working Families with Mortgages
TYPE 11 Affluent Working Couples with Mortgages, New Homes
TYPE 12 Transient Workforces, Living at their Place of Work

GROUP 5
Well-off Workers, Family Areas
TYPE 13 Home-owning Family Areas
TYPE 14 Home-owning Family Areas, Older Children
TYPE 15 Families with Mortgages, Younger Children

CATEGORY C – RISING

GROUP 6
Affluent Urbanites, Town and City Areas
TYPE 16 Well-off Town and City Areas
TYPE 17 Flats and Mortgages, Singles and Young Working Couples
TYPE 18 Furnished Flats and Bedsits, Younger Single People

GROUP 7
Prosperous Professionals, Metropolitan Areas
TYPE 19 Apartments, Young Professional Singles and Couples
TYPE 20 Gentrified Multi-ethnic Areas

GROUP 8
Better-off Executives, Inner City Areas
TYPE 21 Prosperous Enclaves, Highly Qualified Executives
TYPE 22 Academic Centres, Students and Young Professionals
TYPE 23 Affluent City Centre Areas, Tenements and Flats
TYPE 24 Partially Gentrified Multi-ethnic Areas
TYPE 25 Converted Flats and Bedsits, Single People

CATEGORY D – SETTLING

GROUP 9
Comfortable Middle-agers, Mature Home-owning Areas
TYPE 26 Mature Established Home-owning Areas
TYPE 27 Rural Areas, Mixed Occupations
TYPE 28 Established Home-owning Areas
TYPE 29 Home-owning Areas, Council Tenants, Retired People

GROUP 10
Skilled Workers, Home-owning Areas
TYPE 30 Established Home-owning Areas, Skilled Workers
TYPE 31 Home-owners in Older Properties, Younger Workers
TYPE 32 Home-owning Areas with Skilled Workers

CATEGORY E – ASPIRING

GROUP 11
New Home-owners, Mature Communities
TYPE 33 Council Areas, Some New Home-owners
TYPE 34 Mature Home-owning Areas, Skilled Workers
TYPE 35 Low-rise Estates, Older Workers, New Home-owners

GROUP 12
White-collar Workers, Better-off Multi-ethnic Areas
TYPE 36 Home-owning Multi-ethnic Areas, Young Families
TYPE 37 Multi-occupied Town Centres, Mixed Occupations
TYPE 38 Multi-ethnic Areas, White-collar Workers

Exhibit 2.3 continued

CATEGORY F – STRIVING

GROUP 13
Older People, Less Prosperous Areas
TYPE 39 Home-owners, Small Council Flats, Single Pensioners
TYPE 40 Council Areas, Older People, Health Problems

GROUP 14
Council Estate Residents, Better-off Homes
TYPE 41 Better-off Council Areas, New Home-owners
TYPE 42 Council Areas, Young Families, Some New Home-owners
TYPE 43 Council Areas, Young Families, Many Lone Parents
TYPE 44 Multi-occupied Terraces, Multi-ethnic Areas
TYPE 45 Low-rise Council Housing, Less Well-off Families
TYPE 46 Council Areas, Residents with Health Problems

GROUP 15
Council Estate Residents, High Unemployment
TYPE 47 Estates with High Unemployment
TYPE 48 Council Flats, Elderly People, Health Problems
TYPE 49 Council Flats, Very High Unemployment, Singles

GROUP 16
Council Estate Residents, Greatest Hardship
TYPE 50 Council Areas, High Unemployment, Lone Parents
TYPE 51 Council Flats, Greatest Hardship, Many Lone Parents

GROUP 17
People in Multi-ethnic, Low-income Areas
TYPE 52 Multi-ethnic, Large Families, Overcrowding
TYPE 53 Multi-ethnic, Severe Unemployment, Lone Parents
TYPE 54 Multi-ethnic, High Unemployment, Overcrowding

Source: *ACORN User Guide*, CACI Information Services.

Media: Readership of the *Guardian* is 3.2 times higher than average. Other popular papers are the *Mail*, the *Observer*, the *Sunday Times* and the *Independent on Sunday*. ITV viewing and commercial radio listening are extremely light.

Leisure: People here are 88 per cent more likely than average to holiday abroad. They are out and about in pubs, wine bars and restaurants a great deal. Participation in sports is slightly above average. The exception is waterskiing which is done by nearly 5 times more people than average. Art gallery attendance in this group is 18 times more likely than average. Cinema and theatre attendance are 3–4 times higher than average.

Attitudes: People in this type are over 3 times more likely than average to be vegetarian. They love to buy new gadgets, keep up with developments in technology and enjoy television and radio commercials. They believe well-known brands are better than own label.

By far the largest concentration of this type is in inner London in areas such as Kensington and Chelsea. There are concentrations in other parts of Britain, however, such as Bournemouth, Hove and Brighton.[4]

ACORN can become even more effective when used in conjunction with market research data such as BMRB's Target Group Index (TGI) or the National Readership Survey (NRS). The respondents to these surveys can be coded by ACORN so consumption of any product or service can be analyzed.

The Target Group Index

The TGI is a continuous survey which has been carried out in Great Britain every year since 1969, in Northern Ireland since 1992, and in the Republic of Ireland since 1994. The name Target Group Index derives from its primary use: to describe, as accurately as possible, the characteristics of target groups of consumers. For this reason it is heavily used by advertisers, advertising agencies and media owners to help develop more efficient marketing strategies and advertising campaigns. TGI gathers data on the use and purchase by consumers of over 4000 brands within more than 500 product fields.

Reading TGI tables

To show what TGI data look like, an extract is given in Exhibit 2.4.

Referring to the boxed section in Exhibit 2.4, the data should be read as follows:

- Column A – the projected number of people in thousands who are users in that subgroup. Thus 250 000 women aged 55–64 play bingo.
- Column B – the percentage of all those in the group defined by the column label, who also fall into the group defined by the row label. Thus, of all the age groups playing bingo, 13.8 per cent are in the 55–64 category (250 000/1 809 000). This is termed 'profile data'; in media tables it is termed 'coverage data'.
- Column C – the percentage of those in the group defined by the row label who also fall into the group defined by the column label. Thus 8.7 per cent of women aged between 55–64 play bingo (250 000/2 878 000). This is termed 'penetration data'; in media tables it is 'composition data'.
- Column D – an index of selectivity, or the propensity of the group defined by the row label to be included in the group defined by the column label. It is obtained by indexing the percentage figure in column C against the percentage for the universe concerned. An index of 100 equates to parity with the national average; over 100 indicates a greater propensity to fall into the group described by the column heading; under 100 indicates the reverse. Thus for the age group 55–64 the index of 112 is found by dividing 8.7 by 7.7. Thus the incidence of bingo playing in this age group is 12 per cent above the average.

In addition to the above analysis we can conclude that women playing bingo:

- are mainly from socio-economic groups C2, D and E;
- tend to read the *Daily Mirror, Daily Record* and the *Sun* (not shown in Exhibit 2.4);
- are well above-average in terms of cigarette smoking.

As mentioned earlier, ACORN analysis is further enhanced when used along with TGI data. Exhibit 2.5 is an extract from a detailed market analysis of the consumption of Irn Bru.

Exhibit 2.4 Target Group Index data 1994

SPORTS AND LEISURE ACTIVITIES – WOMEN

30052	POPULATION	BINGO				DANCING				FOOTBALL POOLS				BET ON FOOTBALL MATCH				HORSE RACING-BET SHOP			
	'000	A '000	B % down	C % across	D index	A '000	B % down	C % across	D index	A '000	B % down	C % across	D index	A '000	B % down	C % across	D index	A '000	B % down	C % across	D index
ALL WOMEN	23451	1809	100.0	7.7	100	3365	100.0	14.3	100	4347	100.0	18.5	100	1101	100.0	4.7	100	862	100.0	3.7	100
15-19	1710	60	3.3	3.5	46	768	22.8	44.9	313	80	1.8	4.7	25	40	3.6	2.3	50	54	6.3	3.2	86
20-24	1919	175	9.7	9.1	118	670	19.9	34.9	243	238	5.5	12.4	67	53	4.9	2.8	59	66	7.7	3.4	94
25-34	4410	357	19.7	8.1	105	793	23.6	18.0	125	788	18.1	17.9	96	143	13.0	3.3	69	190	22.0	4.3	117
35-44	3756	270	14.9	7.2	93	356	10.6	9.5	66	949	21.8	25.3	136	175	15.9	4.7	99	119	13.8	3.2	86
45-54	3479	280	15.5	8.0	104	244	7.3	7.0	49	837	19.3	24.1	130	232	21.1	6.7	142	146	17.0	4.2	114
55-64	2878	250	13.8	8.7	112	213	6.3	7.4	52	659	15.2	22.9	123	211	19.2	7.3	157	133	15.4	4.6	125
65+	5299	417	23.1	7.9	102	321	9.5	6.1	42	795	18.3	15.0	81	245	22.3	4.6	99	155	17.9	2.9	79
AB	4506	81	4.5	1.8	23	452	13.4	10.0	70	536	12.3	11.9	64	150	13.7	3.3	71	96	11.1	2.1	58
C1	6577	319	17.6	4.8	63	1105	32.9	16.8	117	1172	27.0	17.8	96	265	24.0	4.0	86	206	23.8	3.1	85
C2	5110	467	25.8	9.1	119	758	22.5	14.8	103	1278	29.4	25.0	135	276	25.1	5.4	115	185	21.5	3.6	99
D	3838	505	27.9	13.2	171	595	17.7	15.5	108	868	20.0	22.6	122	250	22.7	6.5	139	206	23.9	5.4	146
E	3421	437	24.1	12.8	166	454	13.5	13.3	92	492	11.3	14.4	78	160	14.5	4.7	100	170	19.7	5.0	135
GREATER LONDON	2829	199	11.0	7.0	91	404	12.0	14.3	99	372	8.6	13.2	71	108	9.8	3.8	82	97	11.2	3.4	93
SOUTH EAST/EAST ANGLIA	5396	289	16.0	5.4	70	663	19.7	12.3	86	901	20.7	16.7	90	229	20.8	4.2	90	168	19.5	3.1	85
SOUTH WEST	1973	90	5.0	4.6	59	351	10.4	17.8	124	278	6.4	14.1	76	85	7.7	4.3	91	82	9.5	4.1	113
WALES	1222	130	7.2	10.7	138	140	4.2	11.5	80	239	5.5	19.6	106	59	5.4	4.9	104	33	3.8	2.7	72
EAST & WEST MIDLANDS	3890	274	15.2	7.1	91	503	14.9	12.9	90	786	18.1	20.2	109	202	18.4	5.2	111	138	16.0	3.5	96
NORTH WEST	2676	227	12.6	8.5	110	409	12.1	15.3	106	615	14.1	23.0	124	156	14.2	5.8	124	140	16.2	5.2	142
YORKSHIRE & HUMBERSIDE	2037	153	8.5	7.5	98	311	9.2	15.3	106	447	10.3	21.9	118	69	6.2	3.4	72	65	7.5	3.2	86
NORTH	1329	166	9.2	12.5	162	231	6.9	17.4	121	300	6.9	22.6	122	70	6.4	5.3	113	65	7.5	4.9	133
SCOTLAND	2100	279	15.4	13.3	172	353	10.5	16.8	117	410	9.4	19.5	105	122	11.1	5.8	124	76	8.8	3.6	98
LONDON	5694	326	18.0	5.7	74	743	22.1	13.0	91	868	20.0	15.3	82	214	19.5	3.8	80	193	22.4	3.4	92
SOUTH	2627	122	6.7	4.6	60	316	9.4	12.0	84	476	11.0	18.1	98	108	9.8	4.1	88	97	11.2	3.7	100
EAST OF ENGLAND	2096	150	8.3	7.1	93	269	8.0	12.8	90	324	7.5	15.5	83	89	8.0	4.2	90	76	8.8	3.6	99
SOUTH WEST	811	46	2.5	5.7	74	124	3.7	15.3	107	104	2.4	12.8	69	37	3.3	4.5	97	30	3.5	3.7	100
WALES & WEST	2211	174	9.6	7.9	102	325	9.7	14.7	102	395	9.1	17.9	96	101	9.1	4.5	97	79	9.1	3.6	97
MIDLANDS	4659	332	18.3	7.1	92	634	18.8	13.6	95	908	20.9	19.5	105	249	22.6	5.3	114	154	17.8	3.3	90
NORTH WEST	3041	247	13.7	8.1	105	439	13.0	14.4	101	679	15.6	22.3	120	167	15.2	5.5	117	144	16.7	4.7	129
YORKSHIRE	2763	207	11.4	7.5	97	398	11.8	14.4	100	603	13.9	21.8	118	101	9.1	3.6	78	95	11.0	3.4	93
NORTH EAST	1410	157	8.7	11.2	145	221	6.6	15.7	109	330	7.6	23.4	126	68	6.1	4.8	102	65	7.5	4.6	125
CENTRAL SCOTLAND	1597	218	12.0	13.6	177	278	8.2	17.4	121	319	7.3	20.0	108	98	8.9	6.1	130	64	7.4	4.0	109
NORTH EAST SCOTLAND	572	81	4.5	14.2	184	84	2.5	14.7	103	109	2.5	19.1	103	35	3.2	6.1	131	17	1.9	2.9	79
BORDER	314	25	1.4	7.9	102	54	1.6	17.1	119	52	1.2	16.6	90	13	1.2	4.2	89	10	1.1	3.0	82
H/D INCOME £35,000 OR MORE	1648	38	2.1	2.3	30	250	7.4	15.2	106	222	5.1	13.5	73	36	3.3	2.2	46	46	5.3	2.8	75
£25,000 - £34,999	2260	98	5.4	4.3	56	312	9.3	13.8	96	459	10.6	20.3	110	76	6.9	3.4	72	65	7.5	2.9	78
£20,000 - £24,999	2063	110	6.1	5.3	69	301	8.9	14.6	102	405	9.3	19.6	106	100	9.1	4.9	103	64	7.5	3.1	85
£15,000 - £19,999	2308	173	9.5	7.5	97	332	9.9	14.4	100	574	13.2	24.9	134	121	11.0	5.2	112	69	8.0	3.0	81
£11,000 - £14,999	2394	165	9.1	6.9	89	361	10.7	15.1	105	555	12.8	23.2	125	130	11.8	5.4	116	82	9.5	3.4	93
£5,000 - £10,999	3796	331	18.3	8.7	113	550	16.4	14.5	101	827	19.0	21.8	118	211	19.1	5.5	118	176	20.4	4.6	126
£4,999 OR LESS	2807	341	18.9	12.2	158	427	12.7	15.2	106	463	10.7	16.5	89	146	13.3	5.2	111	128	14.8	4.5	124
NOT STATED	6176	554	30.6	9.0	116	832	24.7	13.5	94	842	19.4	13.6	74	280	25.5	4.5	97	233	27.0	3.8	102
NO CHILDREN IN HOUSEHOLD	15493	1165	64.4	7.5	98	2033	60.4	13.1	91	2854	65.7	18.4	99	804	73.1	5.2	111	614	71.2	4.0	108
CHILD(REN) UNDER 1 YEAR	639	65	3.6	10.1	131	97	2.9	15.2	106	99	2.3	15.5	84	13	1.2	2.1	45	27	3.1	4.2	115
1 - 4 YEARS	3134	271	15.0	8.6	112	454	13.5	14.5	101	547	12.6	17.5	94	108	9.8	3.5	74	104	12.0	3.3	90
5 - 9 YEARS	3379	319	17.6	9.4	122	532	15.8	15.7	110	660	15.2	19.5	105	101	9.2	3.0	64	116	13.4	3.4	93
10 - 15 YEARS	3977	327	18.1	8.2	107	699	20.8	17.6	122	815	18.7	20.5	111	179	16.2	4.5	96	131	15.2	3.3	89
SMOKE CIGARETTES	6485	851	47.0	13.1	170	1239	36.8	19.1	133	1428	32.9	22.0	119	404	36.7	6.2	133	339	39.3	5.2	142
DRINK ALCOHOLIC DRINKS	20808	1628	90.0	7.8	101	3164	94.0	15.2	106	3967	91.3	19.1	103	1013	92.0	4.9	104	802	93.0	3.9	105
CAR IN H/D,DRIVING LIC,BUY FUEL	18444	1248	69.0	6.8	88	2819	83.8	15.3	107	3624	83.4	19.6	106	868	78.9	4.7	100	657	76.2	3.6	97
HOLIDAY ABROAD IN LAST 12 MONTHS	7935	458	25.3	5.8	75	1370	40.7	17.3	120	1480	34.1	18.7	101	380	34.5	4.8	102	263	30.5	3.3	90

Source: BMRB International.

Exhibit 2.5 Analysis by Scottish ACORN from the Target Group Index 1993/94

PRODUCT: DRINK IRN BRU

Scottish ACORN group	Product (× 1000)	%	Base: Adults Base (× 1000)	%	Penet. %	Index
Affluent Consumers with Large Houses	109	7.8	453	11.2	24.1	70
Prosperous Home-owners	240	17.2	817	20.2	29.4	85
Agricultural Communities	7	0.5	45	1.1	15.6	45
Private Tenements and Flats	178	12.7	470	11.6	37.9	110
Better-off Council Areas, Homes Often Purchased	333	23.8	910	22.5	36.6	106
Council Estates, Less Well-off Families	311	22.2	794	19.6	39.2	113
Council Estates, Older Residents	102	7.3	286	7.1	35.7	103
Poorest Council Estates	98	7.0	215	5.3	45.6	132

Scottish ACORN type	Product (× 1000)	%	Base (× 1000)	%	Penet. %	Index
1 Wealth Families, Largest Detached Houses	6	0.5	82	2.0	7.8	23
2 Wealthy Older Residents, Home-owning Semis	41	2.9	119	2.9	34.1	99
3 Affluent Young Families with Mortgages	23	1.6	118	2.9	19.4	56
4 Affluent Older Couples and Families, Often Rural	39	2.8	134	3.3	29.3	85
5 Better-off Families, Mixed Dwellings	3	0.2	44	1.1	6.6	19
6 Younger Families with Mortgages, Commuters	63	4.5	156	3.9	40.6	117
7 Younger Families with Mortgages, New Homes	24	1.7	80	2.0	29.8	86
8 Older People in Suburban Areas and Small Towns	38	2.8	157	3.9	24.5	71
9 Working Couples, Owner-occupied Terraced Housing	30	2.1	117	2.9	25.2	73
10 Skilled Workers, Owner-occupied Semi-detached Houses	26	1.9	98	2.4	26.7	77
11 Better-off Older Residents, Mainly Villages	56	4.0	165	4.1	34.0	98
12 Home Based Workers, Agricultural Areas	7	0.5	43	1.1	16.6	48
13 Gaelic Speakers, Remote Areas and Islands	0	0.0	2	0.1	0.0	0
14 Younger Couples and Families, Owner-occupied Flats	39	2.8	110	2.7	35.2	102
15 Skilled Workers, Owner-occupied Flats	49	3.5	107	2.6	45.5	132
16 Young Professionals and Students, Private and Rented Flats	12	0.9	38	0.9	32.7	95
17 Elderly People, Private Flats	20	1.4	37	0.9	53.8	156
18 Professionals and Students, Private and Rented Tenements	23	1.6	47	1.1	48.5	141
19 Younger Residents with Mortgages, Tenements	17	1.2	50	1.2	34.4	100
20 Younger Residents with Mortgages, Smaller Tenements	18	1.3	81	2.0	22.8	66
21 Older Residents, New Home-owners	80	5.7	274	6.8	29.3	85
22 Older Residents, Semi-detached, New Home-owners	38	2.7	134	3.3	28.6	83
23 Retired Residents, New Home-owners	17	1.2	45	1.1	38.1	110
24 Older Families, Some New Home-owners	55	3.9	154	3.8	35.7	103
25 Older People, Some New Home-owners	26	1.9	56	1.4	46.9	136
26 Younger New Home-owners, Often New Towns	79	5.6	147	3.6	53.6	155
27 Families in Scottish Homes, Some New Home-owners	38	2.7	100	2.5	37.7	109
28 Younger Families in Flats, Many Children	57	4.1	130	3.2	44.2	128
29 Younger Families in Mixed Dwellings, Some Lone Parents	35	2.5	72	1.8	48.1	139
30 Younger Large Families, Council Terraces	101	7.2	259	6.4	38.9	112

Exhibit 2.5 continued

	Product (× 1000)	%	Base (× 1000)	%	Penet. %	Index
31 Families, Older Children, Terraces	52	3.7	158	3.9	32.9	95
32 Older Large Families, Semi-detached Houses	66	4.7	175	4.3	37.7	109
33 Older Residents, Low-rise Council Flats	17	1.2	49	1.2	35.1	102
34 Retired People, Health Problems, Mixed Dwellings	32	2.3	88	2.2	36.0	104
35 Retired People, Council Terraces	22	1.5	59	1.4	36.7	106
36 Single Pensioners, Health Problems, Larger Flats	23	1.6	73	1.8	31.0	90
37 Single Pensioners, Health Problems, City Centres	8	0.6	17	0.4	48.4	140
38 Poorer Families, High Unemployment, Low-rise Housing	13	0.9	25	0.6	50.2	145
39 Singles, Housing Association Flats, Overcrowding	18	1.3	30	0.7	58.9	171
40 Older Residents, High Unemployment, High-rise Flats	14	1.0	39	1.0	35.8	104
41 High Unemployment, Some High-rise Flats, Scottish Homes	18	1.3	41	1.0	43.9	127
42 Many Lone Parents, High Unemployment, Council Flats	12	0.8	22	0.6	52.7	153
43 Many Lone Parents, Greatest Hardship, Council Flats	23	1.7	58	1.4	40.2	116
44 Unclassified	20	1.4	57	1.4	34.9	101
Totals	1399	100.0	4051	100.0	34.5	100

Source: CACI/BMRB.

Data interpretation follows the same pattern as in Exhibit 2.4. Taking group A as an example: there are 453 000 people in this group of whom 109 000 drink Irn Bru. This represents a penetration figure of 24.1 per cent (109/453). As group A has 7.8 per cent of people drinking the product but 11.2 per cent of the population as a whole, its index figure is 70 (7.8/11.2). Even from the limited figures available we can see that in absolute and index terms groups E and F are the top two favouring Irn Bru.

Income elasticity of demand

One area that has to some extent been overlooked in market analysis is income elasticity of demand. Customer incomes may be outside the control of marketers but changes in income should be anticipated and monitored for their potential impact on the pattern of demand. The sensitivity of demand to changes in income is known as income elasticity of demand. The formula for measuring it is:

$$\frac{\text{Percentage change in quantity demanded}}{\text{Percentage change in income}}$$

Economists cite two types of goods in the demand/income equation of interest to marketers.

- **Normal goods**. It is reasonable to assume that the demand for normal goods (household goods, holidays, entertainment, etc.) will increase as income increases.
- **Inferior goods**. Here an increase in income will result in a fall in demand. An inferior good is generally something which people would rather avoid if they could find a better alternative, e.g. cutting down on sausages and buying more steak as their income rises. Bus transport may be perceived as inferior to taxi rides or even owning your own car. To counter the inferior good effect where income levels are rising, marketers should reposition the product by adding value (emphasizing additional benefits valued by target market(s)), e.g. margarine promoted as healthier than butter and bus journeys as less stressful and more environmentally friendly than car journeys. When incomes are falling in real terms, e.g. during inflation or rising taxation, inferior products tend to sell well as customers trade down to the basic model or brand.

A good can be both a normal and an inferior good depending upon the level of income. Bread may be a normal good for people on low incomes (i.e. they buy more bread when their income increases), but it may be an inferior good for higher income earners. Normal and inferior goods are shown in Figure 2.11.

In the figure, D_1 is the demand for a normal good; it is upward-sloping because demand increases as income increases. D_2 is the demand curve for an inferior good; it is downward-sloping, showing that demand falls as income increases. D_3 is the demand curve for a good which is normal at low levels of income but is inferior at higher levels of income. A normal good will always have a positive income elasticity because quantity demanded and income either both increase (giving a plus divided by a plus) or both decrease (giving a minus divided by a minus). An inferior good, however, will always

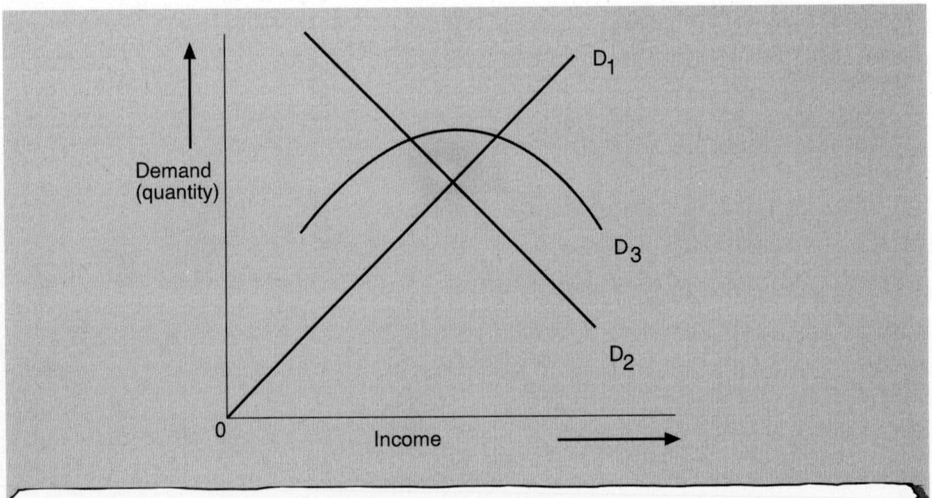

FIGURE 2.11 Normal and inferior goods: income versus demand (see text for key).

have a negative elasticity because the signs on the top and bottom of the income elasticity of demand formula will always be opposite (a plus divided by a minus or a minus divided by a plus, giving a minus in both cases).

For example, if the demand for bread falls by 2 per cent when income rises by 5 per cent then it is an inferior good. Its income elasticity is −2/+5 or −0.4. High income elasticities found in the UK include overseas holidays (3.32), beer (0.51) and car travel (1.23). By contrast, household foods have low income elasticities. Tea has recorded a surprisingly large negative income elasticity (−0.68). As incomes rise households substitute a greater variety of drinks for tea which, per cup, is very cheap. The prime substitute is coffee, which has a positive income elasticity (0.08). A product with a high income elasticity for its category (food) is fruit juices (0.73), an expensive but increasingly popular item of expenditure amongst the more affluent households in the economy.

Forecasting

Forecasting is the art of estimating future demand by anticipating what buyers are likely to do under a given set of conditions. Obviously, accuracy in forecasting will increase where market conditions are relatively stable. Figure 2.12 summarizes some of the more common forecasting methods.

As a crude generalization, trend projections tend to be applied to situations which are either very short-term or very long-term, with causal models applied largely in the medium term. Quantitative methods are used where accurate, quantitative data are already available. Where no past demand figures exist and the factors affecting demand are unknown, qualitative methods, e.g. using a panel of experts, are used. The following material relates solely to quantitative methods.

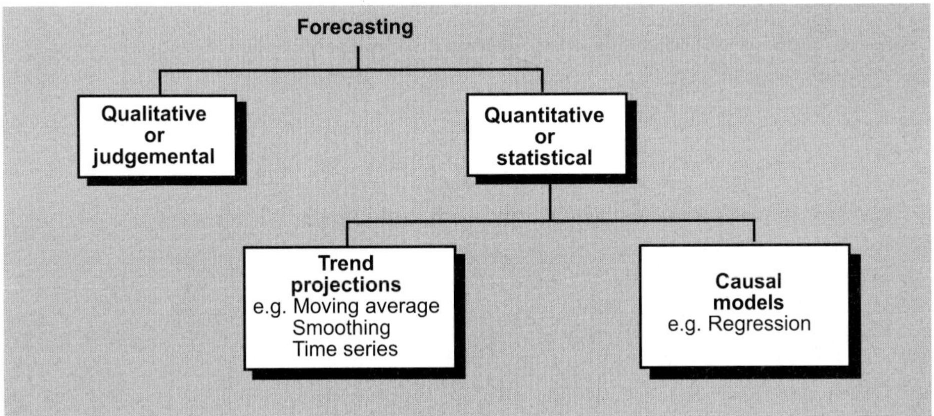

FIGURE 2.12 Forecasting methods.

Correlation

Marketers are interested in the strength of association that exists between variables, as in the following situations:

- How strongly are sales related to advertising expenditure?
- Is there an association between market share and size of the salesforce?
- Are consumers' perceptions of quality related to their perceptions of price?

The degree of association between the pairs of variables above is given by the correlation coefficient (known as r) which is expressed as a number between $+1$ and -1. The closer the coefficient is to either of these two extremes, the better the correlation between the two variables. The nearer it is to 0, the poorer the correlation. A coefficient of $+1$ means that there is an exact linear and positive association, e.g. the relationship between the number of TV sets installed in homes and the number of potential viewers. A coefficient of -1 means there is an exact linear but negative or opposing association, e.g. the relationship between price levels and quantity demanded (Figure 2.13).

In practice, perfect correlations are rare. What usually happens is that the observed values are scattered above and below the lines shown in Figure 2.13. Plotting the variables on what is known as a scattergraph can be a useful first step in establishing the presence or absence of a relationship (Figure 2.14).

Whilst the scatter diagram is useful in providing a graphical, and subjective, assessment about the strength of the relationship between two variables, we clearly need a statistical measure. Pearson's product–moment correlation is the most widely used statistic for this purpose. It is given by the formula:

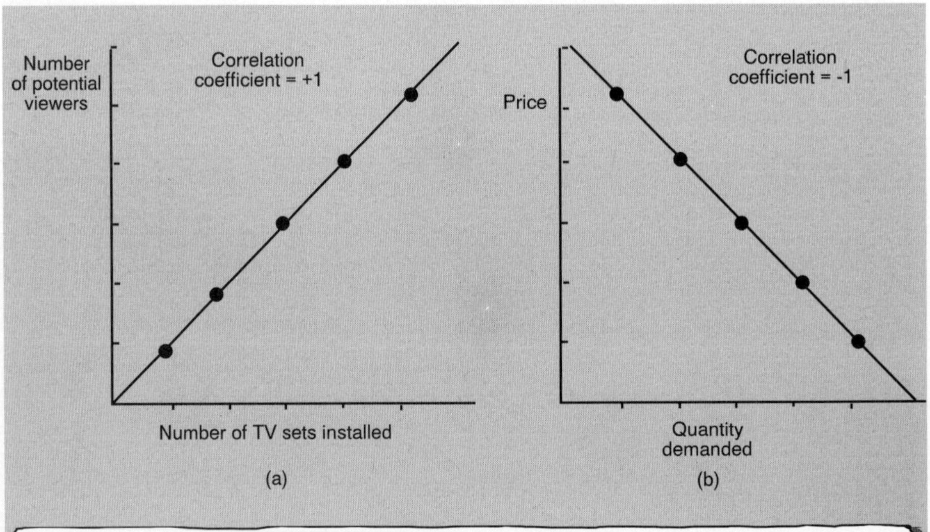

FIGURE 2.13 Perfect positive (a) and negative (b) correlation.

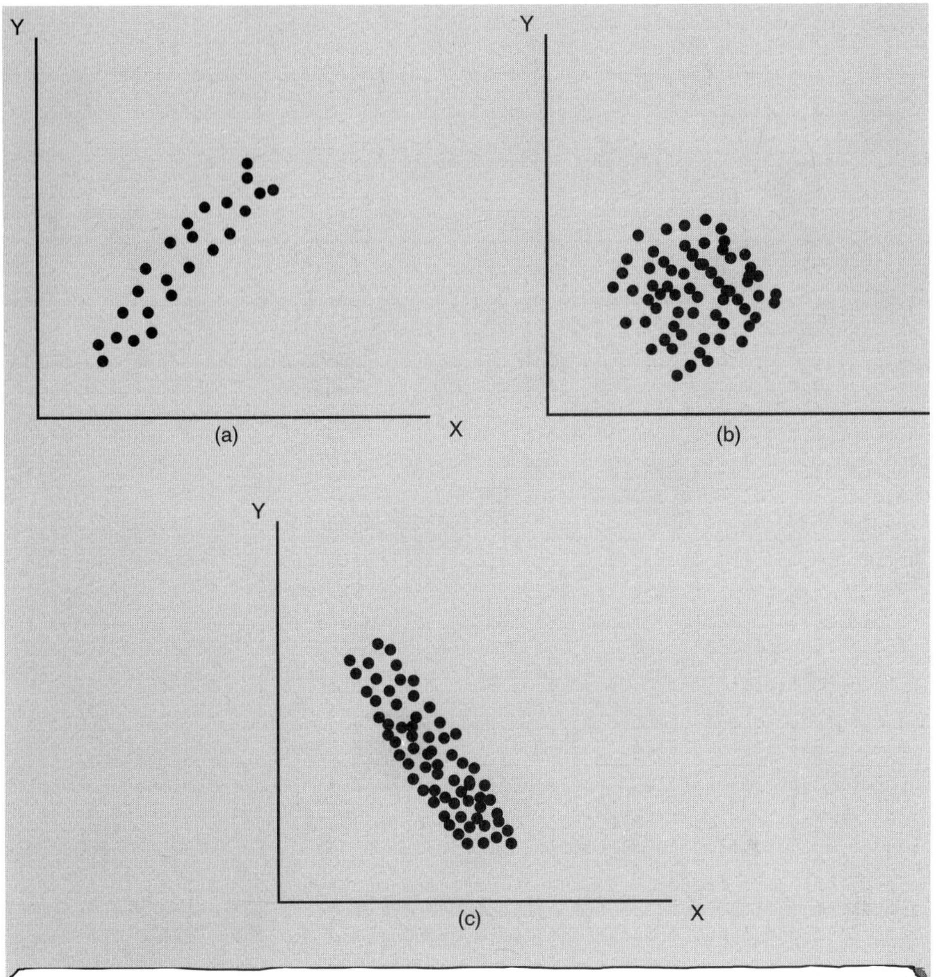

FIGURE 2.14 Scatter diagrams: (a) Positive correlation. (b) Zero correlation. (c) Negative correlation.

$$r = \frac{n\Sigma xy - \Sigma x \Sigma y}{\sqrt{\{n\Sigma x^2 - (\Sigma x)^2\}\{n\Sigma y^2 - (\Sigma y)^2\}}}$$

where x and y are the two variables being compared, n is the number of values in the sample and Σ means 'the sum of'. Consider the data from a salesforce audit which shows the average weekly activity (calls) and performance (orders taken) of six sales representatives (Table 2.6).

The last three columns of Table 2.6 show the calculations of the terms used in the formula:

TABLE 2.6 Average weekly calls and orders taken

Sales representative	Average number of calls per week x	Average number of orders taken per week y	x^2	y^2	xy
1	35	12	1225	144	420
2	23	7	529	49	161
3	29	8	841	64	232
4	33	9	1089	81	297
5	25	6	625	36	150
6	30	8	900	64	240
Totals (Σ)	175	50	5209	438	1500

$$r = \frac{6 \times 1500 - 175 \times 50}{\sqrt{\{6 \times 5209 - (175^2)\}\{6 \times 438 - (50^2)\}}}$$

$$= \frac{250}{\sqrt{80512}}$$

$$= \frac{250}{283.74}$$

$$= 0.88$$

The formula shows a high positive correlation between calls and orders taken. As calls increase, so do orders taken. However, a word of caution: the coefficient measures the strength of the relationship; it does not measure cause and affect. Sales of ice cream are directly related to sales of sunglasses but there is no cause and effect here. The way to increase sales of ice cream is not to increase the sales of sunglasses. Returning to our example, just because calls (x) correlate with orders taken (y) we cannot necessarily deduce that x causes y. However, it does represent a first step in our understanding of how these variables may behave in future periods. In other words, we can expect a statistical connection between the two variables to continue in the future.

Regression analysis

Correlation analysis, as we have seen, is simply concerned with providing a statistical measure of the strength of any relationship between two variables. Regression analysis, on the other hand, is concerned with measuring the way in which one variable is related to another, i.e. how differences in one or more variables help to explain differences in another variable.

As we saw with the scatter diagrams, relationships are often only roughly linear. All of the plotted points do not lie on a straight line (Figure 2.15).

It seems sensible, however, to try to obtain the straight line that comes as close as

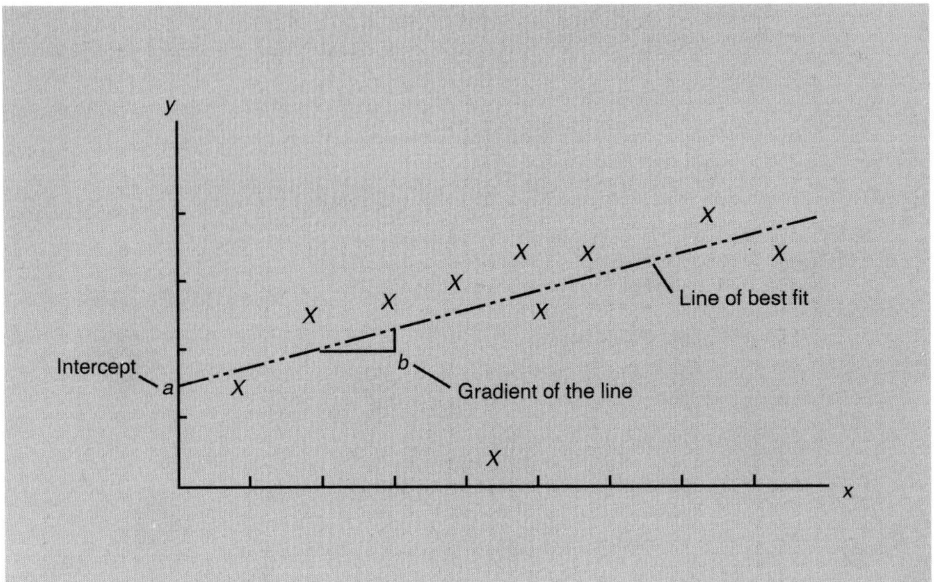

FIGURE 2.15 Scattergraph and line of best fit.

possible to as many points as possible – the line of best fit. The weakness of such an approach lies in its subjectivity, with different people drawing slightly different straight lines. What we need is a more formal way of defining a line of best fit through the data. This is the purpose of linear regression.

The equation of a straight line is:

$$y = a + bx$$

where y is a dependent variable, x an independent variable, a the point where the line intersects the y-axis and b is the gradient of the line. (It is conventional to assume that y varies as x varies. Therefore, y is known as the dependent variable and x as the independent (or explanatory) variable.) The interpretation of the equation above is that as x changes, y changes by b times the change in x, and therefore b measures the slope or gradient of the line. When x takes the value of 0, y has the value of a, which is referred to as the intercept.

The most widely used method of computing the line of best fit is the least squares method. This method works out where to place the line passing through and between the plotted points in a scatter diagram. When the sum of the squared differences between the line and the plotted values is at a minimum, then the line gives the best fit for the two sets of data.

To find the regression coefficients a and b we use the following formulae:

$$b = \frac{n\Sigma(xy) - \Sigma x \Sigma y}{n\Sigma(x^2) - (\Sigma x)^2}$$

$$a = \bar{y} - b\bar{x}$$

where $\bar{y}$ and $\bar{x}$ are the arithmetic means of the y and x values respectively. Once a and b have been determined, we can deduce the equation for the best-fitting line, i.e. $y = a + bx$.

Example

The following data show monthly advertising expenditure (£000) and sales ('000) over a period of 6 months. Estimate the relationship between sales (y) and advertising expenditure (x).

Sales (y)	6	30	12	40	18	50
Advertising expenditure (x)	2	4	6	8	10	12

Solution

The computations involved to determine a and b are as follows:

	x	y	x^2	xy	y^2
	2	6	4	36	12
	4	30	16	900	120
	6	12	36	144	272
	8	40	64	1600	320
	10	18	100	324	180
	12	50	144	2500	600
Totals (Σ)	42	156	364	5504	1304

$$\bar{x} = \frac{42}{6} = 7, \qquad \bar{y} = \frac{156}{6} = 26$$

Using the formulae for b and a cited above, their values are:

$$b = \frac{6 \times 1304 - 42 \times 26}{6 \times 364 - 42^2}$$

$$= \frac{1272}{420}$$

$$= 3.03$$

$$a = 26 - 3.03 \times 7$$

$$= 4.79$$

Therefore, the estimated relationship between sales and advertising expenditure is:

$$y = 4.79 + 3.03x$$

If we assume a linear relationship, this means that for every £1000 increase in advertising expenditure, sales can be expected to increase by 3.03 thousand (i.e. 3030) units on average; with no expenditure on advertising, average sales are likely to be 4.79 thousand (i.e. 4790) units.

Coefficient of determination

Having calculated the regression line we now need to determine how closely the actual points cluster around the regression line (i.e. how good the fit is). We use a measure called the coefficient of determination, usually referred to as r^2. The formula is as follows:

$$r^2 = \left[\frac{n\Sigma xy - \Sigma x\Sigma y}{\sqrt{\{n\Sigma x^2 - (\Sigma x)^2\}\{n\Sigma y^2 - (\Sigma y)^2\}}}\right]^2$$

Using the data in the sales/advertising expenditure example, the coefficient of determination is:

$$r^2 = \left[\frac{6 \times 1304 - 42 \times 156}{\sqrt{\{6 \times 364 - (42)^2\}\{6 \times 5504 - (156)^2\}}}\right]^2$$
$$= \left(\frac{1272}{1910}\right)^2$$
$$= 0.666^2$$
$$= 0.44$$

Therefore, 44 per cent of variation in sales is 'explained' by variation in advertising expenditure, while 56 per cent is 'unexplained' (i.e. caused by other factors). The example above is a simple regression model with only one independent variable. To resolve the '56 per cent unexplained', a multiple regression equation is used where sales (the dependent variable) is a function not only of advertising expenditure, but also of additional independent variables such as prices, product quality and income.

Using linear regression to forecast

The main purpose of linear regression is to predict the value that a dependent variable will take when an independent variable has a particular value. The regression line can be used to give predictions of the value of y for a given value of x simply by reading off the required values from the graph. Alternatively we can enter a value for x into the regression equation to find a corresponding value of y. Using our previous example, let us assume that the company is thinking of spending £7000 on advertising. Can we forecast likely sales? Using the regression equation all we have to do is to substitute the advertising value into the equation that we found relating sales and advertising expenditure, i.e. $y = 4.79 + 3.03x$. This gives:

$$\text{Sales} = 4.79 + 3.03\ (7) = 26$$

That is, on this advertising figure, sales would be forecast at 26 000.

Trend projections

Time series methods examine past patterns and project these patterns forward into the future.

Simple averages

Consider the following sales figures recorded by two retail outlets over the past six months:

Sales (£000)

Month	1	2	3	4	5	6
A	49	50	48	54	50	49
B	90	16	102	8	34	50

Using a simple average of the six months' sales to forecast the sales in month 7 would give us the following:

Retailer A

$$\text{Average monthly sales} = \frac{49 + 50 + 48 + 54 + 50 + 49}{6}$$
$$= 50$$

Retailer B

$$\text{Average monthly sales} = \frac{90 + 16 + 102 + 8 + 34 + 50}{6}$$
$$= 50$$

Although the forecasts are the same we would clearly have more confidence in the first forecast than in the second as the second series is more variable than the first. Using a simple average is easy and works well where the series exhibits constant values. It does not work so well if the pattern changes. Suppose, for example, demand for an item has been constant at 50 units a week for the past year. A simple average would give a forecast demand for week 53 of 50 units. If the actual demand in week 53 rises to 100 units, a simple average would give a forecast for week 54 of:

$$\text{Forecast (week 54)} = \frac{52 \times 50 + 100}{53}$$
$$= 50.94$$

If demand in week 54 continues at 100, the forecast for week 55 would be:

$$\text{Forecast (week 55)} = \frac{52 \times 50 + 100 + 100}{54}$$
$$= 51.85$$

The problem is that old data, which may be out of date, tend to swamp newer, more relevant data. The forecasts are rising but they are nowhere near responsive enough to the actual demand figures. One way round this is to ignore old data and use only a number of the most recent observations. This is known as the principle of moving averages.

Moving averages

Given the task of observing the movement of some variable over time and trying to project this movement into the future, it would seem sensible to try to smooth out any irregular pattern in the historical figures and use this as the basis for future projection. The simplest way of doing this is to calculate a series of moving averages.

Consider the demand for pizzas over a 12 month period and a three-month moving average forecast (Table 2.7).

The three-month moving average is calculated as follows:

$$\text{Month 4} = \frac{70 + 65 + 60}{3} = 65$$

$$\text{Month 5} = \frac{65 + 60 + 55}{3} = 60$$

and so on.

A graph of the moving average forecasts and the actual demand can be seen in Figure 2.16.

The result of the forecast appears to perform reasonably well. However, the choice of the number of periods is important. In practice the choice is to some extent arbitrary. The larger the number of periods in the moving average the greater will be the smoothing

TABLE 2.7 Forecast using moving average

Month	Demand	Three-month moving average forecast
1	70	
2	65	
3	60	
4	55	65
5	40	60
6	55	51.66
7	50	50
8	60	48.33
9	40	55
10	50	50
11	40	50
12	45	43.33
13 (Forecast)		45

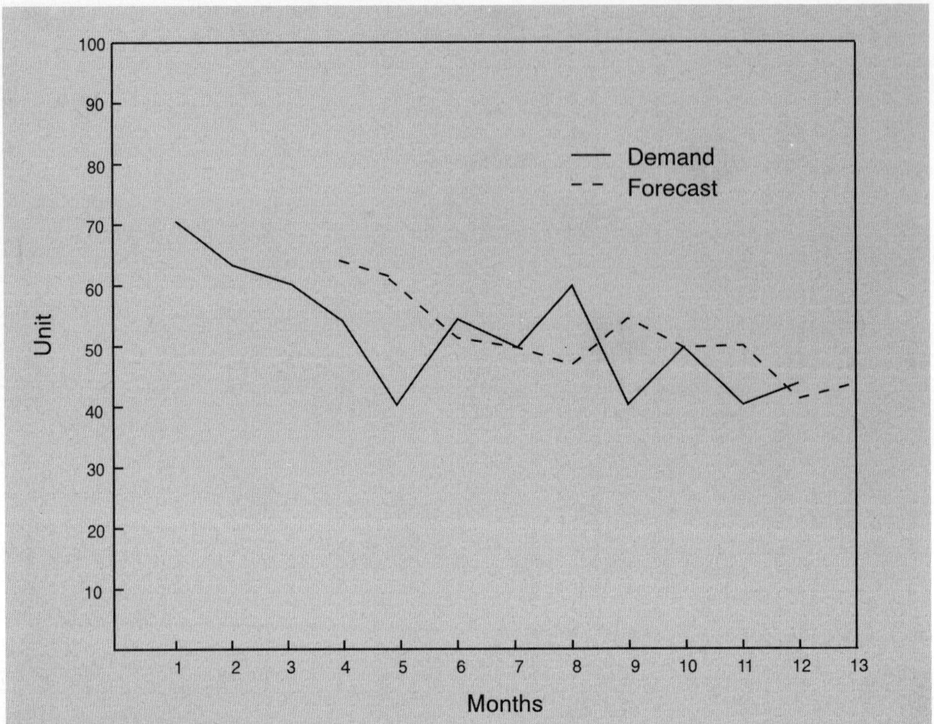

FIGURE 2.16 Actual and forecast demand.

effect of the forecasts, making it relatively unresponsive to recent changes. The forecast will smooth out random variations but may not follow genuine changes in patterns. Conversely, a small number of periods for the moving average will give a responsive forecast that will follow genuine changes but may be too sensitive to random fluctuations.

Moving averages are particularly useful for data that have strong seasonal variations. Consider the following data which exhibit a clear seasonal pattern, peaking every fourth month.

Month	1	2	3	4	5	6	7	8	9	10	11	12
Demand	100	40	30	125	60	35	55	130	75	45	50	135

Using a moving average with two, four and six periods we can calculate the one-month-ahead forecasts (Table 2.8). The pattern can be seen clearly in Figure 2.17.

The two-month and six-month moving averages have responded to the peaks and troughs of demand but neither has got the timing right: both forecasts lag behind demand. The most interesting result is the four-month moving average which has completely deseasonalized the data.

TABLE 2.8 Forecast using moving average (varied periods)

Month	Demand	Forecasts		
		Moving average (months)		
		2	4	6
1	100	–	–	–
2	40	–	–	–
3	30	70	–	–
4	125	35	–	–
5	60	77.5	73.75	–
6	35	92.5	63.75	–
7	55	47.5	62.5	65
8	130	45	68.75	7.5
9	75	92.5	70	72.5
10	45	102.5	73.75	80
11	50	60	76.25	66.66
12	135	47.5	75	65
13		92.5	76.25	81.66

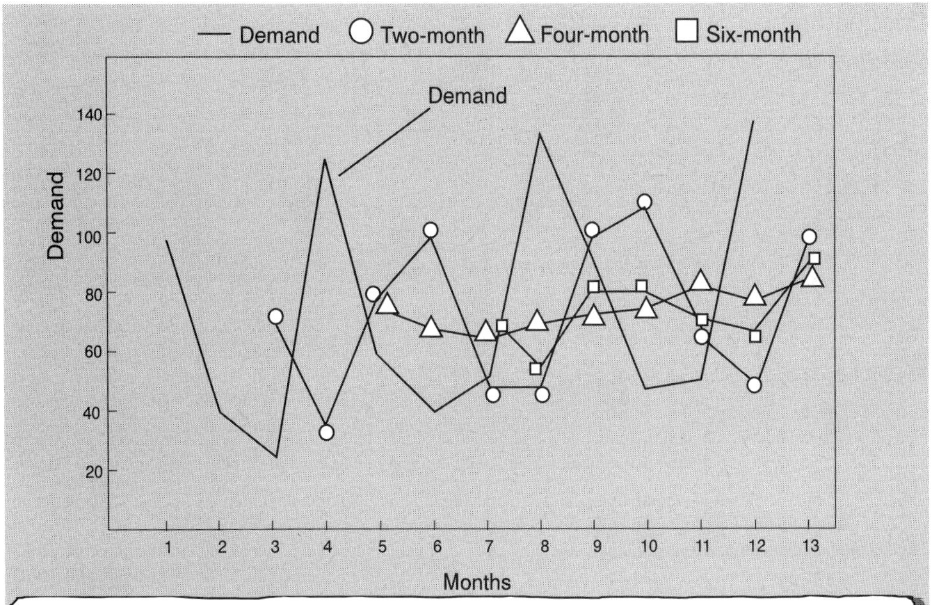

FIGURE 2.17 Moving averages.

Moving averages is an advance on simple averages but several problems remain:

- Moving averages only works well with constant time series (where the data are seasonal it either deseasonalizes or gets the timing wrong, as we have seen).
- All observations are given the same weight.

Exponential smoothing

One arguable weakness of moving averages is that each observation is given the same weight. As data get older, however, they become less relevant to the current situation and should therefore be given less weight. Exponential smoothing is a forecasting method that allocates larger weights to more recent items (Figure 2.18).

Exponential smoothing is a type of moving average technique but has the advantage that it involves little recordkeeping of past data values. The forecast is based on the most recent data value and the previous forecast. The basic exponential smoothing formula is given by:

New forecast = Last period's forecast + α (Last period's actual data value – Last period's forecast)
= Last period's forecast + α (Error in last period's forecast)
≡ Last period's forecast plus a proportion of the error in the last period's forecast

where α (alpha) is a weight or smoothing constant that has a value between 0 and 1. We can illustrate the way in which exponential smoothing adapts to changes in observations with a simple example. Over the past 15 weeks a service station sold the following quantities of oil:

Week	1	2	3	4	5	6	7	8	9	10	11	12	13	14	15
Litres	20	25	28	24	20	27	30	37	30	26	21	18	24	31	26

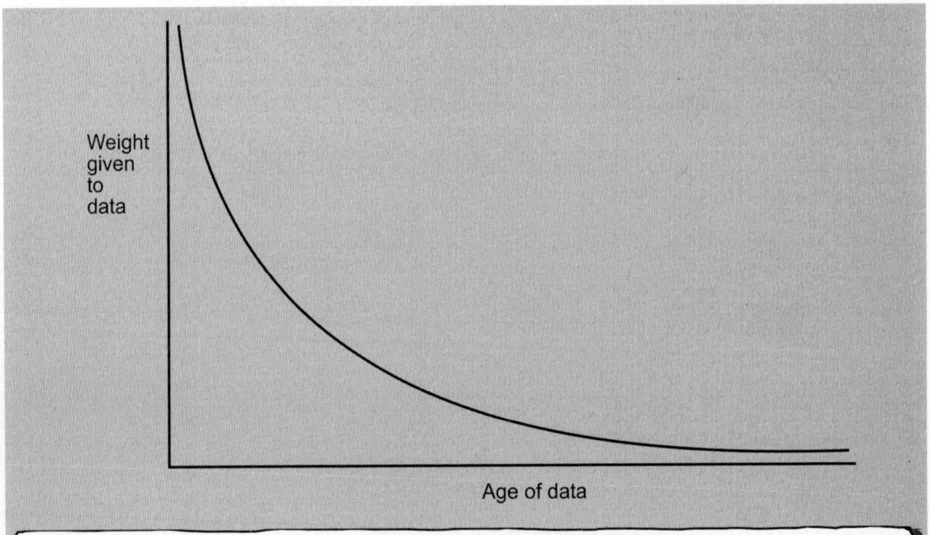

FIGURE 2.18 Weight given to data with exponential smoothing.

Using a smoothing constant of $\alpha = 0.2$ we can forecast one week in advance the number of litres of oil sold by the station (Table 2.9). Thus the forecast for week 16 is 25.74 (26 to the nearest litre). Note that in the absence of further information we have taken the forecast for week 2 to be the demand in week 1.

A large value of α will cause the forecast to change drastically from one period to another, whereas a small value of α will cause the forecast to change more slowly. The value of α is generally found by experimenting with several values and finding the one with the smallest errors. Consider a time series using an initial forecast of 250 to compare exponential smoothing forecasts with varying values of α (Table 2.10).

All the forecasts would eventually follow the sharp increase in period 3 and raise forecasts to around 750. Higher values of α make this adjustment more quickly and give a more responsive forecast; they do not necessarily give more accurate ones (Figure 2.19).

TABLE 2.9 Forecasting using exponential smoothing

Week	Actual number of litres sold	Last period's forecast		α	Error in last period's forecast		New forecast
1	20						
2	25						20
3	28	20	+	0.2	(25 – 20)	=	21.00
4	24	21	+	0.2	(28 – 21)	=	22.40
5	20	22.4	+	0.2	(24 – 22.4)	=	22.72
6	27	22.72	+	0.2	(20 – 22.72)	=	22.18
7	30	22.18	+	0.2	(27 – 22.18)	=	23.14
8	37	23.14	+	0.2	(30 – 23.14)	=	24.51
9	30	24.51	+	0.2	(37 – 24.51)	=	27.01
10	26	27.01	+	0.2	(30 – 27.01)	=	27.61
11	21	27.61	+	0.2	(26 – 27.61)	=	27.29
12	18	27.29	+	0.2	(21 – 27.29)	=	26.03
13	24	26.03	+	0.2	(18 – 26.03)	=	24.42
14	31	24.42	+	0.2	(24 – 24.42)	=	24.34
15	26	24.34	+	0.2	(31 – 24.34)	=	25.67
16		25.67	+	0.2	(26 – 25.67)	=	25.74

TABLE 2.10 Exponential smoothing forecasts with various values of α

Period	Demand	$\alpha = 0.1$	$\alpha = 0.2$	$\alpha = 0.3$	$\alpha = 0.4$
1	240	250	250	250	250
2	250	249	248	247	246
3	750	249.1	248.40	247.9	247.6
4	725	299.19	348.72	398.53	448.56
5	755	341.77	423.97	496.47	559.13
6	750	383.09	490.18	574.02	637.47
7	740	419.28	542.14	626.81	682.48
8	760	451.35	581.72	660.76	705.48
9	750	482.21	617.37	690.53	727.28
10	745	508.98	643.89	708.37	736.38
11	750	532.58	664.12	719.35	739.98
12		555.85	681.29	728.54	743.98

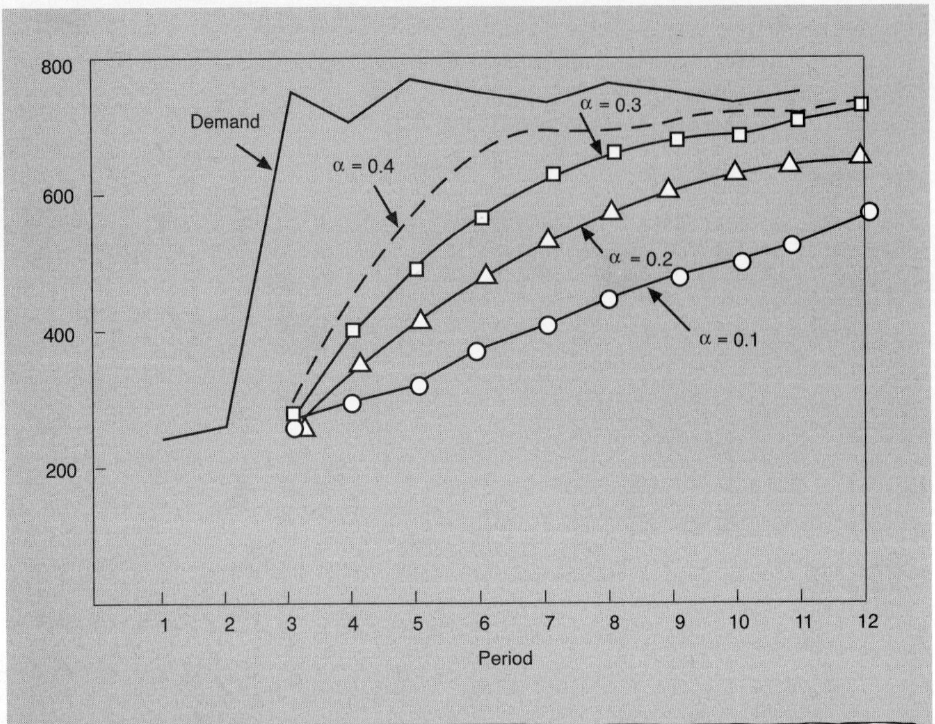

FIGURE 2.19 Exponential smoothing with different smoothing constants. Source: Adapted from Waters, D., *Quantitative Methods for Business*, Addison-Wesley, 1993.

Forecasting with seasonality and trend

To forecast complex time series, observations are split into separate components and a forecast made. The final forecast is found by recombining the separate components. The process of quantifying the components of a time series is often referred to as time series decomposition where an observation is made up of four components:

- Trend (T) is the long-term direction of a time series. It is usually a steady upward or downward movement.
- Seasonal factor (S) is the regular variation around the trend, usually a variation in demand over a year.
- Cyclical factor (C) is a longer-term variation that occurs over several years.
- Random factor (R) whose effects cannot be explained and is unpredictable.

There are two approaches to forecasting:

- The **additive model** where the observation $y = T + S + C + R$
- The **multiplicative model** where the observation $y = T \times S \times C \times R$

As the latter is more widely used and gives better results we shall concentrate on it. Furthermore, as R is generally unknown and data on cycles are invariably lacking, we can exclude both R and C from the forecast.

Forecasting procedure

Historical data are used when we want to

- deseasonalize the data and find the underlying trend, T;
- find the seasonal indices, S;
- use T and S to forecast.

Finding the trend

There are two ways of finding the trend T, both of which have already been explained:

- Linear regression with time as the independent variable.
- Moving averages with a period equal to the length of a season.

Both generally give good results. If the trend is clearly linear, then regression should be used. If it is not clearly linear, then moving averages is better. It is often a matter of individual preference.

Consider the following set of observations over the past 12 periods:

Period (x)	1	2	3	4	5	6	7	8	9	10	11	12
Observation (y)	145	160	71	99	195	206	135	153	246	259	182	194

Using linear regression to deseasonalize the trend

Using linear regression to find the deseasonalized trend, we obtain:

$$n = 12, \quad \Sigma x = 78, \quad \Sigma y = 2045, \quad \Sigma x^2 = 650, \quad \Sigma xy = 14\,588$$

Substituting these into the standard linear regression equation gives:

$$b = \frac{12 \times 14\,588 - 78 \times 2045}{12 \times 650 - 78 \times 78}$$

$$= \frac{175\,056 - 159\,510}{7800 - 6084}$$

$$= 9.06$$

$$a = \frac{2045}{12} - \frac{9.06 \times 78}{12}$$

$$= 111.52$$

TABLE 2.11 Deseasonalized trend values

Period	Value	Deseasonalized trend value
1	145	120.58
2	160	129.64
3	71	138.70
4	99	147.76
5	195	156.82
6	206	165.88
7	135	174.94
8	153	184.00
9	246	193.06
10	259	202.12
11	182	211.18
12	194	220.24

Therefore the line of best fit gives the trend as:

$$\text{Observation} = 73.68 + 13.60 \times \text{Period}$$

The deseasonalized trend values are shown in Table 2.11 and plotted in Figure 2.20. The deseasonalized trend value for period 1 is

$$111.52 + (9.06 \times 1) = 120.58$$

Using a moving average to deseasonalize the trend

Figure 2.20 shows that the values have a clear season of four periods. We can therefore deseasonalize the data by taking a four-period moving average. Deseasonalizing data suggests that average values occur at average times. Looking at the first four periods, the average value of 118.75 (145 + 160 + 71 + 99)/4 occurs at the average time of (1 + 2 + 3 + 4)/4 = 2.5, i.e. it occurs halfway through a period. To find the deseasonalized value at each period, simply take the average of the two values on either side of it. The deseasonalized value for period 3 is therefore the average of the deseasonalized values at times 2.5 and 3.5 (Table 2.12). The graph of the data in Table 2.12 can be seen in Figure 2.21.

Unlike the linear regression, the moving average provides deseasonalized data only for eight periods. However, the two approaches give similar results.

Finding the seasonal indices

In multiplicative models, seasonal variations are measured by seasonal indices. The seasonal index is given by:

$$\text{Seasonal index} = \frac{\text{Actual value}}{\text{Deseasonalized trend value}}$$

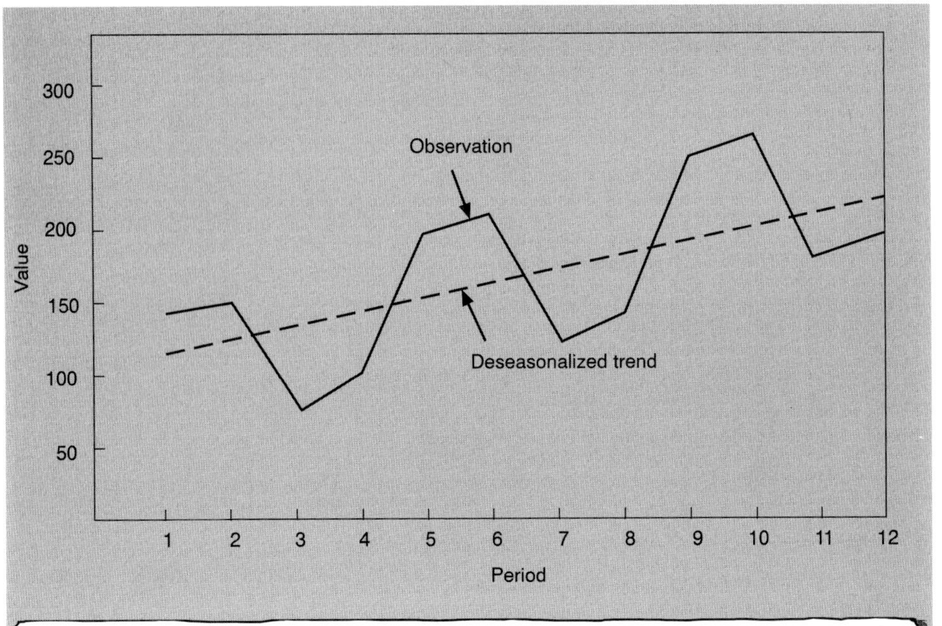

FIGURE 2.20 Using linear regression to deseasonalize the data. Source: Adapted from Waters, D., *Quantitative Methods for Business*, Addison-Wesley, 1993.

TABLE 2.12 Moving average and deseasonalized values

Period	Value	Four-period moving average		Deseasonalized values
1	145			
2	160			
2.5		118.75		
3	71		÷ 2 =	125
3.5		131.25		
4	99		÷ 2 =	136.75
4.5		142.25		
5	195			150.5
5.5		158.75		
6	206			165.5
6.5		172.25		
7	135			178.62
7.5		185		
8	153			191.62
8.5		198.25		
9	246			204.12
9.5		210		
10	259			215.12
10.5		215.12		
11	182			
12	194			

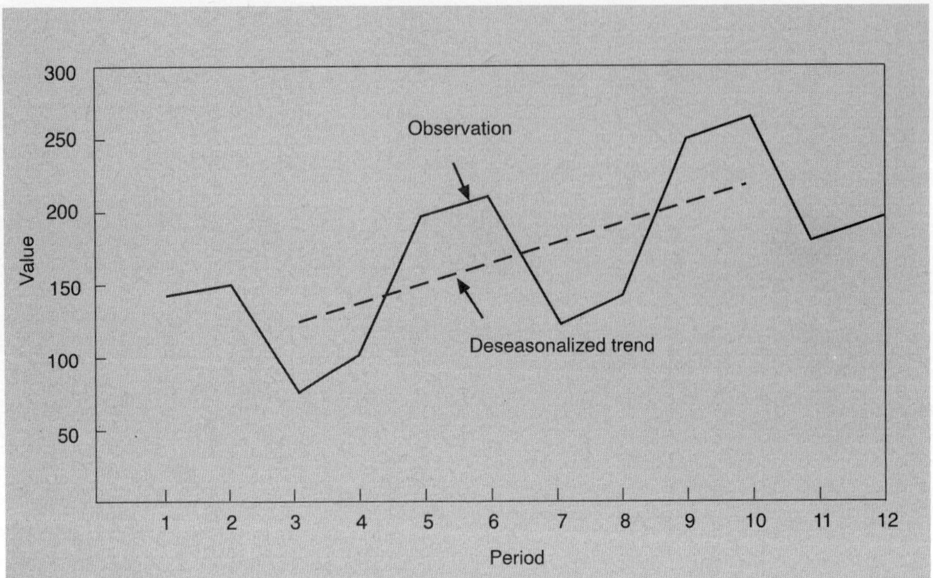

FIGURE 2.21 Using moving averages to deseasonalize the data. Source: Adapted from Waters, D., *Quantitative Methods for Business*, Addison-Wesley, 1993.

We can now determine the seasonal index under both linear regression and moving average values (Table 2.13).

The seasonal index basically states that in period 1, for example, we can anticipate a rise of 20 per cent above the trend (145/120.58). Having calculated a seasonal index for each period, averages can be determined to find more accurate values. From Figures 2.20 and 2.21 we know there are four periods in a season. Therefore, we need to calculate four seasonal indices. For the first period in consecutive seasons (1, 5 and 9) the average seasonal index under linear regression would be:

$$\frac{1.20 + 1.24 + 1.27}{3} = 1.23$$

Moving averages do not give a value for period 1 but the average for periods 5 and 9 is:

$$\frac{1.29 + 1.20}{2} = 1.25$$

Similar calculations should be made for second, third and fourth periods in a season using linear regression and moving averages indices.

Having now found both trend and seasonal index, a forecast can be made. Linear regression is easier to use for this purpose than moving averages where projecting the trend is most easily achieved by drawing a graph of known values and extrapolating from that.

TABLE 2.13 Determination of seasonal indices

Period	Observation	Linear regression		Moving averages	
		Deseasonalized trend value	Seasonal index	Deseasonalized trend value	Seasonal index
1	145	120.58	1.20		
2	160	129.64	1.23		
3	71	138.70	0.51	125	0.57
4	99	147.76	0.67	136.75	0.72
5	195	156.82	1.24	150.5	1.29
6	206	165.88	1.24	165.5	1.24
7	135	174.94	0.77	178.62	0.75
8	153	184.00	0.83	191.62	0.79
9	246	193.06	1.27	204.12	1.20
10	259	202.12	1.28	215.12	1.20
11	182	211.18	0.86		
12	194	220.24	0.88		

Returning to linear regression and the trend found by it, namely

$$\text{Observation} = 111.52 + 9.06 \times \text{Period}$$

the forecast for period 13 would be:

$$\text{Deseasonalized trend} = 111.52 + 9.06 \times 13$$

$$= 229.30$$

$$\text{Seasonal index} = 1.23 \text{ (first period in season)}$$

$$\text{Forecast} = 229.30 \times 1.23$$

$$= 282.04$$

Forecast errors

Forecasts are only estimates and so a forecast error is likely to arise in almost every case. Therefore, any forecast should be viewed as a projection rather than a prediction. The error is equal to the difference between the actual value and the forecast value. We need some method of assessing the overall accuracy of the forecasting method. The two most common ones take the absolute values of errors (and calculate the mean absolute deviation), and the squares of errors (and calculate the mean-squared error).

TABLE 2.14 Forecasting error using mean absolute deviation

Week	Sales	Forecast using 2-week moving average	Error	Absolute deviation
1	197			
2	204			
3	204	200.5	3.5	3.5
4	198	204	−6	6
5	210	201	9	9
6	204	204	0	0
7	205	207	−2	2
8	206	204.5	1.5	1.5
9	198	205.5	−7.5	7.5
10	204	202	2	2
11	205	201	4	4
12	193	204.5	−11.5	11.5
13	203	199	4	4
14	204	198	6	6
15	205	203.5	1.5	1.5
		204.5		
Total				58.5

Mean absolute deviation

This method takes the absolute value of each individual error and averages these absolute errors over the entire period. Consider the data in Table 2.14 and the calculation of the mean absolute deviation.

The total of the absolute deviations is 58.5, giving a mean absolute deviation (MAD) of 4.5 (58.5/13). On average, then, the forecast is 4.5 units away from the actual value. The weakness of this approach is that it attaches no particular importance to large forecast errors like that of week 12 in Table 2.14. Consider a situation where one forecasting method produced a weekly absolute error of 2 units over, say, ten weeks. Another method produces a weekly absolute error of 0 units for nine weeks and 20 units for one week. In both cases the MAD would be the same, namely 2.

Mean-squared error

Rather than taking the absolute value of each error, this method squares the errors before summing and averaging. Applying this to the data in Table 2.14 you will find the mean-squared error (MSE) equals 30.63. Unlike the MAD approach, large forecasting errors (as in week 12) are penalized under this approach. If one or two large errors occur which may be costly to an organization they are far more likely to show up under the MSE approach.

References

1. McDonald, M., *Marketing Plans: How to prepare them, how to use them*, Butterworth/Heinemann, 1995.
2. Ries, A. and Trout, J., *The 22 Immutable Laws of Marketing*, Harper Collins, 1993, p. 18.
3. Smith, D.C., Andrews, J. and Blevins, T.R., 'The role of competitive analysis in implementing a market orientation', *Journal of Services Marketing*, Vol. 6, no. 1, 1992.
4. *User Guide*, CACI Information Services.

CHAPTER 3

Financial aspects of marketing

WHAT IS IT ABOUT?

One area that is probably glossed over during the study, as against the practice of marketing, is finance. It has long been a business tradition that marketing and finance do not see eye to eye; but times are changing.

A good place to begin is the **profit and loss account** with a discussion of what it means for marketing.

As a general rule for getting the best from marketing analysis, it is strongly recommended that data be **disaggregated**. To obtain a finer and more revealing assessment of profitability, the **Pareto effect** (known as the 80/20 rule) reminds us that some customers, products, etc., will be much more profitable than others. If 80 per cent of sales and/or profits comes from 20 per cent of customers discussion is required as to whether such a situation should continue to exist.

Whatever the nature of the activity, be it sales volume, number of patients or commuters, etc., knowledge of how costs and revenue vary with different levels of that activity is required for decision-making. This leads on to **cost/volume/profit analysis**, a valuable tool for examining the relationship between changes in volume and changes in total sales revenue, costs and profit.

One of the most important pieces of information resulting from a profit analysis is the **contribution to sales ratio** or contribution margin ratio. Its calculation and use in various situations are explained.

The concept of contribution has played an important role in marketing control. However, increasing criticism has been directed towards traditional costing systems. If companies wish to have a clearer picture of products, customers and profitability they will evidently need to turn to what is known as **activity-based costing**.

If **cost allocation** can be more finely tuned it will inevitably assist marketing in decisions over whether to drop, retain or invest in customers, products, channels of distribution, etc.

The marketing concept stresses profitability as well as customer satisfaction. To achieve this aim marketers need to be familiar with a certain amount of financial analysis. A good place to start this process is the profit and loss account.

Profit and loss account

The profit and loss account summarizes the profitability of a company for a specific time period, usually one year. It aims to show the profit of the company and the revenues and expenses that led to that profit. There are three main elements to all profit and loss statements:

- Sales of the company's goods and services.
- Costs incurred in making and selling the goods and services.
- Profit or loss, which is the difference between sales and cost.

Table 3.1 shows a profit and loss statement for a company over a five-year period.

Analysis of the profit and loss account

By calculating some statistics and establishing the existence of any trends, an assessment of the company's performance in Table 3.1 can be made (Tables 3.2 and 3.3).

TABLE 3.1 A profit and loss account

	Year 1 £000		Year 2 £000		Year 3 £000		Year 4 £000		Year 5 £000	
Sales		520		780		900		750		780
Less Cost of goods sold										
Opening stock	40		100		80		60		140	
Cost of production	340		380		400		460		500	
Available for sale	380		480		480		520		640	
Less Closing stock	100	280	80	400	60	420	140	380	160	480
Gross profit		240		380		480		370		300
Less Expenses										
Administration										
Salaries	60		63		67		70		70	
Office supplies	15		20		27		32		35	
Miscellaneous	10		13		15		18		20	
Total	85		93		109		120		125	
Marketing										
Selling	40		55		70		75		65	
Advertising	43		79		108		107		57	
Distribution	20		30		45		48		40	
Total	103		164		223		230		162	
Total expenses		188		257		332		350		287
Net profit		**52**		**123**		**148**		**20**		**13**

TABLE 3.2 Horizontal analysis

	Year (% change)			
	1–2	2–3	3–4	4–5
Sales	50	15	−16	4
Cost of production	11	5	15	8
Gross profit	58	26	−30	−23
Expenses				
Administration				
Salaries	5	6	4	0
Office supplies	33	35	18	9
Miscellaneous	30	13	20	11
Marketing				
Selling	37	21	7	−13
Advertising	83	36	9	−47
Distribution	50	50	6	−17
Total expenses	36	29	5	−18
Net profit	**136**	**20**	**−86**	**−35**

Horizontal analysis

Horizontal analysis involves comparing the figures in terms of percentage change from year to year (Table 3.2).

The first point to note from Table 3.2 is the erratic changes over the five years. Sales rose and then fell back. Rising costs of production along with slower turnover of stock (see stock turnover ratio below) has meant a dramatic reduction in gross profit.

As for expenses, only salaries remained fairly stable over the period. After a resounding early increase, net profits fell substantially.

Trend analysis

A clearer picture of how the various elements have behaved over the five years can be sought via trend analysis which indexes year 1 as 100 (Table 3.3).

What emerges from Table 3.3 is whilst sales increased by 50 per cent over the five years, significant increases in expenses meant a large fall in net profits during the last two years.

Ratio analysis

In contrast to horizontal and trend analysis, ratio analysis involves a vertical examination of the profit and loss account, although comparisons from year to year must still be made. Some useful ratios are set out below.

$$\text{Gross profit percentage} = \frac{\text{Gross profit}}{\text{Sales}} \times 100$$

TABLE 3.3 Trend analysis

	Year				
	1	2	3	4	5
Sales	100	150	173	144	150
Cost of production	100	111	117	135	147
Gross profit	100	158	200	154	125
Expenses					
Salaries	100	105	111	116	116
Office supplies	100	133	180	213	233
Miscellaneous	100	130	150	180	200
Selling	100	137	175	187	162
Advertising	100	183	251	248	132
Distribution	100	150	225	240	200
Net profit	**100**	**236**	**284**	**39**	**25**

Gross profit percentage indicates the percentage of revenues available to cover expenses and provide a profit after the cost of goods sold has been paid.

$$\text{Net profit percentage} = \frac{\text{Net profit}}{\text{Sales}} \times 100$$

Net profit percentage indicates how much the company has made after all costs have been subtracted from sales.

$$\text{Stock turnover ratio} = \frac{\text{Cost of goods sold}}{\text{Average stock}}$$

where average stock is usually calculated as:

$$\frac{\text{Opening stock} + \text{Closing stock}}{2}$$

The stock turnover ratio is normally expressed as a number, e.g. 3 or 6, and not as a percentage. A company is anxious to have its stock move quickly or 'turn over'. What is considered a 'good stock turn' will vary by industry.

$$\text{Expenses percentage} = \frac{\text{Expenses}}{\text{Sales}} \times 100$$

Expenses percentage gives some guidance as to how productive £1 spent on, say, advertising or selling is in terms of sales.

From Table 3.4, which illustrates the above ratios, we can see that:

- Company performance in terms of sales and net profit deteriorated after year 3.
- Stock turnover rose in line with increased sales, then fell sharply along with a decline in sales.
- Marketing expenses, in particular advertising, increased over most of the period.

TABLE 3.4 Ratio analysis: expenses percentage

	Year				
	1	2	3	4	5
Gross profit %	46	49	53	49	38
Stock turnover (no. of times)	4	4.44	6	3.8	3.2
Expenses/Sales %					
Selling	7	7	8	10	8
Advertising	8	10	12	14	7
Distribution	4	4	5	6	5
Sales per £1 of marketing expenses	5	4.75	4	3.3	4.8
Net profit %	**10**	**16**	**16**	**3**	**2**

Questions to be asked:

- Are the changes in sales revenue caused by changes in price and/or the number of units sold (sales volume)?
- Is the seemingly high and fluctuating expenses to sales ratio the result of inefficient spending and/or a static, competitive market depressing sales?
- How does performance compare with that of competitors?

Profit sensitivity analysis

Profit sensitivity analysis is a simple technique that gives more insight into how a company makes a profit. Basically it involves calculating for each element in the profit and loss account a profit multiplier that measures the effect on net profit of a change in that element. If, for example, an increase of 10 per cent in price raises net profit by 50 per cent, the profit multiplier for price would be:

$$\frac{\%\text{ change in net profit}}{\%\text{ change in price}} = \frac{50}{10} = 5$$

Similar calculations can be made for other elements, namely number of units sold (sales volume) cost of production and the expenses. It may be that, for a number of reasons, changes to the various elements cannot be made in the short term. However, the main attraction of profit sensitivity analysis is that, given the freedom to act, what changes will have the greatest impact on net profit.

Pareto effect (the 80/20 rule)

Most companies sell more than one product. It may be misleading to judge the performance of the company on the basis of total sales and net profit. A proper analysis

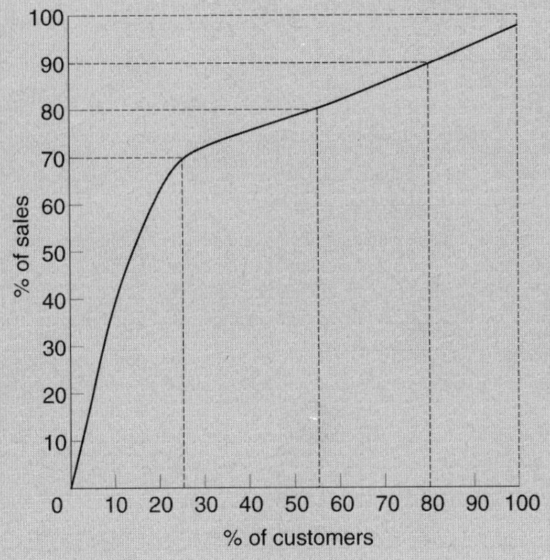

FIGURE 3.1 The 80/20 rule.

requires a breakdown of performance by, for example, product, customer, channel of distribution and sales territory.

The 80/20 rule means that about 20 per cent of customers/products/channels/territories account for about 80 per cent of the business (see Figure 3.1). The figure is not, strictly speaking, always 80/20, but it does signal to companies that much of their business may come from only a few of their customers, etc.

From Figure 3.1 we can see that 25 per cent of the company's customers account for 70 per cent of sales, 55 per cent account for 80 per cent of sales and 80 per cent account for 90 per cent of sales. What this kind of analysis does is to remind a company that its business is not evenly spread across its customer base, and to raise questions over the deployment of its marketing effort. It is not simply a matter of dropping 75 per cent of its customers – some of these will be profitable, some will become more profitable and others will remain small and insignificant.

A basic format for identifying customer profitability is illustrated in Table 3.5. A preliminary assessment of the figures reveals that customer group A, with the highest sales, does not generate the highest profit. This is an important observation in that it is dangerous to assume that large sales invariably lead to large profits. Referring back to Figure 3.1 (the 80/20 rule), a percentage of profit could have been used on the vertical axis and a conclusion drawn as to whether it is the same minority of customers that account for the majority of sales.

A vertical analysis of Table 3.5 confirms the contrast in performance of, for example, customer groups A and C (Table 3.6).

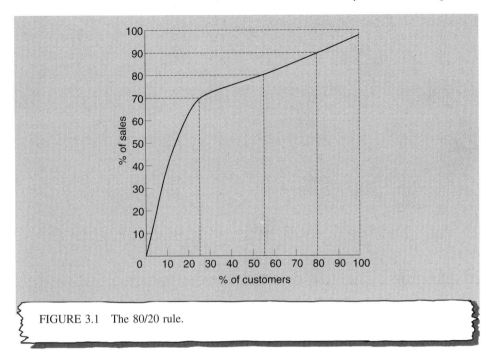

TABLE 3.5 A basic format for customer profitability assessment

Customer group	Sales £000	Cost of goods sold £000	% of sales	Marketing expenses £000	% of sales	Profit £000	%	Total %
A	750	412.5	55	262.5	35	75	10	100
B	250	150	60	70	28	30	12	100
C	450	270	60	67.5	15	112.5	25	100
D	150	82.5	55	45	30	22.5	15	100
Total	1600	915.0		445.0		240.0		

TABLE 3.6 Vertical analysis

	% of sales	% of cost of goods sold	% of marketing expenses	% of profit
A	47	45	59	31
B	16	16	16	13
C	28	30	15	47
D	9	9	10	9
Total	100	100	100	100

Reasons must now be sought as to why customer group A with nearly half of total sales was outperformed in terms of profitability by customer group C. It may well be that difficulties in obtaining sales in group A justified the large amount of marketing expenditure. On the other hand, much of it may be put down to an inefficient use of resources. A list of areas needs to be generalized for the purpose of explaining good and bad performance, for example:

- Allocation and deployment of advertising expenditure.
- Salesforce utilization.
- Pricing – margins, discount structures.
- Service levels – order sizes, delivery frequency.
- Products/services bought by customer groups.

Cost and revenue behaviour

It is important for decision-makers to know how costs and revenues will vary with different levels of activity. For many companies, activity will be measured in terms of sales volume (number of units bought). In the health service, sales volume could be defined as number of patients seen, and for railways number of commuters transported.

Cost behaviour

The basic principle of cost behaviour is that as the level of activity rises, total costs will usually rise. It will cost more to sell 100 000 units than it will to sell 20 000 units. What needs to be understood is the way that costs rise and by how much as the level of activity increases.

Costs are divided into variable and fixed costs.

Variable costs

Variable costs vary in direct proportion to the volume of activity, so doubling the level of activity will double the total variable cost, e.g. expenses for parts, packaging materials, sales commission.

Figure 3.2 illustrates total and unit variable costs. Total variable cost varies proportionally with changes in the level of activity, whilst unit variable cost remains constant whatever the level of activity.

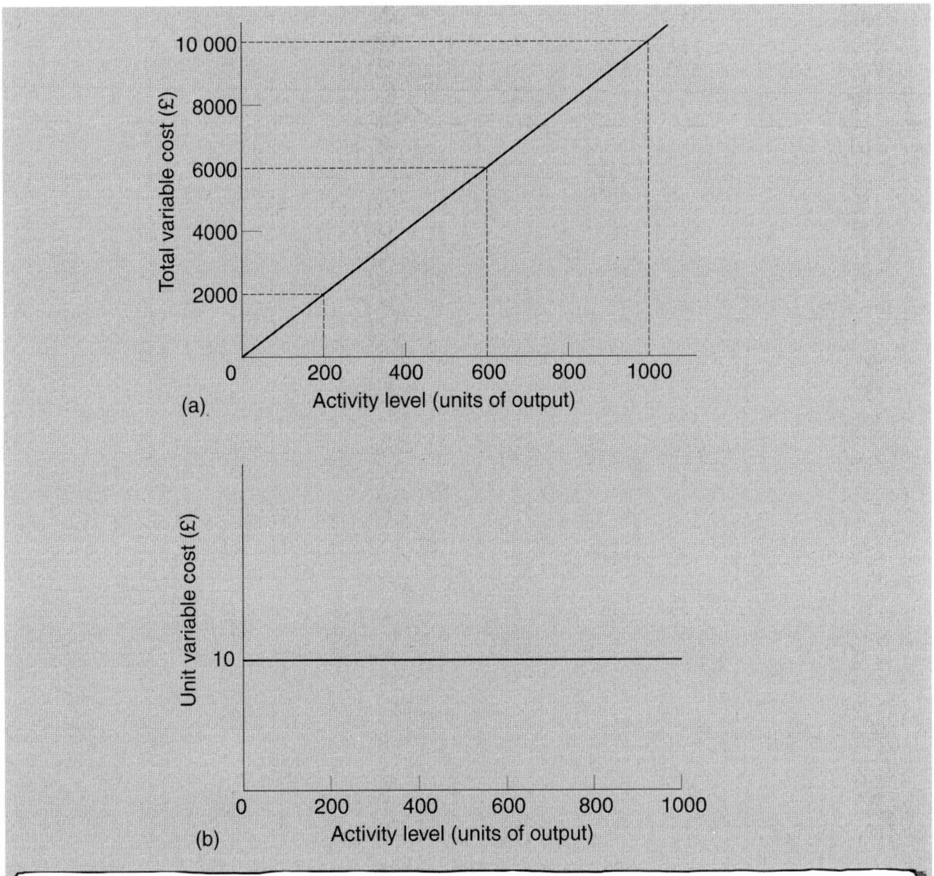

FIGURE 3.2 Total (a) and unit (b) variable costs.

Consider, for example, a company paying its salesforce a commission. As the sales value increases, the commission paid will increase proportionally. If the company pays a commission of 10 per cent of sales value, the total commission paid will be as follows:

Month	Sales value (£)	Commission paid (£)
1	100 000	10 000
2	130 000	13 000
3	140 000	14 000

The variable cost (commission paid) varies proportionally with the level of activity (sales value). The unit variable cost remains unchanged at 10p per £1 of sales.

Fixed costs

Fixed costs remain constant over a wide range of activity for a specified time period, e.g. salesforce salaries, rent, insurance. Figure 3.3 illustrates total and unit fixed costs. Total fixed costs remain constant whereas unit fixed costs decrease proportionally with the level of activity.

If the fixed costs are, say, £10 000 then the unit fixed costs over a range of sales volumes will be as shown in Table 3.7.

Cost structure of a company

Companies need to monitor their competitive position, price levels and profit margins. A vital factor in all of this will be cost variations at different levels of output (Table 3.8). The key column is column 7 as this will be influential when it comes to making decisions in the areas mentioned above (i.e. competitiveness, pricing, profitability).

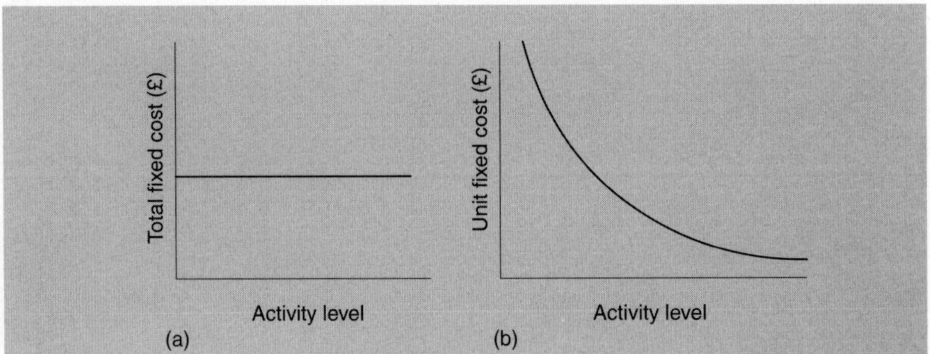

FIGURE 3.3 Total (a) and unit (b) fixed costs.

TABLE 3.7 Unit fixed costs

Units sold	Fixed cost per unit (£)
1	10 000
20	500
50	200
100	100
500	20
2 000	5

TABLE 3.8 Cost structure of a company

(1)	(2)[a] Total fixed costs	(3) Average fixed costs (2 ÷ 1)	(4) Total variable costs	(5) Average variable costs (4 ÷ 1)	(6) Total cost (2 + 4)	(7) Average cost per unit (3 + 5)
0	60 000	–	–	–	60 000	–
20 000	60 000	3	10 000	2	70 000	5
40 000	60 000	1.50	20 000	2	80 000	3.50
60 000	60 000	1	30 000	2	90 000	3
80 000	60 000	0.75	40 000	2	100 000	2.75
100 000	60 000	0.60	50 000	2	110 000	2.60
120 000	60 000	0.50	60 000	2	120 000	2.50
140 000	60 000	0.43	70 000	2	130 000	2.43
160 000	60 000	0.38	80 000	2	140 000	2.38
180 000	60 000	0.33	90 000	2	150 000	2.33
200 000	60 000	0.30	100 000	2	160 000	2.30

[a] To sell more than 200 000 units may necessitate purchasing additional machinery and sales personnel, thereby raising total fixed costs.

Cost/volume/profit analysis

A major decision facing marketing managers is that of profit planning. To plan for profits, information is required about future costs and revenues. What will happen to costs, revenues and, subsequently, profits if, for example:

- the company sells 5 000 more units?
- the company raises or lower its price?
- the company increases occupancy levels by 10 per cent in its hotels?

The solution is to apply cost/volume/profit (CVP) analysis. CVP analysis is a tool for examining the relationship between changes in volume and changes in total sales revenue, costs and profit. It is subject to a number of underlying assumptions and limitations but is, nevertheless, regarded as a powerful decision-making tool.

Relevant formulae and equations

Before embarking on some practical applications, the relevant formulae/equations must be set out and understood.

Net profit

$$\text{Net profit} = \text{Sales revenue} - \text{Total costs}$$

In particular:

$$\text{Net profit} = (\text{Units sold} \times \text{Unit selling price}) - \{(\text{Units sold} \times \text{Unit variable cost}) + \text{Total fixed costs}\}$$

The following symbols can be used to represent the various items in the above equation:

NP = Net profit
x = Units sold
P = Selling price
b = Unit variable cost
a = Total fixed cost

The equation can now be expressed as:

$$\text{NP} = \text{P}x - (a + bx)$$

Contribution

The concept of contribution is extremely important in financial analysis:

$$\text{Contribution} = \text{P} - b$$

or, in aggregate terms:

$$\text{P}x - bx$$

Break-even

Break-even analysis is one of the simplest applications of contribution analysis. It identifies the sales volume and value at which a company makes neither a profit nor a loss but merely covers the total fixed costs. Break-even point (B/E) is expressed as:

$$\text{B/E (sales volume)} = \frac{\text{Fixed cost}}{\text{Contribution per unit}}$$

$$\text{B/E (Sales value)} = \frac{\text{Fixed cost}}{\text{Contribution to sales ratio}}$$

Contribution to sales ratio

Probably the most important piece of information resulting from a profit analysis is the contribution to sales (C/S) ratio, or contribution margin ratio. Note that it does not mean profit in relationship to sales, but the contribution in relation to sales. It is the proportion of sales available to cover fixed costs and profits after deducting varibale costs. It is expressed as follows:

$$\text{C/S ratio} = \frac{\text{Contribution}}{\text{Sales}}$$

The ratio is of further value as it enables the contribution to be calculated from any given level of sales, namely:

$$\text{Contribution} = \text{Sales} \times \text{C/S ratio}$$

Having calculated the contribution we can deduct the fixed costs to arrive at the profit on sales.

Example of cost/volume/profit analysis

Financial data for Alba Ltd are as follows:

Fixed costs per year	£240 000
Unit selling price	£40
Unit variable cost	£20
Existing sales	16 000 units

We can use these data to answer the following questions.

1. What is the existing net profit?
2. What is the output level at which Alba Ltd breaks even?
3. How many units must be sold to obtain £60 000 profit?
4. What is the profit that will result from a 20 per cent reduction in variable costs and a £20 000 decrease in fixed costs, assuming that current sales can be maintained?
5. What is the selling price that would have to be charged to show a profit of £120 000 on sales of 16 000 units?
6. How much additional sales volume is required to cover £40 000 extra fixed costs from a proposed increase in advertising expenditure?
7. What is the contribution from sales of £960 000?

Solutions

1. $$\begin{aligned}\text{Net profit} &= £40 \times 16\,000 - (£240\,000 + £20 \times 16\,000)\\ &= £80\,000\end{aligned}$$

2. $$\text{B/E (sales volume)} = \frac{£240\,000}{£20} = £12\,000$$

$$\text{B/E (sales value)} = \frac{£240\,000}{0.50} = £480\,000$$

As a check, multiply the B/E volume by the price (12 000 × £40) to arrive at the B/E value, £480 000.

3. Applying the contribution approach we must obtain sufficient to cover the fixed costs and the desired profit. Therefore,

$$\text{Units required to achieve desired profit} = \frac{\text{Fixed costs + Desired profit}}{\text{Contribution per unit}}$$

$$= \frac{£(240\ 000 + 60\ 000)}{£20}$$

$$= 15\ 000 \text{ units}$$

4. $NP = £40 \times 16\ 000 - \{£220\ 000 + (£16 \times 16\ 000)\}$

$= £164\ 000$

5. $£120\ 000 = 16\ 000\ P - \{£240\ 000 + (16\ 000 \times £20)\}$

$16\ 000\ P = £120\ 000 + £560\ 000$

$P = £42.5$ (i.e. an increase of £2.50 per unit)

6. $$\text{Additional volume required} = \frac{\text{Extra fixed cost}}{\text{Contribution per unit}}$$

$$= \frac{£40\ 000}{£20}$$

$$= £2000$$

7. Contribution $= £960\ 000 \times 0.50$

$= £480\ 000$

To calculate the profit, deduct the fixed costs of £240 000 from the contribution of £480 000. The contribution to sales ratio of 50 per cent means that for every £1 of sales revenue a contribution of 50 pence is earned. As sales and contribution are in direct proportion to each other, a sales increase of, in this case, 50 per cent would mean an increase in contribution of 50 per cent.

Break-even chart

The data in the above example can be used to construct a break-even chart (Figure 3.4).

A break-even chart is an easy-to-understand visual aid but its weakness is the simplifying assumptions upon which it is based. For example, the straight line of sales

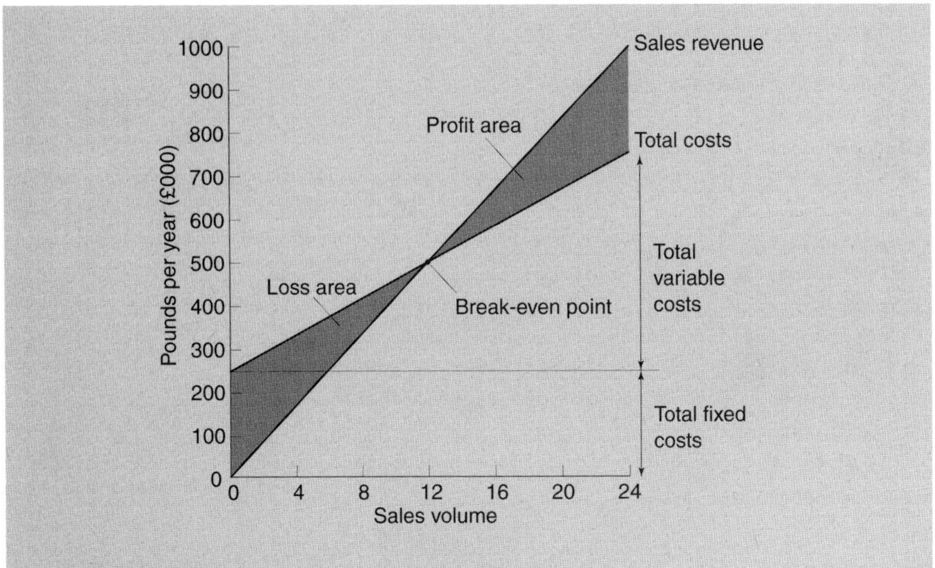

FIGURE 3.4 Break-even chart for Alba Ltd.

revenue assumes that any quantity can be sold at the same price, in this case £40. Similarly, costs can change at different volume levels. The chart can be useful, however, for a small company starting up or a large company launching a new product where, in both cases, price levels are constrained and total costs largely fixed in the shorter term. The break-even point will signal just how much business has to be attained and it will be for the companies to determine, given prevailing market conditions, whether that figure can be reached, let alone exceeded.

Extension of B/E analysis

As we have seen, the B/E chart assumes that each £1 has the same cost, the same C/S ratio and, eventually, the same profit. In the real world, however, things are not quite so straightforward. Over time, changes will occur in costs and prices with resultant changes in profits. In terms of the B/E chart for example:

- A decrease in variable costs will decrease the slope of the total cost line, resulting in a lower B/E point.
- If prices are increased and volume remains unchanged, the result will be a lower B/E point.
- If only fixed costs are increased, the result will be an increase in the B/E point, causing profits to start later.

Profit/volume analysis

The break-even chart does not highlight the profit or loss at different volume levels. To determine the profit or loss figures from a break-even chart you need to establish the difference between the total cost and total revenue lines. The profit/volume graph, although similar to the break-even chart, is a better way of showing the impact of changes in volume on profit (Figure 3.5). The horizontal axis represents the various levels of sales volume, and the profits and losses appear on the vertical axis. From Figure 3.5 you will see that where sales are zero the maximum loss will be the amount of fixed costs incurred. With each unit sold a contribution of £20 is obtained towards fixed costs, and the break-even point is at 12 000 units, when the total contribution (12 000 × £20) exactly equals the total fixed costs (£240 000). With each additional unit sold beyond 12 000 units, a surplus of £20 per unit is obtained. If 20 000 units are sold, the profit will be £160 000 (8000 units at £20 contribution – see dotted line on graph).

It is important to remember the assumptions underlying the construction of the profit/volume graph in Figure 3.5:

- A single product or constant sales mix.
- Fixed costs do not change.
- Total costs and total revenues are linear functions of output.

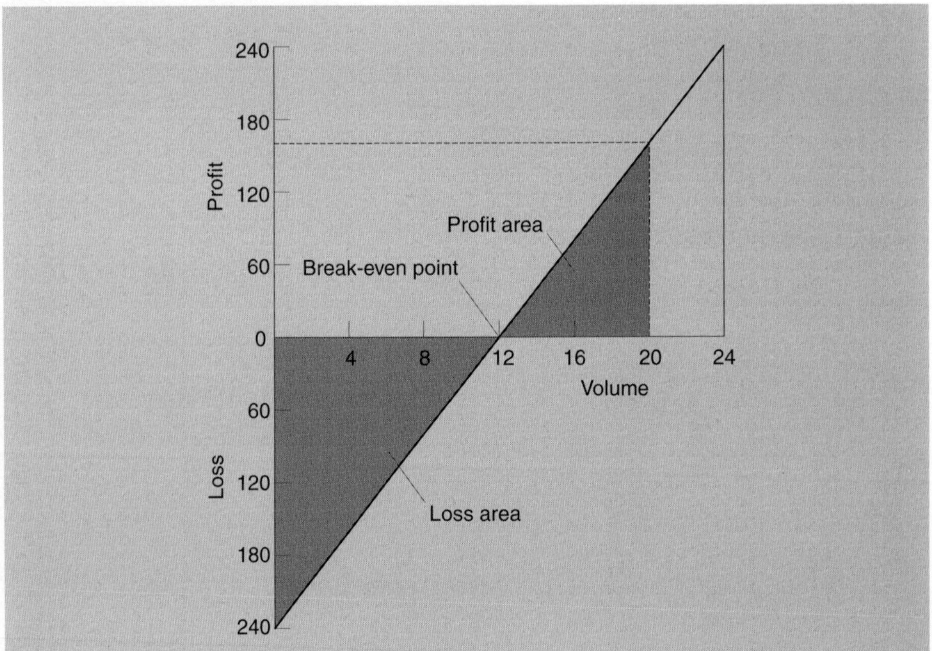

FIGURE 3.5 Profit/volume graph for Alba Ltd.

- Costs can be accurately divided into fixed and variable.
- All the variables, e.g. price, remain constant.

The multi-product situation

Break-even charts are normally constructed with one product in mind. What if the company sells more than one product? Consider the case of a company selling three products A, B and C (Table 3.9).

A break-even chart cannot be drawn as we do not know the proportions of A, B and C in the sales mix. If we assume that sales of A, B and C are in the fixed proportions of 2000 : 4000 : 3000 at all levels of activity a multi-product break-even point can be calculated along with a multi-product cost/volume/profit chart.

TABLE 3.9 Basic financial data

	Products		
	A £	B £	C £
Selling price	8	6	6
Unit variable cost	3	4	5
Unit contribution	5	2	1
Total fixed costs = £10 000			

Break-even calculation

One way to arrive at the break-even point is to calculate the weighted contribution (Table 3.10). Weighting is achieved by multiplying the respective prices, variable costs and contribution by each product's percentage of the total sales mix, e.g. product A's percentage is 22 (i.e. 100 × 2000/9000).

$$\text{Break-even (volume)} = \frac{\text{Total fixed cost}}{\text{Total weighted unit contribution}}$$

$$= \frac{\text{£10 000}}{2.31}$$

$$= 4329$$

TABLE 3.10 Weighted analysis

	A	B	C	Total
Selling price	1.76	2.64	1.98	6.38
Unit variable cost	0.66	1.76	1.65	4.07
Unit contribution	1.1	0.88	0.33	2.31

$$\text{Break-even (value)} = 4329 \times \text{Total weighted unit selling price}$$
$$= 4329 \times 6.38$$
$$= £27\,619$$

Another route to determining the break-even value is through the contribution to sales (C/S) ratio:

$$\text{C/S ratio} = \frac{\text{Selling price} - \text{Variable cost}}{\text{Selling price}}$$
$$= \frac{6.38 - 4.07}{6.38}$$
$$= 36.2\%$$

Hence,

$$\text{Break-even (value)} = \frac{£10\,000}{0.362}$$
$$= £27\,624$$

Multi-product chart

The chart can be constructed using the data in columns 4, 5 and 6 of Table 3.11.

TABLE 3.11

(1) Product	(2) Contribution £	(3) Sales £	(4) C/S ratio %	(5) Cumulative sales £	(6) Cumulative profit £
A	10 000	16 000	62.5	16 000	–
B	8 000	24 000	33.33	40 000	8 000
C	3 000	18 000	16.66	58 000	11 000

In constructing a profit/volume chart it is normal practice to plot the products from left to right in descending order of C/S ratio (Figure 3.6). The dotted line indicates the contribution from each product and the solid line reflects the average profitability of the three products. Break-even could, of course, be achieved through selling only product A – 2000 units at £5 contribution per unit would meet the fixed costs of £10 000. As product A is by far the most profitable in terms of C/S ratio, it might be worth increasing the sales of A even at the expense of C.

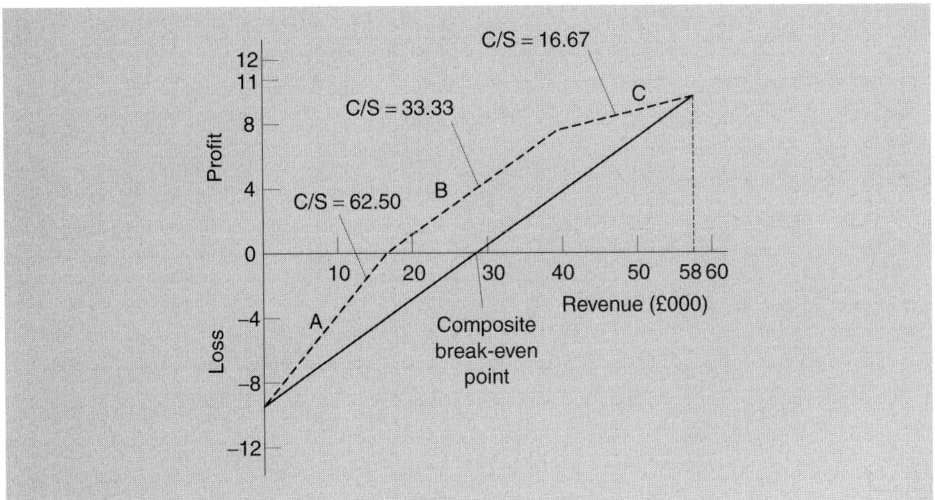

FIGURE 3.6 Multi-product profit/volume chart.

Effect of changes in the sales mix

To illustrate what can happen when a change in the sales mix occurs, consider the figures in Table 3.12.

With fixed costs of £100 000, break-even is:

$$\text{Break-even (sales value)} = \frac{£100\ 000}{0.25}$$
$$= £400\ 000$$

For a total sales revenue of £1m, profits would be:

$$\begin{aligned}\text{Profit} &= (\text{Sales} \times \text{C/S}) - \text{Fixed costs} \\ &= (£1\ 000\ 000 \times 0.25) - £100\ 000 \\ &= £150\ 000\end{aligned}$$

What effect would changing the sales mix (column 3 of Table 3.13) have? The new break-even is:

$$\text{Break-even (sales value)} = \frac{£100\ 000}{0.21}$$
$$= £476\ 190$$

The increase in break-even has come about largely as a consequence of product X which has the best C/S ratio but now contributes less of the sales mix.

TABLE 3.12

(1) Product	(2) C/S	(3) % of total sales Revenue	(4) Weighted C/S (2 × 3)
X	0.40	0.40	0.16
Y	0.20	0.30	0.06
Z	0.10	0.30	0.03
Composite C/S			0.25

TABLE 3.13

(1) Product	(2) C/S	(3) % of total sales revenue	(4) Weighted C/S (2 × 3)
X	0.40	0.20	0.08
Y	0.20	0.50	0.10
Z	0.10	0.30	0.03
Composite C/S			0.21

For a total sales revenue of £1m, profits would be:

$$\text{Profit} = (£1\,000\,000 \times 0.21) - £100\,000$$
$$= £110\,000$$

Hence sales revenue must increase by 19 per cent (4 per cent on 21 per cent to get back to 25 per cent) to recapture the original profit level if the sales mix shifts as indicated.

When, as in this case, a shift in the sales mix results in a poorer C/S, companies may attempt to recover the profit level by across-the-board increases in prices. Although such action helps to restore the original C/S ratio, reaction from competition and consumers could lead to substantial reductions in sales and profits. Shifting emphasis to those products with higher C/S ratio may be a more effective option for recovering some or all of a profit position than increases in prices.

The essential point to remember for any multi-product or multi-service organization is that profitability is affected by four elements:

- Price
- Costs – variable and fixed
- Volume sold
- Revenue sales mix

Cost allocation and profitability

Reference was made earlier in the chapter (see Pareto effect) to the need to analyze sales and profits by customer, product, etc., in preference to total sales and profits. The success and value of any profitability analysis will, however, increasingly depend on how costs are attributed to customers, products and so on. The subject of cost allocation has not received much attention in marketing except for obvious costs that vary directly with sales, namely salesforce commission. The controversy over cost allocation has increasingly been fuelled by criticism of sales as a valid indicator of costs, whether marketing or otherwise. Consider a simple example of a company marketing two products. Sales of product A are £200 000 and of B £400 000. The traditional approach would be to apportion one-third of costs to A and two-thirds to B in order to allocate the costs evenly. However, this may be very misleading if, for example, product A is difficult to sell, requiring two-thirds as against one-third of salesforce resources. If selling costs in this example are a major component of total costs, the correct conclusion would be to regard B as more profitable than A.

Approaches to cost allocation

Full cost approach

All costs are assigned to products, customers, etc. Some of these costs are directly traceable to a product or customer but others (fixed and common costs) are apportioned in some arbitrary way, e.g. percentage of sales (Table 3.14).

The only fixed costs in this case – administration – have been apportioned to products on the basis of percentage of total sales. This is typical of the full cost approach. The question is, 'Should product A be eliminated as it shows a net loss of £1000?' If A were eliminated the administration costs of £6000 would have to be charged to products B and C. The effect on net profit can be seen in Table 3.15.

The result is a reduction in net profit of £5000 since product A previously covered £5000 of the £6000 in administration costs. Furthermore, the reallocation has now rendered product B unprofitable.

TABLE 3.14 Full cost approach

	Product			Total
	A £	B £	C £	£
Sales	100 000	60 000	40 000	200 000
Cost of goods sold	90 000	50 000	20 000	160 000
Gross profit	10 000	10 000	20 000	40 000
Expenses				
Selling	5 000	3 000	2 000	10 000
Administration	6 000	3 600	2 400	12 000
Total expenses	11 000	6 600	4 400	22 000
Net profit (loss)	(1 000)	3 400	15 600	18 000

TABLE 3.15 Cost reallocation

	Product		Total
	B £	C £	£
Sales	60 000	40 000	100 000
Cost of goods	50 000	20 000	70 000
Gross profit	10 000	20 000	30 000
Expenses			
Selling	3 000	2 000	5 000
Administration	7 200	4 800	12 000
Total expenses	10 200	6 800	17 000
Net profit (loss)	(200)	13 200	13 000

Contribution approach

Under the contribution approach only those costs that are directly related to the marketing of a product, serving a customer, etc., are allocated. Should the company drop the product or customer then the allocated costs would disappear. The contribution approach focuses on variable rather than total costs.

Table 3.16 shows a contribution approach using the same data as in the full cost approach above. Note that each product has a positive contribution, in particular product A with a contribution of £5000. This would be the amount lost if product A were dropped (fixed administrative costs are truly fixed – none of them would be eliminated if any of the three products were dropped).

TABLE 3.16 Contribution approach

	Product			Total
	A £	B £	C £	£
Sales	100 000	60 000	40 000	200 000
Variable costs				
Cost of goods sold	90 000	50 000	20 000	160 000
Selling expenses	5 000	3 000	2 000	10 000
Total variable costs	95 000	53 000	22 000	170 000
Contribution	5 000	7 000	18 000	30 000
Fixed costs				
Admin. expenses				12 000
Net profit				18 000

Segmental profitability analysis

The examples in Tables 3.14–3.16 illustrate the basics of full cost and contribution approaches. Furthermore, the analysis by product is of fundamental importance in marketing decision-making. We call this segmented profitability analysis. A segment consists of a product, type of customer, geographical region, channels of distribution, etc.

The earlier reference to Pareto analysis (80/20 rule) suggests a more detailed assessment of performance than simply total company sales and profits. Segmental profitability analysis enables a company to determine whether a segment (product, customer type, etc.) should be expanded or abandoned. The following example builds, in a more detailed way, on the full cost and contribution approaches.[1]

Example of segmental profitability analysis

National Ltd is a wholesaler that sells its products to a wide range of retailers. Marketing is done through three geographical areas: the South, the Midlands and the North. The estimates of the costs and revenues for each sales territory for the next accounting period are shown in Table 3.17. The products are packaged and despatched from a central warehouse, and it is estimated that 50 per cent of the costs are variable and 50 per cent are fixed. All of the selling costs are fixed, with the exception of salesmen's expenses, which are variable with sales revenue. All of the administration expenses of the headquarters are common, unavoidable and without alternatives, and have been apportioned to sales territories on the basis of sales value.

From Table 3.17 you will see that a predicted loss of £56 000 is reported for the Northern area. The question is, therefore, should the Northern area be closed. The profitability analysis shown in the table includes some fixed costs that are common or joint to all three territories. These costs will continue if the Northern area is closed, and are therefore not relevant for decision-making purposes.

What, then, will be the effect of closing the Northern area? The sales revenues, the selling costs and the variable warehousing costs will be eliminated if the area is closed. The remainder of the warehousing costs and all the administration fixed costs will continue and as such are irrelevant to the decision. The financial outcome of eliminating the North is shown in Table 3.18.

TABLE 3.17 Profit analysis by sales territory

	South		Midlands		North		Total
	£	£	£	£	£	£	£
Sales		900 000		1 000 000		900 000	2 800 000
Cost of goods sold		400 000		450 000		500 000	1 350 000
		500 000		550 000		400 000	1 450 000
Gross profit							
Fixed selling costs							
Salesmen's salaries	80 000		100 000		120 000		
Sales office and management expenses	40 000		60 000		80 000		
Advertising	50 000		50 000		50 000		
Salesmen's expenses	50 000	220 000	60 000	270 000	80 000	330 000	
Headquarters administration expenses		80 000		90 000		90 000	
Warehousing costs		32 000		36 000		36 000	
Total costs		332 000		396 000		456 000	1 184 000
Net profit (loss)		168 000		154 000		(56 000)	266 000

Source: Drury, J.C., *Management and Cost Accounting*, ITPS, 1994, p. 240.

TABLE 3.18 Financial consequences of eliminating North territory

	£	£
Sales revenue lost		(900 000)
Less Relevant costs saved		
Cost of goods sold	500 000	
Selling costs	330 000	
Warehousing variable	18 000	
Costs		848 000
Amount lost		(52 000)

The company will lose £52 000 which could have contributed towards the administration and warehousing common fixed costs. If a segment (in this case a geographical area) can contribute towards common and unavoidable fixed costs, there is an argument which suggests that it should not be closed or dropped assuming no better use can be made of the facilities and that sales in other segments are unaffected by the decision.

The problem with the profitability analysis in Table 3.17 is that it is misleading. Fixed costs that are common and joint to all segments have been apportioned to sales territories on an arbitrary basis, namely sales value. The segmental profitability analysis set out in Table 3.19 provides more meaningful information.[2]

This revised approach includes much more than revenue minus variable cost. Contribution margins are computed on a hierarchical basis. At the first level, a short-term contribution is computed by deducting from sales revenue the variable costs traceable to that revenue. At the next level, fixed costs specifically attributable to segments are

TABLE 3.19 Segmental profitability analysis adopting a decision-relevant approach

	South		Midlands		North		Total
	£	£	£	£	£	£	£
Sales		900 000		1 000 000		900 000	2 800 000
Less Variable costs							
Cost of goods sold	400 000		450 000		500 000		
Salesmen's expenses	50 000		60 000		80 000		
Warehousing costs	16 000	466 000	18 000	528 000	18 000	598 000	1 592 000
Contribution to all fixed costs		434 000		472 000		302 000	1 208 000
Less Specific fixed costs							
Salesmen's salaries	80 000		100 000		120 000		
Sales office and management expenses	40 000		60 000		80 000		
Advertising	50 000	170 000	50 000	210 000	50 000	250 000	630 000
Contribution to common fixed costs		264 000		262 000		52 000	578 000
Less Common fixed costs							
Administration							(260 000)
Warehouse							(52 000)
Net profit							266 000

Source: Drury, J.C., *Management and Cost Accounting*, ITPS, 1994.

deducted to derive the contribution to the common fixed costs. Fixed costs that are joint and common to all segments are not apportioned to specific segments. Instead, they are deducted in 'lump sum' to derive the profit for all segments.

It is important that the different segments of the business generate sufficient contribution to cover the common fixed costs that are not specifically attributable to individual segments. For example, if the total contribution to common fixed costs totalled £250 000 instead of £578 000 in Table 3.19, then this would not be sufficient to cover the common fixed costs of £312 000, and a loss of £62 000 would be reported.

Activity-based costing

Increasing criticism has been directed towards traditional costing systems, in particular the full cost approach. If companies wish to have a clearer picture of product, customer, etc. profitability they will need to turn to activity-based costing (ABC), developed by Cooper and Kaplan. The objective of profitability analysis in marketing is to sort out those products and customers to which the company should assign or invest its resources. To make effective decisions as to which segments (customers, products, etc.) should be dropped, harvested, retained and invested in, costs have to be charged appropriately.

The essence of ABC is to appreciate that it is activities which cause costs, and products/customers, etc. which consume activities. There are four stages involved in ABC:

- **Stage 1**. Identify the activities in a company.
- **Stage 2**. Identify the factors that influence the cost of a particular activity. The term 'cost driver' is used to describe any factor that affects the costs of these activities.
- **Stage 3**. Create a cost pool for each activity, e.g. the total costs of all set-ups or sales calls.
- **Stage 4**. Trace the costs of the activities to products/customers, etc. according to their consumption of these activities.

Examples of stages 1 and 2 are given in Table 3.20. Stages 3 and 4 can be illustrated as follows:

Cost pool	*Total cost*	*Number of calls*	*Cost per call*
Sales calls	£50 000	1000	£50

TABLE 3.20 Activities and cost drivers

Activity	Cost driver
Machine set-up	Number of set ups
Purchasing	Number of orders placed
Selling	Number of sales calls (hours)
Travel	Number/location of customers
Distribution	Number of items distributed
Customer service	Number of service calls
	Hours spent servicing products
	Number of products serviced

Let us say customer A received 80 calls, then activity-based costing would allocate £4000 (80 × £50) to that particular customer, this being the amount of that activity (selling) consumed. 'Number of sales working hours' would in fact be a more accurate indicator of cost than number of calls.

Because ABC reveals the links between performing particular activities and the demands that those activities make on the organization's resources, it can give managers a clear picture of how products, brands, customers, facilities, regions or distribution channels both generate revenues and consume resources. The profitability picture that emerges from the ABC analysis helps managers to focus their energy on improving activities that will have the biggest impact on the bottom line. For marketing management, as much emphasis should be given to tracing profitability as to generating sales. If relevant cost drivers can be found and traced to products/customers, etc. then greater understanding of the relationship between marketing effort and profitability will develop.

Cost and profitability analysis

We can gain some insight into activity-based costing by examining a methodology first developed by Sevin. It is essentially a four step process:

- Lay out the overall profit and loss account.
- Convert natural (or primary) costs into functional costs.
- Allocate these functional costs to the marketing segments under study, e.g. product, customer, channel of distribution.
- Prepare a profit and loss account for each segment.

The following example is a simplified version of a possible system that a company might use for activity-based costing.

Example of activity-based costing

Step 1

We start with the profit and loss account (Table 3.21) of a company marketing to three customers. The company wishes to know the profitability of its three customers. To achieve this it must undertake a marketing cost analysis.

TABLE 3.21 Profit and loss account

Sales		£17 000
Cost of sales		11 900
Gross profit		5 100
Expenses		
Salaries	2 500	
Rent	500	
Packaging materials	1 012	
Postage and stationery	50	
Hire of office equipment	100	
		4 162
Net profit		**£ 938**

Step 2

The costs in the five natural accounts (the expenses) must be allocated to four functional accounts – personal selling, packaging and despatch, advertising and invoice, and collection (Table 3.22). (Note, at this point, that these functional accounts can be equated to activities under an activities-based costing system.)

The reasoning behind the allocation is as follows:

- Salaries are divided between thc salesforce, packaging employees and office staff (administration of advertising material and invoicing and collection of debts).
- Rent – 80 per cent of the floorspace is for packaging and despatch (thus £400 allocated) and the remaining 20 per cent is divided between advertising and invoicing and collection which occupy equal amounts of office space.
- Stationery, postage and office equipment charges are split equally to the latter two accounts for the same reason.
- Packaging materials are allocated to the packaging account because these supplies are used in packaging.

TABLE 3.22 Allocating natural accounts to functional accounts

Natural accounts	Total £	Personal selling £	Packaging and despatch £	Advertising £	Invoice and collection £
Salaries	2 500	1 000	900	300	300
Rent	500		400	50	50
Packaging materials	1 012		1 012		
Postage and stationery	50			25	25
Hire of office equipment	100			50	50
Total	4 162	1 000	2 312	425	425

Step 3

The functional costs must now be traced to customers, but more information is required before we can complete this task. Table 3.23 shows that the company's three products vary in cost, selling price and sales volume. The products also have different sizes and the packaging costs are not related to the selling price.

When assigning packaging costs to products, size must be taken into account. For example, product C is six times larger than A and therefore uses a correspondingly higher amount of packaging effort (hence cost) per unit relative to products A and B. Table 3.23 shows how the costs from the functional accounts are to be traced to customers. Note, once again, the reference to activity-based costing in the form of cost driver:

Activity cost	*Cost driver*	*Cost per call*
Personal selling (£1000)	Number of calls (100)	£10 (£1000/100 calls)
Packaging and despatch (£2312)	Number of packaging units (1360)	*Cost per packaging unit* £1.70 (£2312/1360 units) Product A £1.70 × 1 = £1.70 B £1.70 × 3 = £5.10 C £1.70 × 6 = £10.20

TABLE 3.23 Basic data for cost and profit analysis

Products

Products	Cost/unit £	Selling price/unit £	Number of units sold in period	Sales in period £	Relative 'bulk' per unit	Packing 'units'
A	7	10	1 000	10 000	1	1 000
B	35	50	100	5 000	3	300
C	140	200	10	2 000	6	60
			1 110	17 000		1 360

Customers

Customers	Number of sales calls in period	Number of orders placed in period	Number of each product ordered in period		
			A	B	C
Smith	30	30	900	30	0
Jones	40	3	90	30	3
Brown	30	1	10	40	7
Total	100	34	1 000	100	10

Notice that for products A, B and C the calculation of cost per packaging unit takes into account the relative 'bulk' per unit.

Step 4

Calculate the profit and loss for each customer (Table 3.24). The data are now in which the form the company wants them. They are the same data as in the original profit and loss account (step 1), they have simply been rearranged and renamed.

An example of how the figures are arrived at in Table 3.24 is given below.

Customer: Smith			
Sales revenue	900 units of A at £10 each	£9 000	
	30 units of B at £50 each	£1 500	
			£10 500
Cost of sales	90 units of A at £7 each	£6 300	
	30 units of B at £35 each	£1 050	
			£7 350
Sales calls	30 calls at £10 per call	£300	
			£300
Order costs	30 orders at £12.50 per order	£375	
			£375
Packaging costs			
Product A	900 units at £1.70 per unit	£1 530	
Product B	30 units at £5.10 per unit	£153	
			£1 683

TABLE 3.24 Profit and loss accounts for customers

	Smith		Jones		Brown		Whole company
	£	£	£	£	£	£	£
Sales							
A	9 000		900		100		
B	1 500		1 500		2 000		
C			600		1 400		
Total sales		10 500		3 000		3 500	17 000
Cost of sales							
A	6 300		630		70		
B	1 050		1 050		1 400		
C	—		420		980		
Total cost of sales		7 350		2 100		2 450	11 900
Gross margin		3 150		900		1 050	5 100
Expenses							
Sales calls (£10 each)	300		400.00		300.00		
Order costs (£12.50 each)	375		37.50		12.50		
Packaging costs							
A	1 530		153.00		17.00		
B	153		153.00		204.00		
C			30.60		71.40		
Advertising	—		127.50		297.50		
		2 358		901.60		902.40	4 162
Net profit (loss)		**792**		**(1.60)**		**147.60**	**938**

There was no advertising costs charged to Smith. Advertising for this period was for the benefit of only product C which Smith did not buy. For customer Jones, the advertising cost would be:

Advertising cost per unit	Number of units of C bought	Advertising costs for Jones
£42.50	3	£127.50

Analyzing the results

Although sales from Smith's account made up 62 per cent of total sales, they contributed a massive 85 per cent of the total net profit.

As to why Smith buys so much, a whole range of factors deserve consideration. As far as Smith's profitability is concerned, costs and how they arise merit our attention. Cost of goods sold is not relevant here, as for each customer it represents 70 per cent of sales revenue. However, Smith's cost position is more favourable when it comes to packaging. Most of Smith's packaging cost was for product A which has the lowest price per unit. Furthermore, Smith did not buy any of the bulkier packaged product, C, and was not charged any advertising cost. Where the Smith account excelled was the productivity of sales calls in terms of number of orders placed.

References

1. Drury, J.C., *Management and Cost Accounting*, ITPS, 1994.
2. *Ibid*. p. 241.

CHAPTER 4

Quality and design

WHAT IS IT ABOUT?

Quality and design are issues of great concern for consumers. Marketing needs to recognize this fact. Take a simple product like an iron: its look, feel and functioning merit serious consideration.

The chapter begins with a discussion of a number of approaches to defining **quality**. We then look at the dimensions of quality as they relate specifically to products and services. Several examples follow of how we might think about quality in practice.

A range of techniques for **quality control** are then discussed. These techniques are regarded as particularly useful in a service context. Rounding off the quality aspect, the **Business Excellence Model** of the European Foundation for Quality Management stresses the importance of quality throughout the length and breadth of any organization.

The **design** section builds on the issue of quality, and a range of questions is highlighted that should assist a product designer approaching a new project. These questions, along with a few brief case studies, are intended to encourage discussion of how things should look and feel, how well they perform and how easy they are to use.

To bring the chapter to a conclusion, the basic design tool of the management approach known as **quality function deployment** (QFD) is presented. The House of Quality is founded on the belief that products should be designed to reflect customers' desires and tastes – so marketing people, design engineers and manufacturing staff must work closely together from the time a product is first conceived.

What is quality?

There is no generally accepted definition of quality. The various definitions have been categorized into five approaches to quality.[1]

1. *Transcendent approach*

According to the transcendent view, quality is synonymous with innate excellence, a mark of uncompromising standards and high achievement, e.g. a Rolls-Royce car, Rolex watch: in other words, the best possible. The danger of this is that it confuses quality with grade. We often talk loosely about quality. We speak of 'high quality' or 'good quality' without a clear idea of what it is that defines our concept of quality for products and services. We are likely to confuse quality with grade, and when we speak of high quality products, we often mean high grade, or even perhaps, just expensive. The grade and quality of a product or service are quite separate. Grade refers to the product's standard or class, and is reflected on the product specification. Quality refers to the extent to which a product or service is and does what it claims to be and do. It is possible to have products or services of a lower grade that meet the standard laid down. It is no use complaining that a perfectly satisfactory Fiat is not a Rolls-Royce.

2. *Product-based approach*

Quality is viewed as a precise and measurable variable. Products/services can be ranked according to the amount of the desired attribute they possess. Because quality reflects the quantity of attributes that a product contains, and because attributes are considered costly to produce, higher quality goods will be more expensive. A watch for example, may be designed to run without the need for servicing for at least five years while keeping time correct to within five seconds.

3. *Manufacturing-based approach*

The focus here is on the supply side being concerned primarily with engineering and manufacturing practice. It is summed up by the phrase 'conformance to design specifications'. Any deviation implies a reduction in quality. A product or service may not be the best in the world but is regarded as of good quality if it is built or delivered precisely to its design specification.

4. *Value-based approach*

The value-based approach defines quality in terms of costs and prices. Value is the quality you get for the price you pay. Consumers may accept a lower specification quality if the price is low.

5. *User-based approach*

The user-based approach starts from the premise that quality 'lies in the eyes of the beholder'. Goods that best satisfy customer preferences are believed to have high quality. A basic problem with this approach is its equating of quality with maximum satisfaction. A consumer may enjoy a particular brand because of its unusual taste or features yet may still regard some other brand as being of higher quality.

Characteristics of quality

So far we have emphasized the organizational dimension and general approaches to quality. However, to develop, design, produce and deliver a product or service we must look to the characteristics of quality.

Characteristics of quality for products

Eight elements have been proposed:[2]

- **Performance** – the primary operating characteristics. For example, sound and picture clarity in a TV, handling, comfort, acceleration in a car, and cleaning, softening and shining abilities of a shampoo. (*Note*: Performance differences are not necessarily quality differences, e.g. 100 watt and 60 watt bulbs simply belong to different performance classes.)
- **Features** – secondary characteristics that augment the basic function.
- **Reliability** – the probability of a product breaking down; applies particularly to consumer durables, such as washing machines and to industrial machinery.
- **Conformance** – related to reliability as conformance stresses the extent to which a product's design and operating characteristics match pre-established standards. Conformance quality is meaningless if the specifications are not desired by consumers.
- **Durability** – how much use does one get from a product before it breaks down and has to be either repaired or replaced.
- **Serviceability** – the speed and competence of repair, and courtesy received.
- **Aesthetics** – how a product looks, feels, sounds, tastes, smells.
- **Perceived** – because consumers do not always possess complete information about a product's attributes or even understand the information that they do have, they use indirect measures when comparing products, e.g. image, reputation, brand name, etc.

Characteristics of quality for services

There are five established dimensions:[3]

- **Tangibles** – appearance of physical facilities, equipment, personnel and communication materials.
- **Reliability** – ability to perform the promised service dependably and accurately.
- **Responsiveness** – willingness to help customers and provide prompt service.
- **Assurance** – knowledge and courtesy of employees and their ability to convey trust and confidence.
- **Empathy** – caring, individualized attention the firm provides its customers.

Application of quality characteristics

For the purpose of design and control of quality characteristics, consider one example (Table 4.1) as it relates to a product (a car) and a service (air journey).[4]

TABLE 4.1 Quality characteristics for a motor car and an air journey

Quality characteristic	Car	Air journey
Functionality	Speed, acceleration, fuel consumption, ride quality, road-holding, etc.	Safety and duration of journey, on-board meals and drinks, car and hotel booking services
Appearance	Aesthetics, shape, finish, door gaps, etc.	Appearance and cleanliness of aircraft, lounges and crew
Reliability	Mean time to failure	Keeping to the published flight times
Durability	Useful life (with repair)	Keeping up with trends in the industry
Recovery	Ease of repair	Resolution of service failures
Contact	Knowledge and courtesy of sales staff	Knowledge, courtesy and sensitivity of airline staff

Source: Slack, N., Chambers, S., Harland, C., Harrison, A. and Johnston, R., *Operations Management*, Pitman Publishing, 1995.

Some of these characteristics are more easily measurable than others, e.g. the time dimension to reliability. Appearance is much more difficult. For designers and quality engineers the challenge is one of developing specifications and standards that are understood and desired by the consumer. As for courtesy and sensitivity, what consumers expect should be compared with what they perceive is delivered.

Measurement of quality characteristics

Measures used to describe quality characteristics can be either of the following:

- **Variables** – measured on a continuous scale, e.g. length, weight, time.
- **Attributes** – assessed by judgement and have two states, e.g. right or wrong, works or does not work, looks good or does not look good.

Referring back to the car and airline journey, some measures which might be used for the quality characteristics are suggested in Table 4.2.[5]

Looking at some of the points in the table brings out the real problems in arriving at the desired levels of quality. For organizations and consumers thinking about quality, the following questions need to be addressed.

- What is achievable?
- What is acceptable?
- What is reasonable?
- What is practical?
- What is realistic?
- What is cost-effective?

TABLE 4.2 Variable and attribute measures for quality characteristics

Quality characteristic	Car		Airline journey	
	Variable (1–5 scale)	Attribute (Yes or no)	Variable (1–5 scale)	Attribute (Yes or no)
Functionality	Acceleration and braking characteristics from testbed	Is the ride quality satisfactory?	Number of journeys which actually arrived at the destination (i.e. did not crash)	Was the food acceptable?
Appearance	Number of blemishes visible on car	Is the colour to specification?	Number of seats not cleaned satisfactorily	Are the crew dressed smartly?
Reliability	Average time between faults	Is the reliability satisfactory?	Proportion of journeys which arrived on time	Were there any complaints?
Durability	Life of the car	Is the useful life as predicted?	Number of times service innovations lagged competitors'	Generally, is the airline updating its services in a satisfactory manner?
Recovery	Time from fault discovered to fault repaired	Is the serviceability of the car acceptable?	Proportion of service failures resolved satisfactorily	Do customers feel that staff deal satisfactorily with complaints?
Contact	Level of help provided by sales staff	Did customers feel well served?	The extent to which customers feel well treated by staff	Did customers feel that the staff were helpful?

Source: Slack, N., Chambers, S., Harland, C., Harrison, A. and Johnston, R., *Operations Management*, Pitman Publishing, 1995.

Consumer perspective

Consumers' perceptions and evaluation of quality often reflect meanings that are quite distinct from the operational view expressed by organizations. In focus group discussions, consumers understandably see quality in terms of benefits that accrue from usage of a product or experience of a service. This can clearly be seen from the findings of one particular study[6] (Table 4.3).

Consider the first comment in Table 4.3 about laundry detergents. The benefit of getting the job done has to be traced back to the product – what ingredients, how much and in what combinations? In addition, is 'gets the job done' an absolute value or are there degrees of getting the job done? The same applies to refrigerators that are 'well made and durable'. Brands of detergents and refrigerators vary in terms of their capacity to deliver the benefits mentioned here – a brief examination of the Consumer's Association *Which?* magazine will testify to that. However, are the differences a reflection of specification levels, a function of consumer perceptions or a mixture of both (conformance quality versus perceived quality)? As for the services (physicians and restaurants), many of the comments fall within the five dimensions mentioned earlier.

Ishikawa has written and consulted widely on the issue of quality and contends that the first step in quality control is to know what this concept really means.[7] Previously, many Japanese industries did not have answers to the following questions, 'What is a

TABLE 4.3 Meaning of quality for four product or service categories

Product or service category	Responses evoked
Laundry detergents	Gets the job done Does what it's supposed to do Not harsh, not irritating Leaves clothes soft, fresh smelling Good price
Family physicians	Shows concern for patient Communicates with patient Honest Is sensitive, compassionate Not 'out to get money' Trustworthy Knowledgeable, up-to-date Available Good reputation Reasonable fees Efficient office personnel
Refrigerators	Well made, durable Comes with warranty or guarantee Good after-sales service Maintenance-free Energy-efficient Availability of extra features Well-known brand name
Restaurants (dining out)	Treated as special Friendly, unobtrusive service Presence of little 'extras' Efficient, consistent service Positive attitude of service personnel Elegant, comfortable Pleasing atmosphere Not like home Food cooked properly Fresh ingredients

Source: Ellen, D. and Castleberry, S.B., 'Defining and evaluating quality: the consumer's view', *Advances in Consumer Research*, Vol. XIII, 1986.

good car'?, 'What is a good radio'? Product quality can be divided into true and substitute characteristics. Normally, the functions or capabilities of a product are part of its true quality characteristics, e.g. a good car – good styling, easy driving, comfortable riding, good acceleration, stability at high speed, durability, less chance of a breakdown, easy repair, safety.

- What do we mean by easy driving?
- How can we measure it?
- How can it be replaced by numerical values?
- What structure is to be used for the car?
- In what way do tolerances in each part of a car affect the operation?
- How can we determine tolerances?

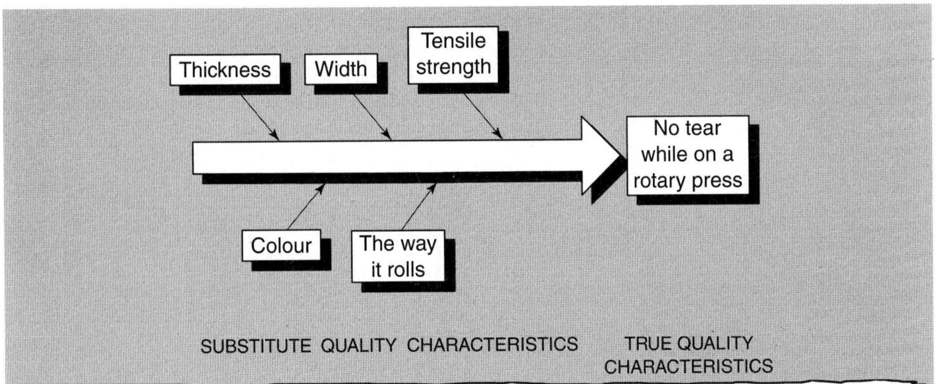

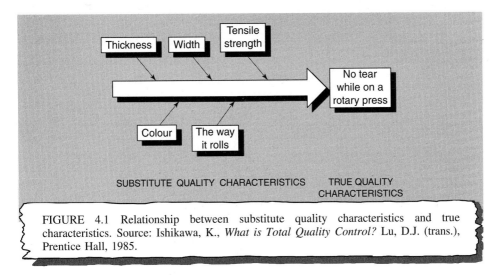

FIGURE 4.1 Relationship between substitute quality characteristics and true characteristics. Source: Ishikawa, K., *What is Total Quality Control?* Lu, D.J. (trans.), Prentice Hall, 1985.

- What raw materials are to be used?
- How can we determine the prices of raw materials?

True characteristics are not always easily measured. Resort is then made to inspecting the substitute quality characteristics to assess their relationship with the true characteristic (Figure 4.1).

Similar assessments could be made of the newsprint roll's capacity to contain the ink on one side only and print clearly. In this example some characteristics can be measured physically or chemically. In general, however, measurement often depends on how characteristics look, feel, taste, sound and smell.

Quality analysis techniques

A commitment to quality is enhanced through the use of a range of techniques designed for monitoring its delivery and acceptability. The following discussion outlines the most frequently mentioned techniques.

Flowchart

Perhaps the simplest yet the most helpful in terms of overall process improvement. It is in essence a pictorial representation of a process (often referred to as blueprinting: see, for example, Figure 8.9 on page 260). Their purpose is to show the sequencing of activities, operations, tasks, materials flow, information flow and movement of people. It is not necessary to use symbols in flowcharting although a fair number are available. Five standardized symbols are shown in Figure 4.2.

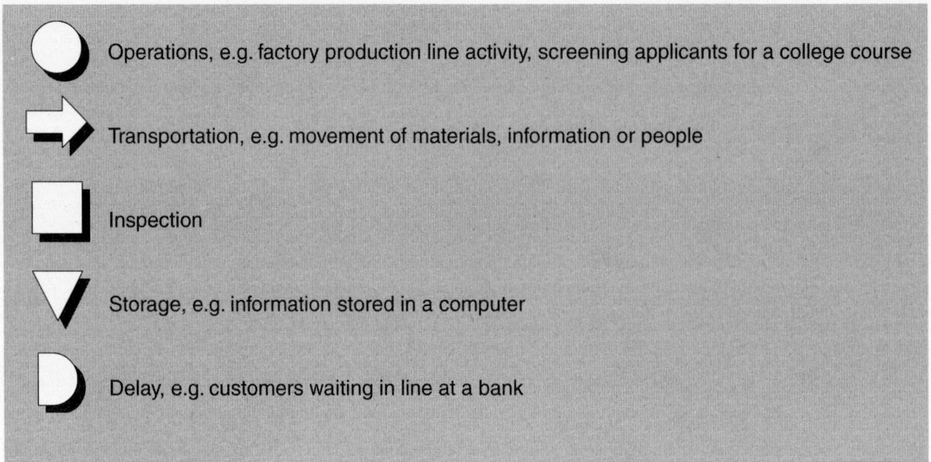

FIGURE 4.2 Process flowchart symbols.

Cause and effect diagram

Sometimes called a fishbone diagram, a cause and effect diagram usually represents the relationships between some quality issue, or effect, and all possible causes affecting this issue (Figure 4.3).

The exact format will vary depending on the situation. However, the diagram helps managers to focus on a specific problem faced in a quality management context, e.g. late deliveries, and to identify the factors contributing to that problem. Within each factor, a range of points could offer an explanation, e.g. under personnel – poor motivation, lack of training.

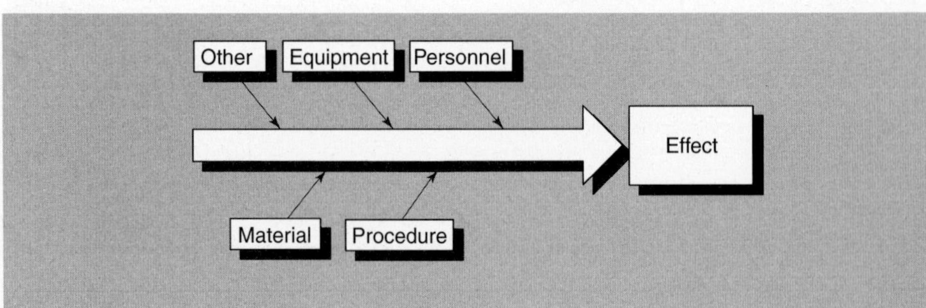

FIGURE 4.3 Cause and effect diagram.

Pareto analysis

A cause and effect analysis (above) may show that the problem has been caused by a few factors, the rest being insignificant. A study done for a pizza parlour experiencing problems with its home delivery service revealed possible causes of failure and their contribution in not meeting target response times[8] (Table 4.4).

A Pareto chart (Figure 4.4) can be constructed from the survey. It shows three factors (d, f and e) which together account for 70 per cent of the causes.

TABLE 4.4 Causal factors with a Pareto distribution

Causes		% contribution to failure in meeting target response times
(a)	Giving order to kitchen	3
(b)	Shortage of drivers	8
(c)	Slowness in preparation of pizzas	3
(d)	Drivers unfamiliar with faster route	30
(e)	Breakdowns in delivery vehicles	15
(f)	Traffic congestion	25
(g)	Weather conditions	6
(h)	Slowness in boxing cooked pizzas	3
(i)	Extent of catchment area	7
		100

Source: Mudie, P.M. and Cottam, A., *The Management and Marketing of Services*, Butterworth/Heinemann, 1993.

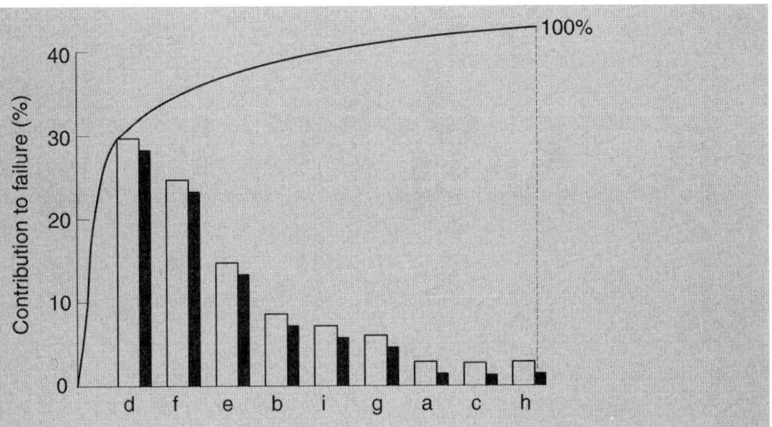

FIGURE 4.4 Pareto chart – causal factors.

Histogram

A histogram is a distribution showing the frequency of occurrences between the high and low range of data. Figure 4.5 shows two histograms illustrating times taken by two organizations to perform a particular service. From the histograms it is clear that the variation of company A's service process is smaller than B's.

The question is, why should the quality of A's service performance be much better than B's. Possible reasons are better equipment, better trained employees and more effective procedures.

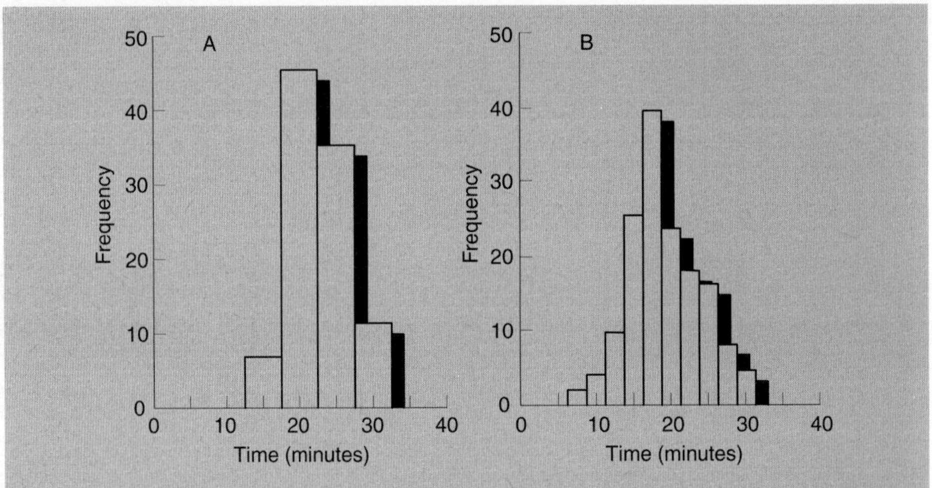

FIGURE 4.5 Time taken by two organizations to perform a particular service.

Run chart

A run chart provides a graphical summary of data in time-order sequence (Figure 4.6). This technique can be used to monitor a system or a process to observe whether its behaviour seems to be changing over time. It uses the same type of data as the histogram but exhibits the data in time-order sequence.

Whatever is being monitored, run charts record the degree of success achieved. Figure 4.6 shows the percentage of meals served in a restaurant within 15 minutes over a twenty-week period. Success is about 50 per cent in week 2 to approximately 95 per cent in weeks 11, 14, 17 and 18. Overall, an upward trend seems to be occurring and this is certainly desirable.

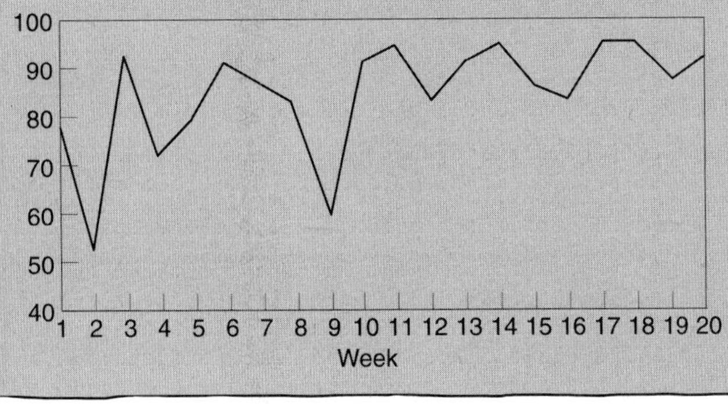

FIGURE 4.6 Run chart.

Control chart

A control chart goes one step beyond the run chart by establishing upper and lower control limits. These limits can represent three types of value:

- **Measurable data**, e.g. time spent in a service or time spent waiting for service.
- **Percentages**, e.g. the percentage of goods damaged or the percentage of customers complaining.
- **Counting data**, e.g. the number of mistakes in an order.

Figure 4.7 shows the run chart of Figure 4.6 converted into a control chart.

Explanations need to be found for the poor performances in weeks 2 and 9. Although one might expect the control chart to contain an upper control limit as well, no 'being served within 15 minutes percentage' is so high as to be a cause for concern. Of course, knowing why actual performance is above control limits still merits investigation.

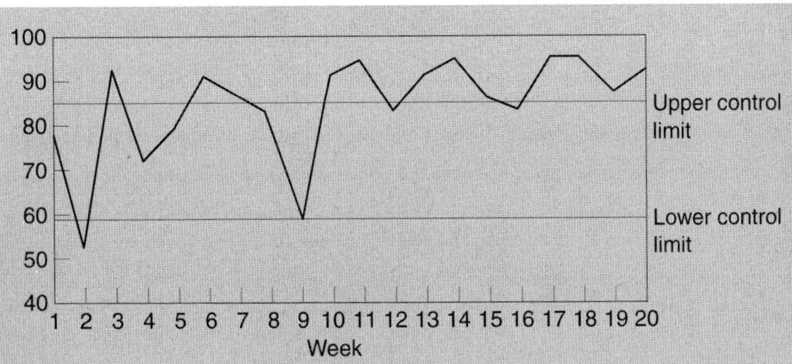

FIGURE 4.7 Control chart.

Checksheet

A checksheet is perhaps the most commonly used method for collecting and compiling data. The checksheet tells how frequently something is occurring. Figure 4.8 illustrates a checksheet recording the incidence of complaints by subject.

Subject of complaint	Number of complaints	Total
Delivery times	~~IIII~~ ~~IIII~~ II	12
Installation	IIII	4
Company personnel	~~IIII~~ III	8
Product	II	2
TOTAL		26

FIGURE 4.8 Checksheet.

Business Excellence Model

Total quality management (TQM) is not a single concept but a convergence of ideas initially developed with the post-war renaissance of Japanese industry, supported by Deming[9] and Juran,[10] among others, which gradually moved from an emphasis on quality control to a deeper concept based on organization-wide principles of the ideal organizational culture. Later, the commercial significance of quality was supported by anecdotal evidence put forward by writers such as Peters and Waterman[11] and the concept that 'quality is free' was developed by Crosby.[12]

By the early 1980s, governmental and industrial leaders in the West were concerned by a lack of productivity leading to a failure to compete in world markets. In the USA, a national productivity study was legislated in October 1982 which led to the recognition of the need for a national quality and productivity award. The process to legislate the award led to the development of a bill which stated, *inter alia*, that it would help to improve quality and productivity by 'establishing guidelines and criteria that [could] be used by business, industrial, governmental and other enterprises in evaluating their own quality improvement efforts'.[13] The Malcolm Baldridge National Quality Award (MBNQA) was established in 1987 with a basic structure of seven categories for self-appraisal. The concept of self-assessment in relation to a model of excellence had been born.

In early 1992, the UK Quality Award (UKQA) Committee was established 'to consider and report ... on the feasibility of developing a new prestige award for British business'. The proposals were to be in a form suitable for self-assessment, in harmony with the European Quality Award (EQA), launched by the European Foundation for Quality Management (EFQM) in 1992, and incorporate the lessons learnt from MBNQA.

The EQA model had been developed from the MBNQA, with the active involvement of UK organizations: to have developed an alternative model for the UKQA could have

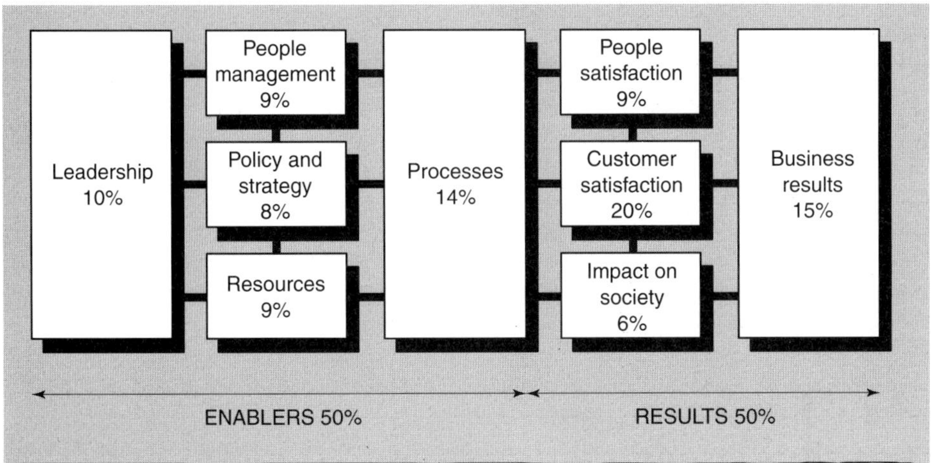

FIGURE 4.9 The Business Excellence Model. Source: British Quality Foundation, London, 1995.

undermined the worldwide TQM development process. The EQA model with its emphasis on self-assessment and improvement planning was therefore accepted by the committee.[14] However, the European award process was not seen as a catalyst to inspire nationally focused businesses, small and medium-sized UK organizations, regional or locally based UK businesses, or the public and voluntary sectors, and therefore there was a need for a new UKQA. This model is now known as a Business Excellence Model, and experience of using the model in a wide range of commercial organizations has shown that it is widely applicable both as a means of assessment and as the basis for planning improvements. The model is based on the premise that customer satisfaction, people (employee) satisfaction and impact on society are achieved through leadership driving policy and strategy, people management, resources and processes, leading ultimately to excellence in business results (Figure 4.9).

Each of the nine elements of the model is a criterion used to assess an organization's progress towards excellence. The percentages shown are those used for the purposes of the UK and European Quality Awards. Both the model and the relative weightings were developed following a wide consultation exercise across Europe, and they are annually reviewed for continuing relevance, criterion and subcriterion definition/deletion/ expansion and relative importance. The model is split on an equal basis between the

- **Enabler** criteria, concerned with **how** and organization approaches its business in each of the areas described by the criteria and subcriteria.
- **Results** criteria covering **what** an organization has achieved and is achieving.

The model criteria

The model is not prescriptive below the level of the criteria. Thus all of the criteria must be addressed but it is accepted that, on rare occasions, it is possible that a subcriterion may be irrelevant in particular organizational circumstances.

- **Leadership**. This criterion relates to the behaviour of all managers in as much as **how** the executive team and all other managers inspire, drive and reflect total quality as the organization's fundamental process for continuous improvement.
- **Policy and strategy**. This criterion reviews the organization's mission, values, vision and strategic direction. **How** the organization's policy and strategy reflect the concept and principles of total quality are used in the formulation, deployment, review and improvement of policy and strategy.
- **People management**. This criterion studies the management of the organization's people and **how** the organization releases the full potential of its people to improve its business and/or service continuously.
- **Resources**. This criterion refers to the management, utilization and preservation of resources and **how** the organization's resources are effectively deployed in support of policy and strategy.
- **Processes**. This criterion analyzes the management of all value-adding activities within the organization, **how** processes are identified, reviewed and revised to ensure continuous improvement of the organization's business and/or service.
- **Customer satisfaction**. Examines **what** the organization is achieving in relation to the satisfaction of its external customers.
- **People satisfaction**. Investigates **what** the organization is achieving in relation to the satisfaction of its people.
- **Impact on society**. Probes **what** the organization is achieving in satisfying the needs and expectations of the community at large.
- **Business results**. Reviews **what** the organization is achieving in relation to its planned business and/or service objectives and in satisfying the needs and expectations of everyone with an interest in the organization.

A full exposition of the model can be found in the *Guides to Self-assessment* published by the British Quality Foundation (1995).

Model characteristics

Within the enabler criteria, assessment addresses the excellence of the approaches used and the extent of the deployment of these approaches, both vertically through all levels of the organization and horizontally to all areas and activities within the organization.

For the results criteria, assessment addresses the organization's results and trends in terms of actual performance, comparison with targets and, wherever possible, by comparison with competitors and the 'best in class' for the results under review. A key distinction within the results criteria is the recognition of both direct feedback data from the relevant stakeholder and the internal measurement of predicative, performance measurements; these two areas are sometimes described as the leading and lagging indicators of performance

Model scoring

Each part of the enabler's criteria is scored on the basis of a combination of two factors:

- the degree of **excellence** of the approach;
- the extent of the **deployment** of the approach.

Each part of the results criteria is also scored on the basis of a combination of two factors:

- the degree of **excellence** of the results;
- the **scope** of the results.

The two systems of scoring are set out in Tables 4.5 and 4.6. In each of the tables one of the five levels, 0, 25, 50, 75 or 100 per cent, or an interpolation may be used. It must be remembered that the conditions described in both Tables 4.5 and 4.6 are additive throughout the table and are not an either/or function.

Self-assessment

The Business Excellence Model is appropriate to any organization, and self-assessment can be applied throughout an organization. Self-assessment is a regular, comprehensive

TABLE 4.5 Scoring the enablers

Approach	Score (%)	Deployment
Anecdotal	0	Little usage
Soundly based Systematic Preventative	25	About one-quarter of the potential
Integrated Review	50	About half of the potential
Refinement	75	About three-quarters of the potential
Role/Model	100	Full potential

TABLE 4.6 Scoring the results

Results	Score (%)	Scope
Anecdotal	0	Little usage
Positive trends Comparison – Targets	25	Some
Comparisons – External Cause and effect	50	Many
Sustained excellence	75	Most
Best in class	100	All

and systematic review of an organization's activities and results against a tangible and relevant model which culminates in the identification of the organization's strengths and areas for improvement which facilitates the development and prioritization of planned improvement actions which can be regularly monitored.

The approach that an organization takes to self-assessment will be influenced by both the structure and culture of that organization but will always involve the following steps:

- Developing the commitment of the leaders to the use of the model and self-assessment.
- Planning the self-assessment process, including the organizational units to be involved.
- Assembling the teams that will manage the self-assessment and training them in the concepts and use of the model and self-assessment.
- Communicating the adoption of the model and self-assessment to the organization through a variety of channels emphasizing the fact that this approach focuses on the customer and on organizational prosperity.
- Conducting the agreed self-assessment(s).
- Establishing action plans, having prioritized the areas for improvement and agreed the owners and milestones for each action.
- Communicating the action plan and strategic direction(s).
- Implementing the action plan(s) and assigning the necessary personnel, financial resources, etc.
- Regularly reviewing progress and developing the plan for the next self-assessment.

Approaches to self-assessment

There are a number of different approaches to conducting self-assessment in use in the UK and across Europe, and six of these approaches are described in broad terms below. However, the key points to remember are that:

- Each approach has its own merits and limitations.
- The paramount objective of self-assessment is continuous improvement.
- The most critical phase is action planning and implementation.

ASSESS

ASSESS was developed by the British Quality Foundation and comes in two forms:

- **RapidScore**, which can be completed with a minimal time investment.
- **ValidScore**, which is more rigorous and time-consuming.

Both processes are based on a questionnaire approach that can be either PC- or desk-based and can be completed individually or in teams. Additionally, the results of these self-assessments are collated on a database at the British Quality Foundation to provide benchmarking information. With the ValidScore approach, the self-assessment is also validated by the Foundation and recognition awarded for the achievement of various scoring levels.

Award simulation

Award simulation involves, the organization undertaking the self-assessment, in writing a full document of up to seventy-five pages based on the analysis of the organization against the criteria and subcriteria of the Business Excellence Model. This document is assessed by 'external' assessors to agree strengths, areas for improvement and a score at each subcriterion level. This is a very comprehensive and accurate approach but is potentially time-consuming and resource-intensive.

Proforma

A set of proforma pages (perhaps one page for each subcriterion) are created on which the strengths, areas of improvement and evidence used during the self-assessment and scoring exercise can be recorded. A well-constructed set of proforma pages is appropriate for all criteria but is particularly suited to addressing the enablers. For larger organizations the proforma pages from various units can be collated and common strengths and areas for improvement identified.

Matrix

An organizationally specific achievement matrix based on the framework of the Business Excellence Model and typically consisting of a series of statements of achievement against the criteria of the model on a nought to ten scale can be created. This approach is simple to use and can be a means of involving everyone in the organization in self-assessment. However, there are significant time requirements during the matrix creation phase.

Workshop

The management team is responsible for gathering the data and presenting the evidence to their peers at a workshop. The workshop is used as a starting point for the team to reach consensus on the strengths, areas for improvement and score of the self-assessment.

Questionnaire

The use of questionnaires is another valid and useful approach to self-assessment which is not resource-intensive, involves many of the organization's people and can be completed quickly. It is an excellent way to gather information on people's perceptions of the organization. ASSESS RapidScore is the best example of this approach.

Benefits of self-assessment

Throughout 1994, universities from six European countries undertook the first pan-European study on self-assessment based on two questionnaire surveys.[15] The research

- determined the extent and knowledge and awareness of self-assessment methods;
- investigated the types of self-assessment taking place in organizations;
- identified the reasons for success and failure of self-assessment methods.

Some of the results were:

- 76 per cent of the respondents found that self-assessment identified opportunities for improvement;
- 75 per cent found that self-assessment directs the improvement process;
- 68 per cent stated that self-assessment provided a new motivation for the improvement process;
- 62 per cent used self-assessment to manage the business.

The key learning points for the organization using self-assessment were found to be the importance of the following:

- senior management review of the improvements;
- the involvement of the CEO;
- training for those carrying out the self-assessment;
- beginning the self-assessment with the senior management;
- agreeing the use of the results at the beginning of the exercise.

What is design?

Is it engineering? Fashion? Products? Styling? Architecture? Advertising?

All six (and possibly some others too) imply that designing involves the control of the form and function of manufactured products, graphic literature and environments. Over £1 billion was turned over by design consultancies in the UK during 1994 and export earnings for the same groups during the same year also topped the £1 billion mark.

Design is about solving other people's problems. It is about quality through caring about people, their needs and aspirations and about improving their quality of living through the responsible designing of quality into their products, environments and communications.

Industrial design is a product of post-Industrial Revolution times and is a child of the twentieth century. Before the introduction of mass production, a craftsman would design a product and make it.

Criteria for the measurement of success of a given design might be:

- **Appearance** – form, colour, pattern and originality.
- **Function** – meeting the objectives set by the brief, convenient to use and easy to maintain, operate and repair.
- **Quality** – efficient and economic use of appropriate materials, manufactured to the highest standards.
- **Safety** – full consideration given to the user and the maker.
- **Appropriateness** – suitability for mass production and economic viability.

The design process

Design involves a process of identifying the problem (**the brief**), collecting relevant data and looking at historic precedent (**research**), formulating, conceptualizing and

Exhibit 4.1 The design process

brief (the problem)
analysis of the brief
research (and data collection)
design
development
engineering
prototyping
evaluation
production
marketing
packaging
distribution
sales
end-user
evaluation
the solution

communicating a response (**sketch design**), developing a model, prototype or testrig (**development**), testing the proposal on the client or market (**evaluation**) and improving the solution following feedback (**final development**). This process is set out in Exhibit 4.1.

The brief

The brief is the critical first step in the process. Consider the example of a client engaging a design consultancy with the following brief: to design a dining table for domestic use. This is viewed as a novel concept as dining tables are associated with the wealthy, large houses, and with the sole purpose of hosting special occasions. The design team in consultation with the client unravels the initial brief and comes up with the list of features set out in Exhibit 4.2.

Designers, in consultation with clients, are particularly adept at developing a brief in such a manner. It is invariably the result of brainstorming sessions using a range of diagrams and matrices. Further illustrations showing the outcomes of such a process can be seen in Exhibit 4.3.

Research

Research involves the following activities:

- Study historical precedent.
- Look at contemporary competition.
- Consider materials and processes.
- Undertake market research.
- What market? Price, customer profile, housing trends, etc.

Exhibit 4.2 Design concepts: the best dining table in the world

The dining table should:

1. adjust in size and configuration (2, 4, 6, 8 settings – rectangle, square)
2. adjust in height (to suit different sized users or for different function, e.g. desk)
3. not have any legs (ease of cleaning underneath – no obstruction to user)
4. have various surface finishes (for differing ambience – breakfast/candlelit dinner)
5. fold away when not in use (space at a premium in modern housing)
6. be self-setting (saving user's time)
7. be self-cleaning (not be susceptible to spillage stains)
8. have built-in waste disposal (enabling crockery stack for removal)
9. allow food preparation and cooking (fondue or barbecue)
10. say 'eat off me', not 'climb up and have your appendix out!' (aesthetic appeal)
11. be inexpensive (highest standard of materials and construction at low cost)
12. be 100 per cent recyclable and made from sustainable resources (green issues)
13. flat-pack for distribution and storage (100 tables per truck)
14. be lightweight (ease of movement or extension)
15. have cable management (enabling task lighting without danger or clutter)
16. be safe in its manufacture and operation (Factory Act – not allow trapped fingers)
17. involve some hand-manufacture to create employment (value-added appeal)
18. be capable of personalization (first time or mature buyer)
19. be appropriate in all environments (Victorian or modern house)
20. allow eye contact to all users (conversation stimulus)

Sketch designs

Drawings, models and computer renderings are produced to communicate design presentations of the product to manufacturers, marketers and consumers for feedback. Concepts are modified and full-size prototype construction ensures.

Development

Development is the proving stage of a design. The model produced by the previous stages is now honed by the team to take account of production, assembly, finishing, packaging, distribution and sales.

Evaluation and feedback

The importance of the evaluation and feedback phase is often overlooked. It is crucial that the designer and marketer co-operate in this phase: customer satisfaction is of paramount importance to the success of a company in a competitive marketplace. Some successful products have had that success through their manufacturers adopting a proactive evaluation process with the customer. Sony Corporation of Japan has been able to launch new products in a limited release, study customer reaction, redesign, retool and relaunch a product in a very short timeframe because of their ability to shorten the design-to-shop-shelf cycle to a few months. Just-in-time (JIT) manufacture is becoming a powerful market influence and designers and marketers have to respond to customer preference, now made possible by advances in technology.

Exhibit 4.3 Design concepts

Disposable wet-razor

performance – a good shave?
features – ergonomically sound?
reliability – is it strong?
conformance – is it always the same?
durability – how many shaves?
serviceability – can you change blade?
aesthetics – does it look/feel good?
perceived – is it as good as Wilkinson/Gillette/electric, etc.?
technology – current materials/Teflon/self-cleaning/retractable
production – is it easily manufactured?
corporateness – does it fit with other company products?
innovation – is it different?
ethics – product lifespan?
futures – 'in' colour?
safety – can you cut yourself?
green – can it be recycled?
demographics – first razor for teenager/lady razor?
globalization – does it suit shaving habits for different ethnic groups?

Coffee-maker

performance – does it make good, hot coffee?
features – can it make cappuccino?
reliability – will it break down?
conformance – is it obvious how to use it, does it have water-level indicator?
durability – is it sturdy enough for a kitchen environment?
serviceability – are components replaceable?
aesthetics – does it look/feel good, clean, appropriate colours – range?
perceived – does it have weight/look as if made from expensive material?
technology – can customer specify individual characteristics?
production – low-tech or high-tech process?
corporateness – part of product range or suitable for customer environment?
innovation – can it clean itself, does it have pre-set timer and warning light?
ethics – can only process coffee from ethically correct sources
futures – will it still appear contemporary in 3 years' time?
safety – can you be scalded?
green – does it use minimum energy?
demographics – are handles, switches suitable for elderly, infirm, partially sighted?
globalization – different voltage settings?

Motor car

performance – does it steer, accelerate and brake adequately?
features – is it comfortable?
reliability – will it break down?
conformance – does it start every morning?
durability – has it got the longevity of a Volvo or Volkswagen?
serviceability – long spells between services? inexpensive, readily available spares?
aesthetics – does it look/feel good, is it quiet, is there a wide choice of colours, extras?
perceived – is it like a Rolls-Royce, Ferrari, Jaguar?
technology – computerized engine management? route-finder?
production – new materials, ceramics, carbon fibre, built by robots?
corporateness – Renault – Nicole/Papa, the talking car, Williams/Renault Formula 1?
innovation – remote locking, car phone, engine immobilizer?
ethics – research on prevention/treatment of automotive injuries?
futures – radar operated control, personal or group transport, roads policies?
safety – passenger/pedestrian protection, abs brakes, air bags, etc.?
green – no emissions, huge mpg, electrically powered, recycled tyres?
demographics – easily adapted for hand-controls, adjustable seat, steering wheel, etc.?
globalization – left-hand drive, customer-specified body – pick-up, saloon, hatchback, van, etc.?

Design also embraces many other disciplines and in the field of consumer products, the designer will of necessity address competition, data collection and interpretation, engineering content, fashion, aesthetics, marketing, production, packaging, distribution and sales.

The recent development of **design management** has promoted the designer as a key player in the previously inaccessible areas of management – finance, planning, production and, especially, marketing. Designers have come a long way since their role was seen as merely styling or the packaging of products.

Perhaps Japanese corporate strategy saw the beginnings of this turnaround during the 1970s. Japanese **teamwork** saw a broader representation of skills at boardroom-level than was evident in the West, where corporate strategy still revolved around the accountant.

Teamwork is probably the keyword in discussing the nature of design. In the simplest model, the team might consist of client, designer and maker; increasingly, the model is far more complex – client becomes market; designer becomes creator, engineering, production, packaging, distribution, advertising, after-sales evaluator, product developer and so on.

Design considerations

The designer has to consider and conform to the eight primary elements in Exhibit 4.3, namely:

- performance
- features
- reliability
- conformance
- durability
- serviceability
- aesthetics
- perceived

Other design considerations which have to be addressed are:

- technology
- production/manufacture
- corporateness
- innovation
- ethics
- future trends
- safety
- green considerations
- demographics
- globalization

Technology

Computers are radically changing the design process as CAD (computer-aided design) and CAM (computer-aided manufacture) become the norm. Computer technology also means that consumers will be involved in the design process as well as in areas such as engineering, production and marketing, collaborating much more closely in the development of new products. On-screen modelling techniques allow the presentation of new concepts to a variety of audiences before a design has left the drawing board. Actual products can be made using software generated by the designer. Publishing has already seen a revolution, with sophisticated graphics and layout being handled in-house and worldwide investment in digital communications sees multimedia presentations as the state of the art.

Production/manufacturing

New materials, manufacturing processes and the plethora of IT present escalating challenges to tomorrow's designers. Prototyping of many products is now achieved by downloading CAD-generated data into a bath of liquid which can, by photographic synthesis form a solid representation of what the designer produced on screen. The designer, through the computer, can issue manufacturing instructions to multipath cutting and forming equipment.

Corporateness

Formerly, the corporate approach to design was largely one of lip service and a new logo every so often. Any company which is design-led uses design not only as a tool for the development and manufacture of its products but also in its presentation of itself through its literature, packaging, distribution, environment and all of its activities. Design, once a bolt-on luxury is now a necessity in marketing, advertising, financial and retail operations.

Innovation

A recent survey demonstrated that many businesspeople believe that innovation is the single most important area to address if their companies are to remain competitive in the future. Many products were once designed for use in, say, five years' time; many products today will be in the high street store within three months. The fashion industry has always had to innovate twice each year. Innovation is defined as to 'renew or to introduce as something new, to make changes'. Renewal is the key to the genesis of the product lifecycle and hence the key to economic success.

Ethics

Are business and ethics compatible? Consumer activism has shown its power at several multinational corporation annual general meetings in recent years. Animal rights groups have had huge successes in stopping testing on animals for the pharmaceutical and beauty products industries. Political correctness is being replaced by a genuine interest in responsible behaviour, and the designer can be at the forefront in helping business to define its own responsibilities. An ethical manifesto perceived as genuine helps to sell products and services. Look at the successes of Body Shop, Virgin and Boots. The five leading clothes retailers in the UK (Burton Group, C&A, Marks & Spencer, Next and Sears Group) have subscribed to Oxfam's Clothes Code which will, it is hoped, outlaw sweatshop environments and minimal wages for overseas workers who manufacture large quantities of 'designer' clothes for their stores.

Future trends

Predicting future trends is a 'design specialism' in its own right. The ability to prophesy what colour will be 'in', what the hemline will be next month, when household products can depart from the accepted norm, when a car manufacturer can depart from the current 'Euro-style' is a valuable asset for a designer. Current fashion equals being competitive. The prediction and compliance with trends has always been a major factor in many areas of design. Designers sometimes see themselves as the trendsetting force, particularly in the fashion industry, but also witness the way that domestic furniture changed after the Memphis group stormed Milan and the partnership between Philips and Alessi has radically altered our perception of household products.

Professional trend prediction agencies, colour consultants and design researchers have a huge impact on design, marketing and long-term socioeconomic trends. A scientific approach to prediction and the creative individualism of designers must now be blended so that manufacturers ensure their products are in harmony with current fashions.

A contrary theory is that nostalgia sells equally well. Consider the 'designer pub' reminiscent of yesteryear and the packaging of consumables in painted tin boxes as were the biscuits, tobacco and powdered drinks of bygone eras.

Safety

Cars, in general, are designed as people-carriers, not weapons of mass destruction. Bull-bars are styling items acknowledged as being very efficient in conveying the most horrendous injuries to children in particular, but we still insist on making our 'fashion statements' despite this knowledge. The designer has an overriding responsibility to both the consumer and the operators of the processes required to manufacture the product, to design safety first into all product development.

Product liability laws protect the consumer; workplace legislation protects the makers. Safety sells: look at the move in automotive product marketing away from sex and speed and towards extolling the virtues of side impact bars, airbags and ABS brakes.

Green considerations

Destruction of rainforests, acid rain, depletion of the ozone layer, wanton pollution and the population explosion are all facts of the late twentieth century. Industrial designers cannot design in traditional ways, with historically traditional materials for traditional markets. Can environmentalism and consumerism be reconciled? Not in a recession, was once the answer; everything, it seems, comes at a price.

Product packaging often displays recycling logos or claims to have been manufactured at no environmental cost. This is equally as often not true. The real green issues have to be addressed at the first conceptual ideas of any design. The source of materials, the product's maintenance requirements, and the re-use of the constituent parts or materials and/or their ultimate disposal. Materials that cannot be recycled must be incinerated to release energy to produce more efficient products. We now recognize the finite nature of many raw materials, the destructive and dangerous implications of some manufacturing processes and the problems associated with the disposal of redundant products. These are major issues at design concept stage, through product development and, increasingly, as major marketing considerations.

Demographics

In Britain at the millenium, most of the population will be over 50 years of age. Indeed, this is the only growing sector of the population. Design should always concern itself with special needs: we are all potentially young, ill, adult and old during our lives. Often by concentrating our efforts on the needs of one particular group, we can arrive at benefits for the other sectors and actually increase market share beyond the original target group. Designers are key players and, in partnership with marketers, can fine-tune the design brief to be adaptable and indeed interactive with the specific sector market.

Globalization

Globalization in the context of design might mean a standardization of products or, perhaps more likely, will provide designers and marketers with the ability to adapt products to suit local markets. Marketing has progressed in recent times through local, provincial, national and international levels to one of a global strategy. Design is a major element in the marketing process. Component manufacture, assembly, distribution and sales no longer rest at 'home base'. Flexible manufacturing systems allow for economic and short production runs and manufacturing is not restricted to the site of raw material extraction.

So-called developing countries form the next great marketplace in the global context, and trends suggest that their aspirations will be to emulate the developed world and that consumer products will be the measure of increased economic prosperity. Is this an amalgam of cross-cultural differences being compromised down to the lowest common denominator and non-controversial 'styling' in the name of internationalization? Or is it the satisfying of the distinctive preferences of the end-user of designed artifacts? Design is becoming a 'global language' where, worldwide, the considerations for form, function, economy, achievability, conservation and regeneration of resources, benefits to mankind and beauty are universally applied and, most importantly, expected by the end-user. Customers are becoming increasingly conscious of their expectations of the design process and are becoming interactive as the sophistication of technological opportunity is presented to an increasingly aware public.

Exhibit 4.4 Benetton Clothes

The quality and design-led ethos of 'reflecting the world of today' encompasses the clothing, cosmetics, eyewear, toys and watches empire that is Benetton, whose keywords in its own publicity material are *innovation* and *flexibility*.

Founded in 1965 in Italy, the United Colors of Benetton has, in thirty-odd years established a truly global market. Producing over 80 million items a year, the company boasts that it is able to satisfy the demands of the marketplace in real time by its highly flexible system of 50 per cent locally owned joint ventures, the company's organization, its technological base, manufacturing facilities, efficient logistics, minimum stock warehousing and design.

Benetton shops are, without exception, 'bright, open and inviting, favouring a direct relationship between client and product'.

Turning the preconception of what advertising design was about, Benetton launched a massive campaign presenting uncomfortable images in the media. As the collage on the next page shows, these controversial advertising campaigns were 'dedicated to themes of universal importance'. Every continent now has gigantic billboards which display photographs that are meant to 'overcome cultural barriers and human indifference'. Advertising can be one of the richest and most powerful forms of communication. Benetton espouses the view that its imagery should make people think and discuss. 'I take pictures, I don't sell clothes', is a quote from Oliviero Toscani, the now infamous photographer of a newborn baby, a cemetery, an AIDS death and the electric chair. Benetton shocked the world by superimposing its logo on these photographs. What was shocking in 1992 is accepted today, and to be memorable and noticed is the intention of any advertising campaign.

An amazingly successful Formula 1 motor racing team is intended to reflect the efficiency of the Benetton organization – up-to-the-minute response to local demands, fashion always on the move, state-of-the-art computer technology and a dynamic 'moving billboard' seen on TV screens worldwide.

Architectural masterpieces form the bricks and mortar of the company headquarters in Ponzano, Veneto. La Ghirada Sports City and the Palaverde Arena demonstrate the company commitment to sport and outdoor living, and the futuristic Fabrica, which is the research and study institute, hosts students from all over the world who have distinguished themselves in applied arts, design, photography, video and graphic design, as well as craftsmanship in fabrics, wood, metal and ceramics. *Colors*, published by Benetton is 'not a catalogue in disguise, or an advertorial', it is a magazine that promotes the company's underlying editorial message that diversity is good. The print run for each issue is over 1 million copies.

Exhibit 4.4 continued

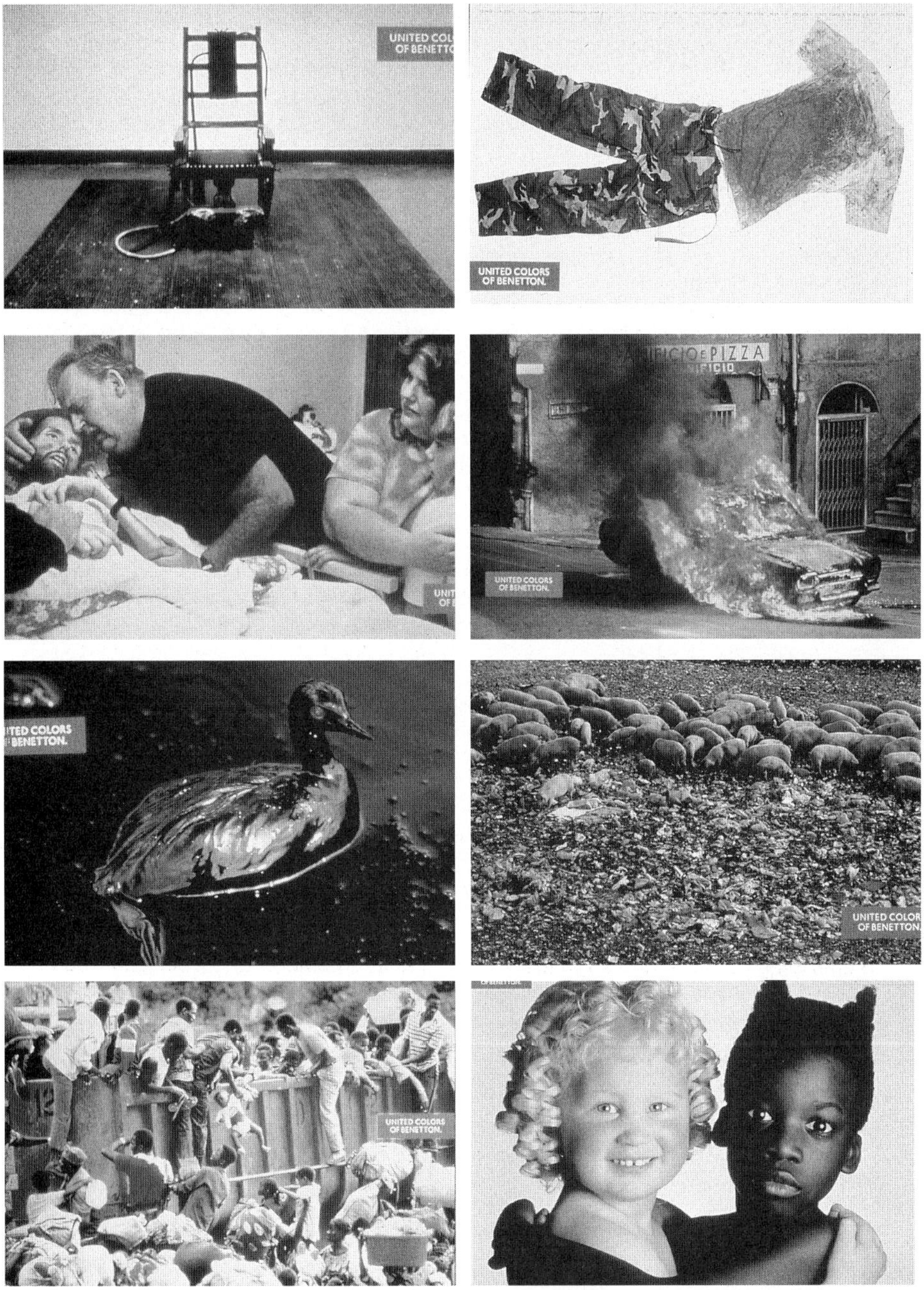

Source: Photographs supplied by Modus Publicity, London, 1997.

Exhibit 4.5 Sony Walkman

A pioneer of innovative quality design for over thirty years, Sony launched the Walkman personal stereo in 1979. It is difficult for the present generation to appreciate the innovative breakthrough that this extraordinary range represented. A major turning point for the company was in the late 1970s when Akio Morita, the company's legendary chairman realized the potential of using industrial designers as initiators of product development. Prior to this, the designer was accepted as last in the line of engineers, sales and marketers. This technically-driven corporation, however, had a design division at the forefront of product inception and development. Cross-fertilization developed across the company divisions and creative reporting ensured the creation of a teamwork approach. At Sony, designers make detailed proposals for marketing and pricing as well as engineering and industrial design concepts. Assembly-line production, plastic constructional parts, a low part-count and easy assembly were design features that led to later price wars with competitors who were eager to share the fortunes created by this phenomenon.

A hand-held, lightweight, shock-resistant, ergonomically styled, coloured, easy-to-use and inexpensive personal hi-fi centre that delivered excellent sound quality was a worldwide success and saw the demise of the other product of this niche at that time – the 'ghetto blaster'. A user analysis would show that this was not only a wanted product, but that with simple retooling it was possible to create a product that could sell for under £20 or for over £200. The user profile was discarded and children's models, 'in the shower' models, Walkmen for joggers, commuters, teenagers and adults were quickly on the shelves. By 1993 there had been three hundred different models of the Sony Walkman, fifty new models each year – a Walkman a week.

This product is a wonderfully successful example of an inspirational or design-led product, rather than a marketing-led conception. Masaru Ibuka, along with Akio Morita is credited with 'wanting to listen to music without disturbing anyone else'. Another anecdote suggests Mr Morita 'wanted to be able to listen to music whilst playing tennis'. The truth is probably that the radio cassette division within Sony was in difficulty (at that time Sony was concentrating its efforts on the video market) and badly needed a saleable new product.

The fledgling prototype was an existing portable tape recorder fitted with headphones. Miniaturization of the stereo amplifier, extensive design development of very small speakers (for earphones) that had sufficient frequency response and a 'rectangular block' case design (dictated by the cassette), and the first working prototype was evaluated. Within months the first range was launched. The product range now demonstrates great product value, well-defined aesthetic appearance and product quality. Hardly larger than the cassette it plays, the Walkman now has added weight (an important quality ingredient in the consumer's point of view), a remote facility and minimalist controls. A luxury item or a contribution to teenage street credibility?

Exhibit 4.6 The Mini

In the wake of the petrol rationing during the post-Suez crisis, the world of transport gave a short-lived boost to the 'bubble cars'. Imported mainly from Germany, these were personal transportation three-wheelers, usually powered by a motorcycle engine. Cheap to purchase and cheap to run, they were incapable of carrying more than one passenger, were unstable and offered little in terms of crash protection.

The then chairman of BMC, Sir Leonard Lord, saw this as a great marketing opportunity and instructed his designer, Alec Issigonis to produce 'a proper car, with four seats, smaller than anything else on the road and using an existing BMC engine'. One of his sketch drawings is reproduced here.

Post-war expectations had been of new roads. Motorways and the end of austerity would mean larger cars and only Issigonis had bucked this trend, designing and developing the Morris Minor, the first British car to achieve sales of one million. This laid the foundation, and the much-loved Minor became the forerunner of the Mini.

A box measuring 10 feet by 4 feet was established as a target volume of which 80 per cent would be given over to passengers and luggage. This would leave only 2 feet in which to accommodate the engine and gearbox. It was immediately apparent to Issigonis that he would have to use very small (10 inch) wheels and independent suspension. His masterstroke was in turning the engine sideways (transverse) and driving the front wheels from the gearbox through connections in the sump of the engine.

For the first time on a road car, subframes were employed to support the drive train, wheels and suspension. Styling was functional. External welded seams made manufacture easy and cheap. The car was only 10 feet long but accommodated four adults; boot space was limited, but the lid hinged down and could be used for extra loads. The door had bin-pockets, made possible because Issigonis insisted on sliding windows so window-winding mechanisms would not reduce available internal width.

The first production cars left the assembly lines in May 1959 after the incredibly short period of just two years of design and development.

The Mini is a design and marketing icon. It openly ignored all of the contemporary fashions in engineering, styling and marketing – yet paradoxically became one of the most fashionable cars ever. As it was not a product of its time, perhaps the Mini's strengths are still relevant today. A car which set out to transport four people without unnecessary waste is still holding its own in terms of economy, performance, handling and character.

Transverse engines and front-wheel drive are now conventional arrangements, but it was the Mini that pioneered and proved the concept that is now the norm.

Selling was almost unnecessary after the product launch as the decade of the mini encompassed all fashion and consumer sectors and the 1960s stood consumer expectation on its head. Minis were equally at home with the jet-set of Chelsea, on the race and rally track, as delivery vans and pick-ups and even as wood-trimmed 'shooting brake' estate cars. The car for everyman also spawned the rage for individualizing cars by the addition of extras, from wide wheels to chequered tape and windscreen stickers.

Issigonis, as well as being a superb engineer, richly deserves his place in history as an innovator of style and fashion alongside Mary Quant, Terence Conran and other 'gurus' of the most important style revolution of the twentieth century.

Exhibit 4.6 continued

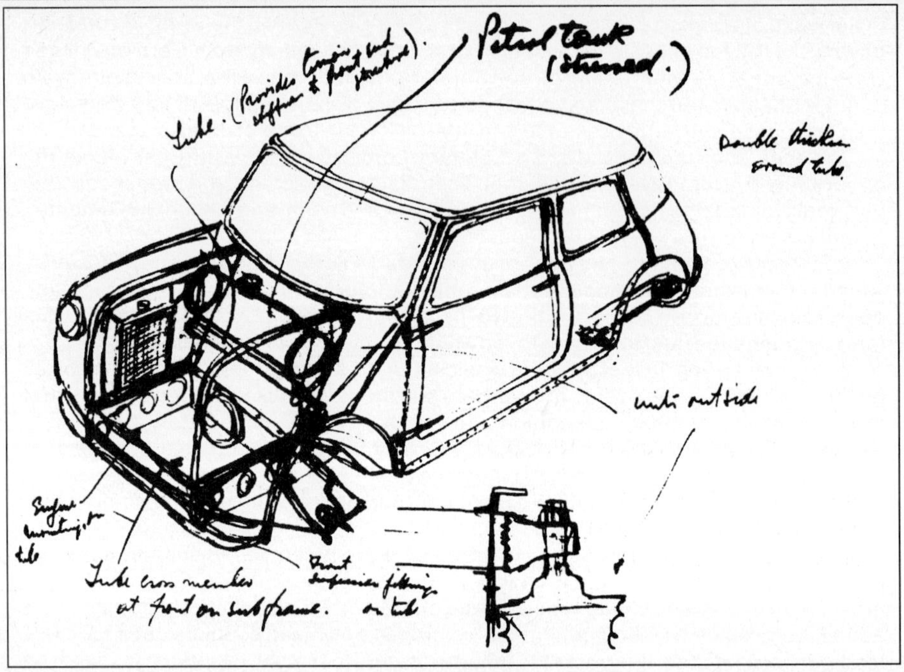

Source: Issigonis' sketch supplied by British Motor Industry Heritage Trust Archive and Library, Warwick.

The stories behind three hugely successful design-led products are told in Exhibits 4.4, 4.5 and 4.6.

QFD and the house of quality

The focus on quality and design has led, in many cases, to the adoption of quality function deployment (QFD). QFD is a product (service) development process based on interfunctional teams (marketing, manufacturing/operations, engineering and R&D) that uses a series of matrices, which look like houses, to consider customer input throughout the design, manufacture and delivery of a service product. QFD originated in 1972 at Mitsubishi's Kobe shipyard and is widely used in both Japan and the USA.

From a marketing perspective, QFD is interesting because it encourages functions other than marketing to use and in some cases perform market research. Each of these functions brings its own uses and its own demands for data. Engineers require greater detail on customer needs than is provided by the typical marketing study – detail necessary to make specific trade-offs in engineering design. For example, the car engineer might want data on customer needs to help place radio, heater, light and air conditioning controls on the dashboard and steering column. However, too much detail can obscure strategic design decisions such as whether the new car should be designed for those interested in sporty performance or for customers interested in a smooth, comfortable ride. Because QFD is an interfunctional process, it requires market research that is useful for both strategic decisions (performance versus comfort) and for operational decisions (placement of the controls). Some of the benefits found to have flowed from adopting a QFD approach are:

- Improved quality
- Improved reliability
- Reduced customer complaints
- Lower costs in design and manufacture
- Increased profits
- Greater effectiveness in decision-making
- Improvements in staff productivity
- A more customer-oriented workforce
- Better reaction to marketing opportunities

QFD uses perceptions of customer needs as a lens through which to understand how product characteristics and service policies affect customer preference, satisfaction and ultimately sales. The essential attraction of QFD is that it uses a visual presentation format (the house of quality[16]) that is easy to use. Working together to develop and deliver a quality and design that meets customers desires and tastes is the foundation upon which the house of quality was built.

Essential elements of the house of quality

Figure 4.10 illustrates the basic structure of the house of quality.

Customer requirements

Establishing what customers want is the logical place to begin the process of developing a product or service. Already in this chapter you will have come across a range of examples of what customers are looking for in a product or service. Take, for instance, a visit to the laundry. Customers would want, at the very least, their clothes to be properly cleaned, perfectly pressed with a quick turnaround and delivered in a friendly manner. The bottom line for a computer customer might be 'easy to read what I'm working on'. The fact that customer requirements are gathered in the customers' own words makes for difficulties when it comes to interpretation. For example, what does a customer really mean by friendly service or easy to use? Breaking such concepts down such that organizations can give them operational significance is a challenge for the marketers, engineers and designers alike.

A computer monitor team might be tempted to focus on the size of the monitor to affect the size of the characters on the screen. However, the size of the characters is only one of the design attributes that affects the customer requirements of 'easy to read'. It may also depend on the ambient room light and reflections, the colours that the software

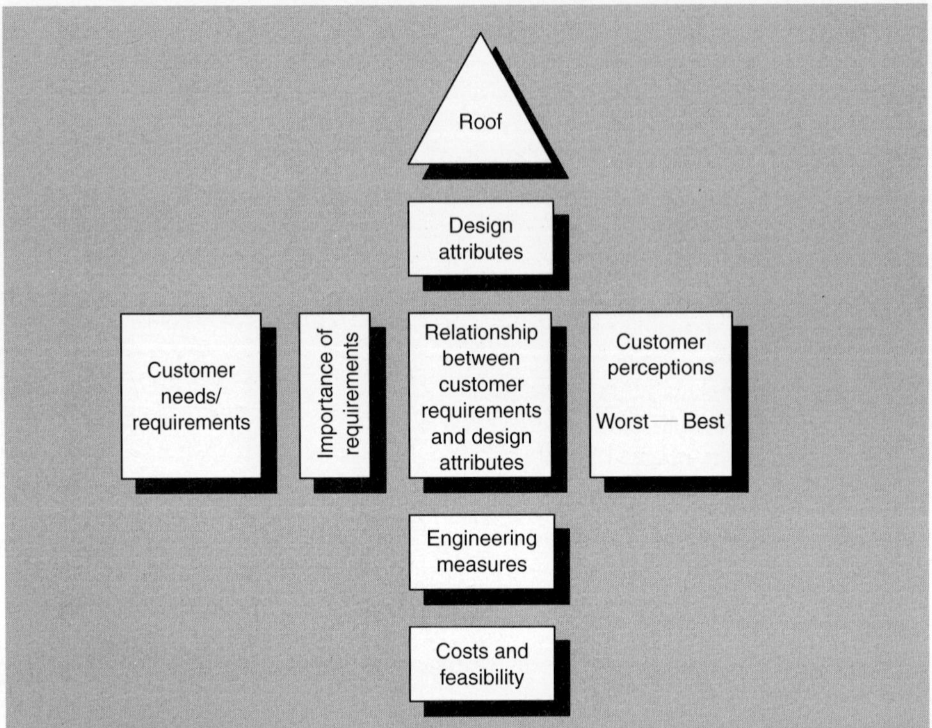

FIGURE 4.10 The house of quality from quality function deployment.

designer chooses, the ratio of the height of lower case letters to capitals and so on. Much of this has been recognized with the introduction of different font sizes and styles.

Importance of requirements

Discussions with customers could reveal a long list of requirements. As it is impossible to satisfy all of them, customers are asked to rank the requirements in order of importance.

Customer perceptions

To design a successful product or service any organization needs at least to meet or preferably to exceed competition on requirements that customers regard as important. On the right-hand side of the house, therefore, customers are surveyed for their views of competing products or services. An organization will then have a picture of how consumers view its performance relative to its nearest competitors. Marketers will recognize this approach as being akin to perceptual mapping and positioning. Finding out which products/services best fulfil which requirements, just how well these requirements are fulfilled, and whether there are any gaps between the 'best' and a potential product provides further information for development decisions to be made by a QFD team.

Design attributes

Once the customers' requirements have been identified the product or service must be translated into the language of the designer, engineer or operational expert. In the case of a laundry service, operational characteristics might be training, washing/bleaching formulation, washing programme, tumbler filters, moisture prior to calendering and equipment maintenance. Standards or tolerances, e.g. temperature values for meeting customer requirements, will need to be set for each operational step in the process. For a product, the engineering/design characteristics need to be set out in measurable terms, e.g. what weight should a household iron be so that it is easy to use and lift but such that it does not compromise its functional capability.

Roof

The roof specifies the operating or engineering relationships amongst the design attributes. For example, in the laundry a medium relationship would exist between good equipment maintenance and clean tumbler filters/correct moisture prior to calendering. Relationships can be non-existent, positive or negative, and trade-offs may need to be made where the presence of one design attribute adversely affects the operation of others, e.g. space configurations in a service setting could impact negatively on traffic management, customer/employee communications and so on.

Relationships between customer requirements and design attributes

The body of the house lies at the heart of the whole process as it indicates how each design attribute affects each customer requirement. Relationships are portrayed either by way of a number (from a statistical study) or a symbol (a tick or a cross) based on judgement or intuition. Normally, only the strongest relationships are specified. Returning to the laundry example, the customer requirement of completely clean would be strongly related to washing/bleaching formulation, wash programme, tumbler filters and equipment maintenance.

Engineering measures

Once the design attributes are established for meeting customer requirements, engineers and highly trained technicians work out specific measures for lifting/opening strengths, sound levels, heat emissions, lighting illumination, etc.

Costs and feasibility

As already mentioned, customers rank their requirements. A QFD will use these priorities

Exhibit 4.7 The house of quality

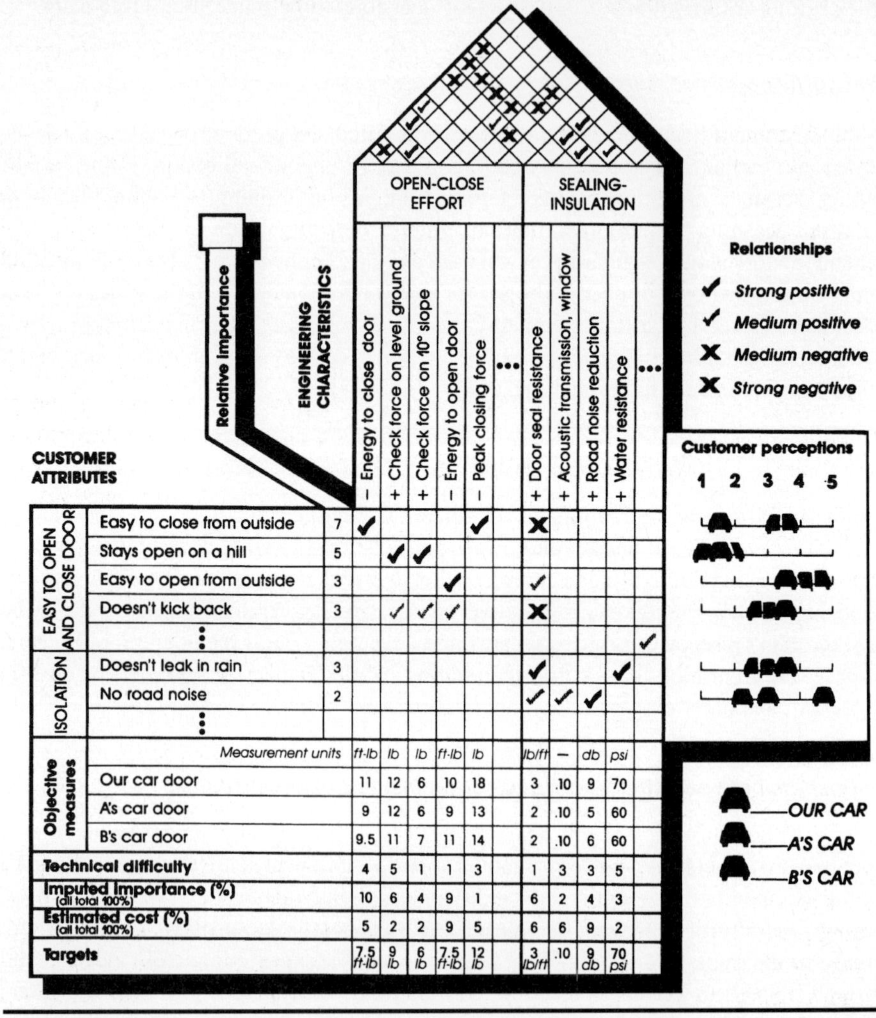

Source: Reprinted by permission of Harvard Business Review. An exhibit from 'The House of Quality' by Hauser, J.R. and Clausing, D., *Harvard Business Review*, May/June 1988. Copyright 1988 by the President and Fellows of Harvard College.

to make decisions that balance the cost of fulfilling a customer requirement with the desirability (to the customer) of fulfilling that need.

A house of quality example

Exhibit 4.7 illustrates how a QFD team used the house in the design of a car door.[17] A number of observations merit attention:

- **Customer perceptions**. Our existing doors are perceived as being much more difficult to close from the outside than those on competitors' cars.
- **Importance**. As customers regard 'closing the door' as important, the company needs to investigate further.
- **Relationship house**. This section allows the company to identify the engineering characteristics that affect this customer requirement, namely energy to close the door, peak closing force and door seal resistance. The engineers judge both the energy to close the door (the negative sign means engineers hope to reduce the energy required) and the peak closing force as good candidates for improvement together because they are strongly positively related to the customers' desire to close the door easily.
- **Roof**. The company identifies which other engineering characteristics might be affected by changing the door-closing energy requirement. Door-opening energy input and peak closing force are positively related (see the two ticks on the extreme left of the roof, squares 3 and 4 up). Other engineering characteristics (check force on level ground, door seals, window acoustic transmission, road noise reduction) are bound to be changed in the process and are negatively related.
- **The decision**. After consideration of competitors' doors, customer perceptions, cost and technical difficulty, the design team decides that the benefits outweigh the costs. A new design target is set for the door of the new car – 7.5 ft-lb of energy. This target will lead to a door which customers perceive to be superior and an important customer benefit.
- The further consideration was 'no road noise' and its relationship to acoustic transmission 'road noise' is only mildly important to customers and its relationship to the characteristics of the window is not strong.
- Window design helps only so much to keep things quiet. Decreasing acoustic transmission usually works. If we look at the roof of the house we can see that more weight would have a negative impact on characteristics (open and close energy plus both check forces). These characteristics are already strongly related to customer requirements ('easy to close', 'stays open on a hill'). Finally, the customer perception map shows our car as better on road noise than competitors.

The major attraction of the house of quality is the recognition it accords to the voice of the consumer in the design and delivery of quality products and services.

References

1. Garvin, D.A., 'What does "product quality" really mean?', *Sloan Management Review*, Fall, 1984.
2. *Ibid.*

3. Zelthaml, V.A., Parasuraman, A. and Berry, L.L., *Delivering Quality Service: Balancing Customer Perceptions and Expectations*, Free Press, 1990.
4. Slack, N., Chambers, S., Harlans, C., Harrison, A. and Johnson, R., *Operations Management*, Pitman Publishing, 1995, p. 694.
5. *Ibid.* p. 692.
6. Ellen, D. and Castleberry, S.B., 'Defining and evaluating quality: the consumer's view', *Advances in Consumer Research*, Vol. XIII, 1986.
7. Ishikawa, K., *What is Total Quality Control?*, Lu, D.J. (trans.), Prentice Hall Business Classics, 1985.
8. Mudie, P.M. and Cottam, A., *The Management and Marketing of Services*, Butterworth/Heinemann, 1993, p. 98.
9. Deming, W.E., *Out of the Crisis. Quality, Productivity and Competitive Position*, Cambridge University Press, 1986.
10. Juran, J.M., *Juran on Quality by Design: The New Stops for Planning Quality into Goods and Services*, Maxwell Macmillan International, 1992.
11. Peters, T.J. and Waterman, R.H., *In Search of Excellence: Lessons from America's Best Run Companies*, Harper Collins, 1991.
12. Crosby, P.B., *Quality is Free*, Penguin, 1980.
13. de Carlo, N.J. and Kent, S.W., 'History of the Malcolm Baldridge national quality award', *Quality Progress*, March 1990.
14. Henderson/Quality Award Committee, *Report on the Feasibility of a New UK Total Quality Award*, DTI, 1992.
15. British Quality Foundation, *Guide to Self-assessment*, 1995.
16. Griffin, A. and Hauser, J.R., *The Voice of the Customer*, Marketing Science Institute Working Paper, Report no. 92–106.
17. Hauser, J.R. and Clausing, D., 'The house of quality', *Harvard Business Review*, May/June 1988.

CHAPTER 5

Pricing

WHAT IS IT ABOUT?

What is price? How should we view it? How is a price arrived at? These are some of the questions addressed in this chapter. Examples cited of how a final price is reached might surprise people in terms not only of the elements involved but also of the contribution of each to the final price.

As price becomes a **perception of value** and a **determinant of quality**, illustration of how these relationships might be portrayed in practice are discussed.

The case of value and price for industrial products merits special attention as industrial consumers are concerned about **total lifecycle costs** and how this is reflected in price.

For many consumer products, price develops from a manufacturer's unit cost through to the final price paid by the customer. **Mark-ups** and **margins** figure in this process. How these fit in to arriving at the final price is calculated.

The role of cost in the price-setting process is demonstrated using the example of an orchestra performance.

Sensitivity is a key element in price formulation in terms not only of the factors that affect it but also of the economics of price sensitivity conveyed through the concept of the **elasticity of demand**.

Changes in price affect not only demand but also **profitability**. How to calculate the effect is explained.

Discounts and **price discrimination** feature too – both are significant everyday concerns for anyone involved in pricing.

Perceived value

The normal way of giving expression to what a product or service is worth is to put a price on it. Only then has a potential customer a yardstick against which to make a judgement about whether the product/service is worth the price or not. Customers' judgements or perceptions of product/service value represent their summary evaluations of it, taking into account the benefits that they perceive as offered and the price they perceive as required to obtain these benefits. Therefore,

Perceived value = Perceived worth − Perceived price

Perceived worth is what customers feel they should pay for the benefits they receive. Perceived price is the price that customers believe they will be charged. Whenever perceived price is lower than perceived worth, customers feel that they got more than they paid for, in other words 'a good deal'. Where perceived price exceeds perceived worth, customers regard the product/service as not good value, in other words 'a rip-off', 'too expensive' or 'poor value for money'. Judgements as to perceived value will naturally, vary from individual to individual.

Consider an analysis of where consumers' money went on a typical £31 bottle of perfume:

	£
Ingredients	1.57
Packaging	3.13
Advertising	3.96
Administration	3.96
Profit for company	3.87
Retail mark-up (60%)	9.89
VAT ($17\frac{1}{2}$%)	4.62
	31.00

A more recent example relates to a bicycle helmet. A cycle helmet costs about £6.27 to manufacture:

	£
Compacted polystyrene	1.50
Plastic shell	1.00
Four foam pads	0.80
Webbing and buckles	1.40
Velcro	0.02
Labels	0.50
Transport	0.30
Packaging	0.75
Cost to manufacture	6.27 approximately

By the time the helmet reaches the shop, mark-up can inflate the price for purchasers by more than 600 per cent. The average price lies between £18 and £30 but the flashy, expensive versions of top brands sell for more than £100. According to the chairman of the British Cycle Helmet Manufacturers Association, higher prices do not necessarily mean better protection.

Apart from consumer judgements possibly being different, seeing the above breakdown illustrates the essential two elements in price:

- **Basic price** – what consumers will pay for the core product.
- **Premium price differential** – what consumers will pay for the extended or augmented product.

For products like wheat, the basic price is the total price. There is little or no opportunity to 'add value' beyond the core product. At the other extreme, the chemicals in perfumes have little value. The premium price differential makes up most of the price. What consumers will pay for perfumes is largely a function of the image created by brand names, advertising and packaging. We can get an indication of perceived value through simple measurement.

Numerical example of perceived value pricing

A sample of consumers is asked to rate four brands of suction cleaners to determine the perceived value of each in relation to its price. Research indicates that consumers weight the importance of the attributes as follows:

Cleaning power	0.35
Portability	0.25
Versatility	0.20
Handling	0.20
	1.00

Consumers are asked to rate the attributes by dividing 100 points among the four brands for each attribute. The results, together with importance weights, can be seen in Table 5.1. The perceived value is calculated by multiplying the importance weights by the attribute ratings. For example, brand A is:

$$(0.35 \times 30) + (0.25 \times 25) + (0.20 \times 30) + (0.20 \times 20) = 26.75$$

Next, the perceived value of each brand is divided by the average perceived value and then multiplied by the average price of a suction cleaner. In this example with four brands, the average perceived value is 25 (100/4). Say that the average selling price of suction cleaners is £40. The calculation would be:

TABLE 5.1 Perceived value pricing: importance and attribute ratings

Weighted importance	Attribute	A	B	C	D	Total
0.35	Cleaning power	30	15	35	20	100
0.25	Portability	25	25	25	25	100
0.20	Versatility	30	15	40	15	100
0.20	Handling	20	20	30	30	100
1.00		26.75	18.5	32.5	22.25	

$$\text{Price proportional to the brand's perceived value} = \frac{\text{Perceived value of a specific brand}}{\text{Average perceived value}} \times \text{Average selling price}$$

For brand A, this works out to:

$$\frac{26.75}{25} \times 40 = £42.80$$

If the actual price of brand A is higher than £42.80, there is a danger that it will be perceived as overpriced. If the actual price of brand A is lower than £42.80, there is an argument for saying the brand is underpriced, although it may be seen as a bargain or excellent value for money.

The main objective should be to price proportional to perceived value. Thus, for brand A, it would be as near to £42.80 as possible.

Is there a relationship between price and quality?

There is probably no more important determinant of perceived value than perceived product or service quality. Customers are likely to choose the product that they perceive as having the highest quality among a set of products viewed as having comparable prices. A simple exercise can illustrate the 'relationship' between price and quality: respondents are asked for their estimate of quality and standing of five brands. The results, along with the respective prices, are in Table 5.2.

An index is calculated for each price and each percentage by dividing the figures by the average. Thus, the price index for brand A is 35/39.88 = 0.88. A's quality index is 70/75 = 0.93. The indices for all five brands can now be plotted on a graph (Figure 5.1).

There does seem to be a general relationship between perceived quality and price. However, brand C seems to be overpriced, whereas brand B seems to be in a good position.

Most price-perceived quality research has been exploratory and has not succeeded in resolving the question of when price is used to infer quality or even whether a relationship exists. Price may be used where consumers are unable, through insufficient

TABLE 5.2 Price and quality standing

Brand	Price £	Price index	Average estimate of quality and standing %	Quality index
A	35.0	0.88	70	0.93
B	40.0	1.00	85	1.13
C	38.5	0.96	70	0.93
D	56.0	1.40	95	1.26
E	29.9	0.74	55	0.73
	199.4		375	
Average	£39.88		75%	

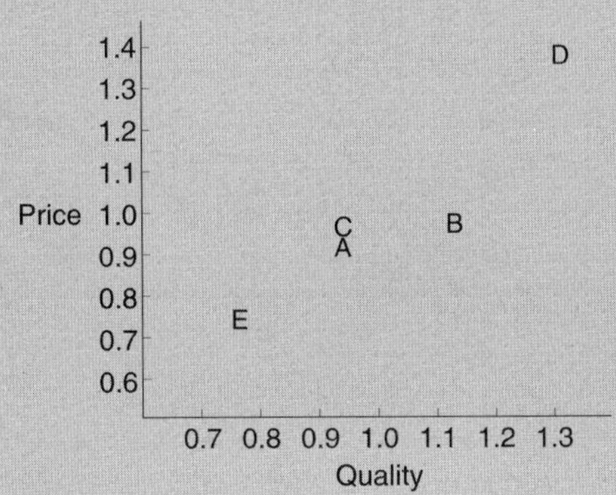

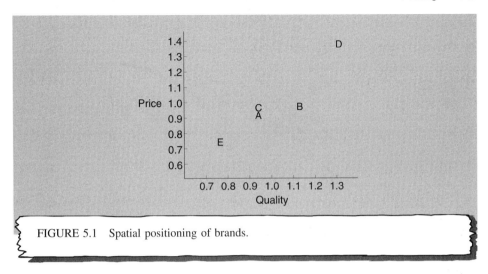

FIGURE 5.1 Spatial positioning of brands.

product knowledge, to understand the variation in quality. Equally, where price and perceived quality levels in a product category are regarded as great, price is used as a guide. Price will inevitably vary in importance depending on the type of customer and product. Buyers of industrial products, for example, do consider value in terms of a relationship between price and performance.

Value pricing for industrial products

Pricing-setting for industrial products takes on a somewhat different form from that for consumer goods, though it still embraces the concept of perceived value. Industrial companies can use a tool called **economic value to the customer** (EVC) to increase perceptions of value. It is regarded as an appropriate method of pricing for this particular market. The terms used in this approach are defined as follows:

- **Reference product**. In principle, any product that is either accomplishing the same function or meeting the same need as the product whose EVC is to be calculated. In practice, this will normally be the (competing) product that the customer is currently using.
- **Lifecycle cost**. This is the sum of a product's purchase price, start-up costs, and post-purchase costs.
- **Purchase price**. This is the total amount paid by the customer. Apart from the product itself, purchase price may include transport, insurance, installation charges and any initial technical training required by the customer.
- **Start-up costs**. Initial costs not included in the purchase price are the start-up costs, e.g. the cost of modifications to the customers existing system and lost production

while the product is being installed. Also, costs of installation and technical training may occur here rather than be included in the purchase price.

- **Post-purchase costs**. These are all the costs incurred by the customer once the product has been installed and is in use, e.g. repair and maintenance, continued technical training, operating costs (labour, power consumption, etc.). These costs, because they represent outlays over time, should be discounted back to the present time using an interest rate that reflects the customer's desired return on investment.

- **Incremental or improvement value**. This represents the potential incremental satisfaction or profits that the customer can expect from this product over the reference product. This may derive from attributes of the product that improve productivity (reduce costs or increase output per unit of time) or increase the value of the customer's output and potentially the output's price. Incremental value may also come from other elements of the total 'package', such as delivery reliability, service responsiveness, and even brand name.

Figure 5.2 illustrates the calculation of EVC.[1] A company is developing two products, Y and Z, to compete with X (the reference product) currently being used by potential customers.

The start-up and post-purchase costs for new product Y amount to £40 000, yielding savings of £30 000 over product X. The EVC of product Y is (100 000 – 40 000) = £60 000. The EVC is the amount that a customer would have to pay to make the total lifecycle costs of the new and reference products the same. The maximum acceptable price of £60 000 would represent an economic indifference point to customers. Some might switch but others will have a degree of inertia. Customers may have to be offered an inducement. One solution could be to set Y's price at £45 000. The manufacturer of Y would obtain a price premium of 50 per cent over product X (15 000/30 000) and the customer would save £15 000 in total lifecycle costs (45 000 + 10 000 + 30 000 = 85 000).

The attractiveness of product Y was its lower costs. The other side of the coin is where a product raises a customer's revenues, e.g. a better machine may produce more and/or improved-quality products. New product Z has more features or performance characteristics than product X or Y. This converts to an incremental value of £30 000. In addition there is a saving of £10 000 in post-purchase costs over product X. The economic value to any customer is therefore £70 000 (130 000 – 20 000 – 40 000 = 70 000). Considering that a customer is willing to pay £30 000 for X (the reference product), he should be prepared, in principle, to pay up to £70 000 for product Z (that same £30 000 plus the £10 000 savings in post-purchase costs plus the £30 000 worth of incremental value it offers). The question again arises as to what price to set for product Z. A possible solution[2] can be seen in Figure 5.3.

If we assume that it costs £40 000 to make the product then any price in excess of that will return a 'profit' (contribution to fixed costs) to the manufacturer. Any price under £70 000 will give the customer a better deal than he can get from X (the reference product). The £30 000 range bracketed can be regarded as the manufacturer's competitive advantage. The manufacturer then has discretion to price within this range. At a price of

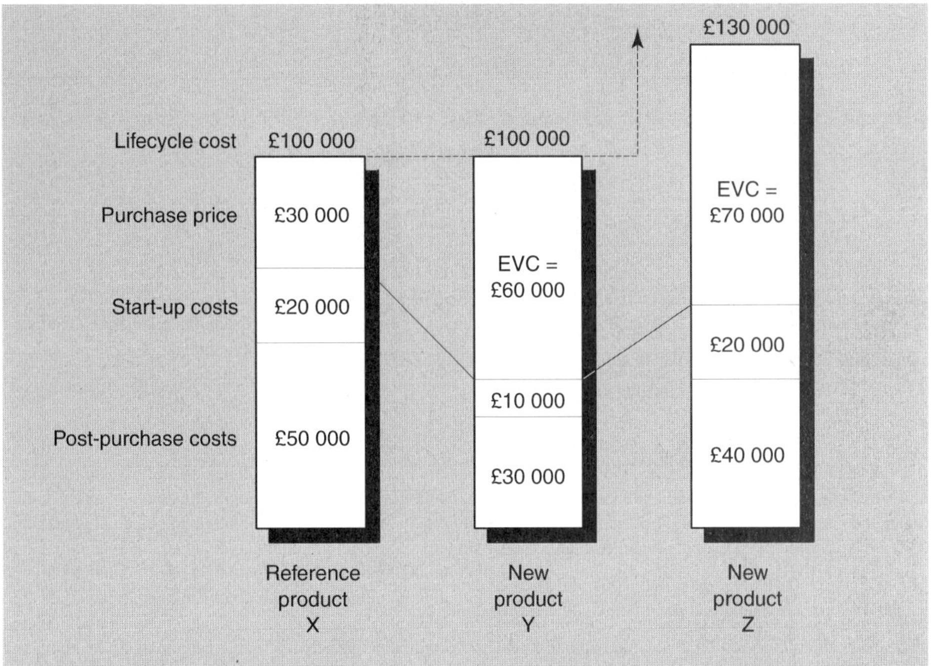

FIGURE 5.2 Economic value to the customer. Source: Forbis, J.L. and Mehta, N.T., *Economic Value to the Customer*, McKinsey Staff Paper, McKinsey & Co., February 1979.

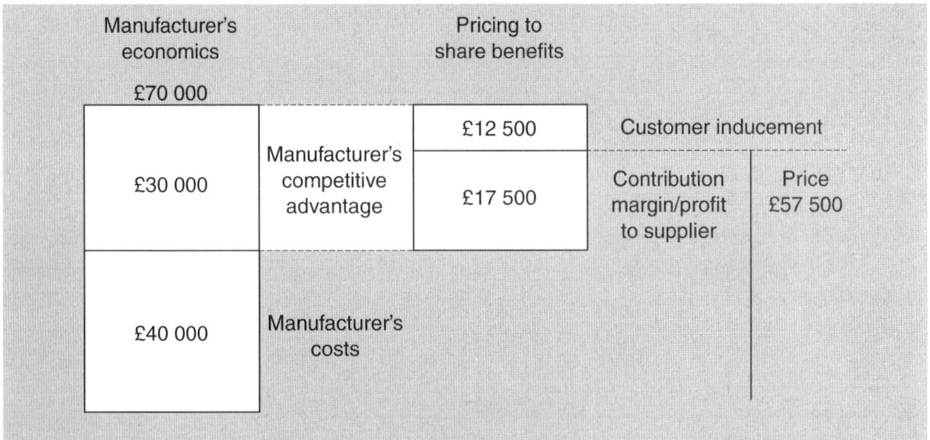

FIGURE 5.3 Setting the price of product Z. Source: Forbis, J.L. and Mehta, N.T., 'Value based strategies for industrial products', *Business Horizons*, May/June 1981.

£57 500 the manufacturer obtains a £17 500 profit, or contribution margin, while offering the customer an economic advantage of £12 500 over the reference product. We term this last amount the 'customer inducement'. Calculations such as these demonstrate that the EVC concept can certainly be regarded as a valuable tool in the pricing of industrial products.

Price and cost at levels in the channel of distribution

We have already seen the anatomy of price in the example of perfume. Now consider the general picture of how price develops from the manufacturer's unit cost to what the final consumer pays. A simple example will illustrate the process.

Manufacturer
Unit variable cost = £5
Total fixed costs = £150 000
Expected sales volume = 50 000

The manufacturer's unit cost for the product is:

$$\text{Unit cost} = \text{Unit variable cost} + \frac{\text{Total fixed costs}}{\text{Expected sales volume}}$$

$$= £5 + \frac{£150\,000}{50\,000}$$

$$= £8$$

The mark-up is 25 per cent giving a selling price of £10 (8+2). Another way of expressing the same figures is to say that the manufacturer requires a 20 per cent margin. Unlike mark-up, which is a percentage of the cost price, margin is a percentage of the selling price, namely:

$$\text{Selling price} = \frac{\text{Unit cost}}{1 - \text{Contribution margin}}$$

$$= \frac{8}{1 - 0.20} = £10$$

The manufacturer's selling price becomes the wholesaler's buying price. He also marks-up by 25 per cent or a 20 per cent margin:

$$\text{Mark-up price} = 10 + 2.5 = £12.50$$

or

$$\text{Margin price} = \frac{10}{1 - 0.20} = £12.50$$

The wholesaler's selling price in turn becomes the retailers buying price. He marks-up by

50 per cent, or a 33.3 per cent margin:

$$\text{Mark-up price} = 12.50 + 6.25 = £18.75$$

or

$$\text{Margin price} = \frac{12.50}{1 - 0.33} = £18.75$$

Hence, by knowing his unit cost and the respective mark-ups/margins of channel members, a manufacturer can establish the final retail selling price. Equally, a retailer can reverse the process by working backwards. In the manufacturer's case, working back from a retail price can also be helpful as it will guide him on what his unit cost and profit margin will have to be. For the manufacturer, however, achieving the 20 per cent profit margin rests on realizing the expected sales. If, in fact, only 30 000 units were sold, the profit would disappear as the unit cost would now equal £10, i.e. £5 + £150 000/30 000 = £10.

Target return pricing

A variant of the cost-plus or mark-up approach of the previous section is called target return pricing. It is in essence the preserve of large companies wanting to achieve a target return (profit) on their investment, usually over the long term. Although demand is reckoned to fluctuate during the period, the companies take the view that the fluctuations will even themselves out, enabling the target return to be achieved. The following formula is used to obtain the selling price:

$$P = UVC + \frac{F}{X} + \frac{rK}{X}$$

where P is selling price, UVC is unit variable cost, F is fixed cost, X is standard unit volume, *r* is profit rate desired and K is capital employed.

For example, unit variable costs are estimated to be £4.20 on a standard volume of 500 000. Fixed costs are £500 000 and a 15 per cent rate of return on £1m in capital employed is desired. The selling price is £5.50. In equation form:

$$\begin{aligned} P &= £4.20 + \frac{£500\ 000}{500\ 000} + \frac{15\%(£1m)}{500\ 000} \\ &= £4.20 + £1.00 + £0.30 \\ &= £5.50 \end{aligned}$$

'Limits' framework

In establishing a price one needs to estimate the range within which the product/service can be profitably sold (Figure 5.4).

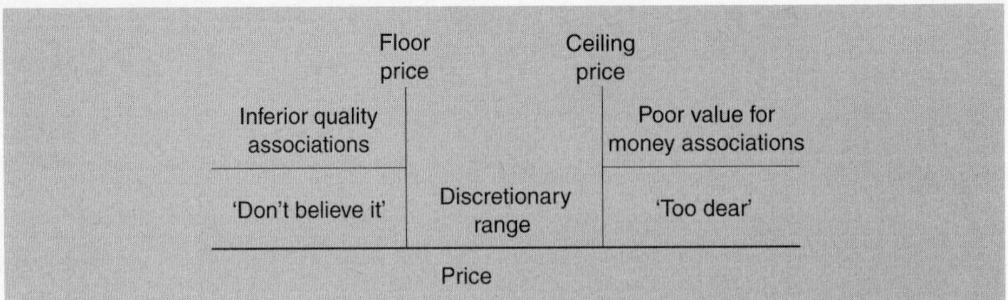

FIGURE 5.4 The limits concept.

- **Price floor**. In normal circumstances, this is the lowest price that will not result in a loss on the product. As it is based on a particular volume level, an estimate must be made of how large the market will be. Consumers will inevitably question the quality of any product or service priced lower than this.
- **Price ceiling**. This is the upper limit beyond which it will be difficult to stimulate demand. Consumers may perceive any price higher than this as a rip-off.

It is the price-setter's task to determine the limits and how wide or narrow the range is likely to be. The width of the range will vary substantially depending on the situation, giving the price-setter a great amount of, or very little, discretion. The limits might be reasonably close together if both price-setters and consumers shared their beliefs and knowledge about costs, profit requirements, use values, etc. However, this they do not do. The correct price will lie within a range that is limited by the price that a company believes it requires and the price that the consumer thinks he can afford. How much freedom a company has to price (the discretionary range) will be determined by a number of factors:

- Stage in the product lifecycle
- Nature of demand
- Product differentiation
- Competitors' prices
- Costs

Costs and pricing

Costs should never determine price, but they do have an important role to play in the price-setting process. It is price that determines sales levels. Costs, however, will be incurred in delivering these sales, so decisions about what to sell and in what quantities will, to a large extent, be influenced by cost considerations. We saw in chapter 3 how costs are generally divided into fixed and variable. It is not quite as simple to say that one varies with sales and the other does not. To overcome the limitation of costs being either fixed or variable, one can refer to incremental costs, which are costs associated with changes in pricing and sales. Variable costs will always be incremental for pricing, and fixed costs will be so on some occasions, e.g. the fixed cost to a restaurant to print menus with new prices.

To illustrate the importance of properly identifying the incremental costs when making a pricing decision, consider the problem faced by the business manager of a symphony orchestra.[3] The orchestra usually performs on two Saturday evenings each month during the season, with a new programme for each performance. The following costs are incurred for each performance:

Fixed overhead costs	£1500
Rehearsal costs	£4500
Performance costs	£2000
Variable costs (e.g. programmes, tickets)	£1 per patron

The business manager is concerned about the very thin profit margin. The current ticket price is £10. At full capacity (1100 seats) profit would be:

Sales revenue	£11 000 (1100 × 10)
Less Total costs	£9 100 (1500 + 4500 + 2000 + 1100)
Profit	£1 900

Unfortunately the usual attendance is only 900 patrons, resulting in an average cost per ticket of £9.89 (£8900/900). This is perilously close to the £10 admission price. The total profit per performance is only £100 (£9000 – £8900). The manager is now considering three proposals aimed at increasing the profit. They are as follows:

1. A 'student rush' ticket priced at £4 and sold to college students half an hour before the performance on a first come, first served basis. The manager estimates that 200 such tickets could be sold to people who would otherwise not attend.
2. A Sunday matinee repeat of the Saturday evening performance with tickets priced at £6. The manager expects to sell 700 of these but 150 would be to people who would otherwise have attended the higher priced Saturday performance. So the net increase would be 550.
3. A new series of concerts to be performed on the alternate Saturdays. Tickets would be priced at £10 and sales of 800 tickets are estimated. However, 100 of these would be sold to people who would attend the new series instead of the old. The net figure is therefore 700.

The question now is, which, if any, of these proposals, should the orchestra adopt? An analysis of the options[4] is set out in Table 5.3. The most profitable option is the student rush even though it is the lowest priced and yields the least amount of additional revenue. The lesson to be learnt here is that profitable opportunities can be missed if the focus is on average rather than incremental costs. The current average cost of £9.89 per patron would drop to £8.27 (£8900 + £200)/1100 if option 1 (the student rush) were adopted. However, the student rush tickets priced at £4 each would cover less than half the average cost per ticket. It is this concentration on average costs which includes costs that are not

TABLE 5.3 Analysis of three proposals for the symphony orchestra

	1 Student rush	2 Sunday matinee	3 New series
Price	£4	£6	£10
× Unit sales	200	700	800
= Revenue	£800	£4200	£8000
– Other sales forgone	(0)	(£1500)	(£1000)
Revenue gain	£800	£2700	£7000
Incremental rehearsal cost	0	0	£4500
Incremental performance cost	0	£2000	£2000
Variable costs	£200	£550	£700
Incremental costs	£200	£2550	£7200
Net profit contribution	£600	£150	(£200)

Source: Nagle, T.T. and Holden, R.K.. *The Strategy and Tactics of Pricing*, Prentice Hall, 1995.

incremental and thus irrelevant which could result in forgoing a profitable opportunity. Offering a low price can therefore make good business sense in terms of contribution to profit, and the smaller the incremental addition to costs, the larger the profit.

Price sensitivity

Analysis of price sensitivity is regarded as a key element in the formulation of price. It not only assists the development of marketing strategy but also helps identify segments with different price sensitivities and the range within which price should be set. Ten factors affecting price sensitivity have been identified.[5]

- **Perceived substitutes effect**. Buyers are more sensitive the higher the product's price relative to the prices of perceived substitutes, e.g. local residents may avoid the area's higher priced restaurants frequented by tourists (who are unaware of alternatives).
- **Unique value effect**. Buyers are less sensitive to a product's price the more they value any unique attributes that differentiate the offering from competing products, e.g. many consumers exhibit unswerving loyalty towards products like Heinz Ketchup and Volvo cars.
- **Switching cost effective**. Buyers are less sensitive to the price of a product the greater the added cost of switching suppliers. This is often a characteristic of industrial marketing where a buyer has made substantial investments in training and systems, etc., which could be very costly to change with a new supplier. On a more positive side, relationship marketing has meant customers experiencing the benefits of remaining with their present supplier.
- **Difficult comparison effect**. Buyers are less sensitive to the price of a known or reputable supplier when they have difficulty comparing alternatives. Buyers may

seek loyalty with an approved supplier or established brand names. However, with increasing access to consumer reports like *Which*? magazine 'difficult comparisons' are now less of a problem.

- **Price quality effect**. Buyers are less sensitive to a product's price to the extent that a higher price signals better quality. A direct relationship between price and quality is not always conclusive. The purchase of a high priced item may simply reflect the buyer's ego and desire for prestige. Within certain ranges, however, the average customer is sensitive to differences in price, whilst in others less so. For example, changes in the price of whisky are expected to be matched by differences in quality. Petrol prices, on the other hand, may vary substantially across the country but the quality is expected to be the same.

- **Expenditure effect**. Buyers are more price-sensitive when the expenditure is larger, either in money terms or as a percentage of income. This is particularly relevant in low income households for whom most expenditure is a source of concern.

- **End-benefit effect**. Buyers are less sensitive the less the expenditure is to the total cost of the end-product. This occurs frequently in industrial markets, e.g. a manufacturer's price-sensitivity towards materials for making office furniture will vary according to the strength of demand for office furniture.

- **Shared cost effect**. Buyers are less price sensitive when part of the cost is borne by another party. The classic case here is that of sales representatives for whom expenditure incurred is usually compensated. Outwith their business role they may be much more price sensitive.

- **Fairness effect**. Buyers are more sensitive to a product's price when it is outside the range they perceived as fair or reasonable. This falls under the rip-off category and must inevitably be linked to customers perceiving suppliers enjoying undue profits and exploiting situations, e.g. selling drinks and ice cream at inflated prices where there is no immediate competition and the temperature is very high.

- **Inventory effect**. Buyers are less price sensitive when they cannot store the product, e.g. a supermarket discounting canned tomatoes for one week can reasonably expect the percentage increase in sales of canned tomatoes to exceed the percentage increase when it features fresh tomatoes with a similar price cut.

Economics of price sensitivity

The factors that affect price sensitivity are clearly crucial when it comes to undertaking a price analysis. However, we need a more operationally useful definition of price sensitivity in order to analyze price changes. The definition commonly used is called the price elasticity of demand. It is the percentage change in quantity demanded divided by the percentage change in price. The price elasticity of demand (E) is calculated using the following formula:

$$E = \frac{\%\text{ change in quantity demanded}}{\%\text{ change in price}}$$

E is generally a negative number since price increases generally result in a reduction in quantity demanded, and price decreases generally result in an increase in quantity demanded.

If, for example, the elasticity of demand for overseas holidays is estimated to be −1.83 one would expect that a 5 per cent decrease in price would increase the quantity demanded by 9.15 per cent. Demand is said to be elastic where E is greater than 1 and inelastic where E is less than 1. Both types of demand are shown in Figure 5.5.

The significance of price elasticity of demand can be seen in the effect on revenue, which is the price multiplied by the quantity demanded. From Figure 5.5 we can determine the effect on revenue of a price decrease and increase:

	% change in P	% change in Q	E	Change in total revenue £000	%
Elastic demand					
Price decrease (50 → 45)	−10	+62.5	−6.25	+9250	+46.2
Price increase (45 → 50)	+11	−38.4	−3.49	−9250	−31.6
Inelastic demand					
Price decrease (60 → 45)	−25	+14.2	−0.56	−300	−14.2
Price increase (45 → 60)	+33.3	−12.5	−0.37	+300	+16.6

It is evident from these figures that elastic demand favours a price decrease whereas inelastic demand favours a price increase. One must be aware, however, that a product's price sensitivity is not the same at all levels. The degree of price elasticity often depends on the direction and size of the price change. Demand may be inelastic for a small change but elastic for a more dramatic change. Consider a possible demand schedule for house cleaning (Figure 5.6).

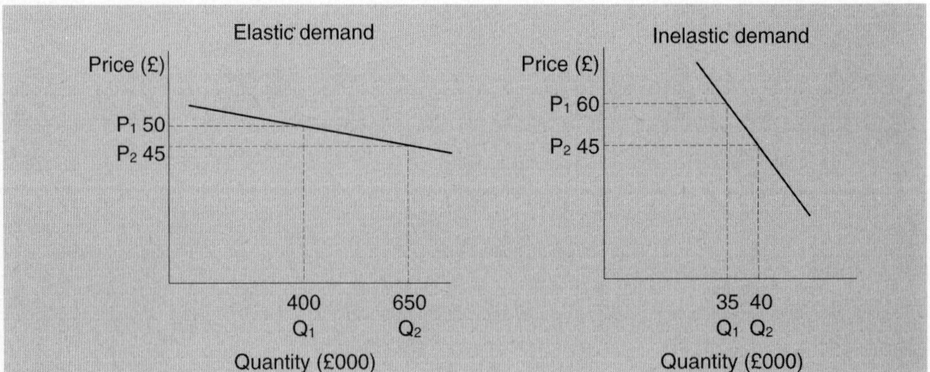

FIGURE 5.5 Elasticity of demand.

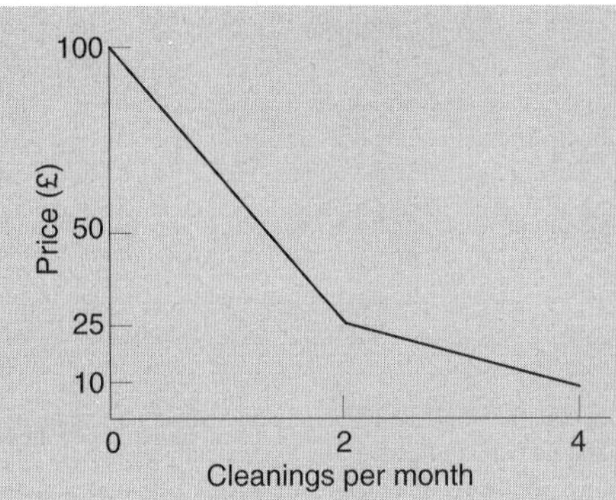

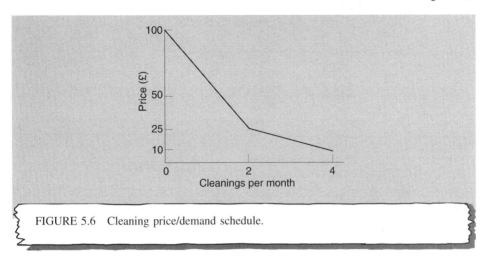

FIGURE 5.6 Cleaning price/demand schedule.

Consumers might be willing to pay a cleaner £10 per week, but might have the house cleaned only every two weeks if the price rose to £25. In the unlikely event of price rising to £100, cleaning would become a DIY activity.

Demand may, of course, shift without any change in price. An increase in marketing expenditure, particularly promotion, along with an improvement in the economy could move the demand curve to the right (Figure 5.7).

Two further demand schedules with implications for pricing merit attention: prestige pricing and product line pricing. Prestige pricing (Figure 5.8) occurs when buyers want the very best quality that money can buy. Buyers' sensitivity to product performance increases more than their sensitivity to price. They believe you get what you pay for, and therefore they will pay more with the expectation of getting more. Owning top quality goods gives people confidence in their purchases and security in themselves. High priced products are more exclusive to own and therefore become more desirable to those who only want the best.

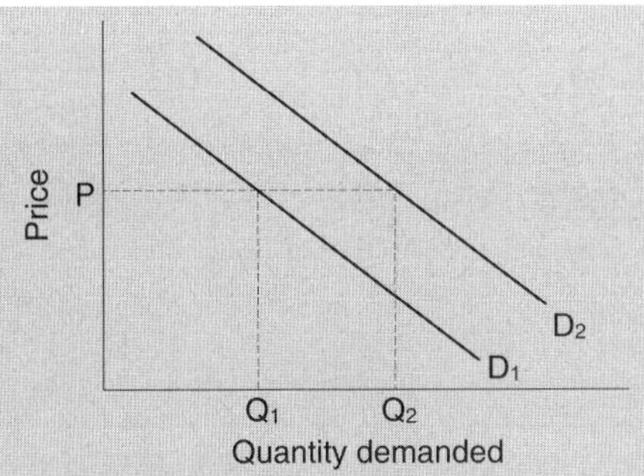

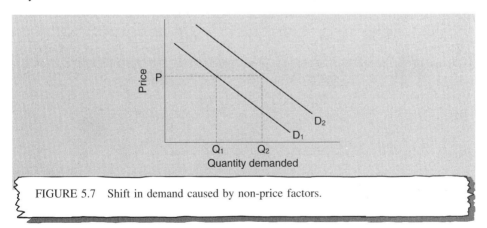

FIGURE 5.7 Shift in demand caused by non-price factors.

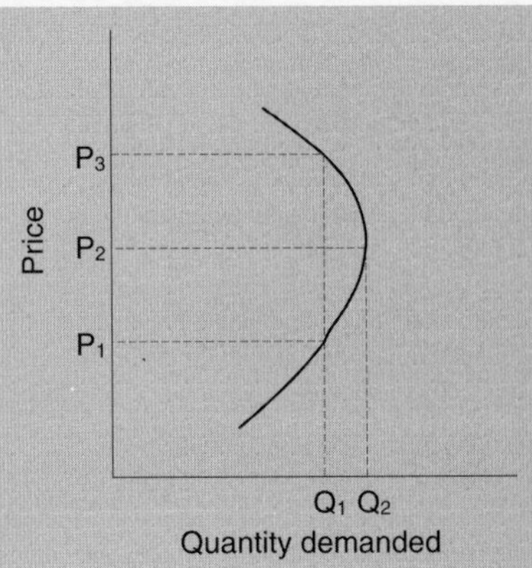

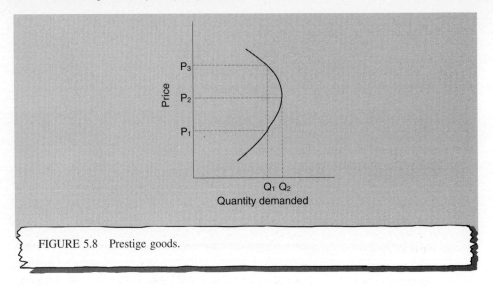

FIGURE 5.8 Prestige goods.

As a consequence of prestige pricing, the demand curve for prestige goods sometimes slopes upward. Raising price from P_1 to P_2 may increase demand. If too high a price (P_3) is charged then demand will fall.

Often a company that is selling not just a single product but a line of products may price them at a number of different pricing points, which is called price lining. It is practised by clothing retailers in particular: men's trousers may be priced £19.99, £29.99 and £39.99. Figure 5.9 shows the demand curve assumed by these retailers.

The assumption in Figure 5.9 is that a good number of trousers will be sold at £39.99, but if the price is lowered, not many more will be sold until the price reaches the next price-point, £29.99. Similarly, if the price is raised from £19.99 there will be a rapid drop

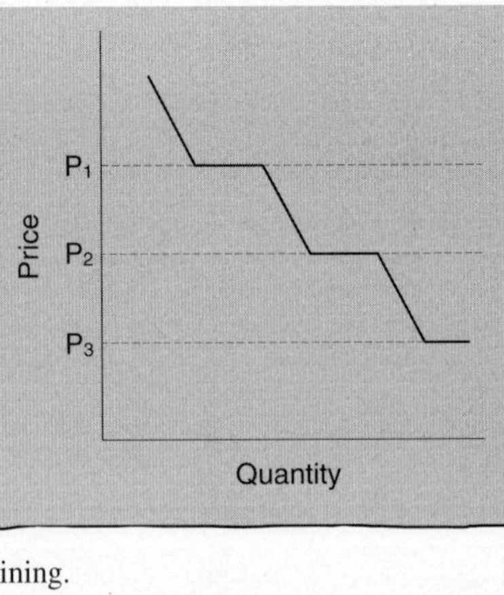

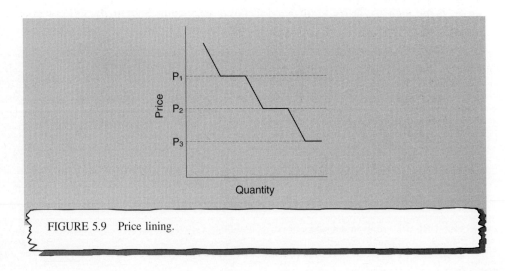

FIGURE 5.9 Price lining.

in sales until the next strong price-point is reached. Price lining simplifies consumers' buying decisions. Shoppers can first select a price-point and then choose from the assortment in the price line based on colour, style or other product characteristics. It also simplifies the retailer's decisions about what specific prices should be selected. The number of price-points is usually limited to three or four.

Profitability and pricing

Contribution, as we saw in chapter 3, remains an important concept in marketing management. When it comes to price-setting, the size of the contribution is important as it is the share of price that either adds to profit or reduces losses. The percentage contribution is the contribution divided by the price and is a measure of the leverage between a company's sales volume and its profit. Sales volume thus becomes an important marketing objective.

To make an informed, profitable pricing decision we need to know the cost structure of an organization. An illustration of the importance of this can be seen in Table 5.4 showing the cost structures of two contrasting organizations, an airline and an electrical contractor.

Although at current sales volumes each organization earns the same net profit, the effect on each of a change in sales volume can be dramatic. For the electrical contractor, only 20 pence of every additional £1 increases profit or reduced losses. For the airline that figure is 80 pence in the pound. As a change in sales is often attributable to a change in price, would a change in price improve the situation? More precisely, we should ask:

- How much would sales volume have to increase to profit from a price reduction?
- How much could the sales volume decline before a price increase becomes unprofitable?

Answers to these questions will depend on the percentage contribution. For a price decrease, the necessary volume increase before profitability is enhanced is given by:

$$\%\text{ volume increase} = \left(\frac{X}{CS - X}\right)100$$

where X is the percentage price decrease and CS is the percentage contribution.

Similarly, for a price increase the permissible volume decrease before profitability is harmed is given by:

TABLE 5.4 Cost structures and contribution (% of selling price)

	Airline	Electrical contractor
Variable cost	20	80
Fixed cost	70	10
Net profit	10	10
Contribution	80	20

$$\% \text{ volume decrease} = \left(\frac{X}{CS + X}\right) 100$$

To illustrate these two formulae, consider the case of a company deliberating between a price reduction of 2.5 per cent or a price increase of 2 per cent. The present price is £15 and the unit variable cost is £9. Which option should be recommended, and why?

For the price reduction the percentage volume increase is:

$$\% \text{ volume increase} = \left(\frac{0.025}{0.4 - 0.025}\right) 100$$

$$= 0.066$$

$$= 6.6\%$$

For the price increase the percentage volume decrease is:

$$\% \text{ volume decrease} = \left(\frac{0.02}{0.4 + 0.02}\right) 100$$

$$= 0.0476$$

$$= 4.76\%$$

(See Appendix A, for values of minimum and maximum volume, and Exhibit 5.1 for an explanation of break-even sales analysis.) The two figures, 6.6 and 5.2, indicate the level of price sensitivity indicated by the company's cost and margin structure. To determine what action to take we need to get some indication as to the level of price sensitivity in the market and compare it with our own figures. Let us say that research shows an elasticity of demand in the market of –2. On the basis of the company's price options, elasticity would be:

Price decrease	*Price increase*
$E = \dfrac{6.6\%}{2.5\%}$	$E = \dfrac{4.76\%}{2.0\%}$
$= 2.64$	$= 2.38$

Based on the market elasticity, the price increase should be selected, as the reduction in quantity demanded would only be 4 per cent against the 4.76 per cent permissible before profitability is harmed (E(–2) = 4.0% ÷ 2.0%). In the case of the price decrease, demand in the market will rise by only 5 per cent against the 6.6 per cent required, and therefore a price decrease should be rejected (E(–2) = 5.0% ÷ 2.5%).

Referring back to the data in Table 5.4 we can now see the impact of contribution on pricing decisions (Table 5.5).

For the electrical contractor, with a relatively small percentage contribution, to profit from a 5 per cent price cut, sales must increase by more than 33 per cent. Compare that with the 6.7 per cent for the airline with its much larger percentage contribution. Therefore, building sales volume through price cuts will be much more difficult for the

Exhibit 5.1 Break-even sales analysis

The logic behind the implications of a price increase or decrease is set out below. Consider the case of a company where:

Selling price	=	£25
Variable cost	=	£15
Present sales	=	12 000 units

A price cut of £1.50 is under review. The financial trade-offs can be seen in the diagram.

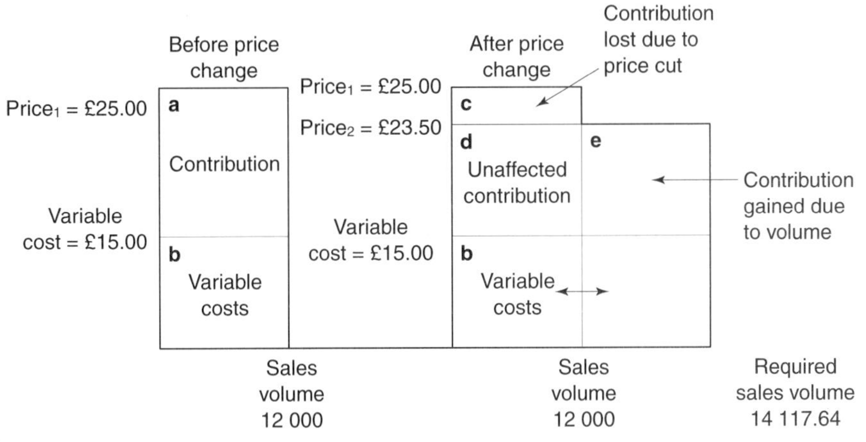

Before any price change:

$$\text{Total revenues} = 12\,000 \times £25 = £300\,000$$

From this, variable costs must be subtracted:

$$\text{Total variable costs} = 12\,000 \times £15 = £180\,000$$

$$\therefore \text{Total contribution} = £(300\,000 - 180\,000)$$
$$= £120\,000$$

A price decrease of £1.50 is recommended. For that to be profitable, contribution after the price decrease must be greater than £120 000. After the price decrease of 6 per cent (£1.50) the company receives a price of only £23.50 or £1.50 less contribution per unit.

As sales are normally 12 000 units, the total loss in contribution would be £18 000 (12 000 × 1.50). This is called the **price effect**. To balance this, however, a price decrease is expected to increase sales.

The contribution earned from that increased volume, known as the **volume effect**, is unknown (box e). The price reduction will be profitable, however, when the volume effect (box e) exceeds the price effect (box c). Basically what this means is that for the price reduction to be profitable the gain in contribution from the increased sales volume must be greater than the loss in contribution resulting from the decrease in price.

The purpose of break-even sales analysis is to calculate the minimum sales volume necessary for the volume effect (e) to balance the price effect (c). If sales exceed that minimum amount then the price cut will be profitable.

Exhibit 5.1 continued

Therefore, to determine the break-even sales change: the last contribution due to the price effect (c) is £18 000 which means that the gain in contribution due to the volume effect (e) must be at least £18 000 for the price cut to be profitable. Since each new unit sold after the price cut results in a contribution of £8.50 (23.50 − 15) the company must sell at least an additional 2117.64 (18 000/8.5) to make the price cut profitable. This represents an increase of 17.65 per cent over existing sales of 12 000 units. (You can verify this figure from Appendix A.)

What if price were increased by £1.50?
The gain in contribution would be £18 000 (12 000 × £1.50) – the price effect. The loss in contribution due to the volume effect must not, therefore, exceed £18 000 for the price increase to be profitable. Since each new unit sold after the price increase results in a contribution of £11.50 (26.50 − 15) the company must not allow the sales volume to fall by more than 1565.21, a reduction of 13.04 per cent. (Once again you can verify this figure from Appendix A.)

TABLE 5.5 Impact of contribution on pricing decisions

	Airline	Electrical contractor
Minimum sales increase for A (%)		
5% price reduction	+6.7	+33.3
10% price reduction	+14.3	+100.0
20% price reduction	+33.3	–
Maximum sales decrease for A (%)		
5% price increase	−5.9	−20.0
10% price increase	−11.1	−33.3
20% price increase	−20.0	−50.0

electrical contractor. The opposite conclusion follows from price increases. The electrical contractor can afford to lose many more sales than the airline and still profit from higher prices. (See Appendix A for the percentage volume changes necessary to offset percentage price changes.)

Circumstances favouring a price change

Several circumstances favouring either a price decrease or a price increase are said to exist. For a price decrease they are:

- Spare capacity
- Elastic demand
- Declining market share
- Cost advantage over competitors

For a price increase they are:

- Cost inflation
- Excess demand
- Inelastic demand

Response to price changes

A number of parties may express more than a passing interest in a price change, e.g. government, suppliers, competitors, consumers. In particular, reactions from final consumers may not be as straightforward – price up/demand down and price down/demand up – as one might expect.

A number of consumer reactions to price changes have been found. Consumers may believe that a price decrease signals that:

- The item is about to be replaced by a later model.
- The item has some fault and is not selling well.
- The company is in financial trouble and may not stay in business to supply future parts.
- The price will come down further and it pays to wait.

For a price increase, they may believe that:

- The product is going into short supply, so they had better buy some now.
- It is especially good value.
- The company is greedy.

Particular dangers for a price increase are how much and how often. Whatever the decision, providing a sound and true explanation is an absolute necessity. It has been known for organizations to adopt an 'equivalence perspective', e.g. an increase in the television licence is equivalent to only a few pence extra per week; or a price increase that is equivalent to one night's entertainment. Whether such tactics work remains a mystery.

Discounts and the final price

According to one survey of 2463 companies, price increases typically have three to four times the effect on profitability as proportionate increases in volume. For example, in a company with average economics, increasing unit volume by 1 per cent yields a 3.3 per cent increase in operating profit, assuming no decrease in price. However, a 1 per cent increase in price, assuming no loss in volume, increases profit by 11.1 per cent.[6] Aside from the wider difficulties of arriving at the right price, companies can do much to manage the full range of components that contribute to the final price. Much of this focus will fall on the question of discounts. Most companies offer discounts of one sort or another to their customers. They are used by suppliers as a mechanism for encouraging customers to modify their behaviour in a way that will be beneficial to the supplier.[7] A range of devices for 'rewarding' customers is used by companies. The most commonly encountered are:

- **Trade discount**. This is given to a channel intermediary in return for the service he makes available, e.g. a wholesaler, providing such services as bulk-breaking, transporting, storage, etc. might qualify.

- **Quantity discount**. This is a discount which is offered in relation to the size of the order: the larger the order, the larger the discount.
- **Promotional discount**. This is given where other members of the channel (wholesalers, retailers, etc.) join the manufacturer in promoting the sale of that manufacturer's products.
- **Cash discount**. This is offered to customers who pay their bills on time. It is often stated in a format such as 2/10, n/30, which means that if the buyer pays the amount in full within 10 days, a 2 per cent discount will apply. Otherwise the full amount (n = net) will be due in 30 days.

When the various discounts and allowances are properly taken into account, the difference between list price and what is termed 'pocket price' (the revenues left in a company's pocket) can be substantial.[8] Figure 5.10 shows how revenues cascade down from list price to invoice price to pocket price. It is called the pocket price waterfall. Each element of the price structure represents a revenue 'leak'.

Management may be surprised not only by the width of this range but also by which customers are getting which allowances and discounts and who is paying the highest and lowest prices at the ends of the range. Some customers are more sensitive to certain types

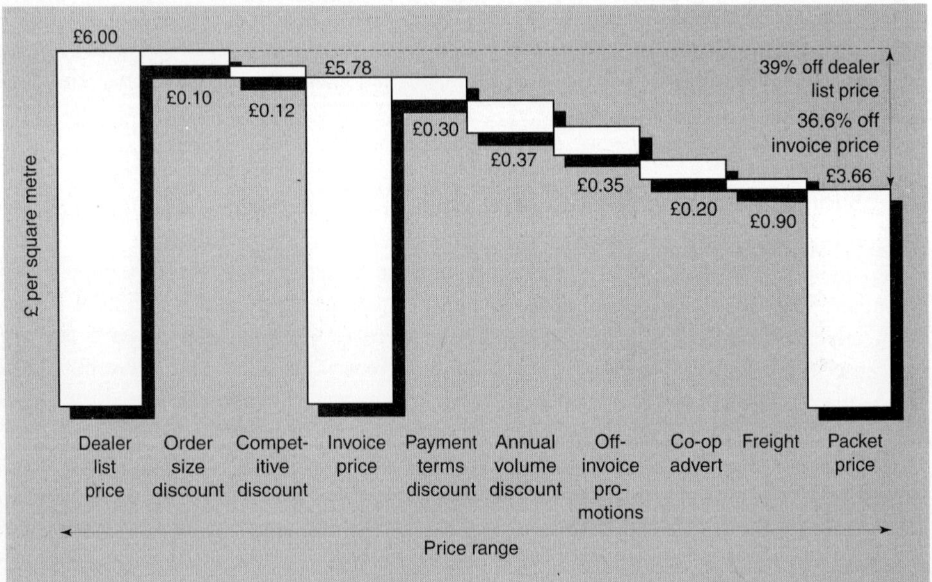

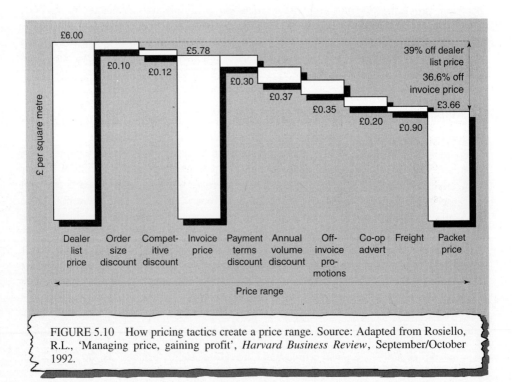

FIGURE 5.10 How pricing tactics create a price range. Source: Adapted from Rosiello, R.L., 'Managing price, gaining profit', *Harvard Business Review*, September/October 1992.

of discount than are other customers. If a supplier wishes to raise or lower price, he must take into account customer sensitivities when making adjustments to any of the elements. One company found no correlation between pocket prices and account sizes. Some small accounts were buying at very low pocket prices, as were some very large accounts, whilst some very large accounts were buying at high pocket prices. There was clearly no economic justification for this situation. It had arisen through long-established customers obtaining favourable treatment over the years. An interesting consequence of relationship marketing.

Price discrimination

As we have already seen, companies will adjust their prices, through discounts and allowances, to reward buyers for certain responses. Similarly, in the consumer market adjustments can be made to allow for differences in certain areas. It is a recognition of differing sensitivities that have been found to exist in many markets. Price discrimination takes the following forms:

- **By customer**. Different prices for the same product or service are offered to different groups, e.g. admission at different rates for students or pensioners. Low incomes mean price sensitivity.
- **By product or service**. Different versions are priced differently. There is frequently little or no cost difference in the different versions, e.g. calculators range in price depending on the number of features – this range reflects more the demand and price sensitivities of different buyers than any reference to costs of production. Similarly, airlines capitalize on the difference between the price-insensitive business traveller who requires flexibility and the mass of holidaymakers whose demand for the service is established well in advance.
- **By location**. At a range of events, different seat locations attract different prices. Place utility rather than cost is the deciding factor. Customer income will of necessity be a constraining factor in choice.
- **By time**. Prices vary by season, day of the week, time of day, etc. Time sensitivity occurs when demand varies at different times but the product is not storable. It is often referred to as peak-load pricing where variable costs and customer demand are considered in determining the price level at a given point in time. It can be used to help an organization smooth out demand placed on its capacity or facilities. A good example is the telecommunications industry for which almost all the costs are capacity costs. These costs are relevant only for the pricing of peak period sales when lowering price to serve more customers would require adding more capacity. Raising prices during peak periods to serve fewer customers allows an organization to avoid building new capacity. Price-sensitive customers are moved to off-peak hours allowing the organization to operate with less total capacity.

Price bundling

Broadly defined, bundling is the practice of marketing two or more products and/or services as a single package for a special price.[9] Technically, many firms employ mixed price bundling: buyers are given the choice of buying two products in a package or buying the products individually. Buyers who place a low value on one of the two products will avoid the bundle. However, the economic incentive of a lower price on one item will lead to additional sales of both products to some buyers who would otherwise buy only one. If the products are in some way related, e.g. complementary, the effects and the incentive of the special price are even greater.

Rationale for price bundling

Organizations with a high fixed to variable cost ratio benefit from price bundling. Several of their products/services can be produced and marketed using the same facilities, equipment and person. Therefore the direct variable cost of a particular offering is usually relatively low, meaning that it has a relatively high C/S (contribution to sales) ratio. The costs of selling additional units are therefore low relative to the organization's total costs.

Furthermore, price bundling allows an organization to exploit the 'consumer surplus', which is the difference between what the consumer is willing to pay (maximum price) and what is actually paid. Where the price of a product/service is less than the maximum acceptable, the price of a second product or service may be greater than the willingness to pay. If some of the consumer surplus from the first, highly valued offer can be shifted to the less highly valued offer then there is an opportunity to increase the total contributions to profitability. Table 5.6 provides an example of this point of shifting consumer surplus.

The table shows four customers, two products (A and B) and the reservation prices (RP) of the customers for the products. Customer 1 is willing to pay up to £8 to acquire product A but only £1 to acquire product B, a combination of £9. Customer 2 is willing to pay only £3 for product A but up to £6 for product B, a combination of £9.

Customers 3 and 4 also value the two products differently, with customer 3 willing to spend a total of £15 but customer 4 willing to spend a total of only £7.

TABLE 5.6 Economic principle of bundling (independent demand)

	Maximum acceptable reservation prices (RP)		
Customer	Product A	Product B	A + B
1	8	1	9
2	3	6	9
3	8	7	15
4	5	2	7

Source: Adapted from Guiltinan, J.P., 'The price bundling of services: a normative framework', *Journal of Marketing*, Vol. 51, April 1987, pp. 74–85.

If the price of A (P_A) is £7 and the price of B (P_B) is £4 then:

- Customer 1 will buy A only
- Customer 2 will buy B only
- Customer 3 will buy A and B
- Customer 4 will buy neither

Total revenue would equal £22 (7 + 4 + 7 + 4). If, however, A and B are offered as a bundle and set at a price of £9, then:

- Customer 1 buys the bundle
- Customer 2 buys the bundle
- Customer 3 buys the bundle
- Customer 4 buys nothing

Total revenue would now equal £27 (3 × 9), an increase of nearly 23 per cent.

The relevance of consumer surplus relates to consumers 1 and 2. For consumer 1 there is a deficit of £3 between RP_B and P_B, but the surplus of £1 from $RP_A - P_A$ plus the discount of £2 from the individual prices total (£11) minus the bundled price (£9) effectively closes that gap. Similarly, for consumer 2 there is a deficit of £4 between RP_A and P_A but the surplus of £2 from $RP_B - P_B$ plus the discount of £2 wipes out that gap. In both cases the consumer surplus has been transferred from the highly valued product to the less valued.

References

1. Forbis, J.L. and Mehta, N.T., *Economical Value to the Customer.* McKinsey Staff Paper, McKinsey & Co., Inc., Chicago, February 1979.
2. Forbis, J.L. and Mehta, N.T., 'Value based strategies for industrial products', *Business Horizons*, May/June 1981.
3. Nagle, T.T. and Holden, R.K., *The Strategy and Tactics of Pricing*, Prentice Hall, 1995.
4. *Ibid.*
5. *Ibid.*
6. Marn, M.V. and Rosiello, R.L., 'Managing price, gaining profit', *McKinsey Quarterly*, Vol. 4, 1992, p.18.
7. Blois, K.J., 'Discounts in business marketing management', *Industrial Marketing Management*, Vol. 23, 1994, p.94.
8. Rosiello, R.L., 'Managing price, gaining profit', *Harvard Business Review*, September/October 1992.
9. Guiltinan, J.P., 'The price bundling of services: a normative framework', *Journal of Marketing*, Vol. 51, April 1987.

CHAPTER 6

Communication

WHAT IS IT ABOUT?

Although this chapter is entitled 'communication' it is not the intention to cover the full array of tools that comprise communication. Instead it focuses on three aspects of communication: salesforce, media planning for advertising and direct marketing. The reasons for this partial coverage are that:

- Each is a major aspect of communication.
- Each often figures in case study analysis.
- Each has its own statistical framework and is therefore susceptible to control and evaluation.

The **salesforce** focuses on evaluation of performance: the causes of variations in performance and the application of ratios for determining how well salespeople have performed. Exhibit 6.2 in particular offers scope for discussion.

The section on **media planning** seeks to explain the terminology used in this area and illustrate media scheduling. Figures are provided of what it costs to advertise. Knowledge of media rates is crucial for deciding where one can advertise, when and how often. In other words, given a certain budget for advertising, how can it be spent? To round off, the overall factors to consider in media selection are detailed.

The increasing attention being given to relationship marketing and customer loyalty has given rise to databases enabling organizations to profile customers and target them accordingly – the activity known as **direct marketing**. Just as with the salesforce and media planning, there are vital statistics for direct marketing which enable the monitoring of a campaign. For those interested in drawing up a direct marketing campaign budget, a sample is provided.

With the rise of the database comes the potential for measuring **customer loyalty** and **lifetime value**. Knowing how much customers are worth over a period of time is obviously a valuable step when analyzing the nature of relationships between an organization and its customers.

Control and evaluation of the salesforce

Salesmen and women are commonly portrayed as unloved, foot-in-the-door creatures, whose superiors provide motivation principally in the form of alternate bouts of public humiliation and recognition. Confirmation of problems that seem to beset the salesforce comes from a survey conducted by Kinnaird Communications Group. It questioned about 1000 salespeople in the UK, France, Italy and Germany, examined sales records and sought the views of chief executives, supervisors and customers.[1]

One, perhaps unexpected, revelation from the survey is that only 5 per cent of field sales staff 'possess the requisite natural selling skills that make them stand out as professionals', whilst 35 per cent 'just manage to pay their way', leaving 'an astounding 60 per cent just there for the beer'.

The top 5 per cent achieve about five times the sales performance level of the poorest employees whilst many of the rest 'have drifted into the profession, attracted by the freedom, car, and expense account'. Whilst there will be people for whom success in selling comes naturally, the need for detailed analysis and evaluation of sales performance is necessary.

Why salespeople fail

There has not been a great deal of research into why salespeople fail, which is perhaps surprising given the impact of increased competitive activity and rising selling costs. However, two studies in particular attempted to shed some light on this issue. In the first study,[2] sales management, salespeople and students were asked to identify factors associated with failure. Of the three groups, sales management gave the clearest view of what causes failure:

- Lack of initiative
- Poor planning and organization
- Lack of enthusiasm
- Lack of customer orientation
- Lack of personal goals

The second study[3] asked sales executives to rate on a five-point scale the significance of a number of factors in determining salesperson failure. The findings in terms of what was most significant reflected those of the earlier study:

- Poor listening skills
- Failure to concentrate on top priorities
- A lack of sufficient effort
- Inability to meet customer needs
- Lack of planning for sales presentation
- Inadequate product/service knowledge

The conclusion to be drawn from these studies is that factors mentioned as contributing to failure can be influenced by sales management through training and motivation.

Determinants of sales performance

In contrast to the lack of research on salesperson failure, there is an abundant literature on the factors that evidently affect job performance. According to Churchill and colleagues,[4] there are five factors that influence a salesperson's job behaviour and performance:

- **Role perception**. To perform adequately, a salesperson must understand what the job entails and how it is supposed to be performed. There are three aspects to role perception:
  - *Role conflict* exists when the salesperson is caught between incompatible demands of customer and company, e.g. a customer demands a delivery schedule or credit terms that the salesperson believes will be unacceptable to the company.
  - *Role ambiguity* exists when salesperson believes there is not the information necessary to perform the job adequately, e.g. not knowing if price negotiation is permissible.
  - *Role inaccuracy* exists when salesperson thinks something is permissible when it is not, e.g. believing price is negotiable when it is not.
- **Aptitude**. Ability to perform the activities of the job is influenced by the individual's personal characteristics, such as personality, intelligence, analytical ability.
- **Skill levels**. Salespeople must have the necessary skills, e.g. product knowledge, how to make an effective sales presentation, etc., to carry out the tasks.
- **Environmental variables**. Ability to reach a certain sales volume can be affected by such things as market demand, the number and aggressiveness of competitors, state of the economy, etc. Equally, other factors, under company control, such as product quality, advertising effectiveness, customer service can affect a salesperson's ability to obtain sales.
- **Motivation**. Motivation, according to one view,[5] is the amount of effort the salesperson desires to expend on each activity or task associated with the job, e.g. calling on potential new accounts, developing sales presentations, filling out reports. The conceptual framework behind this view of motivation is known as expectancy theory and provides a useful framework for sales management aiming to motivate their sales force. The basic model is shown in Figure 6.1.

Expectancies are the salesperson's perceptions of the link between job effort and performance. For example, a salesperson might think, 'If I increase my calls on potential new accounts by 10 per cent (effort) then there is a 50 per cent chance (expectancy) that my volume of new account sales will increase by 10 per cent during the next six months (performance level).'

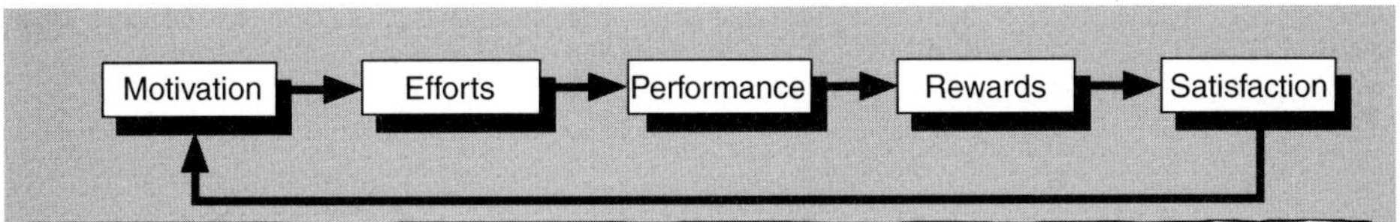

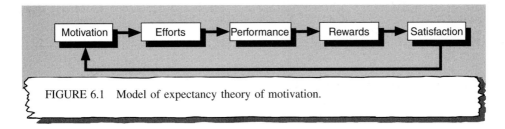

FIGURE 6.1 Model of expectancy theory of motivation.

If we assume that the expectancy model is valid, sales managers need to be concerned with the following:

- Building a motivational climate that will encourage effort. What this means in practice, according to one study,[6] is providing motivational techniques that salespeople value highly, namely:
  - Product quality and reliability
  - Image and reputation of the company
  - Back-up and support
  - Introduction of new products
  - Product training
  - Advertising programmes directed at your customers
  - Commission rate

  There were echoes of this in the findings from the Kinnaird survey when salespeople complained of inadequate marketing and advertising support for products from head office, poor sales literature, and products or services provided more cheaply by competitors.

- The extent to which a salesperson believes that increased effort, properly directed (i.e. working smarter rather than harder) will influence ultimate job performance.

- The salesperson's perceptions of the link between job performance and various rewards, namely what chance that an improvement in performance on some dimension will lead to a specific increase in a particular reward, e.g. more pay, promotion to a better territory, winning a sales contest. Management must communicate to the salesforce how performance is to be evaluated and the rewards obtainable for various levels of performance.

- The salesperson's perceptions of the desirability of the rewards from increased performance. Are some rewards consistently valued more highly than others? Unlike other occupations, the evidence points to salespeople placing a higher value on receiving more pay than any other reward.

In summary, it is the responsibility of salesforce management to ensure that salespeople perceive positive links between the various elements in the basic expectancy model of motivation.

Performance measures

The performance of the salesforce can be measured quantitatively and qualitatively.

Quantitative measures

Quantitative measures fall into three categories: output measures, input measures and ratio of output and/or input measures.

Outputs

- Sales revenue and volume achieved
- Profits generated
- Number of potential accounts
- Number of active accounts
- Number of new accounts
- Number of lost accounts
- Number of orders
- Size of orders

Inputs

- Number of calls made
- Days worked
- Calls per day
- Selling time versus non-selling time
- Expenses

Ratios

To obtain a measure of performance the above outputs and inputs can be combined in selected ways in the form of ratios. For example:

$$\text{Order/Call ratio} = \frac{\text{Orders}}{\text{Calls}}$$

$$\text{Expenses/Sales ratio} = \frac{\text{Expenses}}{\text{Sales}}$$

$$\text{Penetration ratio} = \frac{\text{Sales}}{\text{Potential}}$$

These are simply illustrative, as a fuller ratio analysis (including figures) will be discussed later – see Exhibit 6.2. As the list of outputs, inputs and ratios can be extensive, it has been suggested that the following simple model of salesforce evaluation, with just four measures of performance, is adequate:

$$\text{Sales (£)} = \text{Days worked} \times \frac{\text{Calls}}{\text{Days worked}} \times \frac{\text{Orders}}{\text{Calls}} \times \frac{\text{Sales (£)}}{\text{Orders}}$$

The model indicates nicely what the salesperson must do to increase sales:

- Increase the number of days worked.
- Make more calls per day.
- Secure an order on a given call.
- Increase the size of those orders.

Care should be exercised in using the model because of the interactions amongst the factors. Calls, for example, have a positive relationship with sales, but often a negative relationship with sales per order. This means that even though sales increase as calls increase, at some point the size of the order begins to decline, as there is less time to spend with each customer. It is really a matter of determining the optimum number of calls.

Ranking procedures

A useful framework to assist salesforce evaluation is a ranking procedure. An example of the performance of each salesperson ranked over a range of measures is set out in Table 6.1.

The first factor used to evaluate performance is sales. It is a good overall measure but it can be deceiving, e.g. Smith had the highest total sales but was last on sales to potential, suggesting that this high volume was owing to a large territory. Gray, on the other hand, had low volume and high sales to potential, indicating good coverage of a limited market. The performance of the five salespeople varied widely across the ten factors and each person ranked first on two criteria and last on at least one factor. When the rankings are added, Jones, Brown and Adams had total scores close to 30, the expected value. Gray is the best performer and Smith the worst. However, care must be exercised in interpreting the rankings because the assumption is that all ten criteria are equally important. Furthermore, the difference between the ranks is almost certainly not equal.

Graphs

The performance of each salesperson can be plotted on graphs, similar to the examples illustrated in Figure 6.2.

What relationship, if any, should we expect between the two variables on each of the three graphs, and why?

Qualitative measures

The quantitative measures described above focus on what people do, whereas qualitative measures reflect how well they do what they are doing. A framework that highlights qualitative factors and how they may be measured is used by the Testor Corporation (Exhibit 6.1).

TABLE 6.1 Ranking salespersons on performance criteria

Salesperson	Sales £	Sales to potential	Sales to quota	Sales per order	Number of calls	Orders per call	Gross margin %	Expenses £	New accounts	Number of reports turned in	Total of ranks
Smith	1	5	5	5	2	4	5	4	1	4	36
Jones	2	3	4	1	5	2	1	3	4	3	28
Brown	3	4	2	4	1	5	3	5	2	1	30
Adams	4	2	1	3	3	3	4	1	5	5	31
Gray	5	1	3	2	4	1	2	2	3	2	25

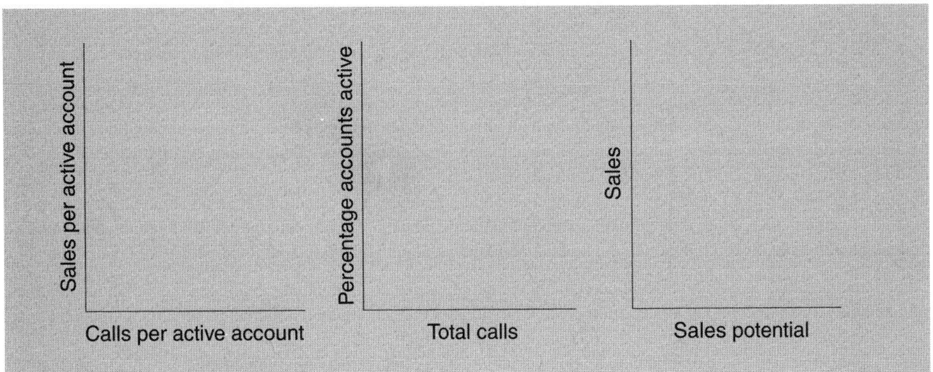

FIGURE 6.2 Salesforce graphs.

Exhibit 6.1 Sales personnel inventory used by the Testor Corporation

SALES PERSONNEL INVENTORY

Employer's Name ____________________ Territory ____________________

Position Title ____________________ Date ____________________

INSTRUCTIONS (Read Carefully)

1. Base your judgement on the previous six-month period and not upon isolated incidents alone.
2. Place a check in the block which most nearly expresses your judgement on each factor.
3. For those employees who are rated at either extreme of the scale on any factor – for example, outstanding, deficient, limited – please enter a brief explanation for the rating in the appropriate space below the factor.
4. Make your rating an accurate description of the person rated.

FACTORS TO BE CONSIDERED AND RATED:

1. Knowledge of Work (includes knowledge of product, knowledge of customer's business)	☐ Does not have sufficient knowledge of products and application to represent Company effectively.	☐ Has mastered minimum knowledge. Needs further training.	☐ Has average amount of knowledge needed to handle job satisfactorily.	☐ Is above average in knowledge needed to handle job satisfactorily.	☐ Is thoroughly acquainted with our products and technical problems involved in this application.

Comments ____

____

Exhibit 6.1 continued

	☐	☐	☐	☐	☐
2. Degree of Acceptance by Customers	Not acceptable to most customers. Cannot gain entry to their offices.	Manages to see customers but not generally liked.	Has satisfactory relationship with most customers.	Is on very good terms and is accepted by virtually all customers.	Enjoys excellent personal relationship with virtually all customers.
	Comments ______				
3. Amount of Effort Devoted to Acquiring Business	Exceptional in the amount of time and effort put forth in selling.	Devotes constant effort in developing business.	Devotes intermittent effort in acquiring moderate amount of business.	Exerts only minimum amount of time and effort.	Unsatisfactory. Does not put forth sufficient effort to produce business.
	Comments ______				
4. Ability to Acquire Business	Is able to acquire business under the most difficult situations.	Does a good job under most circumstances.	Manages to acquire good percentage of customer's business if initial resistance is not too strong.	Able to acquire enough business to maintain only a minimum sales average.	Rarely able to acquire business except in a seller's market.
	Comments ______				
5. Amount of Service Given to Customers	Rarely services his accounts once a sale is made.	Gives only minimum service at all times.	Services accounts with regularity but does not do any more than he is called on to do.	Gives very good service to all customers.	Goes out of his way to give outstanding service within scope of Company policy.
	Comments ______				
6. Depend-ability – Amount of Supervision Needed	Always thoroughly abreast of problems in his territory, even under most difficult circumstances.	Consistently reliable under normal conditions. Does special as well as regular assignments	Performs with reasonable promptness under normal supervision.	Effort occasionally lags. Requires more than normal supervision.	Requires close supervision in all phases of job.

	Rises to emergencies and assumes leadership without being requested to do so.	promptly. Little or no supervision required.			

Comments ____

____

7. Attitude Toward Company – Support Given to Company Policies	☐ Does not support Company policy – blames Company or factors that affect his customers unfavourably.	☐ Gives only passive support to Company policy – does not act as member of a team.	☐ Goes along with Company policies on most occasions.	☐ Adopts and supports Company viewpoint in all transactions.	☐ Gives unwavering support to Company and Company policies to customers even though he personally may not agree with them.

Comments ____

____

8. Judgement	☐ Analyses and conclusions subject to frequent error and are often based on bias. Decisions require careful review by supervisor.	☐ Judgements usually sound on routine, simple matters but cannot be relied on when any degree of complexity is involved.	☐ Capable of careful analyzing of day-to-day problems involving some complexity and rendering sound decisions. Decision rarely influenced by prejudice or personal bias.	☐ Decisions can be accepted without question except when problems of extreme complexity are involved. Little or no personal bias enters into judgement.	☐ Possesses unusual comprehension and analytical ability. Complete reliance may be placed on all judgements irrespective of degree of complexity. Decisions and judgements are completely free of personal bias or prejudice.

Comments ____

____

9. Resource-fulness	☐ Work is consistently characterized by marked originality, alertness, initiative, and imagination. Can be relied on to develop	☐ Frequently develops new ideas of merit. Handling of emergencies is generally characterized by sound decisive	☐ Meets new situations in satisfactory manner. Occasionally develops original ideas, methods, and	☐ Follows closely previously learned methods and procedures. Slow to adapt to changes. Tends to become confused in new situations.	☐ Requires frequent reinstruction. Has failed to demonstrate initiative or imagination in solving problems.

new ideas and techniques in solving the most difficult problems.	action.	techniques.

Comments ____

____

To be more effective on present job, this employee should:

1. Be given additional instruction on ______________________________
2. Be given additional experience such as ______________________________

____

3. Study such subjects as ______________________________

____

4. Change attitude as follows: ______________________________

____

5. There is nothing more that I can do for this employee because ______________________________

____

6. Remarks

The attractiveness of the Testor Corporation assessment form is the anchors or verbal descriptions for each point on the scale and the opportunity for further comment.

The salesforce is rated by management on each scale but it may be helpful to allow for ratings from the customers and salesforce itself. Figure 6.3 illustrates a hypothetical outcome of assessments using the Testor Corp. form.

Given the differences of view from Figure 6.3, the following questions arise:

- Are the differences significant enough to warrant further investigation?
- Why do these differences exist (related to the first question)?
- Which party's view comes closest to the 'truth'?

Whatever the outcome, the whole process of assessment should be handled properly. As one commentator puts it:

> For an evaluation and control system to work efficiently, it is important for the sales team to understand its purpose. For them to view it simply as a means for management to catch

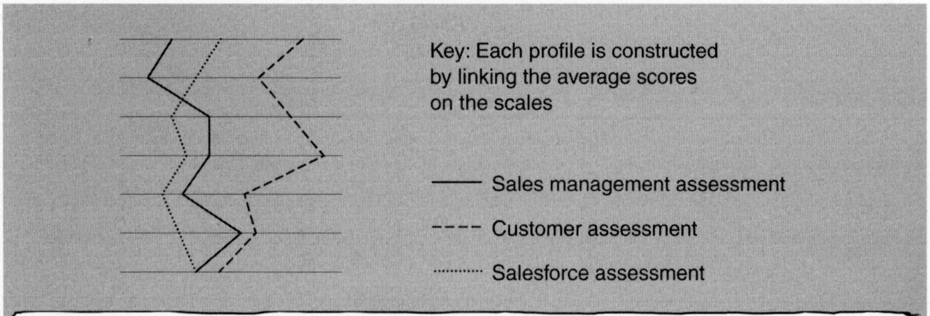

FIGURE 6.3 A multi-party assessment of salesforce performance.

them out and criticize performance is likely to breed resentment. It should be used, and be perceived, as a means of assisting people in improving performance. Indeed, the quantitative output measures themselves can be used as a basis for rewarding performance when targets are met. In essence, controls should be viewed in a positive manner, not a negative one.

Example of salesforce evaluation

The following example is an extract from a comprehensive case on salesforce evaluation.[7] It highlights a range of performance measures and typifies the issues present in overall management and control. The performance of three salespeople out of a force of nine, along with the average performance, is set out in Exhibit 6.2.

Summary comment on the performance

Of the three salespeople, Halbert's performance is vastly superior, although he does benefit from being in an attractive territory in terms of potential and workload. Anderson, on the other hand, with ten years in sales, is a disaster. With a sales potential of 16 per cent above average and the smallest land area (out of the nine) he can only manage 12.2 per cent penetration against an average of 20.6 per cent (a key figure). Furthermore, given the potential of expenses to further sales, Anderson 'managed to achieve' the lowest recorded figure of expense per account sold. Vereker's performance is not good (sales 30 per cent below average) and yet it is not all bad.

To what can we attribute good and bad performance? That is the challenge for salesforce management. In the case of Anderson with long experience and a good territory, one might understandably conclude that he does not possess the main qualities that make a successful salesperson – charisma, sense of humour, good planning and preparation, initiative and belief in oneself and the company. In the search for reasons, however, nothing must be discounted, for example an otherwise successful salesperson may suffer as a consequence of a strong competitor entering the market with an excellent product.

Media planning

Every advertiser must decide where to place its advertisements. The range of media available for selection includes the following:

- Press and newspapers
- Magazines
- Television
- Outdoor – poster, transportation
- Radio
- Cinema

Exhibit 6.2 Salesforce quantitative performance

	Units	Average	Halbert	Vereker	Anderson
Territory			Greater London	Midlands East	North West
Age	Years		54	29	37
Years selling	Years		24	4	9
Territory potential					
Sales potential = Mkt. × Ppn. of pupils	£000	788	887	655	915
Potential accounts	No.	663	570	653	699
Sales potential per account	£	1,190	1,560	1,000	1,310
Land area sq. km.	000	25.7	1.6	28.2	7.3
Accounts per 000 sq. km.	No.	26	356	23	96
Sales potential per sq. km.	£000	31	554	23	125
Sales and account performance					
Sales	£000	162 (121)	258 (118)	112 (114)	112 (115)
Penetration = Sales/Potential	%	20.6 (102)	29.0 (100)	17.1 (97)	12.2 (98)
Active accounts	No.	363 (99)	239 (86)	353 (99)	398 (97)
% Accounts active	%	55	42	54	57
Sales per active account	£	446 (123)	1,079 (137)	317 (115)	281 (120)
Margin performance					
Gross margin	£000	56 (117)	75 (109)	41 (114)	39 (115)
Gross margin %	%	35 (97)	29 (91)	37 (100)	35 (100)
Call effectiveness					
Calls per year	No.	1,225 (101)	1,230 (98)	1,409 (109)	1,450 (103)
Calls per active account	No.	3.4 (103)	5.1 (113)	4.0 (111)	3.6 (106)
Sales per call	£	132 (119)	210 (122)	79 (104)	77 (112)
Sales as % of account potential	%	37	69	32	21
Gross margin per call	£	45.1	61.0	29.1	26.9
Expense analysis					
Expense	£	3,120	1,980	3,820	1,940
Expense/Sales ratio	%	1.9	0.8	3.4	1.7
£ per 000 sq. km.	£	122	1,237	135	266
£ per account sold	£	8.6	8.3	10.8	4.9
£ per call	£	2.5	1.6	2.7	1.3

Note: Bracketed indices, previous year = 100. So, for example, under the Average column, sales are up 21% on the previous year and active accounts are down 1%.
Source: Simmonds, K. (ed.), *Strategy and Marketing: A Case Approach*, Philip Allan, 1982.

- Exhibitions
- Direct mail, i.e. mailing the message
- Telemarketing, i.e. telephoning the message
- Directories

In producing a media plan, several basic questions come to mind:

- Which media to select – TV, radio, press, cinema, posters?
- Should a combination of media be used, e.g. press and TV, radio and cinema?
- Which media vehicles to select – specific magazine title, newspaper, television programme?

- How many times should the advertisement be seen, heard or read?
- When and over what period of time should the adverts appear?

Media planning glossary

Media planning has its own jargon. The following short glossary of terms is valid for most media.

Target audience. Who is the campaign to be aimed at? The target audience is the people identified as the most likely to respond to the advertising by buying the product or service. The target audience can be defined in a variety of ways:

- Demographically, e.g. aged 25–34
- Socio-economic, e.g. ABC1
- Occupation, e.g. nurse
- Lifecycle, e.g. young families, retired
- Lifestyle, e.g. active, outdoor pursuits
- Geographically, e.g. all families in Edinburgh, consumers within a certain distance of a retail outlet.

Identifying the correct target audience is vital not only for directing the media selection (which titles to use, which TV spots to buy) but also for deciding the content of the creative message.

A product may have more than one target audience. If we find that the majority of users of a product are housewives with children but there are still significant numbers of retired people using the product, we may define the *primary* target audience as 'housewives with children' and a *secondary* target audience as adults aged over 60.

Impacts (opportunities to see). Impact is defined as one person experiencing one exposure to an advert. It is not realistic, however, to determine the exact number of people who saw an advertisement. What can be achieved is to measure the number of people who have an opportunity to see (OTS), i.e. being in the room during the screening of a commercial, or being a reader of a particular publication in which the advert is printed. Definitions of OTS differ according to which media are being used.

Coverage or reach. Coverage (reach) is defined as the percentage of the target audience that saw at least one advertisement of the campaign. If the target audience is ABC1 adults in Newcastle and 70 per cent coverage is achieved, one could claim that 70 per cent of all ABC1 adults in Newcastle have been exposed to the campaign. The major objective must be to select media that are seen, heard or read by as many of the target audience as possible.

Frequency. Frequency is defined as the number of times the target audience is exposed to the advertising message. If an average frequency of 5 is achieved then it can be claimed that, on average, the target audience saw the campaign five times. Frequency targets are important – too low a frequency and the campaign may not be effective, too high and money is wasted. As a very broad guide, a two-month campaign achieving only an average frequency of 2 is very light, and one achieving an average frequency of 50 is too heavy.

Coverage and frequency figures are quoted with media schedules as a measure of performance against the target audience. A short example of what these figures show is detailed below.

	Individuals A	B	C	D	E	F	G	H	I	J	Average OTS
No. of ads seen	1	0	5	2	7	6	3	3	5	0	4

Campaign performance: 80% @ 4 OTS
Average OTS or frequency = 32/8 = 4

The total coverage of the campaign is 80 per cent as 8 out of the 10 individuals saw at least one advertisement.

On an aggregate level, a newspaper advert may reach 10 000 of its 50 000 readers once, 20 000 of them twice, 15 000 three times and 5 000 four times. The average frequency would be:

$$\frac{(10\,000 \times 1) + (20\,000 \times 2) + (15\,000 \times 3) + (5\,000 \times 4)}{50\,000} = \frac{115\,000}{50\,000} = 2.3$$

As you can see, average frequencies disguise a wide range of frequencies. In media planning, frequency data are usually considered cumulatively, i.e. we count those who see a campaign at least once, those who see it at least twice, those who see it at least three times, etc. This is usually referred to as 1+ coverage, 2+ coverage, 3+ coverage and so on.

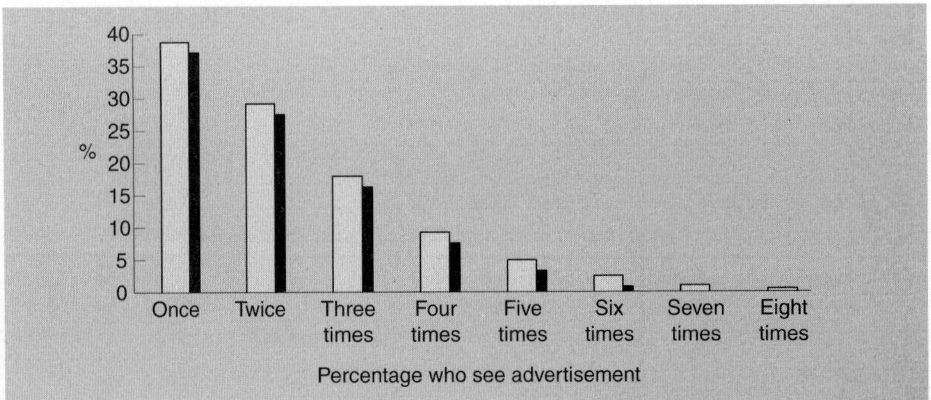

FIGURE 6.4 Cumulative frequency distribution. Source: Monkman, M., 'The basic concepts of media planning', *MRG Guide to Media Research*, Media Research Group, 1995.

TABLE 6.2 Example of cost per thousand

Title	Adult coverage		Page monochrome	CPT
	000	%	£	
Daily News	3 000	60	10 000	3.33
The Press	2 000	40	5 000	2.50

This type of data can be shown in the form of a chart[8] (Figure 6.4). If we specified an average OTS of 3, the schedule would deliver 3 OTS only in a minority of cases.

Cost per thousand (CPT). Cost per thousand is defined as the cost, expressed in pounds and pence, to reach the target audience. It is often used as a method of measuring cost effectiveness within any given media. A theoretical example, using press, is shown in Table 6.2.

The table shows that the *Daily News* is read by 3 million adults, 60 per cent of the total universe of 5 million. If a full-page (black and white) advert were to cost £10 000, the cost per thousand would be £3.33 (10 000/3 000). On the basis of cost per thousand, *The Press* newspaper is more cost effective at £2.50. Caution must be exercised, however, in opting for the lowest cost per thousand. The figures must be adjusted for the following factors:

- *Audience quality*, e.g. the profile of the *Financial Times* is more favourably disposed towards a target audience of senior executives than the *Daily Mirror*.
- *Audience attention probability*, e.g. could readers of *Country Life* pay more attention to advertisements than readers of the *Sunday Times*?
- *Editorial quality* – the credibility and prestige of a particular magazine may affect the exposure value of an advert.
- *Placement* – positioning and size of the advert.

Positioning and size. For the press, there is some evidence supporting the greater effectiveness to advertisers of the right-hand page over the left, the front of a magazine over the back and so on. Size and colour also play a role. For television, the number of commercials in a break, their respective length, location in the break and the programme during which they are shown must be considered.

Research suggests that, in the press, adverts work better if they are:

- In colour
- Large as a percentage of the page size
- Facing editorial rather than another advertisement
- On a back or inside cover
- Early in the publication
- Accompanied by fewer adverts in the publication

Evidence suggests TV advertisements work better if they are:

- Long
- In short breaks

- Early in the break
- Within certain kinds of programme

All media come in a large range of space sizes. The media will usually indicate on their rate card which sizes are available. In newspapers, sizes smaller than full-page and half-page are generally expressed in terms of single column centimetres or SCCs. Newspapers are divided into columns. In a tabloid there are normally seven columns to a page. Each newspaper sets an SCC rate card cost for advertising space. If the current cost in the *Daily News* is £40.50, a 20 × 2 advertisement will cost £1620, i.e. £40.50 × 20 cm × 2 columns. These, of course, are rate card costs and may be negotiated downwards.

Magazines split their space by proportions of a page, e.g. $\frac{1}{8}$, $\frac{1}{4}$, $\frac{1}{2}$, whole page. Posters operate sheet size multiples of a single sheet, for example, 48 sheet (20′ × 10′), 36 sheet (13′4″ × 10′), 16 sheet (6′8″ × 10′), 4 sheet (40″ × 60″).

Radio, cinema and television operate by multiples of seconds, e.g. television normally offers 10, 20, 30 and 60 second time lengths.

Specific media

Television

TVRs (television ratings). A TVR is defined as the percentage of adults watching a particular programme at any moment. If the programme *Take the High Road* achieves a TVR of 45 adults on Scottish Television, this means that 45 per cent of all the adults within that region were watching at a given time. TVRs are differentiated by target audience, so that a programme that achieves 45 all-adult TVRs may only achieve 20 ABC1 adult TVRs, but may achieve 50 housewife TVRs, i.e. 50 per cent of all housewives are watching. Such a programme may be *Coronation Street*. This appeals particularly to housewives and is watched less by an upmarket (ABC1) audience.

Gross rating points (GRP). Media planners will look at a media schedule's GRP, which is the product of its reach and frequency. A particular figure for GRP can be achieved in a variety of ways, e.g. 360 GRPs can be achieved as follows:

Reach	*Frequency*
90	4
60	6
45	8

Press

Average issue readership. This is defined as the number of people who have read or looked at any copy of the publication within its publishing interval, counting back from the day of the interviews, e.g. daily newspaper – reading any issue during the day before the interview; weekly publication – reading any issue during the preceding seven days. There is also a frequency of reading measure.

Cinema

Terms similar to press/TV, namely **coverage** or **reach** (proportions going to the cinema) and **frequency** (how often do you go and when was the last occasion).

Radio

Buying radio time uses terminology similar to that for other media.
Day part. The radio day is divided into five day parts:

0600–1000	Morning drivetime
1000–1500	Daytime
1500–1900	Afternoon (or evening) drivetime
1900–0000	Night-time
0000–0600	All night

Audiences for all-night listening are measured but there are not many listeners.

Weekly reach. This is the number of people who are listening to a specific station during any 15 minute period of any given day part.

Consider the example[9] of Sunset Leisure wanting to use radio advertising in the Sheffield area through the placement of spots on Radio Hallam which has an average quarter-hour listening estimate (Monday–Sunday, 6am–midnight; persons over 12 years old) of 4200 people. The agency handling the account found that the total average quarter-hour listening audience for all stations in the Sheffield catchment area is 48 900. Sunset Leisure can conclude that:

- Radio Hallam's average quarter-hour share is 8.6 per cent:

$$\frac{4200}{48\,900} = 0.086 \quad (8.6\%)$$

- Radio Hallam's average quarter-hour rating is 0.7 per cent:

$$\frac{4200}{600\,000} = 0.007 \quad (0.7\%)$$

Sunset Leisure wants to run twenty-five spots on Radio Hallam during a two-week period. This would mean:

$$\text{Gross impressions} = 105\,000(4200 \times 25)$$
$$\text{Gross rating points} = 17.5(0.7 \times 25)$$

Obviously this depends on where spots are placed – morning drivetime delivers much greater audience than 1am in the morning.

Outdoor posters

As with other media, **reach** and **OTS** (opportunity to see) are used. The difference between posters and other media is that the poster audience is less captive. Outdoor Site

Classification and Audience Research (OSCAR) was launched in 1985 and is funded by the OAA (Outdoor Advertising Association) which represents the poster contractors. Then came OSCAR II, and amongst a host of factors, it provided data that distinguished poster panels in terms of the following:

- Geodemographics
- Size, angle, distance from kerbside
- Height above ground-level
- Visibility distance
- Type of road
- Flow of traffic (vehicle and pedestrian)
- Proximity to a main shopping centre
- Whether on a bus route
- Whether traffic lights nearby

In May 1996 came the latest development in the poster industry – the arrival of POSTAR. It now claims to measure audiences of roadside poster sites in the most sophisticated fashion outdoor has ever managed. Under POSTAR, advertisers will know how many people have really looked at their poster, rather than merely passed by. POSTAR translates an 'opportunity to see' figure for sites into a 'likely to see' one. It will deliver smaller audience figures but with data that can at least be believed.

A note on OTS

The purpose of advertising is to make an impact of some kind, e.g. sales, awareness, attitude change. The problem is determining how much repetition is required to achieve the stated objective. Much of what we known about how people respond to different amounts of advertising is of a very imprecise nature.

The concave curve

Response functions are generally agreed to curve downwards. The curve is either totally concave or S-shaped (Figure 6.5).

The totally concave curve points to the first OTS having the biggest effect, whereas there is relatively little effect from the first OTS in the S-shaped curve. The challenge for the media planner is to deliver enough OTS to achieve the desired impact – not too little and not too much.

Most of the research evidence suggests that the concave response curve is the commonest. There is little evidence of increasing returns to advertising as demonstrated by the S-shaped curve. In recent research on the amount of media exposure necessary to increase short-term sales, one exposure was found to generate the highest proportion of sales, and additional exposures added very little to the effect of the first.[10] The advertising response function, the research concluded, was concave downwards, demonstrating diminishing returns in the clearest possible way.

There is no simple way to calculate the amount of advertising, and its scheduling

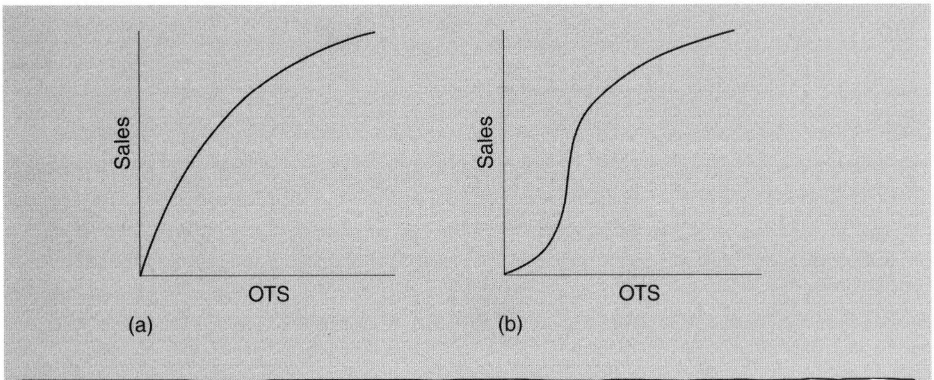

FIGURE 6.5 Response functions: (a) Concave (b) S-shaped.

over time, that is considered to have the optimum effect: enough to make the impact wanted, but not so much as to be wasteful. The choices range between a concentrated burst of advertising to a steady ('drip') schedule. The 'most effective pattern' will depend on a range of factors including campaign objectives, the nature of the product, buyer behaviour and competitive behaviour.

A new brand may require a concentrated burst, as too may a product with a seasonal demand. On the other hand, a successful fast-moving consumer good benefits from a steady drip that reinforces its image and maintains market share.

Media scheduling and planning in practice

What does a media schedule look like? The following fictitious example illustrates a media schedule involving five newspapers covering a population of 180 000 adults[11] (Table 6.3) The average frequency or average OTS of this schedule is the gross impressions divided by the net coverage. In this example, column G 1 758 000 gross impressions is divided by the net coverage 163 800 to give a figure of 10.7. Hence anyone reached at all by this campaign will have an average of 10.7 opportunities to see the advertising. The range of opportunities to see will go from 1 to 26 (the total number of insertions) but the average is 10.7.

A media planning case study is presented in Exhibit 6.3 (pages 190–2).

Media rates

The crucial question for any company with a specific budget to spend in the media is, 'What can we get for our money?' Furthermore, students are often required to confront this situation in exams and case study analysis. What follows, therefore, is a guide to how much space/time can be obtained for varying amounts of money. Many of the rates quoted below are of the standard variety as quoted in media rate cards. However, there is a range of packages available to suit individual customer needs. The bible of media rates

TABLE 6.3 Demonstration media schedule

A Title	B No. of insertions	C Cost/ page £	D Total cost £	E AIR 000	F AIR %	G Gross impressions 000	H Cost/ 1000 £
The Trader	6	2000	12 000	108	60	648	18.52
The Chronicle	6	1448	8 688	72	40	432	20.11
The Advertiser	6	1458	8 748	63	35	378	23.14
The Review	4	1250	5 000	41	23	164	30.49
The News	4	1000	4 000	34	19	136	29.41
Totals	26		£38 436			1758	£21.86

A Name of title; B Number of insertions (this schedule gives a total of 26); C Page rates; D Page rates × insertions gives total cost of schedule; E Average issue readership expressed in thousands; F Average issue readership expressed as a percentage; G Total number of individual opportunities for a campaign to be seen, column B × column E, (1 758 000 for this schedule); H Cost per thousand, calculated by dividing the total cost by the thousands of gross impressions, i.e. £38,436/1758 = £21.86.
Source: Holland, R., 'Regional press measurement – JICREG', in *Guide to Media Research*, Monkman, M. and McDonald, C. (eds), Media Research Group, 1995.

is, of course, BRAD (British Rate and Data). In addition, each radio/TV station, newspaper, poster contractor, etc. will provide a rate card. The lists that follow are a selection.

Newspapers and magazines

Tables 6.4–6.6 list the rates for a selection of publications.

The rate for full page mono in regional newspapers ranges from approximately £1500 to £7500, with one notable exception: *London Evening Standard*, £12 075.

TABLE 6.4 National newspaper rates

	SCC[a]	Full page rate (£)	
		Mono	Colour
The Sun	136	32 300	39 700
Daily Mirror	100	25 900	32 800
Daily Mail	90	22 680	32 760
Daily Express	85	20 825	31 500
Daily Telegraph	83	36 500	45 000
Daily Record (Scotland)	38.95	10 200	12 730
Scotsman	18.50	8 019	
Glasgow Herald	22	10 700	12 050
Daily Star	38.50	9 433	15 092
The Times	39	17 000	23 000
Today	24	5 712	6 188
Guardian	36	15 500	17 000
Financial Times	69	30 912	39 000
Independent	32	14 000	18 000

[a] SCC Single column centimetre.
Source: BRAD, August 1995.

TABLE 6.5 National Sundays' rates

	SCC[a]	Full page rate (£)	
		Mono	Colour
News of the World	144	35 700	46 400
Sunday Mirror	110	28 500	36 250
The People	83	21 750	28 000
Mail on Sunday	107	28 300	38 350
Sunday Express	105	29 864	38 623
Sunday Times	105	47 000	55 000
Sunday Post (Scotland)	41	9 275	11 100
Sunday Mail (Scotland)	41	10 745	13 650
Sunday Telegraph	60	27 000	31 500
The Observer	51	23 750	28 100
Independent on Sunday	32	14 000	18 000
Sunday Sport	18	4 000	5 500

[a] SCC Single column centimetre.
Source: BRAD, August 1995.

TABLE 6.6 Magazine rates

	Frequency	SCC	Full page rate (£)	
			Mono	Colour
Antiques Trade Gazette	Weekly	8	840	
Car Stereo and Equipment	9 issues per year		830	1 560
Motor Boat and Yachting	Monthly		1 190	2 495
CD ROM	Monthly			1 279
Internet	Monthly		1 105	1 300
Country Life	Weekly	26.25	1 925	3 150
Big Issue in Scotland	Fortnightly	12.50	960	1 400
Get Active	Bimonthly	12	1 200	1 750
Gardeners' World	Monthly	32.50	3 200	5 400
Readers Digest	Monthly		16 700	23 000
Gay Times	Monthly	5.50	850	11 500
Car	Monthly		2 642	5 950
Woman's Own	Weekly		16 600	23 650
Personal Computer World	Monthly		2 400	
The Engineer	Weekly	52	2 125	
Marketing Business	10 issues per year		2 500	3 800
Supermarketing	Weekly		1 900	2 625
Vogue	Monthly		10 800	12 000
Cosmopolitan	Monthly	76		12 075
People's Friend	Weekly		3 180	4 720
Melody Maker	Weekly	12.40	2 275	4 555
The Economist	Weekly		4 450	7 850
Caterer & Hotel Keeper	Weekly	18	2 105	3 240

Source: BRAD, March 1996.

Exhibit 6.3 Media planning case study

The Bank of Scotland commissioned Baillie Marshall Advertising to develop communication strategies (including media schedules and plans) for a range of financial services. Mortgages will be used as an example.

The target audience was deemed to be ABC1C2 adults aged 25–54. This was quite a wide group and by no means homogeneous. In the main, however, they were medium to light TV viewers (including Channel 4), mediumweight cinema-goers (more so in the younger age groups) and they listened to local radio and had a good exposure to outdoor poster sites. In press, they were best reached, in numerical terms, by the *Daily Record, Sunday Mail* and *Sunday Post*, and they also had a high propensity to read the Scottish quality dailies.

Baillie Marshall recommended the use of Scottish press and radio.

Newspapers

Five press schedules were considered (see table).

Schedule evaluations (newspapers)

Target audience	:	ABC1C2 aged 25–54
Universe	:	1 394 300
Sample size	:	1477
Size	:	25 × 5 and equivalent

Title	Cost	Number of insertions				
		1	2	3	4	5
Sunday Mail	4805	2	0	0	0	1
Daily Record	4920	1	2	2	0	1
Sunday Post	4440	1	0	0	0	1
Herald	3360	2	2	3	4	3
Scotsman	2408	2	2	3	4	3
Scotland on Sunday	2352	1	1	1	0	0
Dundee Courier	1764	2	2	2	2	2
Aberdeen P&J	2170	2	2	2	2	2
Daily Express (S)	2375	0	1	1	0	0
Glasgow Eve Times	2500	0	1	0	2	0
Edinburgh Eve News	1785	0	1	0	2	0
Aberdeen Eve Express	875	0	1	0	1	0
Sunday Times (S)	1680	0	0	0	0	0
Cum. net cover[a] (000)		1197.9	1136.6	1093.3	751.6	1180.2
Cum. net cover (%)		85.9	81.5	78.4	53.9	84.6
Gross OTS[b] (000)		3 749	2 750	2 635	1 932	3 139
Average frequency		3.13	2.42	2.41	2.57	2.66
Cost of schedule[c] (£)		40 726	40 811	39 739	40 385	39 337

[a]Cum. net cover $= \dfrac{\text{Cum. net cover}}{\text{Universe}} = \dfrac{1\,180\,200}{1\,394\,300} = 84.6$

[b]Gross OTS = Reach × Frequency = 1180.2 × 2.66 = 3139

[c]Cost of schedule = Sum of individual publication cost × Number of insertions

Source: NRS April 1991–March 1992.

Exhibit 6.3 continued

Although schedule 1 performed well in terms of overall coverage and frequency, Baillie Marshall recommended schedule 5 for qualitative reasons. This schedule increased the number of insertions in the core quality property titles – the *Herald* and the *Scotsman*. The *Sunday Mail* and *Sunday Post* contained 54.2 and 41.7 per cent respectively of the target market and had to be included in the schedule. The *Daily Record* with a strong property section also performed well, with 46 per cent cover. The quality Sunday newspapers were regarded as less appropriate for this product. The overall coverage for each eight-week schedule was 89 per cent, with 5 OTS.

Radio

Scottish radio reached 56.3 per cent of the target group. The medium was recommended to increase the frequency of the mortgage message at peak property periods. The campaign was designed to achieve the following:

Target audience:	ABC1C2	25–54 years
Universe:	1 237 000	

The results of a three-week campaign are shown in the table below.

	Week 1	Week 3
Ratings	250.0	750.0
Impacts (000)	3088.0	9264.0
Reach (000)	476.0	591.0
Reach (%)	38.5	47.8
Average frequency	6.5	15.7

Source: JICRAR, October–December 1991.

So, over a three week campaign, the message reached nearly half (47.8 per cent) of the target audience an average of 15 times. The actual media plan for the mortgages campaign is set out here.

Rationale for media selection

The Bank of Scotland had been using television heavily, promoting a corporate message rather than specific products. The press had been used largely for products, targeting the English market more than the Scottish. This was against the trend of its major competitors – Royal Bank of Scotland and Clydesdale Bank – which had virtually withdrawn from television advertising to concentrate on products, targeting specific markets.

The Bank of Scotland believed its advertising needed to be much more direct and highly targeted. There was a desire to continue television advertising but budgetary restraints negated this. The major objective for the campaign described above was to reach target groups more cost-effectively. The main recommendation was use of the press plus selective use of radio and outdoor. The arguments cited in favour of the press were:

- High levels of coverage achievable.
- Measurable results (in terms of coupon response) obtainable.
- An appropriate editorial environment.
- Relatively inexpensive production costs.

Exhibit 6.3 continued

Media plan

Client Bank of Scotland — **Product** Mortgages

Target: ABC1C2 25–54
Universe: 1 394 300

Version 1 — **Date** 29/6/92 — **Campaign** 1993

Press		Jan	Feb	Mar	Apr	May	Jun	Jul	Aug	Sept	Oct	Nov	Dec	£K
Sunday Mail	25 × 5			X	X				X	X				19 220
Daily Record	25 × 5			X	X				X	X				19 680
Sunday Post	24 × 5				X	X				X	X			17 760
Herald	28 × 6			X	XXX	XX			X	XXX	XX			40 320
Scotsman	28 × 5			XX	XXX	X			XX	XXX	X			28 896
Dundee Courier	28 × 6			X	XX	X			X	XX	X			14 112
Press & Journal	28 × 5			X	XX	X			X	XX	X			17 360
Coverage per burst – 89%													PRESS	157 348
Average frequency – 5													LESS 24% DISCOUNT	37 348
													TOTAL PRESS & EXPENDITURE	120 000
Radio: 40 second commercial														
Scottish Radio														
Target audience: ABC1C2 25–54					3 WEEKS					3 WEEKS				
Radio ratings					750					750				
Planned expenditure					21 000					21 000			RADIO	42 000
Adult cost per thousand 0.85p														
Spot laydown				COVERAGE	47.8%				COVERAGE	47.8%				
Mon–Wed 0700–0900 × 3 spots/day				AVERAGE O.T.H.	15.7				AVERAGE O.T.H.	15.7				
Thur–Fri 0700–0900 × 4 spots/day														
Sat: 0800–1200 × 3 spots/day				REACH (000)	591				REACH (000)	591				
Sun: 0800–1100 × 3 spots/day				IMPACTS (000)	9264				IMPACTS (000)	9264				
No. of spots per week: 23														
250 ratings per week													TOTAL PLANNED EXPENDITURE	162 000

Television

There are thirteen TV regions plus Channel 4. They are: Grampain, Scottish, Border, Tyne Tees, Ulster, Granada, Yorkshire, Central, HTV, Anglia, Carlton/LWT, Meridian and West Country.

For the purposes of schedule management the transmission day is divided into the following segments.

0925–1229	Coffeetime
1230–1714	Afternoon
1715–1924	Early peak
1925–2329	Late peak
2330–2629	Late night
2630–close	Moonlight
1715–2329	Peak

To illustrate the amounts of money involved, Exhibit 6.4 relates to Scottish and Grampian regional rates. Discounts on spot and package rates may be available. In addition, advertisers who can demonstrate a significant increase in their levels of annual commitment may qualify for cashback incentives.

As well as standard rates, premium rates are available in selected programmes. These can be significantly higher than standard rates, e.g. Meridian television covering the South and South East England has premium rates of £25 000–£33 000 for 30 seconds. On the other hand, premium rates for West Country Television covering the South West are in the range £5400–£7200. Meridian reaches 5 386 000 individuals against 1 661 000 for West Country Television.

To see what a proposal from an ITV contractor might look like, consider Exhibit 6.5. The 1+ cover means that 1.65 million adults (43.6 per cent of the total universe) has an opportunity to see the commercial at least once. A specification cover of 2+ would mean seeing the advert at least twice, and so on. By combining a range of spots, maximum coverage of the target audience can be achieved. Against each spot will be a TVR figure. On a regional basis the cover will depend on the potential number of ratings bought, but as a guide one can expect the following:

Rating campaign	200	300	400
Cover achieved	70%	75%	80%

Television is traditionally seen as an expensive medium, particularly for a small company. However, just like buying a car, the final cost of a campaign is determined only by the specifications required – not so much as in a car stereo or sunroof, but as a combination of the following:

- Which audience do I wish to target?
- What type of programming is suitable?
- When do I want to advertise?
- How many times do I need people to see my commercial?

Exhibit 6.4 ITV standard regional rates

Rate code	Grampian 30 seconds £	Scottish 30 seconds £
SGR	2550	8700
10	2295	7830
20	2040	6960
25	1913	6525
30	1785	6090
40	1530	5220
50	1275	4350
60	1020	3480
65	893	3045
70	765	2610
75	638	2175
80	510	1740
85	383	1305
90	255	870
95	128	435
97	85	290
98	60	174
99	26	87

Guaranteed spot packages

Segment[a]	Spots	30 seconds	
LN&ML (2330–2959)	10	45	150
DT (0925–1714)	3	230	800

The following factors will apply by the time length with the rates rounded to the nearest £1:

	10s	20s	30s	40s	50s	60s
Divide by	2.00	1.20	1.00	0.75	0.60	0.50

[a] LN Late night; ML Moonlight; DT Daytime.
Note: Local rates are also available.
Source: Scottish and Grampian Regional Rate Card, 1996.

Sales consultants are on hand to advise on schedule construction and tailor a proposal to fit individual budgetary requirements. A small company could, for example, be attracted by the cost of the following sample proposal from Grampian television:

Grampian Television Local Rate Card Proposal

Number of spots	Peak	4
	Daytime	10
	Late night/Moonlight	6
Total number of spots		20

Exhibit 6.5 Sample airtime proposal (Grampian and STV)

Ratecard:	Local (GPN and STV)	
Target audience:	Adults	
Commercial length:	30 seconds	
Campaign duration:	September 1996	
Universe:	962 000 GPN and 2 821 000 STV	
Day part requirement:	50% peak; 40% daytime; 10% late night	
Scottish Television Local Rate Card Proposal		
Number of spots	Peak	4
	Daytime	10
	Late night/Moonlight	6
Total number of spots		20
Total Rate Card Cost:	£15 801	
Total discounted cost:	£10 271	
Approx. total cover:	1.65 million adults (1+ cover)	
Approx. ratings	100 TVRs	

Source: *Television Sales Scotland, Scottish and Grampian Regions*, 1996.

Total rate card cost:	£3000
Total discounted cost:	£4000
Approx. total cover:	575 000 adults
Approx. ratings:	100 TVRs

Note on commercial production: Approximate costs are from £500 for a 30 second slide-based production and a minimum cost of £2000 for a 30 second live-action commercial, depending on creative requirements.

Radio

Planning radio airtime schedules

One of the key findings from radio audience research is that the vast majority of radio listening is habitual rather than programme-led, as is the case with television. In other words, listeners normally tune in on the same days each week and the same time each day which results in listening not fluctuating greatly between seasons. It follows from this that to reach the maximum number of those within the defined target audience (a typical requirement in combination with a frequency objective), spots should be spread through as many appropriate timebands. Furthermore, since new listeners are constantly tuning in, there is good reason to maintain a presence.

Airtime costs

The cost of advertising varies considerably but generally reflects the following factors:

- Length of commercial
- Size of audience in preferred timebands
- Degree of flexibility slotting
- Time of year
- General trading conditions of the station
- Special offers and promotions available

Radio Forth has two stations: Forth FM targeting under 40s and Max AM targeting over 35s. Consider Radio Forth's local business package for companies with a single outlet which operate exclusively in the transmission area (Exhibit 6.6).

The local rates for Forth FM and Max AM are as follows:

30-second commercial

0700–1000	Monday–Friday	£165	Peak
0800–1300	Saturday–Sunday		
1600–1900	Monday–Friday	£65	Drivetime
0600–0700	Monday–Friday	£20	Off-peak
0600–0800	Saturday–Sunday		
1900–2400	Monday–Sunday		
0700–1900	Monday–Sunday	£75	Run of day
0600–2400	Monday–Sunday	£55	Run of schedule

Production costs include:

Single voice fee	
10–30 seconds	£65
40–60 seconds	£75
Additional voice	£25
Library music per production/station	from £55
Jingles	from £800
Sound effects	£15 each

Exhibit 6.6 Radio Forth's local business package

	No. of weeks			
	1	4	7	13
Total number of commercials	20	80	140	260
Reach	270 000	381 000	405 000	421 000
Opportunities to hear (OTH)	3.1	8.7	14.3	25.5
Total impacts	827 000	3 310 000	5 792 000	10 756 000
Cost	£1000	£3600	£5600	£9100

Suggested schedule	Mon	Tues	Wed	Thur	Fri	Sat	Sun
Forth FM	3	3	3	3	3	3	2
Max AM	3	3	3	3	3	3	2

These local business package rates are for 30-second commercials. Other commercial lengths are available and costs in relation to the 30-second rate at 60 s + 80%, 50 s + 65%, 40 s + 30%, 20 s – 20%, 10 s –50%.

Source: Radio Forth.

Cinema

Airtime is available in weekly blocks running Friday to Thursday. There are several buying options including:

- **Screen by screen**. Each cinema or screen within a cinema can be bought individually or in any combination with a minimum exhibition of one screen for one week. The average 30-second screen-by-screen weekly rate is:

Greater London	£121
Rest of UK	£76
National average	£83

- **Film packages**. Campaigns can be coordinated demographically (e.g. certificates), by type of cinema (e.g. art houses) or around particular types of film (e.g. Disney release). Standard rates are listed in Table 6.7.

TABLE 6.7 Cinema standard rates

ISBA area	Admission share %	Number of screens	Weekly cost all screens (30 seconds)
London	27.2	429	23 256
Southern	7.6	159	6 498
Eastern England	5.4	116	3 219
Midlands	14.6	294	9 775
Yorkshire	8.4	159	5 006
North	5.0	81	2 668
Lancashire	13.1	226	7 807
Wales and West	5.9	151	3 081
South West	1.5	59	894
Border	0.5	19	270
Central Scotland	6.5	108	3 359
Northern Scotland	1.3	29	689
Northern Ireland	3.0	89	1 789
	100	1 919	£68 311

Source: BRAD, March 1996.

Posters

More O'Ferrall Adshel Ltd is a major contractor in the outdoor posters market. There are two broad categories: **supersites** (sites in key, prestigious locations) and **superlites**. Rates for a two-week campaign at each type of site are set out in Tables 6.8 and 6.9.

Large organizations have used both supersites and superlites successfully over the years. Smaller companies can still use a poster campaign, e.g. a few superlite panels. In terms of coverage and frequency, the new Postar model[12] would suggest the following for a two-week fast-moving consumer goods (FMCG) and main roads campaign:

	FMCG 5000 1+ coverage	Average frequency OTS	Main roads 3000 1+ coverage	Average frequency OTS
All adults	36%	12	35%	10.5

TABLE 6.8 Supersite rates for a two-week campaign

Campaign	Number of panels 40ft × 10ft	Range of rates £000
National Gold Standard	200	160–200
London Gold Standard	50	50–80
Conurbations	150	113–158
National	200	140–200
270 Network	500 (27ft × 10ft)	175–315

Note: Rates vary according to month of year.
Source: Rate card, More O'Ferrall Adshel Ltd, 1996.

TABLE 6.9 Superlite rates for a two-week campaign

Campaigns	Number of panels 6ft × 4ft	Range of rates £ per panel
Broadcast		
National	5000	90–125
London	1000	95–145
TV areas	400	95–145
Shopping		
FMCG[a]	5000	95–145
London FMCG	600	100–175
Local shopping	4000	80–115
Premium		
Main roads	2000	105–155
National key locations	2000	110–160
London key locations	500	175–250
Youth	1000	150–215

[a] FMCG fast-moving consumer goods.
Source: Rate card, More O'Ferrall Adshel Ltd, 1996.

Bus

Rates from an established, contractor are shown in Table 6.10.

TABLE 6.10 Bus advertising

	Price per space per month (£)		
	1 month	2–11 months	12 months
T-shape	170	140	110
Superside	100	80	60
Bus rears	60	50	45
Interior panel	10	7	5

Source: BRAD, March 1996.

Overall factors to consider in media selection

Usually, in practice, a media planner will start with a budget. That will clearly set limits as to where advertisements can be placed and how often. Knowing just how far the money will go is the bottom line in media planning.

Clearly, the size and composition of the audience will be crucial in media selection. How much of an organization's target audience does a particular medium cover? To answer this, the media habits of the target market will need to be researched. If the organization are advertising to teenage girls, you do not use *Women's Weekly* whose target readership is aged over 55. Equally you would not buy TV spots during *News at Ten*.

The type of product can often dictate, to an extent, the media to be used. Fashions, for example, are best advertised in colour magazines. Family products tend to be advertised on TV, women's products in women's magazines and so on.

Different types of message may require different media. For example, a big sale announcement is likely to appear on the radio or television or in the newspapers. A message with a lot of technical data might require magazines or direct mail.

What the competition is doing may come in for consideration. The choice is between competing in the same media as competitors because, 'we must be seen to compete' or because it is the most appropriate medium; or to try to avoid the competition and dominate a reasonable alternative medium.

Candidate media

There may just be one obvious, immediate candidate in the media selection process. Alternatively there may be just a few or even a whole host. For example:

- A local company wishing to recruit office staff – the obvious choice would be the local newspaper.
- A software company advertising a specialist package to solicitors on a fairly limited budget may consider one or more of the following: the Law Society's *Gazette*, direct mail, trade marketing.
- A local restaurateur, again with a quite small budget, has a number of options – local newspaper and radio, Yellow Pages, posters, leafleting, direct mail to business customers.

Media characteristics

Knowledge of media characteristics can assist the selection process. The following is a summary of the major categories.

National daily newspapers
- High readership
- Flexibility
- Timeliness

- Range of titles each with its own audience profile
- Short life
- Intensity of readership, i.e. read closely

Magazines
- Selective and targeted
- Strong fit between product and marketplace
- Long life
- Credibility and prestige
- Long advertisement purchase leadtime

Television
- Combines sight, sound and motion
- High impact, visibility and the power to demonstrate
- Audience can be selected by programme type or time of day
- High absolute cost
- Fleeting exposures
- Less audience selectivity

Direct mail
- Capacity to go direct to the target
- High selectivity of audience
- Flexibility by time, audience, message, area
- Capacity for testing on a small sample before being extended
- Outstanding importance in business-to-business markets

Radio
- Capacity to localize
- Beneficial to local advertisers for short-term news and announcements, etc.
- Lower attention than television
- Fleeting exposure

Cinema
- Gives sound coverage of younger age groups (16–24)
- Has impact and a captive audience
- Has colour, sound, movement and the ability to demonstrate
- Can be localized, if required

Outdoor
- Does not have the immediacy and impact of, say, television
- Wide geographical coverage
- Very high repetition
- Ability to locate near types of distributor
- Low cost
- Low competition

- No audience selectivity

Exhibitions
- Provide specific audiences for specific markets, e.g. the Boat Show
- Provide opportunities to make personal contact, take orders and sell
- Could be self-financing if sufficient orders can be obtained

Telemarketing
- Ability to target selectively using a variety of lists (business-to-business markets in particular)
- Personal contact
- Ability to operate nationally or locally
- Telephone may be used to sell, or to develop sales leads, or to make appointments for the salesforce
- Highly flexible and can be mounted rapidly

Directories
- Retained for long periods
- Prime source amongst readers for information and reference
- High coverage and frequency of message
- Can be highly selective providing specialist coverage against specialist industries and audiences
- For targeted audiences with targeted messages, can be highly cost-effective and provide substantial pulling power

Direct marketing

Direct marketing is a method of marketing that uses a range of media to bring about a measurable response. Through direct response advertising media it aims to acquire customers with whom it is hoped to build a long-term relationship. From direct mail to electronic shopping, prospects are encouraged to buy, directly, whatever is on offer. Organizations are then able to build a customer database from which future business can be obtained. The whole purpose of direct marketing is to enable organizations to profile their customers and prospects and to target customers based on a knowledge of purchasing patterns, lifestyle and propensity to buy. The database is the key tool for enabling this interactive approach to marketing.

The database

The essential distinction between direct marketing and other forms of marketing communication is the database. Its very existence allows organizations to target prospects and customers individually and limit the waste of expenditure found in more traditional marketing methods.

What information should be held on a database?

Information will obviously vary but should include the following:

Consumer markets	*Business markets*
Name	Name
Age	Company
Marital status	Position
Number of children	Status, e.g. buyer, influencer, authorizer
Income bracket	Area of business (SIC code)
Occupation	Telephone, fax, e-mail
Lifestyle (more difficult)	Number of employees
Media area	Turnover range
Geodemographic	Import/export activity
Classification (if possible)	Address

For both consumer and business markets, two further crucial types of information are necessary: activity data and accounts data.

Activity data – how the customer behaves

Financial institutions have long been known for analyzing accounts in terms of the amount of activity taking place. For database marketing, activity is not simply purchases made: what needs to be monitored are:

- When was the last purchase?
- How much has been purchased?
- How often is a purchase made?
- Has a trial offer been accepted, a competition entered?

Accounts data – financial status

There are two aspects to financial status:

- Direct marketers must consider a prospect's ability to pay.
- An existing customer's record of meeting his financial obligations must be monitored.

For what purposes should the database be used?

To acquire and maintain an accurate, healthy database is an investment in time, effort and money. Quite naturally one would expect a return on that investment. The major route to achieving this is through encouraging good prospects to become loyal customers who will in turn recommend the company to other good prospects. You will no doubt remember from chapter 1 the financial benefits that can accrue from customer retention. Activity on the database will allow a company to do all of the following:

- Identify the good and poor customers.
- Cross-sell related products.
- Launch new products to receptive prospects.
- Convert occasional purchasers to lifetime customers.

Measurement: the vital statistics of direct marketing

Consider the simple factors that might be used to describe a mailing:[13] cost of mailing (C) and number mailed (N). There are also two simple factors that might be used to describe the response to it: number of responses (n) and value of responses (v).

These four simple factors may be combined in several different ways:

$$\text{Response rate (R)} = \frac{n}{\text{N}}$$

$$\text{Cost per response (CPR)} = \frac{\text{C}}{n}$$

$$\text{Return on investment (ROI)} = \frac{v}{\text{C}}$$

$$\text{Average mailing value (AMV)} = \frac{v}{\text{N}}$$

$$\text{Profit} = v - \text{C}$$

Hence for a mailing of 10 000 that cost £5000 and to which 250 people responded generating sales of £10 000, the vital statistics would be:

$$\text{Response rate} = 2.5\%\ (250/10\ 000)$$

$$\text{Cost per response} = £20\ (£5000/250)$$

$$\text{Return on investment} = 2\ (£10\ 000/£5000)$$

$$\text{Average mailing value} = £1\ \frac{(£10\ 000)}{10\ 000}$$

$$\text{Profit} = £5000\ (£10\ 000 - 5000)$$

ROI is the ratio of cost and revenue, so an ROI of 1 means that a promotion is performing at break-even; 2 means that for every £1 spent on a promotion, £2 is coming in; 1.1 is a return of just 10 per cent on a mailing.

The above analysis assumes that all responses were purchases, but it may be that only a percentage of those who responded actually bought. We call this the **conversion rate**. As a consequence, a further measure, **cost per sale**, can be determined.

We can see in Table 6.11 various measures come together in a typical response analysis.[14]

Looking along the results in Table 6.11 we can conclude that a better performance is obtained from publication C.

TABLE 6.11 Response analysis

Publication	Issue date	Space size	Copy code[a]	ABC[b] 000	Total cost	No. of responses	Response rate[c]	No. of sales	Conv. to sales[d]	Cost per sale[e]	Sales value[f]	Return on £1 investment[g]
A	10 Jan.	25 × 4	pr 1	660	£2000	132	0.02%	18	13.6%	£111.11	£7200	£3.60
C	20 Jan.	15 × 2	d 11	1750	£1800	175	0.01%	24	13.7%	£75	£9600	£5.33

[a] Copy codes represent a unique letter/numbering system included in all insertions to identify bookings and to match them with results. The copy code will be included on all response coupons, and with telephone response generation all respondents will be asked to quote the reference number at the time of enquiry.
[b] ABC refers to the publication circulation; the price of the item is £400.
[c–g] Using publication A figures: [c] 132/600 000 = 0.02%; [d] 18/132 = 13.6%; [e] £2000/18 = £111.11; [f] 18 × £400 = £7200; [g] £7200/£2000 = 3.60.

Source: Barker, B., 'Direct response advertising and direct mail research', in *Guide to Media Research*, Monkman, M. and McDonald, C. (eds), Media Research Group, 1995.

Allowable cost per sale

One of the simplest measures used to control direct marketing activity is the allowable cost per sale, or order. To arrive at this figure we need to build a mini profit and loss account for an average sale including the desired profit but excluding the promotional costs. The result is the amount that can be afforded to obtain the sale. The calculation is as follows:[15]

Selling price		50.00
Less Returns		5.00
Net order value		£45.00
Costs:		
Cost of goods sold	15.00	
Fulfilment	5.00	
Bad debt	2.25	22.25
Contribution to break-even		22.75
Desired profit		5.00
Allowable promotional cost		£17.75

(*Note*: Fulfilment costs are copy, artwork, the product, handling, packaging and posting costs.) Once the allowable cost per sale has been calculated, the response required to produce a desired profit may be determined. If the total cost of the promotion is, say, £12 000 then the sales needed to meet that cost would be:

$$\frac{£12\,000}{£17.75} = 676$$

If 50 000 people were to be mailed, the response rate required would be:

$$\frac{676}{50\,000} = 1.35\%$$

The basic concern over the allowable cost approach is that promotion is assumed to be a function of price and sales – namely, the more that is sold and the higher the margin, the more that can be spent on promotion. The reality, as we all know, is that sales are meant to be a function of promotion. The key, in terms of an overall campaign, lies in estimating a likely response rate and the financial consequences.

Campaign budget

The final step, as with other areas of marketing, is to draw up a campaign budget.[16] This is in essence a projected profit and loss account. An illustration is given in Exhibit 6.7.

Lifetime value of a customer

The lifetime value of a customer is the total revenue received from a customer during his

Exhibit 6.7 Sample campaign budget

1	Mailing quantity		50 000	
2	Expected responses	10.0%	5 000	
3	Expected returns/rejects	10.0%	500	4 500
		per item		**total**
4	Average sales value	£75		£375 000
5	Returns	£75	£37 500	£337 500
6	Cost of goods sold	£30	£135 000	£202 500
	MAILING PACK PRODUCTION	**Cost per 1000**	**Actual cost**	
7	List rental	£90.00	£4 500	
8	Computer processing	£50.00	£2 500	
9	Printing	£50.00	£2 500	
10	Lasering	£60.00	£3 000	
11	Enclosing	£40.00	£2 000	
12	Postage	£170.00	£8 500	£23 000
	RESPONSE & RETURNS HANDLING			
13	Freepost	£175.00	£875	
14	Datacapture & processing	£100.00	£500	
15	Despatch costs	£30.00	£150	£1 525
	FIXED COSTS			
16	Creative and artwork, fees		£10 000	£10 000
17	**TOTAL COSTS**			£34 525
18	**REVENUE**			£202 500
19	**TOTAL COSTS**			£34 525
20	**CONTRIBUTION**			£167 975

Source: Weetch, R., 'Budgeting, costing, evaluation for non-financial managers', *The Practitioner's Guide to Direct Marketing*, Direct Marketing Centre Ltd, 1992.

'lifetime' with a company, less the costs of servicing and marketing that customer. It is the total profit received from having that customer over time. Where there is a difficulty in calculating profit, sales revenue or contribution margin (revenue minus variable cost) can be used.

Lifetime value in practice

A relatively simple scenario using contribution margin (CM) as the financial measure of success will demonstrate lifetime value calculation in practice[17] (Table 6.12). From an initial acquisition of 1000 new buyers, the lifetime value over a twelve-year period is determined.

In year 1 the company acquires 1000 new buyers. The average contribution margin

TABLE 6.12 Lifetime value

	Acquisition year											
	1	2	3	4	5	6	7	8	9	10	11	12
Buyers	1000	250	150	105	84	67.20	53.76	43.01	34.41	27.53	22.02	17.62
Retention (%)		25	60	70	80	80	80	80	80	80	80	80
Contribution margin (CM) per buyer	£1	£20	£20.40	£21.01	£21.85	£22.95	£24.09	£25.30	£26.56	£27.89	£29.28	£30.75
CM % increase			2%	3%	4%	5%	5%	5%	5%	5%	5%	5%
Total CM	£1000	£5000	£3060	£2206	£1836	£1542	£1295	£1088	£914	£768	£645	£542

Source: Wang, P. and Splegel, T., 'Database marketing and its measurements of success', *Journal of Direct Marketing*, Vol. 8, no. 2, 1994.

per buyer (CM/buyer) is £1 owing to a large proportion of the contribution margin having been used to cover the cost of new customer acquisition. Therefore, the total annual contribution for these buyers is £1000. The following year, 250 of the original 1000 buyers made repeat purchases from this company. The retention rate is therefore 25 per cent for year 2. The average contribution per customer increases to £20. The increase in the contribution margin is due to the significant decrease of variable marketing costs by the second year. Over subsequent years we witness an increase in the average contribution per buyer due to the improving quality of repeat customers. From year 6, a contribution margin of 5 per cent is sustained till year 12. The lifetime value of this customer group over the 12 years is £19 896, being the sum of the 12 yearly contributions.

The scenario above assumes that customers would be acquired through the use of a single method each year. However, customers can be acquired by different methods, e.g. some may be offered a promotional discount if they make an initial purchase whilst others may pay the full price. Some may be recruited through direct mail, others by mass-media advertising.

Present value

The problem with Table 6.12 is that we are unable to make direct comparisons between the cash received in year 12 and that received in year 1 in terms of how much each is worth. Clearly £542 received today is worth much more than £542 received in 12 years' time. In fact, £542 invested today for 12 years at an annual interest rate of 10 per cent would give a cash amount of £1701 (i.e. £542 $\times$ 1.10^{12}). We have in effect converted today's money (£542) into an equivalent amount (£1701) 12 years in the future by using a rate of interest.

A better way of making all the cash flows comparable is to bring all of them back to today's values rather than to project forward. The technique uses the same logic but in reverse: the objective is to find an equivalent present value for any future cash flow. Instead of applying compounded interest we apply a negative interest rate to reduce the future value to its value now. This negative interest rate (or **discount rate**, as it is called) is the annual cost associated with having to wait to receive the cash. The present value (PV) of a future sum is given by the formula:

$$\mathrm{PV} = \frac{1}{(1+r)^n}$$

where r equals the rate of interest per period and n the number of the periods to be discounted. Returning to the £542 in contribution received in year 12, in today's terms (present value) it would be worth,

$$£542 \times \frac{1}{(1+0.10)^{12}} = £172 \qquad \text{(see Appendix B)}$$

What does this £172 means? It gives you some sense of how much a customer is worth to you in today's money. Furthermore, it guides the amount that can be spent today on acquiring a customer. Spending any sum around £172 today on acquiring customers would do little for the company's profitability.

A further example should make it crystal clear. A company is wondering whether to spend £180 000 now on an advertising campaign, in order to obtain cash profits as follows:

Year	*Profits (£000)*
1	60
2	80
3	50
4	10

The company requires a return of 10 per cent per annum (rate of interest). In order to assess whether the advertising project is viable, a table of present values is drawn up (Table 6.13).

The present value is negative: the value, today, of the future profits is £14 700 less than the money to be invested in advertising. Obviously, the project is not viable.

In a comprehensive study of newspaper subscription,[18] present value calculations formed an integral part of the analysis offering guidance on how much could be spent acquiring additional subscribers. An extract from the data is given in Table 6.14.

Although nearly a quarter of the newspaper's readers are in the South zone (there are five zones in total), they represent the lowest revenue per customer and are last in terms of the final present value calculation. The implication for management is that circulation efforts in this zone must be mindful of acquisition costs to avoid eroding already modest revenues.

It is important to note that present value as we have calculated here does not take into account inflation and variations in the interest rate. Even so, it brings lifetime values back to present-day values and in so doing enables direct marketers to establish how much to invest in acquiring and retaining customers.

TABLE 6.13 Present value of proposed advertising campaign

Year	Cash flow £	Discount factor 10%	Present value £
0	(180 000)	1.00	(180 000)
1	60 000	$1/1.10^1 = 0.91$	54 600
2	80 000	$1/1.10^2 = 0.83$	66 400
3	50 000	$1/1.10^3 = 0.75$	37 500
4	10 000	$1/1.10^4 = 0.68$	6 800
			(14 700)

TABLE 6.14 Using present value to assess future levels of expenditure

Year	Net income	Zone: South Acquisition cost	Total	Present value
0	312	(55)	257	233.63
1	17	0	17	14.04
2	19.58	0	19.58	14.71
3	22.42	(62.38)	(39.97)	(27.29)
4	25.53	0	25.53	15.85
5	28.95	0	28.95	16.34
	425.48	117.38	308.89	267.28

Discount rate = 10%

References

1. Kinnaird, Communications Group, Glasgow, 1994.
2. Johnson, M.W., Hair, J.F. and Boles, J., 'Why do salespeople fail?' *Journal of Personal Selling and Sales Management*, Vol. 9, 1989.
3. Ingram, T.N., Schwepker, C.H. Jr and Hutson, D. 'Why salespeople fail', *Industrial Marketing Management*, Vol. 21, 1992.
4. Churchill, G.R, Jr, Ford, N.M. and Walker, J.C. Jr, *Sales Force Management*, Irwin, 1993.
5. *Ibid.* p.541.
6. Berry, D. and Abrahamsen, K. 'Three types of salesmen to understand and motivate', *Industrial Marketing Management*, Vol. 10, 1981.
7. Simmonds, K. (ed.), *Strategy and Marketing: A Case Approach*, Philip Allan, 1982.
8. Monkman, M., 'The basic concepts of media planning', in *MRG Guide to Media Research*, Monkman, M. and McDonald, C. (eds), Media Research Group, 1995.
9. Moutinho, L., *Problems in Marketing*, Paul Chapman Publishing, 1991.
10. Jones, J.R., 'Single-source research begins to fulfil promise', *Journal of Advertising Research*, May/June 1995.
11. Holland, R., 'Regional press management – JICREG' in *MRG Guide to Media Research*, Monkman, M. and McDonald, C. (eds), Media Research Group, 1995.
12. More O'Ferrall Adshel Ltd.
13. Ozimek, J., *Targeting for Success*, McGraw-Hill, 1993.
14. Barker, B., 'Direct response advertising and direct mail research' in *MRG Guide to Media Research*, Monkman, M. and McDonald, C. (eds), Media Research Group, 1995.
15. Weetch, R., 'Budgeting, costing, evaluation for non-financial managers', *Practitioner's Guide to Direct Marketing*, Direct Marketing Centre Ltd, 1992.
16. *Ibid.*
17. Wang, P. and Splegelt, T., 'Database marketing and its measurements of success', *Journal of Direct Marketing*, Vol. 8, No. 2, 1994.
18. Keane, T.J. and Wang, P., 'Applications for the lifetime value model in modern newspaper publishing', *Journal of Direct Marketing*, Vol. 9, No. 2, 1995.

CHAPTER 7

Customer service

WHAT IS IT ABOUT?

Customer service used to be regarded as the 'cinderella' of marketing. Now that is all changed, with organizations falling over backwards in the race to provide service and care. The reality, unfortunately, does not always match the promises.

As to the meaning of customer service there is still no clear definition. It began as a branch of physical distribution, and Lalonde and Zinszer were the first to expand the concept beyond the physical distribution framework. Whatever the service is, the level at which it is delivered brings with it variations in costs, sales and profits.

To meet customer expectations, organizations are turning to **standards-setting** across a range of activities vital for the achievement of customer service. One area that has been around for a long time and will remain so, is **stock control**. How this element of customer service should be managed is explained.

In addition to **order cycle time**, delivery reliability, stock control, etc. is the human side of service. How should the service provider interact with, and care for, the customer?

Mystery shopping, that well known method for gathering information on customer service, is discussed, and some evidence is presented of how well a range of organizations have performed.

No discussion of customer service can take place without reference to that much maligned buzzword, **empowerment**. The controversy surrounding the role of the front-line employee continues to be the subject of much debate.

Finally, **complaints** – the bane of all organizations. How should they be handled?

How often have you heard the following comments from customers?

- 'I called your office to straighten out the order, but I couldn't get anyone who knew how to handle my problem.'
- 'The shipment arrived late, and as a result we had all kinds of problems.'
- 'When the order arrived it wasn't right and we had to have it redone.'
- 'This bill isn't correct – we don't owe you so much!'
- 'Nobody cared about my problem.'
- 'They didn't keep their promise.'

Comments like these are all too familiar. What organizations have failed to recognize is that satisfied/loyal customers value *how* something is sold as well as what is sold. That means that they value such things as reliability, courtesy, flexibility and speed of response.

It all comes down to customer service, that much neglected area which, historically, has been defined in the narrow sense of physical distribution activity and after-sales service. This is not meant to play down the significance of these areas, particularly when one reads of the experiences that buyers of personal computers have had. One PC company admitted to receiving more than 100 000 calls a month from frustrated customers, and others confirmed a similar story. The problem was not so much product quality but the inexperience of novice home computer users. Customers expect support and information as well as a reliable product.

An editorial in *Marketing*[1] reflecting on the subject of customer service drew a parallel with BS 5750 (now ISO 9000) certification. Receipt of that award is not proof of quality being delivered: all it proves is that the systems are in place to produce quality – not that it is actually happening. The editorial went on to highlight the case of a company that carries out service and repairs on products under warranty from a high street retailer. The contrast between the promise, 'pick up a phone and an engineer will solve the problem', and the reality, 'a two week saga of repeated telephone calls and three days off work waiting for engineers who never arrived' sums up the gulf between what companies say they will do and what they actually do.

The many meanings of customer service

The discussion so far has given some insight into the areas that may fall within customer service. Unfortunately, customer service is an aspect of business for which there is no general agreement as to what it is or might cover. The phrase is used, in at least five different ways:[2]

- The activities involved in ensuring that a product or service is delivered to the customer on time and in the correct quantities.
- The interpersonal working relationship between the staff of a supplier and a customer.
- The provision of after-sales repair and maintenance facilities.

- The department of an organization which handles complaints.
- The order-taking department of an organization.

Customer service developed from a focus on 'order cycle' related activities into a much more general and all-embracing approach. Lalonde and Zinszer were the first to expand the concept beyond the strictly order-cycle-related components. They defined customer service as, 'Those activities that occur at the interface between the customer and the corporation which enhance or facilitate the sale and use of the corporation's products or services.' Their contribution was to divide customer service into the temporal sequence: pre-transaction elements, transaction elements and post-transaction elements.[3]

Pre-transaction elements establish a climate for good customer service, and include:

- Written customer service policy – is the policy communicated internally or externally, is it understood, is it quantified where possible?
- Accessibility – are we easy to contact/do business with?
- Organization structure – is there a customer service management structure in place? Does its personnel have appropriate authority and responsibility?
- Systems flexibility – can the system be adapted to meet particular customer needs? Can the system continue to function in the face of unexpected problems, e.g. strikes, adverse weather conditions.

Transaction elements are those that directly result in the delivery of the product to the customer, for example:

- Order cycle time – what is the total elapsed time from initiation of the order by the customer until delivery to the customer?
- Stock availability – what percentage of demand for each item can be met from stock?
- Order status information – how long does it take to respond to a customer query with the required information? Is the customer informed of problems or do customers contact the company to hear of problems?

The transaction elements of customer service are the most visible because of the direct impact they have on sales.

Post-transaction elements represent the array of services needed to support the product in the field:

- Availability of spares – what are the in-stock levels of service parts?
- Call-out time – how long does it take for the engineer to arrive? What is the 'first call fix rate'?
- Product tracing – are we able to recall potentially dangerous products from the marketplace?
- Warranty – can we maintain/extend the warranty to customers' expected levels?
- Customer complaints – how promptly are complaints and returns dealt with? Do we measure customer satisfaction with our response?

The work of Lalonde and Zinszer is still regarded as the most comprehensive treatment of customer service. It reminds us of the opportunity to deliver customer service throughout the company/customer relationship. Nevertheless, it has to be said that customer service is a notoriously difficult area on which to reach agreement as to meaning. A possible solution is to think of it in terms of two essential activities undertaken by organizations:

- **Primary activities**, e.g.:
  - car manufacturer – design, produce and sell cars
  - restaurant – cooking and selling meals
  - bus operator – providing buses on which customers travel
  - hotel – providing rooms to rent
- **Secondary activities**, e.g.:
  - physical distribution
  - complaint handling
  - after-sales service
  - provision of information to customers
  - terms of payment

Primary activities are the basics, the minimum necessary to enter and compete in the market. The secondary activities listed, and many others besides, form the basis of customer service. As customers become unable to distinguish among the core products under primary activities, the competitive arena into which more companies will move is service to the customer. People are now deciding to do business based on how they expect to be treated. The following questions are typical of those likely to arise:[4]

- Has the selling company paid close attention to making a product or service easy to use and effective from the customer's standpoint?
- How difficult is it to do business with the company?
- What happens when something goes wrong?
- Do people who come into contact with the buyer behave as if they are working mainly for the company, or for the customer?

Just how well companies deliver service or respond to failure may be measured on what, rather humorously, has been called the customer serviceometer.[5] It would operate like a thermometer, measuring customer service as opposed to temperature (Figure 7.1).

Figure 7.1 illustrates what a reading may look like when 'plugged in' to a particular company. The desired level may be the company's choice or even the consumer's; the actual level may be the findings from a customer survey. The challenge for management would be to account for the gap.

Cost versus service

Each level of service has an associated cost level. The basic relationship between the level of service and the cost is usually shown as a steeply rising curve (Figure 7.2).

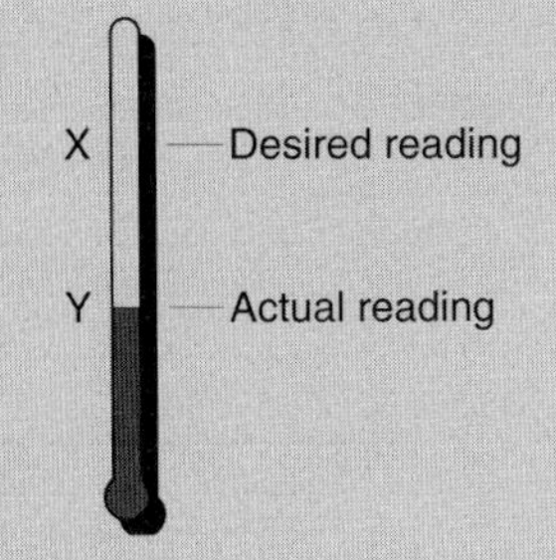

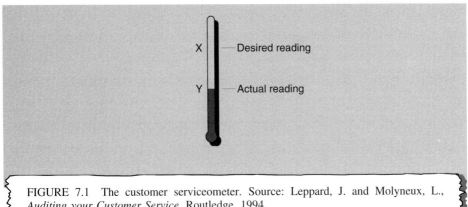

FIGURE 7.1 The customer serviceometer. Source: Leppard, J. and Molyneux, L., *Auditing your Customer Service*, Routledge, 1994.

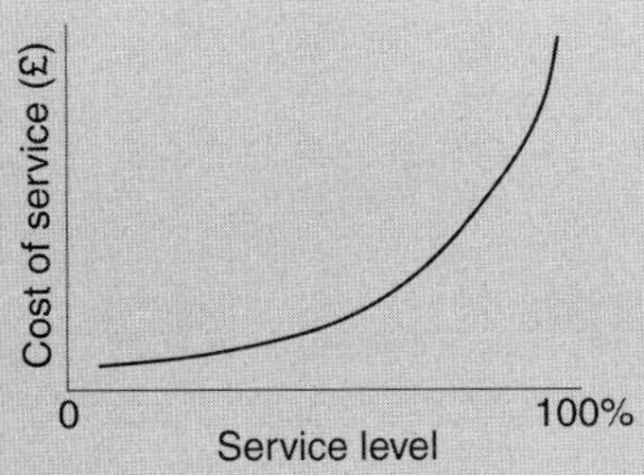

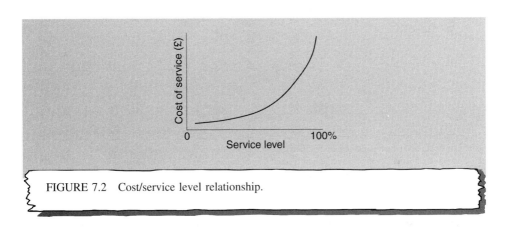

FIGURE 7.2 Cost/service level relationship.

This phenomenon is largely due to the increased costs of movement and storage associated with increases in service level. The other side of the coin is how sales respond to variations in the service level (Figure 7.3).

As in other areas of marketing, sales response to service level is said to be S-shaped. The curve begins with a minimum level of service that is regarded as just acceptable and no more (the service threshold). After that, sales respond significantly to increases in service level until we reach a point where additional expenditures on service are not rewarded in terms of sales.

Bringing the cost and revenue curves together highlights the trade-off between cost and benefit in service level determination (Figure 7.4). The maximum profit point typically occurs between the extremes of low and high service levels.

From an individual customer's perspective, however, there are only two levels of service, either 100 per cent or 0 per cent – the customer gets exactly what he ordered at the time and place required or he does not. If a customer urgently requires 20 items, and

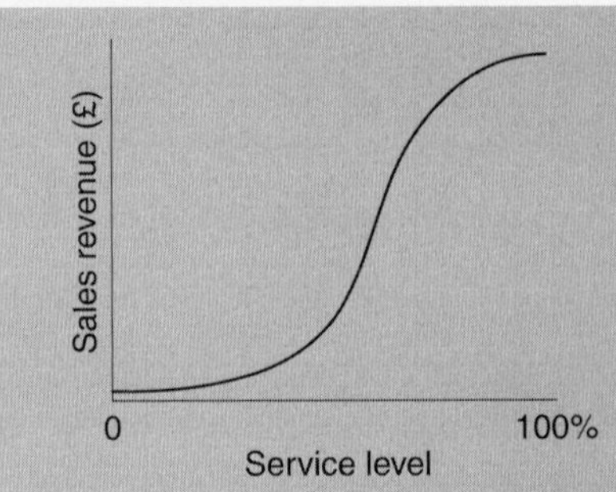

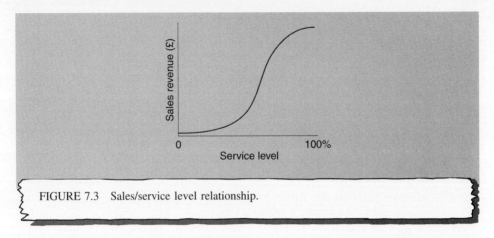

FIGURE 7.3 Sales/service level relationship.

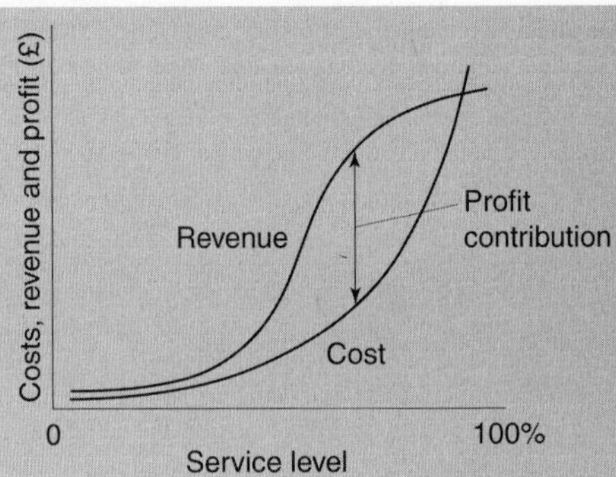

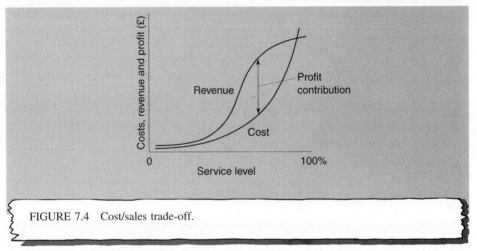

FIGURE 7.4 Cost/sales trade-off.

19 are shipped, the supplier could record that as a 95 per cent service level. However, as all 20 were required, the customer would regard it as a zero service level. A primary objective of stock management is to ensure that a product is available at the time and in the quantities desired. This is usually expressed in terms of the probability of being able to meet a request from current stock. This probability is the service level, which, for a single item can be defined as:

$$\text{Service level} = 1 - \frac{\text{Expected number of units out of stock annually}}{\text{Total annual demand}}$$

If we return to the customer order for 20 items where each item is carried in stock at the 95 per cent level of availability, the probability that the complete order can be filled is just over one-third ($0.36 = 0.95^{20}$). In one study[6] of how well a manufacturer satisfied his dealers, the customer service criteria (as set out by the dealers) were whether the manufacturer answered telephone calls promptly (within four rings), supplied the order in full, packed the order correctly, shipped the order on-line and priced it accurately. At this particular manufacturer, these things were being achieved 23 per cent of the time. In other words, there was a one-in-four change that all five criteria would be satisfied in a single transaction. The chance of satisfying a dealer completely three times in a row would be only 1.2 per cent (0.23^3). No doubt shocked at the findings, the manufacturer set a goal of increasing transaction integrity from 23 per cent to 95 per cent. If the manufacturer could accomplish that, then in three consecutive transactions the chance of satisfying the dealers would be 86 per cent (0.95^3).

Developing customer service level standards

Developing customer service level standards requires a company to determine the types of service that its customers desire, the cost of providing alternative services and measures for evaluating service performance. Below are some of the key areas where standards are essential.

- **Order cycle time** – the time from customer order to delivery. Often a company will state these standards as a given percentage of deliveries completed within a given number of days after order receipt, e.g. 90 per cent of deliveries (service level) made within three days (service standard) after the seller receives the order. Only 10 per cent will take longer.
- **Product availability** – the percentage of demand for a given item that can be met from available stock. The standard for this element may combine timeliness with availability to derive a measure such as '95 per cent or orders to be shipped on time and complete'.
- **Frequency of delivery** – how often do customers require shipments to their premises?
- **Flexibility of the supplier** – e.g. willingness of supplier to meet a special request outside the frequency cycle.
- **Ordering convenience** – may be related to the last point, e.g. in meeting special needs. In wider terms, how accessible and 'easy to do business with' is the supplier.
- **Documentation quality** – what is the error rate on invoices, delivery notes and other communications?
- **Order status information** – can we inform customers at any time on the status of their order? Customers often require quick, accurate and detailed answers. Hotlines and 'appropriate procedures' allow customers to be informed of potential problems on stock availability and delivery time status.
- **After-sales support** – what support is provided to customers after the sale? Are helplines available? A supplier would benefit from developing time standards for

shipping repair parts to customers. Thus, a measurable standard such as '95 per cent of all repair parts shipped on the same day as order is received' would promote customer confidence in a company's commitment to this type of customer service.

Stock control

Managing the stock is clearly a major activity in the process of delivering customer service. Every organization holds stocks of some kind to act as a buffer between supply and demand. If small stocks of an item are kept, they will be insufficient to meet all demand and there will be shortages. Conversely, if high stocks are held there is less chance of a shortage but stockholding costs are higher. The problem is one of trying to minimize the costs incurred on the one hand and on the other trying to ensure that a stockout (running out of stock) does not happen.

Costs incurred in stock management

- **Order costs** – all the costs involved from the placement of an order to payment.
- **Purchase costs** – the actual cost of obtaining the stock item from the supplier.
- **Holding costs** – costs incurred in storing the items. The obvious cost is for tied-up money that is either borrowed (with interest payable) or could be put to another use (opportunity costs). Also, storage costs (heating, rent, lighting) insurance, obsolescence, depreciation, etc.
- **Stockout costs** – if an item is needed but cannot be supplied from stock, there is usually a cost involved. In the simplest case, profit from a sale is lost but the effects may be more widespread, e.g. goodwill damaged and loss of potential future sales might be added as well as an element for loss of reputation. This goodwill cost is, however, difficult to quantify. Also included in the shortage costs might be allowances for positive action to counteract the shortage, e.g. sending out emergency orders, paying for special deliveries or using alternative, more expensive suppliers. For the purposes of the basic stock control model, shortage costs will be ignored as they are difficult to quantify.

The stock control decision

Two matters need to be resolved:

- How much stock to order.
- How frequently stock should be reordered.

Consider the following example, where the annual demand (D) for an item is 500 units, the order cost (OC) is £25, the holding cost (HC) for an item is £10 and Q is the size of order to be placed. Table 7.1 shows the order costs, holding costs and total costs (TC) for a range of order sizes Q.

TABLE 7.1 Costs and order sizes

Q	No. of orders	OC	HC	TC
5	100	2500	25	2525
10	50	1250	50	1300
20	25	625	100	725
40	12.5	312.5	200	512.50
50	10	250	250	500
75	6.66	166.5	375	541.5
100	5	125	500	625
125	4	100	625	725
150	3.33	83.25	750	833.25
175	2.85	71.25	875	946.25
200	2.5	62.50	1000	1062.50
250	2	50	1250	1300
500	1	25	2500	2525

An underlying assumption in Table 7.1 is that as the last item of any order is despatched, the next order arrives from the supplier so that a stockout never occurs. As a further consequence, being overstocked does not arise. At any one time the average number of items held in stock will be Q/2 (at the beginning there will be Q items, at the end 0 items). The holding costs will therefore be:

$$Q/2 \times HC = 5/2 \times 10 = £25$$

The important point from Table 7.1 is that the two cost elements move in opposite directions as Q moves from 5 to 500. How much to order at any one time will be the amount (Q) that minimizes the total costs (TC) involved in stock. The answer from Table 7.1 is an order quantity of 50 (OC = HC, and TC is at its minimum).

Economic order quantity

The illustration above is known technically as the **economic order quantity (EOQ) model**: establishing the value for Q that minimizes total cost. The formula for Q is:

$$Q = \sqrt{\frac{2 \times OC \times D}{HC}}$$

Substituting the data from our example gives:

$$Q = \sqrt{\frac{2 \times 25 \times 500}{10}} = 50$$

Reorder level

From the EOQ calculation we can determine what is known as the reorder cycle – the frequency or timing or orders throughout the year. Calculating the cycle is straightforward. The number of orders each twelve-month period will then be:

$$500/50 = 10 \text{ orders}$$

The number of days between each order will be:

$$365/10 = 36.5 \text{ days}$$

Assumptions of the EOQ model

The key assumptions underlying the calculations so far have been:

- Demand is known for certain.
- Demand is constant over time.
- Orders are received as soon as they are made.
- An order is made when stock levels reach zero.
- Order quantity remains constant over time.
- All costs are constant.

Obviously, these assumptions are unrealistic in many stock control decisions. However, as a model, the EOQ can be adapted to allow some of these assumptions to be relaxed, and it does illustrate the basic principles involved.

Incorporating leadtime

One assumption of the EOQ model that orders are made when stock levels reach zero is a feature of the just-in-time (JIT) inventory system. By co-ordinating demand and supply, stock arrives just in time for use – neither any earlier nor any later. In many cases, however, JIT is not required or is irrelevant. Instead there will be a leadtime which is the time that elapses between an order's placement and its receipt.

Let us consider a situation where a stock order may take up to two weeks to arrive and assume there are 50 working weeks in the year. As demand equals 500, ten items of stock will be used each week. Given this weekly usage, stocks must be reordered when stock levels reach 20 items. The calculation is:

$$\begin{aligned} \text{Reorder level} &= \text{Demand} \times \text{Leadtime} \\ &= 10 \times 2 \\ &= 20 \text{ items} \end{aligned}$$

The reorder model is shown in Figure 7.5.

The reorder level will vary according to:

- the variability of the order leadtime (LT);
- fluctuations in consumer demand (D);
- the customer service standard.

The higher the variability, fluctuations and service standard, the higher the reorder level.

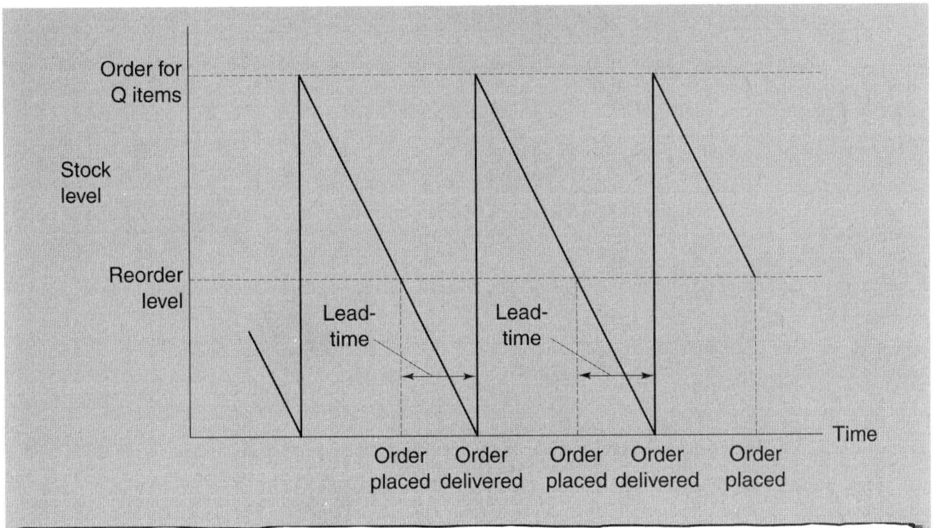

FIGURE 7.5 The reorder model.

Probabilistic demand

The analysis described so far assumes that demand is constant and known exactly. In practice this is rarely true, and demand for almost any item varies over time. Where uncertainty is small, the EOQ model gives widely used results. Variations are sometimes too large, necessitating the use of other approaches, e.g. a model for demand that is normally distributed.

For the management of stock under variable demand, a service level is used in which the desired probability that a demand can or cannot be met from stock is specified. A company might specify a service level of 95 per cent, implying a probability of 0.05 that a demand is not met.

The probability of not running out of stock in a stock cycle is sometimes called the **cycle service level**. Under constant demand, the reorder point was found from **leadtime demand** (LT×D). If this is normally distributed it will be greater than the mean value on half the occasions. This means that there will be shortages in 50 per cent of stock cycles. Conversely, leadtime demand will be less than the mean in 50 per cent of stock cycles, and this will give spare stock.

To give a cycle service level greater than 0.5, a safety stock must be added so the reorder level becomes:

$$\text{Reorder level} = \text{Mean leadtime demand} + \text{Safety stock}$$

The size of the safety stock depends on the service level specified. A high service level requires a high safety stock. When leadtime demand is normally distributed, the calculation of safety stock becomes:

$$\text{Safety stock} = \text{Z} \times \text{Standard deviation of leadtime demand}$$
$$= Z\sigma\sqrt{L}$$

Here Z is the number of standard deviations that the safety stock is away from the mean demand. Any value in a distribution can be converted into a Z-value by subtracting the mean of the distribution and dividing the difference by the standard deviation. For example, when the mean is 50 and the standard deviation is 10, a raw score of 60 would have a Z-value of (60–50)/10 = 1: that is, the score 60 is 1 standard deviation above the mean score. Corresponding probabilities are to be found in normal distribution tables. For example:

- If Z = 1, a shortage will occur in 15.9 per cent of stock cycles.
- If Z = 1.5, shortages will occur in 6.7 per cent of stock cycles.
- If Z = 2, shortages will occur in 2.3 per cent of stock cycles.
- If Z = 2.5, shortages will occur in 0.6 per cent of stock cycles.
- If Z = 3, shortages will occur in 0.1 per cent of stock cycles.

If demand varies widely, the standard deviation of leadtime demand will be high, and very high safety stocks would be needed to ensure a service level near to 100 per cent. Arriving at a final service level will inevitably be subject to the potentially conflicting pressures of cost and customer expectations. It may be that, for important items, a service level close to 100 per cent is set; for other items the level may be around 85 per cent.

Stock control example[7]

Demand for an item is normally distributed with a mean of 200 units a week and a standard deviation of 40 units. Reorder cost (including delivery) is £200, holding cost is £6 a unit a year and leadtime is fixed at 3 weeks.

1. Describe an ordering policy that will give a 95 per cent cycle service level.
2. What is the cost of holding the safety stock in this case?
3. By how much would the costs rise if the service level is raised to 97 per cent?

Solution
Listing the values we know that:

Demand, D	= 200 units a week
Standard deviation, σ	= 40 units
Reorder cost, R_c	= £200 an order
Holding cost, H_c	= £6 a unit a year
Leadtime, L	= 3 weeks

(a) Substituting these gives:

$$\text{Order quantity } Q_o = \frac{2R_cD}{H_c} = \frac{2 \times 200 \times 200 \times 52}{6}$$
$$= 833$$
$$\text{Reorder level ROL} = LD + \text{safety stock} = 3 \times 200 + \text{safety stock}$$
$$= 600 + \text{safety stock}$$

For a 95 per cent service level:

$$Z = 1.645 \text{ standard deviations from the mean}$$

(To find out how this is determined see Exhibit 7.1.) Then:

$$\text{Safety stock} = Z\sigma\sqrt{L} = 1.645 \times 40 \times \sqrt{3}$$
$$= 114$$

The best policy is to order 833 units whenever stock declines to 600 + 114 = 714 units. On average, orders should arrive when there are 114 units remaining.

(b) The expected cost of the safety stock is given by:

$$\text{Safety stock} \times \text{Holding cost} = 114 \times 6 = £684 \text{ a year}$$

(c) If the service level is raised to 97 per cent, Z becomes 1.88 and:

$$\text{Safety stock} = Z\,\alpha\sqrt{L} = 1.88 \times 40 \times \sqrt{3} = 130$$

The cost of holding this is:

$$\text{Safety stock} \times \text{Holding cost} = 130 \times 6 = £780 \text{ a year}$$

The human side to service

Much of the discussion so far has focused on the logistical aspects of customer service – order cycle time, frequency of delivery, etc. There is, however, a fundamental aspect of customer service that involves people and their behavioural styles. Whatever the organization, management is increasingly recognizing the pivotal role played by its front-line employees in the delivery of customer service. These people are the key to success during what Jan Carlzon calls the 'moments of truth'. We often limit these 'moments of truth' to the fast-food business, airlines, hotels and the like. However, it has equal relevance in what may be described as a more industrial context. Consider the case described in Exhibit 7.2 of a sales engineer deliberating how to respond to a customer, the outcome of which may have a significant impact on future relationships.[8]

The most effective answers are (b) for situation 1 and (d) for situation 2. You may care to reflect on why and also give reasons as to why the remainder of the responses are ineffectual.

Exhibit 7.1 How to obtain the Z value

Under the standard normal distribution curve (see figure below), the level at which demand can be met in the example on page 222 is 95 per cent. There is a 5 per cent probability of not being able to meet demand.

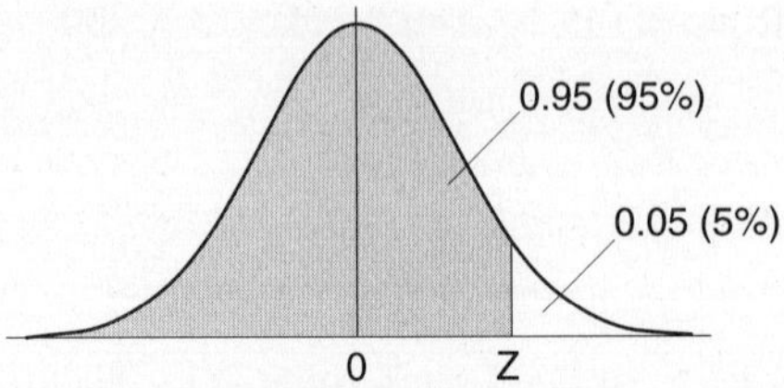

We need to find the Z value such that the area to the left of this value is 0.95. One approach to this is to split the above curve into 2 areas of 0.5 and 0.45 as shown below.

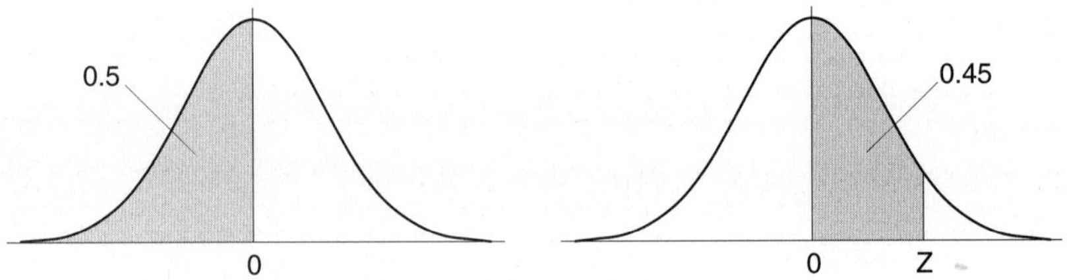

Then using the standard tables (Appendix C) look up 0.45 in the main body of the table and this will give the corresponding Z value of 1.645.

Tack Training International who devised the situations above is a world leader in sales, marketing and management training. From its work on situations like the above it categorized behavioural styles under four main headings[9] (Exhibit 7.3).

Although the compromise style is regarded as the best because both company and customer are satisfied, the other approaches cannot be discounted.

The range of customer service situations is wide and the circumstances surrounding each often different. Apart from the 'script' in the examples cited above, there is also the manner of communication. In other words, the distinction between what is said and how it is said. Invariably the script and its delivery will go together. The three typical behaviours that characterize the responses of front-line employees are:

- **Submissiveness.** The employees allow themselves to be dominated, withhold opinions and feelings, are indecisive, apologize constantly and have poor eye contact and posture.

Exhibit 7.2 Behavioural styles

Situation 1

CUSTOMER: Why are your products so unreliable?

How should the engineer reply?

(a) 'They're not! They're as good as anything else in the market!'
(b) 'Sorry about the trouble you've had; but believe me, it is most unusual, but I've given it a good check and I'm certain it will be OK now.'
(c) 'I wouldn't know about that, I only service them.'
(d) 'I'm really sorry you've been so unlucky with this one. I know it is not the top of the range, but there are plenty worse. I don't know why it has given so much trouble.'

Situation 2

CUSTOMER: Why are your charges so high?

(a) 'Prices are nothing to do with me, so I can't comment.'
(b) 'They're not high when you compare them with our competitors. None of them could give you this service at a lower price.'
(c) 'I know they are a bit on the high side, but they keep telling me that overheads are increasing all the time. I suppose someone has to pay.'
(d) They aren't bad when you compare them with the cost of downtime. We find that customers like yourself rely on a quick response, and recognize that such a service is good value for money.

Source: Tack, A., *Profitable Customer Care*, Butterworth/Heinemann, 1994.

Exhibit 7.3 Four behavioural styles

A = Avoiding

CUSTOMER: 'That new engineer has rather a quick temper, hasn't he?'

ENGINEER: 'I really can't say – I hardly know him.'

B = Bountiful

CUSTOMER: 'If you haven't got it in your van stock, how long will I have to wait?'

ENGINEER: 'Don't worry, I can pick it up from the depot this evening, and drop it off first thing in the morning.'

C = Compromising

CUSTOMER: 'Why don't you ever have the right parts with you when you come to do repairs?'

ENGINEER: 'I understand your concern and I shall certainly mention it to the boss when I get back, but I've just checked, and this is only the second time in the last year that I have not had the right parts. But I do agree its two too many.'

D = Determined

CUSTOMER (being insistent): 'I'm certainly not signing for three hours labour charge. You were only working on the machine for two hours. The rest of the time you were on the phone!'

ENGINEER: 'I'm sorry, but the phone calls were necessary, to check out some technical details with the factory. I'm sure you will understand that the time was devoted to your repair, and agree that the hours will have to stand.'

Source: Tack, A., *Profitable Customer Care*, Butterworth/Heinemann, 1994.

- **Assertiveness**. The employees state their wants and needs directly, give opinions and feelings, are decisive, confront issues and have good eye contact and posture.
- **Aggressiveness**. The employees interrupt, conceal information and opinions, dominate and are poor listeners, are loud, blaming and sarcastic and have intense and glaring eye contact and dominant posture.

The above stances can, of course, be equally applicable to customer behaviour. The following customer service situations illustrate the types of action that characterize submissive, assertive and aggressive employees[10] (Exhibit 7.4).

What should now be evident in the delivery of customer service is the need for standards to be set and monitored. 'Hard' as well as 'soft' standards may be set. **Hard standards** are quantifiable, e.g. 90 per cent of deliveries to be made within 3 days of receipt of order. **Soft standards** are qualitative, e.g. to be courteous and polite to customers. As one observer puts it,

> In many businesses, the real action often takes place in the first 60 seconds of interaction with customers. Do employees make the right impression? Is the company perceived as being considerate and helpful? It is important for employees to know what role they are expected to play and be aware of what the customers expect.[11]

Some of the principles of public service behind the Citizens' Charter offer a valuable framework for any business devising a customer service policy. For example, it is good

Exhibit 7.4 Assertiveness and customer care

You have to telephone a customer to explain that your company cannot deliver when the customer had hoped. You expect the customer to be disappointed and possibly even angry (even though it is not your fault). Would you:

- Postpone making the call because you are anxious about upsetting them? (**submissiveness**)
- Think how you could break the news in a simple and honest manner and then make the call straight away? (**assertiveness**)
- Give it no special consideration as it is one of these things that have to be done now and again? (**aggressiveness**)

Staffing an enquiry desk, you are in the middle of a lengthy conversation with a customer sorting out a serious complaint. There is no-one else to help you. The telephone rings. Would you:

- Ask the customer to bear with you while you answer it. Sort out the telephone enquiry then return to your customer? (**aggressiveness**)
- Ask the customer to bear with you one moment, explain to the customer on the phone that you are with a customer, take their name and number, promise to return their call within one hour. Return to your other customer thanking them for their patience? (**assertiveness**)
- Try to hurry up the face-to-face customer so that you can get to the telephone because a ringing telephone bothers you? (**submissiveness**)

Source: Gillen, T., *Twenty Training Workshops for Customer Care*, Gower, 1990.

Charter practice to do the following:

- Set specific standards for the maximum time that people should have to wait for services, and make sure these are met.
- Offer fixed appointments, and to apologize if people are kept waiting.
- Ask people what they think of the services they use and what they see as priorities for improvement.
- Make sure that people can find out easily everything they want to know [about public services] through clear and effective communications.
- Ensure that where people have to deal with a large organization, or more than one part of it, a single, named individual should be responsible for making sure that customers receive all the help they need.
- To set specific standards for the maximum time that people have to wait for a response to their enquiries.
- Make sure that there are swift, effective and easy-to-use ways of putting things right when they go wrong.
- Respond positively when mistakes are made or services do not meet the standards customers can reasonably expect.

Mystery shopping

There is a range of methods for gathering information on customer service. One method gaining in importance is mystery shopping, in which an independent assessment is made of service levels. As mystery shoppers can be viewed as snoopers, spies or detectives, the method's use requires careful handling. The ethos of mystery shoppers should be to reward staff for good service, not to castigate them for poor, and the method should be used in conjunction with other forms of customer feedback.

Excellent customer service may be the aim of all companies, but there is a wide variation in its delivery according to a report from the Grass Roots Group based on a survey of the service levels of 2500 business operations.[12] *The Front Line Survey* (1995) is the first in a series of annual reports which will examine the basics of customer service in sectors ranging from petrol stations and department stores to British Rail and estate agents. The survey is about basics: Are staff friendly and polite? Do they say 'thank you'? Do they smile? Are the toilets clean? How long were the queues?

The assessors provide a service rating and a performance index on each outlet visited. The **service rating** is based on marks out of ten awarded by the shopper to reflect his or her opinion of the overall standard of service experienced. The **performance index** is a more objective calculation whereby points are allocated for each action or attribute in an outlet in a given sector. For instance, four points might be given for a smile, a maximum of six points may be available for toilets, two points for being smartly dressed, etc. There can therefore be differences between the service rating and the performance index scores. The performance index is a much more precisely measured and objective assessment, the components of which are used by clients to identify specific shortcomings so that remedial action can be taken. The summary of results by market sector can be seen in Exhibit 7.5.

Exhibit 7.5 *The Front Line Survey: overall results*

Service rating league table			Performance index league table		
Rank	Sector	Score (max. 100)	Rank	Sector	Score (max. 100)
1	Electricity showrooms	80	1	Building societies	94
2	Travel agents	79	2	Banks	93
3	Estate agents	79	3	Electricity showrooms	91
4	Gas showrooms	79	4	Post offices	91
5	Electrical retailers	78	5	Travel agents	88
6	Off licences	77	6	Gas showrooms	87
7	British Rail	77	7	Off licences	86
8	Fast-food restaurants	75	8	Petrol stations	84
9	Building societies	75	9	Pubs	83
10	Post offices	74	10	Supermarkets	83
11	Banks	74	11	Fast-food restaurants	82
12	Pubs	73	12	Electrical retailers	82
13	Petrol stations	73	13	Estate agents	81
14	Department stores	73	14	Music shops	81
15	Variety stores	72	15	Department stores	76
16	Music stores	71	16	Variety stores	75
17	Newsagents	69	17	British Rail	74
18	Supermarkets	67	18	Newsagents	71
	National average	76		National average	82

Source: Grass Roots Group plc.

An interesting conclusion from the survey was that newsagents are the least friendly and least helpful shops in the high street, music store assistants are the least likely to smile and fast-food chains McDonald's and Burger King, despite their carefully cultivated images, performed worse than the much maligned banks and British Rail. The specific findings for newsagents are shown in Exhibit 7.6.

Grass Roots admits to being puzzled as to why the newsagents, which included W.H. Smith and Menzies, got the thumbs down. Grass Roots hopes to provide answers to this and other questions as the survey develops in the future. It is, of course, always worth speculating about possible explanations:

- **Knowledgeable**. What do we expect newsagent employees to be knowledgeable about? Given the mundane nature of many of the purchases, is it unreasonable to expect that consumers should know what they need!
- **Helpful**. In what respects can newsagent employees be helpful? Does the very nature of the activity require much in the way of helpfulness apart from say giving directions within a large establishment?
- **Smiling**. Given the volume of customer throughput, particularly in large, centrally located establishments, employees would need to have a permanent smile on their face no matter what. In other, less busy outlets, sheer boredom may account for a less than happy demeanour. It may simply be an 'inappropriate personality' for front-line activity.

Exhibit 7.6 *The Front Line Survey*: findings for newsagents

Shopper's task: Make a normal purchase.

	Newsagents	National average
Service rating (%)	68%	76%
Performance index	74	82

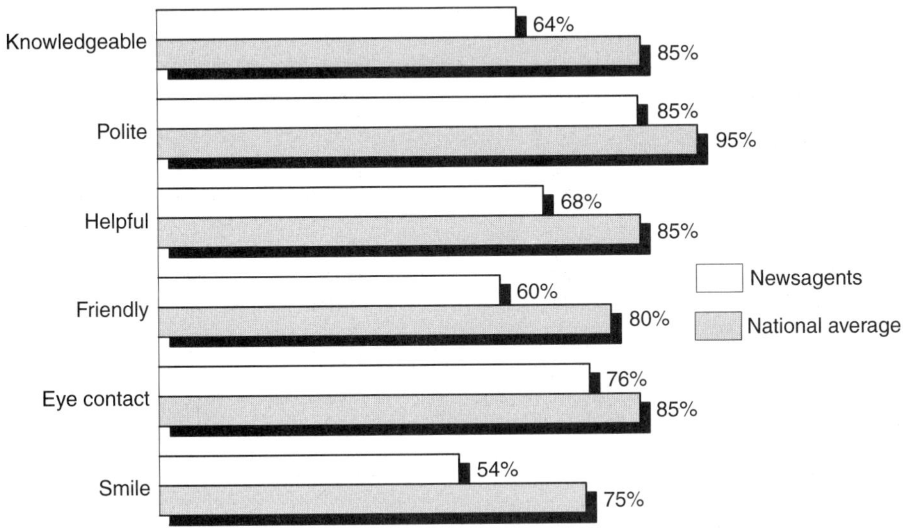

Total number of visits = 195

Detailed performance

			%
When making a purchase, did the staff:	Greet you?	Yes	52
		No	48
	Say thank you?	Yes	86
		No	14
How long did you have to queue for?	Less than 1 minute		54
	Between 1 and 3 minutes		36
	Between 3 and 5 minutes		9
	Longer than 5 minutes		1
How many people were in the queue in front of you?		0	34
		1	30
		2	23
		3 or more*	13
* If there were 3 or more people in front of you, were all the positions (tills) open?		Yes	51
		No	49

Source: Grass Roots Group plc, 1995.

Rude, arrogant, unreasonable customers cannot be excluded from the frame. Further study, according to Grass Roots, is required. What is often neglected in customer service surveys are the views of the front-line employees themselves: the survey invariably seeks just the views of consumers and management. Until this imbalance of opinion is redressed, the symptoms will remain largely unexplained.

Empowerment

Although front-line employees are not often canvassed for their views and opinions, recognition in recent years of their importance in customer service has given rise to another buzzword – **empowerment**. Historically, there has been a paradox: front-line employees are often the most important determinant of service quality but they are normally the least appreciated in any company. So we have to tread carefully when examining this sudden 'interest' by management in the workers.

Some arguments for action in this area are particularly incisive and worth documenting. Consider first:

> One of the most potent ways to get started on the service-quality journey is to 'thin the rule book'. Many organizations operate with thick policy and procedure manuals that have the effect of strangling service initiative and judgement. These thick manuals benefit neither customer nor service provider, producing a regimented service when a flexible one is needed, a by-the-book when a by-the-customer one is required.
>
> Too many policies and procedures take the fun out of servicing. For one thing, delivering inflexible service when the situation calls for flexible service angers customers, and interacting with angry customers is no fun for employees. Also problematic is the frustration many employees feel when they know certain operating procedures keep them from doing good jobs in serving their customers.
>
> Many firms are unwittingly tying their employees up in knots, saying to them with the thick rule book that they are supposed to be robot servers rather than thinking servers. And in the process, these firms are reducing employees' perceived control and sapping their willingness and ability to serve customers effectively. Why on earth would a company's management choose to operate in such a dysfunctional way? Often it is for the worst of reasons:
>
> - because many managers do not trust employees' judgement, they make all kinds of rules that in effect represent management's judgement; and
> - because thinking employees appear to threaten management prerogatives, control and power.[13]

Next, from another leading authority:

> It is necessary to 'dehumiliate' work by eliminating the policies and procedures (almost always tiny) of the organization that demean and belittle human dignity. It is impossible to get people's best efforts, involvement, and caring concern for things you believe important to your customers and the long-term interests of your organization when we write policies and procedures that treat them like thieves and bandits.[14]

What, then, does empowerment really mean? In simple terms it has been defined as 'removing the barriers that prevent workers from exercising judgement and creativity'.[15] It is said to involve giving employees more information and knowledge, rewards based on company performance and power to make decisions. There are benefits as well as costs (Table 7.2).

It is argued[16] that empowerment is not an either/or but rather a choice of three options each of which involves differing amounts of knowledge, information, rewards and power. They are:

- **Suggestion involvement**. Where the word 'empowerment' is used merely to dress up consultation. Management retains the power to decide, employees simply suggest, e.g. McDonald's.
- **Job involvement**. This entails extensive job redesign so that employees use a variety of skills, often in teams. They have considerable freedom in deciding how to do the necessary work. However, overall strategic decisions remain senior management's responsibility.
- **High involvement**. Employees become involved in the whole organization's performance. Virtually every aspect of the organization is different from that of a control-oriented organization. Employees develop extensive skills in teamwork, problem-solving and business operations. They participate in work-unit management decisions. There is profit-sharing and employee ownership, e.g. Federal Express.

Whether the term 'empowerment' should be applied to all three is debatable. The greatest challenge for all those interested in the welfare and needs of front-line employees lies with the first option: their plight is indeed a cause for concern[17] as they are caught between management and customer. For those set on researching the signs of an empowered/unempowered workplace, understanding the feelings of those directly affected, the front-line workers, would be an admirable place to begin.

TABLE 7.2 Empowerment: benefits and costs

Benefits	Costs
• Quicker response times to customer needs • Quicker response times to complaints • Employees fell better about themselves and their jobs • Employees interact with customers with more warmth and enthusiasm • Empowered employees can be a great source of service ideas • Great word of mouth advertising and customer retention	• Greater investment in selection and training • Higher labour costs • Slower, inconsistent service delivery • Violations of 'fair play' • Giveaways and bad decisions

Source: Bowen, D.E. and Lawler III, E.E., 'The empowerment of service workers: what, why, how and when', *Sloan Management Review*, Spring 1992.

Complaints

This chapter began by citing comments relating to customer service. Things do go wrong, problems will occur, and mistakes will be made. Each one of a whole range of issues has the potential for eroding customer satisfaction and destroying customer loyalty, for example faulty goods, lengthy waiting times, promises made and not kept, poor staff attitudes and inappropriate or poorly applied procedures.

The main concern of customers is how effectively organizations respond to their complaints. The Citizens' Charter stresses that if things do go wrong then public services should offer an apology, a full explanation and a swift and effective remedy. Unfortunately this is not always the case, as evidenced by findings from an Office of Fair Trading report on consumer loyalty.[18] A number of comments summed up the feelings of customers about organizations to which complaints were made:

- 'They messed me around.'
- 'No replies to letters or telephone calls.'
- 'They did not take my complaint seriously.'
- 'Responsibility passed on to others.'
- 'Verbal, not written apology.'
- 'Lack of interest, poor attitudes.'

Clearly, organizations are perceived as not having adequate procedures for handling complaints. The consequences for both effective and ineffective complaint handling has been extensively studied. A model developed by the Technical Assistance Research Programs Institute (TARP) for the US Office of Consumer Affairs portrays the implications[19] (Figure 7.6).

The aim for any organization should be to develop a system of effective complaint management. Such a system of on-going steps or actions would allow an organization to both:

- respond efficiently and effectively to the complaints of individual customers, and
- collect, aggregate and analyze complaint data to pinpoint and correct the root causes of customer problems.

Front-line handling of a complaint or problem

In the first instance, complaints and problems are generally made to front-line staff either in person or by telephone. A substantial responsibility thus falls on the front-line employee to represent the organization and to act in a fair and professional manner towards the complainant. The most important thing to do is make sure the customer knows that the complaint is being taken seriously and that efforts will be made to find a solution. A useful ten-stage approach has been suggested for the front-line employee:[20]

- Stay calm – remember the irritation is generally not aimed at you.
- Avoid admitting any liability at this stage – express concern and sympathy that a problem exists, e.g. 'I'm sorry there is a problem. Let me see what I can do.'

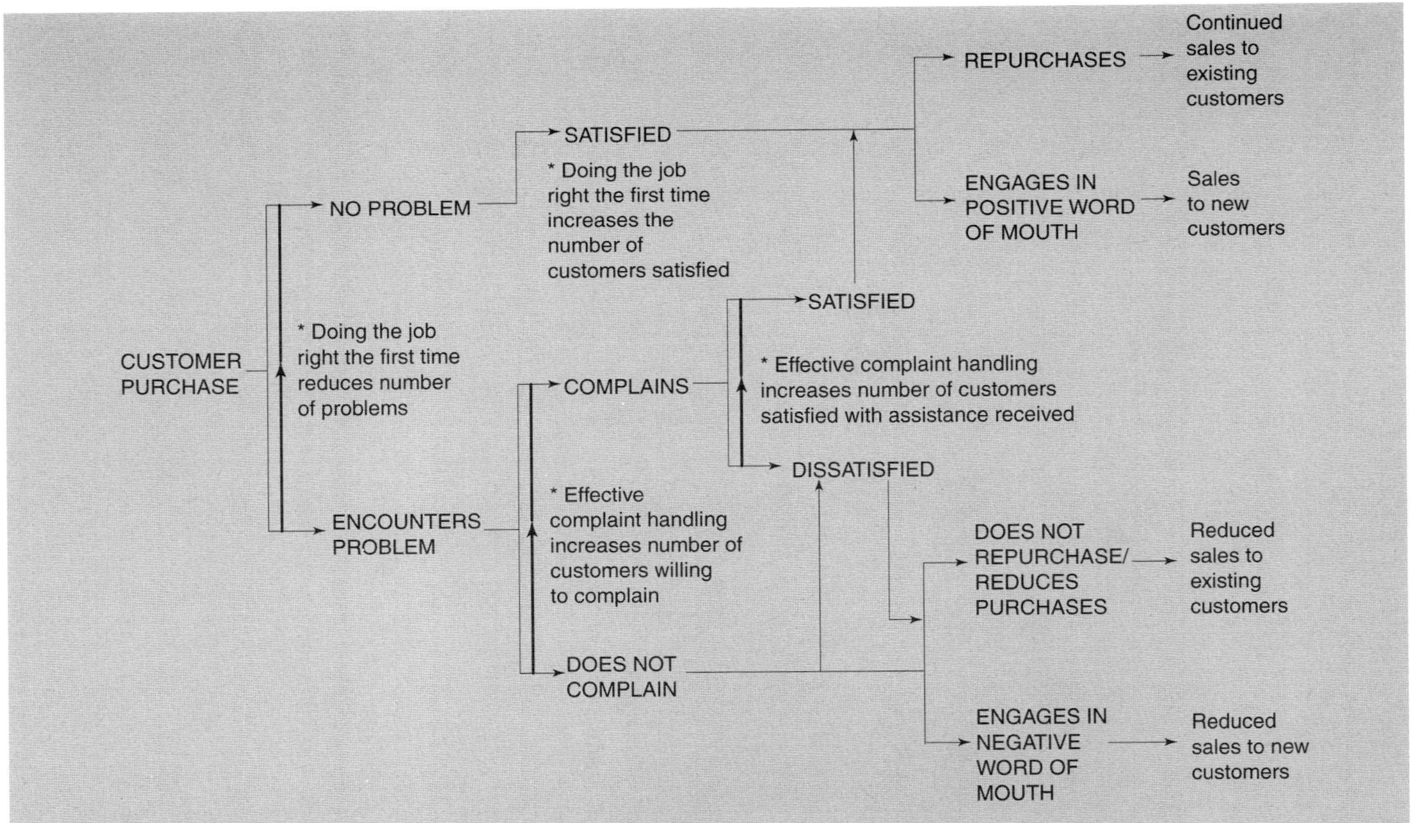

FIGURE 7.6 The TARP model for complaints handling. Source: Adamson, C., 'Complaint handling: benefits and best practice', *Consumer Policy Review*, Vol. 1, pt 4, 1991.

- Let the customer get the story off their chest – do not interrupt – this will only cause irritation.
- Get the facts – use questions and careful listening to find out what the real, whole problem is.
- Find out what the customer wants – often the customer knows what will satisfy them.
- Identify the appropriate action to take – bearing in mind the policy, the customer's expectations and what is possible.
- Take action to solve the problem if you have the authority to do so – if you have not, involve the manager but make sure that you brief the manager on the situation so the customer does not have to start from scratch again.
- If the corrective action cannot be carried out immediately, tell the customer what will be done and when. Be realistic on promised timescales. It is better to under-promise and over-perform than the other way around.
- Record action to be taken and inform anyone else in the organization involved.
- Follow up – broken promises cause further irritation.

To have any hope of success in dealing with complaints and angry customers, organizations must provide a supportive environment for its front-line employees. This will involve training in both procedures and interpersonal skills. It has also been said that, 'employees should be empowered, feel highly valued and their importance to the success of the company recognised'.[21] These are indeed lofty ideals for which many organizations have a long way to go to achieve.

Consumer evaluations of responses to complaints

A great deal of attention is often given to how the organization and its employees should respond to a complaint. Although the ten-point plan and the like cited above are designed with customer satisfaction in mind, little effort is given to how the complainant views the whole process. Are organizations often guilty of assuming that they know what redress will satisfy the customer?

Psychological equity theories may help organizations to understand and develop approaches to complaint response. Equity theory states that people will become angry when equity principles are violated. Discomfort occurs whether one is a victim of unfair practice, observes another who is victimized, or treats another unfairly. Research has found that people who experience, observe or even create unfairness will try to reduce their discomfort by trying to restore either physical or psychological equity: that is, they will want to make restitution by tangible repayment, e.g. refund for damaged merchandise, or else rearrange their perceptions of a situation ('maybe I didn't use the product correctly').

In a complaint setting, the organization is seen as being 'in the dock' and the complainant the 'victim'. Restitution by the company restores physical equity. Blaming the customer restores psychological equity! Most importantly, equity in handling complaints means violations of 'fair play'. Customers with the same or a similar complaint expect to be treated equally.

Further aspects of equity theory which merit consideration in complaint handling are:

- **Distributive fairness**, which for complaint management raises the question, what do consumers deserve in terms of recompense or restitution?
- **Procedural fairness** is a matter of how the decision was arrived at. Apart from a natural desire to express feelings and opinions (often referred to as 'voice'), complainants hope that publicizing their complaint might affect an organization's choice of compensation. However, opportunities for 'letting off steam' may be perceived as a sham if the impact on how the complaint is resolved is nil. Organizations are criticized for merely giving an impression of participation.
- **Interactional fairness** is very much concerned with how the complainant is treated, in other words the style of organization's behaviour and communication. Rudeness is clearly unacceptable whereas an apology is said to restore a degree of psychological equity to the complainant; the legitimacy of the complaint is acknowledged and the complainant's self-esteem enhanced.

In developing systems and procedures for handling complaints, concepts like equity theory from the psychological literature should be considered. The convenience of the organization should certainly not be considered as primary over that of the customer. Otherwise, what is the customer paying for?

References

1. Editorial, *Marketing*, 15 December 1994.
2. Peel, M., *Customer Service*, Kogan Page, 1987, p. 22.
3. Lalonde, B.J. and Zinszer, P.H., *Customer Service: Meaning and Measurement*, National Council of Physical Distribution Management, 1976.
4. Davidow, W.H. and Uttal, B., *Total Customer Service: The Ultimate Weapon*, 1990, p. 26.
5. Leppard, J. and Molyneux, L., *Auditing Your Customer Service*, Routledge, 1994, p. 77.
6. Kotler, P., 'Marketing's new paradigm: what's really happening out there', *Planning Review*, September/October 1992, p. 51.
7. Waters, D., *Quantitative Methods for Business*, Addison-Wesley, 1994.
8. Tack, A., *Profitable Customer Care*, Butterworth/Heinemann, 1994.
9. *Ibid.*
10. Gillen, T., *Training Workshops for Customer Care*, Gower, 1990.
11. Turpin, D.V., *Beyond Product Excellence*, Financial Times Mastering Management Series, no. 17, p. 8.
12. *The Front Line Survey*, Grass Roots Group plc.
13. Zeithaml, V.A., Parasuraman, A. and Berry, L.L., *Delivering Service Quality: Balancing Customer Perceptions and Expectations*, Free Press, 1990, p. 151–52.
14. Tom Peters quoted in *The Service Edge: 101 Companies that Profit from Customer Care*, R. Zemke and D. Schaaf, New American Library, 1989, p. 68.
15. Bowen, D.E. and Lawler III, E.E., 'The empowerment of service workers: what, why, how and when', *Sloan Management Review*, spring 1992.
16. *Ibid.*
17. Mudie, P., 'Internal marketing: cause for concern', *Quarterly Review of Marketing*, Spring/Summer 1987.

18. *Consumer Loyalty: A Report on a Research Survey*, Office of Fair Trading, May 1990.
19. Adamson, C., 'Complaint handling: benefits and best practice', *Consumer Policy Review*, Vol. 1, Pt 4, 1991.
20. Bailey, D., 'Service recovery: a ten stage approach in the training of front-line staff', *Training and Management Development Methods*, Vol. 8, 1994.
21. Cook, S., *Customer Care*, Kogan Page, 1992.

CHAPTER 8

Retailing

WHAT IS IT ABOUT?

A crucial decision for every potential retailer is where to locate. A number of techniques for **site assessment** are discussed. One technique already discussed in chapter 2, namely **geodemographics**, is particularly useful in location analysis.

Retailers also need to determine what stock to carry, how much, when to reorder and so on. This is the domain of **merchandise planning**.

Once a company has located and arranged its stock, a retailer requires a range of measures to evaluate performance. One measure best suited to supermarkets – **direct product profitability** is discussed in some detail.

Retailing is an industry where people are prominent. Therefore how people should be treated warrants consideration. Reference to established theory assists discussion.

Although much of the material up to this point applies to retailing in general, service retailers possess unique characteristics that deserve separate consideration. A substantial part of this chapter is therefore devoted to the issues raised by these characteristics.

Where to locate?

There is a saying in the retailing industry that only three things matter: location, location and location. Site your shop in the right spot and the world will beat a path to your door! Of course, this is not entirely the case – product variety, presentation, price, etc., are also determinants of success. How do retailers know what the right site is, though, and more importantly, how do they go about finding it? Consumers are attracted towards one location or another – one of the earliest exponents of this 'pulling effect' was W.J. Reilly who published his law of retail gravitation in 1929. The law's purpose is to establish a point of indifference between two cities or communities so that the catchment area can be determined. The crucial task in retail location is to delineate the catchment area which can be defined as the geographical area from which a retailer draws his custom. Reilly's law may be expressed as:

$$D_{AB} = \frac{d}{1 + \sqrt{\frac{P_B}{P_A}}}$$

where D_{AB} is the limit of city A's catchment area measured in miles along the road to city B, d is the distance in miles along a major roadway between A and B, P_A is the population of city A and P_B is the population of city B.

Based on this formula, a city with a population of 450 000 (A) would draw people from three times the distance that a city with 50 000 (B) could manage. If the cities are 20 miles apart, the catchment area for city A extends to 15 miles and for city B, 5 miles (Figure 8.1).

Reilly's law rests on two major assumptions:

- The two competing areas are equally accessible from the major road.
- Retailers in the two areas are equally effective.

Consequently, the law has its limitations. Not only is the focus on distance rather than travel times but also, actual distance may not correspond with the consumer's perception of distance, e.g. a store that offers few conveniences and few services may be at a greater perceived distance from one with an attractive, pleasant environment.

However, despite its weaknesses, Reilly's law still represents an important contribution to our understanding of retail location. In particular, it reminds us of some of the basics of location:

- **Spatial convenience** – travel time and distance (Reilly) to destination stores or market centres – places limitations on market size.
- **Range** is the maximum distance that customers are willing to travel to a shopping destination.
- **Threshold** refers to the smallest market size needed to support a certain type of store or shopping centre (see the section on index of retail saturation on page 242).

Factors in the location decision

In order to determine possible catchment areas, to forecast sales and calculate likely

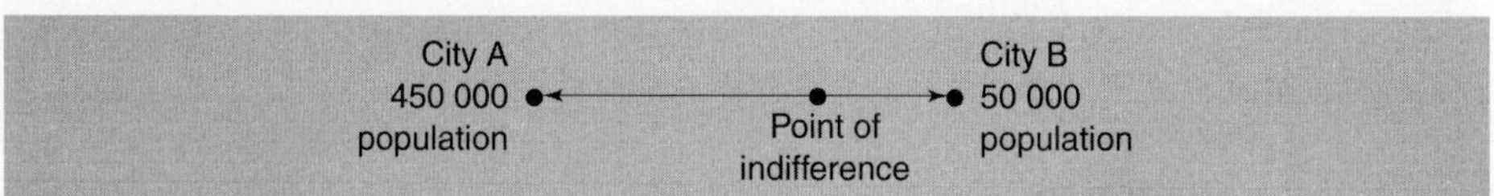

FIGURE 8.1 Catchment areas of two cities.

TABLE 8.1 Sample of location factors

Customers	Accessibility	Competition	Costs
Amount	Site visibility	How much	Building costs
Income	Pedestrian flows	Type	Rates payable
Spending patterns	Public transport	Saturation index	Labour rates
Demographics	Road network	Proximity of key	Delivery costs
Lifestyles	Parking	traders, e.g. Boots,	
Car ownership		Marks & Spencer	

profitability, a substantial number of factors may need to be investigated. The list in Table 8.1 is merely a sample.

Two types of retailing in location decisions

Two broad types of retailing figure in the location decision: proximity retailing and destination retailing.[1]

- **Proximity retailing** is all about being where the consumer is – at work, on the move, near the home or at home, e.g. petrol stations, chemists, small grocery shops, newsagents, video outlets, fast-food outlets, mail order and teleshopping. For retail outlets in this category, finding sites with maximum passing traffic and visibility is crucial, as well as the characteristics of people working/living in the immediate vicinity.
- **Destination retailing** is based on drawing consumers to your store, e.g. the major multiple grocers, Marks & Spencer in clothing, Toys R Us, B & Q and 'discount' retailing in general. Mobile, car-owning consumers pressed for time are attracted by this type of retailing, e.g. out-of-town shopping centres.

The criteria for deciding which category a retailer falls into can be seen in Figure 8.2.

Location assessment techniques

Techniques for assessing a location of a retail outlet range from simple to sophisticated. One retailer of convenience stores and tobacconists swears by a very simple method of assessing a site's viability: he counts the passers-by during a five minute period at the busiest time of the week, invariably between 11am and 1pm on a Friday or Saturday. He commented that,

> If we had a site where 100 people passed within five minutes, then that would equate to £10 000 turnover a week. Two hundred people would represent £20 000. As a rule of thumb it is pretty accurate.[2] Other factors would come into play such as a preference for being next to shops with a high customer flow, e.g. bakers or greengrocers. It may not be very scientific according to the retailer, but it worked.

The next step up would be to use a checklist of factors similar to those in Table 8.1. For a potential site each factor could be rated on a scale of 1 to 10 (1 = poor, 10 =

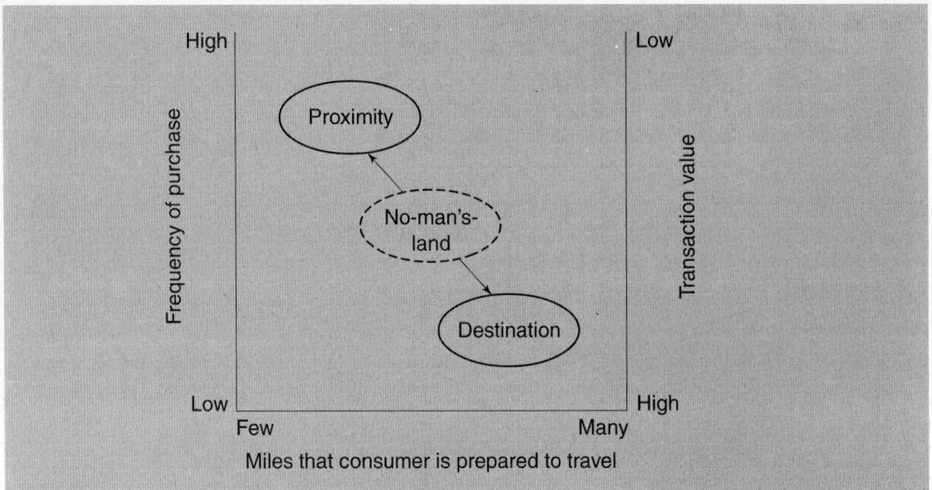

FIGURE 8.2 Polarization: consumer behaviour, retail offer. Source: Wileman, A., 'Destination retailing', *International Journal of Retail and Distribution Management*, Vol. 21, no. 1, 1993.

excellent). The final score would serve as a basis for deciding whether or not to proceed. This approach would be regarded as grossly inadequate for locating superstores, largely because of the size of the investment involved and the profit required to secure a return on that investment. Destination retailing, as previously referred to, requires much greater accuracy in determining a location.

Catchment area analysis

Catchment area analysis coupled with the analogue method (a comparison of similar stores in the group) together serve as a useful basis for forecasting sales of a proposed superstore. A superstore wanting to locate a new site may turn to catchment area analysis. The basic framework is shown in Table 8.2.

The columns of Table 8.2 require some explanation:

- Column 1: although expressed in time bands it could equally be stated in terms of distance.
- Column 2 could be broken down into socio-economic groups, age bands, car ownership, etc.
- Column 3 would initially be calculated by multiplying per capita expenditure on food by the population figure. More detailed analysis would determine per capita expenditure in different consumer categories multiplied by the number of such consumers in the various time bands. The superstore, for example, may be looking to attract the higher socio-economic groups.
- Columns 4 and 5 enable an assessment to be made as to whether the area is over-stored, under-stored or about right (see index of retail saturation later in this chapter).

TABLE 8.2 Framework for catchment area analysis

(1) Travel time (minutes)	(2) Population	(3) Weekly potential sales	(4) Competition (total square footage)	(5) Square footage per head	(6) Forecast sales
0–9.9					
10–19.9					
20–29.9					

- Column 6: comparing data from a number of similar stores in the group (analogue method) will allow a forecast to be made. The forecast will show the levels of penetration in each of the travel bands, taking competition into account. Whether or not the store development proceeds will depend on the sales required to make it a viable proposition.

Regression analysis

Superstores may also turn to regression analysis for forecasting sales. Once again, existing stores similar to the proposed new store are used to estimate an equation relating variations in sales to a set of variables, e.g. population, competition store size. A hypothetical example will illustrate the procedure. Let:

Y = retail sales
X_1 = population (within 20 minutes' drive time)
X_2 = competition (floorspace of all stores over 20 000 ft^2 within 20 minutes' drive time)
b_1, b_2 = regression coefficients
a = intercept value

Twenty-five observations from analogous stores give us the following regression equation:

$$\begin{aligned} Y &= a + b_1X_1 - b_2X_2 \\ &= 200\,000 + 0.74X_1 - 1.35X_2 \end{aligned}$$

The overall explanatory power of the regression equation above is known as the **coefficient of determination**, r^2, which for this equation is 0.83. (This figure of 0.83 is in turn the squared value of the correlation coefficient, r, which in this example would be 0.91. Therefore $0.91^2 = 0.83$.)

What does $r^2 = 0.83$ mean? An r^2 of 0.83 means that 83 per cent of the differences in sales amongst the 25 analogous stores can be explained by variations in population and competition. Only 17 per cent is left unexplained (owing to some other factors, e.g. income levels, promotional expenditure, product range). Thus a very positive relationship exists between sales and population competition.

For the regression coefficients: b_1 is equal to 0.74, which means that for an increase of one in the population sales will increase by 0.74. On the other hand, a b_2 of -1.35 means that for an increase of one square foot in floorspace, sales will decrease by 1.35. Using its own population and competition figures, a proposed new superstore can use the above equation to estimate sales.

Whereas superstores look at travel times and distance proximity, retailers look to geodemographic profiles for understanding catchment areas. More specifically, proximity retailers wish to know the types of people in the immediate vicinity of the proposed site, as it is from here that the vast proportion of its business will come. Geodemographic systems like ACORN can provide detailed information on the catchment area, e.g. consumer characteristics, consumption patterns, suggestions on product ranges. Statistical data and maps can show the preponderance and distribution of, say, ACORN types within a city, town or village. Further analysis leads on to market size and sales potential.

Index of retail saturation

The retail opportunity in an area cannot be accurately assessed unless the competitive structure is studied. A catchment area can be under-stored, over-stored, or saturated. An under-stored area has too few stores selling specific goods or services to satisfy the needs of its population. An over-stored area has so many stores that some retailers are unable to earn an adequate profit. A saturated area has just enough retail facilities to satisfy the needs of its population.

One general ratio that has been developed to measure store saturation in an area is the index of retail saturation. The calculation can be made as follows:

$$\mathrm{IRS}_i = \frac{\mathrm{C}_i \times \mathrm{RE}_i}{\mathrm{RF}_i}$$

where

IRS_i = index of retail saturation for area i
C_i = number of customers in area i for the product/service category
RE_i = retail expenditures per customer in area i for the product/service category
RF_i = total retail square footage in area i allocated to the product/service category

Consider the following example of food stores saturation in a catchment area. There are 18 000 consumers in the area and they spend, on average, £15 per week in food stores. There are three stores serving the market with a total of 30 000 square feet. Hence:

$$\mathrm{IRS} = \frac{18\,000 \times £15}{30\,000} = £9$$

The revenue of £9 per square foot of selling area measured against the revenue per square foot necessary to break even provides the measure of saturation.

TABLE 8.3 Using the index of retail saturation

	Catchment area		
	1	2	3
Number of customers buying annually	60 000	30 000	10 000
Average annual purchases per customer	£60	£75	£100
Total square footage (including the proposed store)	20 000	15 000	7 500
Index of retail saturation (including the proposed store)	180	150	133
Total square footage (excluding the proposed store)	15 000	10 000	2 500
Index of retail saturation (excluding the proposed store)	240	225	400

The use of the IRS can also be illustrated by an analysis of three catchment areas under consideration by a home furnishings retailer. The company has predetermined that its sales must be at least £160 per square foot of store space to be profitable. The catchment area chosen will be the one that yields the best index of retail store saturation. In this case, the retailer selects catchment area 1 which has an index of saturation of £180 (Table 8.3).

When calculating the index, the retailer must remember to include the proposed store. If that store is not included, the relative value of each area may be distorted. If the proposed store is excluded in Table 8.3, then area 3 has the best level of sales per square foot (£400). However, this area is not desirable after the prospective store is added to the computation. It should be noted that sales per square foot decline most when new outlets are added to a small area. The retailer should also examine whether a new store will expand the total market or not. The data in Table 8.3 assume that sales will remain the same. In the food retailing industry there is a rule of thumb which states that there should be one square foot of retail space for each head of population living in a catchment area. So 50 000 people should attract 50 000 square footage, but it does not always work out as neatly as that.

Merchandise planning

Retailers need to determine what stock to carry, how much, when to reorder and so on. In addition, they need to ensure a balance between stocks and sales. Estimates of sales form the basis of the merchandise plan, and to ensure that actual purchasing is done according to that plan retailers maintain what is known as an open-to-buy (OTB) control. Retailers aim to:

- Limit the amount of stock held
- Improve stock turnover
- Avoid out-of-stock situations

The OTB system is used by many retailers to control the quantities purchased within particular time periods and product groups.[3]

Calculating OTB in value terms

It is a straightforward calculation expressed by the following equation:

Open-to-buy = Merchandise needed − Merchandise available

More specifically it is calculated as:

Merchandise needed:		Planned sales
	+	Planned reductions
	+	Planned EOM stock
	=	Total merchandise needed
Merchandise available:	−	Planned BOM stock
	=	Planned purchases
	−	Outstanding orders
	=	£ Open-to-buy

where 'planned reductions' includes employee discounts, shrinkage and markdowns, EOM means end of month and BOM means beginning of month. The buyer must therefore plan purchases to ensure sufficient stock to cover sales, reductions and EOM inventory.

Calculating OTB in volume terms

Volume open-to-buy is the desired number of items to be purchased. To obtain this figure we must consider the following:

- **Reserve (R)**. A safety factor in the event that sales exceed expectations; expressed in either number of weeks or as a specific quantity.
- **Delivery period (DP)**. The time between the date of order and receipt of delivery.
- **Reorder period (RP)**. Represents the frequency with which a particular item will be reordered.
- **Rate of sale (S)**. The quantity of an item that the buyer anticipates will sell during a particular period of time.
- **Minimum stock (Min)**. Indicates the amount to be on hand at all times to avoid out-of-stock before delivery. It can be calculated in weeks or units:

  Min stock (weeks) = Reserve + Delivery period (R + DP)
  Min stock (units) = Reserve + Delivery period × Rate of sale (R + DP)S

  Maximum stock (Max) is equal to the minimum stock available at all times plus the amount of stock that might be sold during the time elapsing before the next reorder point. It too can be calculated in weeks or units:

$$\text{Max stock (weeks)} = R + DP + RP$$
$$\text{Max stock (units)} = R + DP + RP \times S$$

It is now possible to determine the OTB in units as follows:

$$\begin{aligned}\text{OTB (in units)} &= \text{Merchandise needed} - \text{Merchandise available}\\ &= \text{Max (units)} - (\text{Stock on hand} + \text{Stock on order})\\ &= \text{Max (units)} - (\text{OH} + \text{OO})\end{aligned}$$

Two further equations complete the picture:

$$\text{Average stock} = \text{Reserve} + \tfrac{1}{2}\,\text{Reorder period}$$

$$\text{Stock turnover} = \frac{\text{Sales}}{\text{Average stock}}$$

Example using the formulae

A retail departmental buyer wants to determine the unit OTB and the unit annual stock turnover for a £19.95 item. The following information is available:

Rate of sale (S)	20 per week
Reserve (R)	3 weeks
Delivery period (DP)	3 weeks
Reorder period (RP)	5 weeks
Stock on hand (OH)	72 units
Stock on order (OO)	24 units

Solution

$$\text{OTB} = \text{Max} - (\text{OH} + \text{OO})$$

$$\begin{aligned}\text{Max} &= (\text{R} + \text{DP} + \text{RP}) \times \text{S}\\ &= (3 + 3 + 5) \times 20\\ &= 220 \text{ units}\end{aligned}$$

$$\begin{aligned}\therefore \text{OTB} &= 220 - (72 + 24)\\ &= 124 \text{ units}\end{aligned}$$

$$\text{Stock turnover} = \frac{\text{Sales}}{\text{Average stock}}$$

$$\text{Annual sales} = 52 \times 20 = 1040$$

$$\begin{aligned}\text{Average stock (weeks)} &= \text{R} + \tfrac{1}{2}\,\text{RP}\\ &= 3 + (\tfrac{1}{2} \times 5)\\ &= 5\tfrac{1}{2} \text{ weeks}\end{aligned}$$

$$\text{Average stock (units)} = 5\tfrac{1}{2} \times 20$$
$$= 110$$
$$\text{Annual stock turnover} = \frac{1040}{110}$$
$$= 9.5$$

Planning model stocks

The planning of the merchandise assortment in terms of its breadth and width can be accomplished by a retailer in one of two ways, depending on the type and classification of merchandise.

Basic stock list

This type of planning is found primarily in staple merchandise (books, confectionery, hosiery, cosmetics) where a greater degree of stability exists in the various selection factors. It is also referred to as a periodic fill-in or staple stock list. The maintenance of the stock is dependent on a system of periodic reordering of the units by controlling the upper and lower limits of the assortment. Since the periodic fill-in of staple stock is the process of building to a maximum stock, you will recall from the previous section that:

$$\begin{aligned}\text{Maximum stock} &= \{\text{Reserve (weeks)} + \text{Delivery period (weeks)} \\ &\quad + \text{Reorder period (weeks)}\} \times \text{S} \\ &= (\text{R} + \text{DP} + \text{RP}) \times \text{S}\end{aligned}$$

and

$$\text{Open-to-buy} = \text{Max} - (\text{OH} + \text{OO})$$

Example of periodic fill-in

The buyer of a ladies hosiery department uses a system of periodic reordering for her £4.99 price line of ladies tights. Table 8.4 shows the data available. For a period of, say, three weeks the reorder form would be as shown in Table 8.5.

The amount of stock on order (100) or open-to-buy is the same amount that had been sold during the previous period. Under this plan of periodic reordering, the retailer is constantly building to a maximum and subsequently replacing items which would have been sold.

Model stock plans

This type of planning for a store's merchandise assortment is used primarily for items classified as shopping goods for which consumers shop around to compare prices,

TABLE 8.4 Ladies hosiery department

	Short	Medium	Long	Extra long
Rate of sale	24	40	30	12
Delivery period (weeks)	1	1	1	1
Reorder period (weeks)	2	2	2	2
Reserve (weeks)	1	1	1	1

TABLE 8.5 Periodic reorder form

Size	Maximum stock	Weeks								
			1			2			3	
		OH	OO	S	OH	OO	S	OH	OO	S
Short	96	48	48	21	75	21	36	60	36	30
Medium	160	90	70	36	124	36	48	112	48	40
Long	120	70	50	24	96	24	40	80	40	36
Extra long	48	10	38	12	36	12	18	30	18	15

quality, colours and any other selection factors deemed important. Such goods include furniture, shoes and clothing. The importance of this type of planning becomes evident when the selection problem of the buyer is realized, namely choosing from the ever-increasing number of colours, styles, patterns, fabrics, etc. Figure 8.3 is a model stock plan for a sweaters classification.[4] Assume that only two customer-attracting features are important – synthetic and natural fibres.

Even though the illustration is simple, Figure 8.3 shows that in order to offer customers only one sweater in each assortment-width factor (in both synthetic and natural fibres), 270 sweaters (2 × 5 × 3 × 3 × 3) are needed. The depth plan involves deciding how many sweaters are needed in each of the five assortment factors. If the retailer believes that 90 per cent of sales will be in synthetic fibres, then 720 sweaters will be needed (800 × 0.9 – 720). You can also see that the retailer will have 144 of size A, 58 in colour A, 29 at price point A and 12 in design A.

On the surface, the model stock plan (in units) appears a rather routine approach to planning. However, reaching decisions as to the percentage relationships amongst the various assortment factors represents a challenge. Being out of stock or left with significant amounts of unsold stock are situations that retailers wish to avoid. Sales forecasting accuracy and effective stock replenishment policies aim to minimize the occurrence of such situations.

Performance measures in retailing

A range of measures is used to evaluate performance. The appropriateness of each measure will depend on the retailing situation. However, the following are most commonly in use:

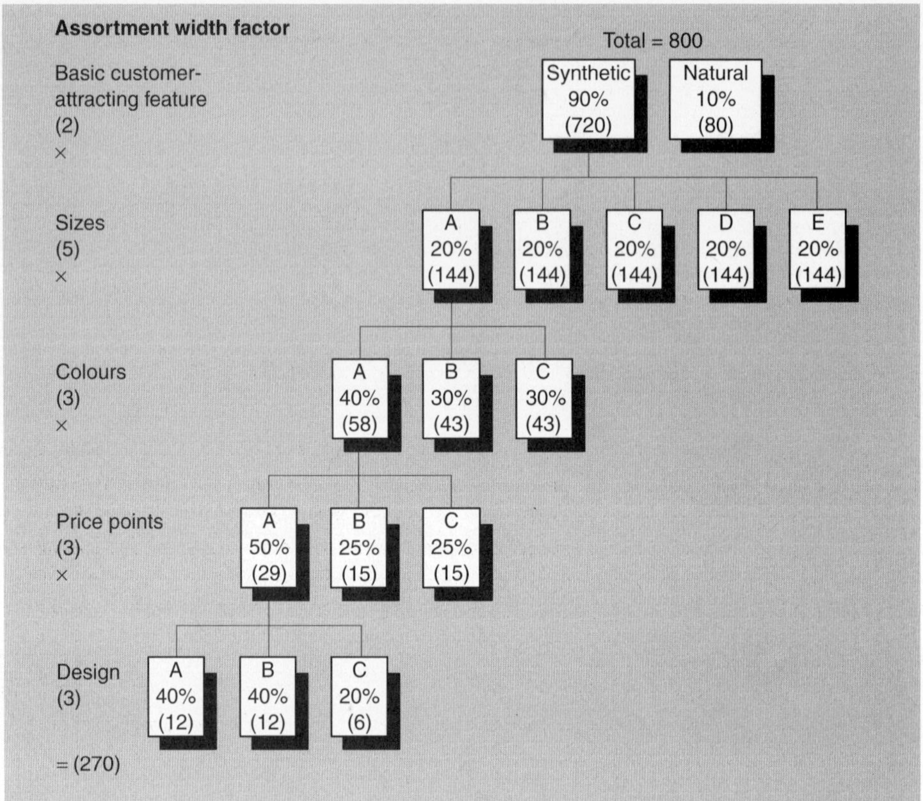

FIGURE 8.3 Model stock of sweaters. Source: Mason, J.B., Mayer, M.L. and Ezell, H.F., *Retailing*, Business Publications, 1988.

- **Profit (or sales) per square foot**. Whatever the type of retail outlet, this is the longest established measure as it indicates how well a retailer uses its main asset, space[5] (see Table 8.6).
- **Direct product profitability (DPP)**. DPP is becoming more popular as it is seen as a better measure than sales or profit per square foot because more factors are involved. The measure is particularly attractive to superstores selling fast-moving items, e.g. groceries. (See section on DPP below.)
- **Profit (or sales) per employee**. This is a productivity measure which is more appropriate in non-food retailing as employees are in a position to influence the level of sales.
- **Average transaction value**. This is total sales divided by the number of transactions. A useful measure of success, as a high figure implies that the product offer matches

TABLE 8.6 Sales per square foot

Food[a]	£	Non-food	£
Sainsbury	18.53	Richer Sounds	5840.3
Tesco	17.00	Dixons	653.5
Safeway	12.86	Scottish Power	450.0
Asda	12.38	Comet	432.9
KwikSave	9.10		

[a] In supermarkets, sales per linear foot is also used, recognizing the number of facings allocated to any item.
Source: *Corporate Intelligence on Retailing: The Retail Rankings*, 1995.

the customer's expectations and that the width and depth of the store's offer are about right.

- **Customer flow**. The busier the store, the more chance of a sale. Various gadgets are now in operation to assess the flow of shoppers. They can be used to gauge the effects on trade of seasonal factors, such as the weather and school holidays, and promotional activity. In stores, knowing customer flow can give an indication of how many sales staff are needed at particular times. Customer flow gadgets can also record the number of times that shoppers pick up and put down products and show which areas of a store draw in the most customers.
- **Percentage of takings**. This measure shows how sales are distributed across the range on offer. It may well be that a large percentage of the takings comes from a quite small number of items (the Pareto effect).
- **Shrinkage**. This is the percentage of potential sales that was never achieved owing to theft, spoilage, etc.

To further the analytical process a table can be drawn up with the performance measures along the top and products, or even stores, down the side. Data can then be entered and an assessment made. It is important to remember that the performance data above cannot provide real insight into the reasons for good or bad performance. For that we need to look elsewhere, e.g. site characteristics, catchment area characteristics.

Direct product profitability

For many years food retailers in particular have wanted to know the profitability of the products that they sell through each store. The answers were based on gross profits which provided only a general idea about which products were profitable; they could not identify loss-makers at the till-end of the business. The concept of direct product profitability (DPP) has been with the food industry since the 1960s. Developments in computer technology have enabled DPP to be taken seriously by manufacturers and retailers as a viable decision support tool. Recent developmental work on DPP applications has been undertaken by Alison Pinnock formerly of the Institute of Grocery Distribution.

What is DPP?

One of the simplest ways to describe DPP is to view it as a system for refining gross margins into net contributions, where the contributions are to overheads and profit for individual stock-keeping items.

In simple terms, a DPP analysis draws a profit and loss statement for each product or category considered. Only those costs which are being directly incurred by the product are allocated, e.g. the cost of taking it off the lorry, storing it, unpacking it, stacking it on the shelves, even how much shelf space it takes up and how long it takes to shift.

Calculation of DPP

As already stated, the traditional method of calculating a product's profit contribution has long been gross profit, defined as:

$$\text{Sales price} - \text{Invoice costs} = \text{Gross profit}$$

The weakness of this approach is that it does not take account of the direct cost borne by the retailer. DPP allows such costs to be captured and accounted for. The calculation of DPP is portrayed in Figure 8.4.

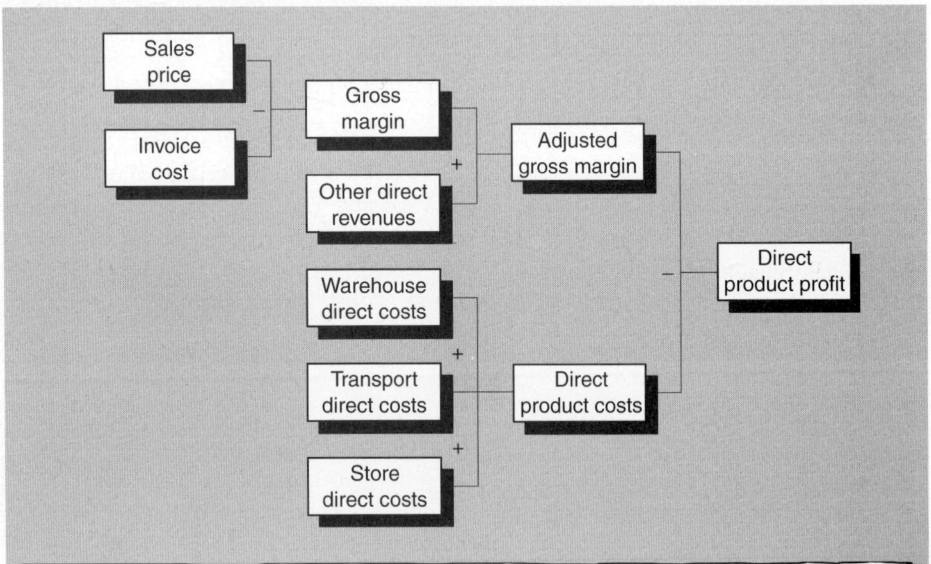

FIGURE 8.4 Calculation of direct product profitability. Source: Institute of Grocery Distribution.

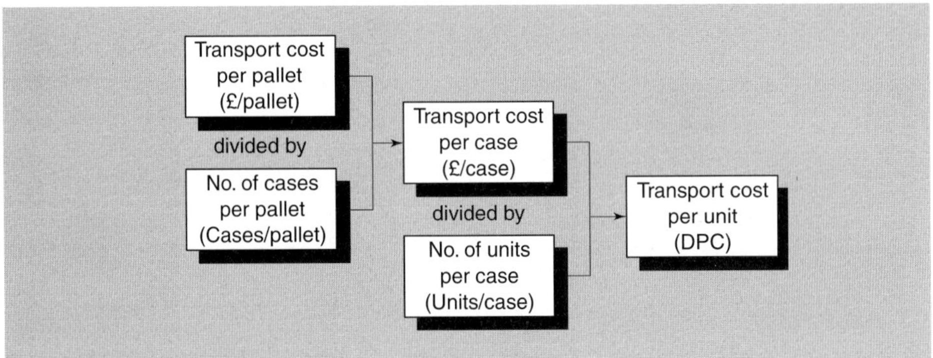

FIGURE 8.5 Direct product cost analysis: transporting goods from warehouse to store (single-product pallet). Source: Euro DPP Model.

The gross margin is calculated, and to this any other direct revenues are added. These might include manufacturer deals, promotions, allowances, prompt payment discounts, etc., to reflect the true prices paid for the product. As can be seen, the crux of DPP lies in the direct product costs in the areas of warehouse, transport and store. Within each of these it is necessary to identify and measure costs that are directly attributable to the handling of each item. For example, when the supplier delivery arrives at the warehouse, each pallet is unloaded, and a handling cost is incurred. The whole journey of each product needs to be followed in this way in order to find the true direct costs of handling and storage. Figure 8.5 illustrates how the cost of transporting a product between the warehouse and store is allocated.

Where two items have the same gross margin, say 20 pence, a retailer is indifferent as they both appear to contribute the same amount towards fixed costs. A DPP analysis shows a very different picture (Table 8.7). Item A may be on a shrinkwrapped tray of 12, delivered into central warehouse. Item B may be in a carton of 24, delivered direct to store only once every 3 weeks. Obviously the retailer would prefer to sell more of item A since it is more profitable.

TABLE 8.7 DPP calculation

	Item A £	Item B £
Gross margin	0.20	0.20
DPCs	0.05	0.15
	0.15	0.05

DPP merchandising decision matrix

When conducting a DPP study, one of the most useful tools to use is the decision matrix (Figure 8.6).

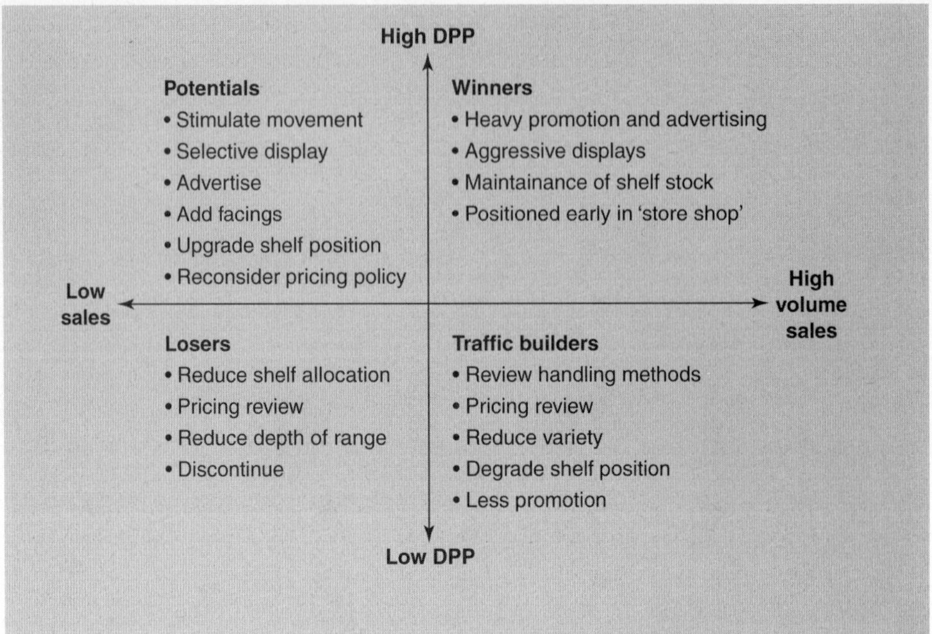

FIGURE 8.6 DPP decision matrix. Source: Institute of Grocery Distribution.

The most desirable sector of the matrix for a product to be located is in the winners category, an example of which is health and beauty. Clearly, every retailer has a range of performers in its portfolio. Some products have to fall into one of the three other quadrants on the matrix, e.g. sugar in traffic builders, chilled ready meals in potentials. To help improve their performance, managers can investigate the variety of responses shown.

In the retail sector, shelf space management currently is, and is expected to remain, the principal use of DPP. Major supermarkets, for example, have thousands of product lines: Sainsbury 19 000, Tesco 38 000, Asda 22 000. When the different types of packaging – such as twin-packs, four-packs – of each is taken into account, the total number of different stock keeping units (SKUs) can rise to around 100 000 or more. With a DPP study needing to be done for each, there is clearly still a long way to go before the nut is finally cracked. Control of shelf space is a preoccupation of fast-moving consumer goods (FMCG) manufacturers because for low value purchases, presence in-store is often a critical influence. Certain shelf space is proven to sell more goods than others: 130–130 cm (4.3–4.5 ft) off the ground on the left is considered the key site, and supermarkets often ask suppliers for a cash inducement or extra discount to place their products there. End-of-aisle sites are also key selling areas as sales are often five times higher from here than from a mid-aisle position. Stores often move goods that they particularly want to sell, such as those nearing their sell-by date, to these sites.

Space management, then, is the maximization of sales, profit and stock turn from a predefined space. Apart from the standard square footage measure of space utilization, superstores look to shelf management and sales per linear foot as a measure of performance. The focus of attention is the planogram, which is a map of how products should be displayed on a fixture (Figure 8.7). Specifically, retailers need to address the question of how many facings per item, e.g. Golden Wonder Ready Salted, and how many items should be stocked in each facing.

Importance of people

However well a retail outlet locates itself, carries desirable merchandise at attractive prices and provides a pleasing environment, the people who work within it (management and employees) merit attention. The culture of any establishment ('the way we do things around here') deserves study not only for its impact on sales and customer service but also for the related and equally important matter of morale, motivation and general job satisfaction. How employees are treated by management should form an important part of any such study. The competence of the management/supervisory team will be crucial.

In recognition of the need for standards in management, the Management Charter Initiative (MCI) was formed in 1988. It is a non-profit organization and its aim is to improve the performance of UK organizations by improving the quality of the work of their managers. The MCI management standards are nationally recognized yardsticks measuring good management practice. The focus is on whether managers are competent to do their job. Competence is gained from:

- The experience of actually doing the job.
- Knowledge about and understanding of the management function, e.g. from training course, textbooks.
- Personal qualities, e.g. judgement, self-confidence, communication skills and the ability to work constructively with colleagues.

Notwithstanding the MCI's admirable objectives, the question of management standards will remain a thorny issue.

'Bottom-up' assessment

Few companies use one of the most practical and efficient methods for diagnosing management problems and improving performance: employee appraisals. Who, after all, knows the quality of a manager better than those who are managed? The retailer W.H. Smith is one of the few to have moved into this area. The format for an employee survey varies. Exhibit 8.1 illustrates one approach.[6]

At the very least, bottom-up assessment provided feedback to managers that they would not ordinarily have. Management will learn about 'what's really on the minds of the employees'. If there is a discrepancy of view, it is much better that it is brought to the surface. In one study,[7] managers who perceived themselves to be effective at 'providing

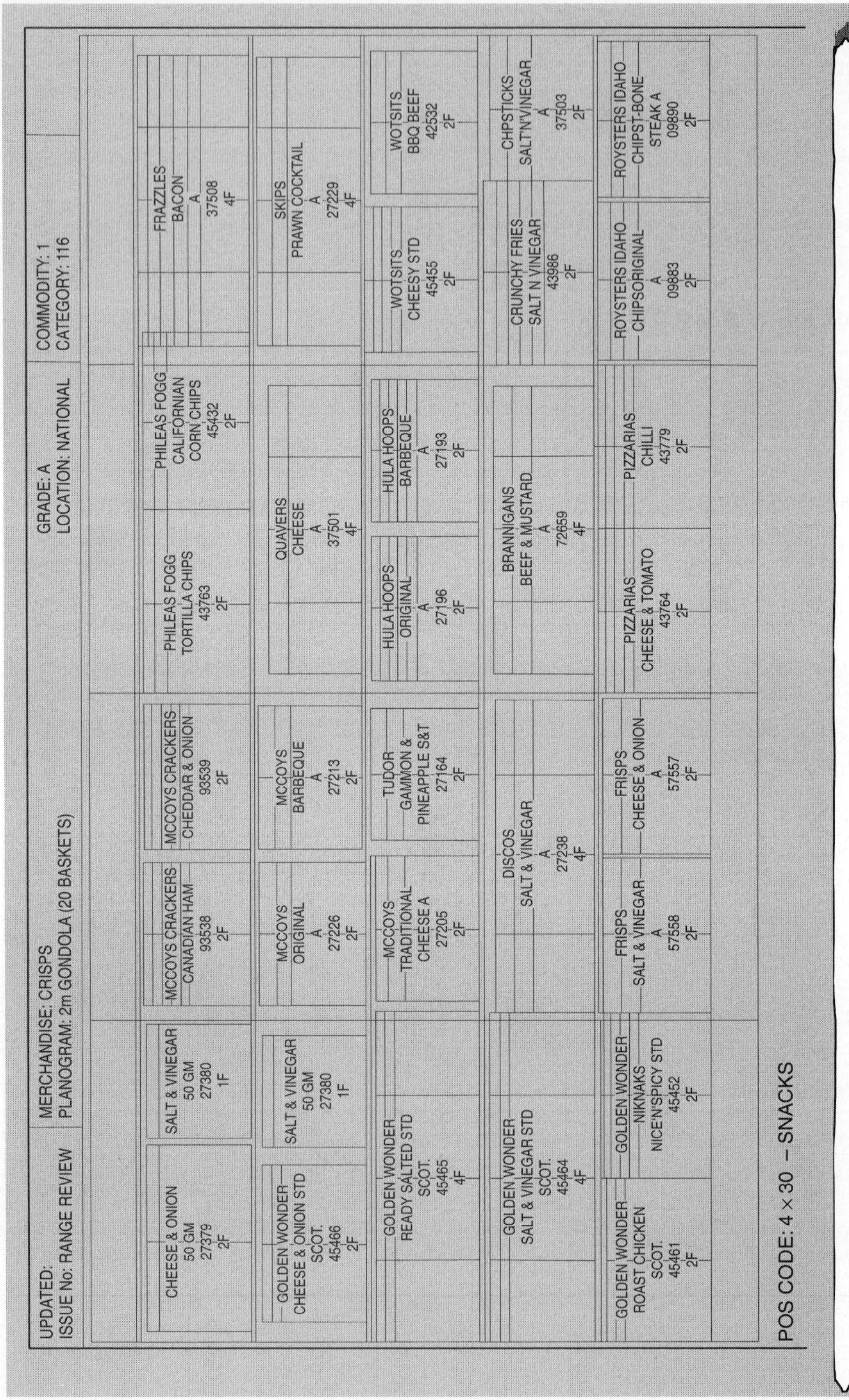

FIGURE 8.7 Planogram for snacks.

Exhibit 8.1 Format for employee appraisal of boss

Is your boss . . .	Agree strongly 1	Agree slightly 2	Neither agree nor disagree 3	Disagree slightly 4	Disagree strongly 5	Not applicable 6
Prepared to listen to you						
Approachable						
Someone to turn to if you have a work-related problem						
Someone who makes you feel you matter						
Courteous						
Someone who keeps you motivated						
Able to maintain discipline						
Prepared to make decisions						
Honest with you						
Consistent						
Fair						
Prepared to praise where praise is due						

Source: Thompson, F., 'Keeping bosses up to the mark', *Financial Times*, 10 February 1992.

clear instruction and explanation to employees when giving assignment' were not perceived as such by those persons supposedly on the receiving end of the instructions.

Leadership styles

Whenever the subject of the role of management surfaces, people often resort to the question, 'are you Theory X or Theory Y?' According to McGregor,[8] a US academic, managers were likely to hold one orientation or other. A Theory X manager would hold the view that people do not like work, avoid it, have little ambition, try to avoid responsibility and need firm direction, control and coercion. A Theory Y manager would maintain that under the right conditions people not only work hard, showing commitment and talent, but also seek increased responsibility and challenge. (Use Exhibit 8.2 to test yourself to see if you are X or Y.[9] Give yourself 4 points for strongly agree, 3 for agree, 1 for disagree and 0 for strongly disagree.)

Exhibit 8.2 Theory X or Y believer

1. Almost everyone could probably improve his/her job performance quite a bit if he/she really wanted to.
2. It is unrealistic to expect people to show the same enthusiasm for their work as for their favourite leisure-time activities.
3. Even when given encouragement by the boss, very few people show the desire to improve themselves on the job.
4. If you give people enough money, they are less likely to worry about such intangibles as status or individual recognition.
5. Usually when people talk about wanting more responsible jobs, they really mean they want more money and status.
6. Being tough with people will usually get them to do what you want.
7. Because most people do not like to make decisions on their own, it is hard to get them to assume responsibility.
8. A good way to get people to do more work is to crack down on them once in a while.
9. It weakens a person's prestige to admit that a subordinate has been right and he/she wrong.
10. The most effective supervisor is one who gets the results that management expects, regardless of the methods used in handling people.
11. It is too much to expect that people will try to do a good job without being prodded by the boss.
12. The boss who expects his/her people to set their own standards for superior performance will probably find they do not set them very high.
13. If people do not use much imagination or ingenuity on the job, it is probably because relatively few people have much of either.
14. One problem in asking for the ideas of subordinates is that their perspective is too limited for their suggestions to be of much practical value.
15. It is only human nature for people to try to do as little work as they can get away with.

- **Score under 20** and you are an optimist.
  You probably trust your subordinates and use a wide range of rewards. You may prefer group participation in decision-making and like people to be well informed.
- **Score 21–30** and we see more caution with substantial, but not complete, confidence and trust in subordinates. You wish to keep control of most important decisions.
- **Score 31–45** and some may consider you a benevolent autocrat. You have a rather condescending confidence and trust such as a master has in a servant. You tend to believe in economic motives and do not fraternise with your staff.
- **Score 45 and above** and face it, you are a cynic about the average worker: all stick and no carrot.

Source: Furnham, A., 'Are you an optimistic or pessimistic boss?', *Financial Times*, 1 September 1993.

Some would argue that the truly supportive boss employs what has been termed Theory Z (the contingency approach: it depends). The argument is that, of the three (X, Y, Z), it is the only one that makes practical sense. If a manager treats all employees or circumstances in an autocratic (Theory X) or a democratic (Theory Y) fashion, he or she would be likened to the doctor who gives the same treatment to all patients, regardless of their condition. For some the treatment may be helpful; for others it may do harm. The most effective treatment will be dependent upon the individual patient's condition.

Transaction analysis

One tool that aids understanding of various management philosophies and leadership styles is transaction analysis. Developed by Eric Berne,[10] a Canadian psychologist, it is a communication-based theory. Through watching people interact he noticed that sometimes people act like children, sometimes like adults and sometimes like parents. Each represents an ego state which is defined as a consistent pattern of feeling, thinking and behaving.

Parent ego state

The parent ego state is divided into two parts: critical and nurturing. The former tends to put people down whereas the latter tends to build them up. The critical parent is often out to 'nail' an employee. The nurturing parent is in the business of finding solutions rather than faults.

- 'I give you a simple job to do and what do you do – you don't do it the right way.' (critical parent)
- 'OK, here's the problem. How can I help you correct it?' (nurturing parent)

Child ego state

We are all 'kids at heart' the saying goes. The child ego is the feeling part of the personality. Again it is divided into two parts: the adapted child and the free child. The adapted child with whom managers or supervisors have to contend is either the overly submissive or dependent employee or the overly rebellious one. The former refuses to stand on his or her own two feet and must constantly check with the boss even regarding trivial matters. The overly rebellious feels compelled constantly to work against authority even for no logical reason. When told to do A, he or she will invariably do B. The critical parent and the adapted child often go together.

The free child is able to express feelings the way they really are, not adapted to meet the wishes of the critical parent. Their expressions are often of a more mature nature. Of course, managers/supervisors act as adapted or free children. An adapted child manager would be one who would not be able to make his or her own decisions ('a wishy washy manager'). A free child supervisor may say, 'I'm really excited about your work and its impact on sales.'

Adult ego state

This is the non-feeling part of the personality: it might be likened to a computer bringing in and analyzing information before generating and selecting alternatives. It is the thinking and rational side to human nature and is reflected in the individual who remains cool under fire. A supervisor can readily delegate to the adult employee. Basically, adults will be asking questions like who, what, where, when, why and how.

How managerial/supervisory styles and transaction analysis relate to each other can be seen in Figure 8.8. An explanation of the diagram follows.

In **quadrant 1** the subordinate is treated as a mature worker. Suggestions are not only appreciated but encouraged. The employee becomes involved in important decisions regarding his or her own job.

In **quadrant 2** the subordinate is viewed as lacking the competence and maturity to assume any reasonable amount of independent judgement. The managerial style is very much top-down, which often breeds what it intends to avoid – irresponsible, overly dependent workers or apathy. Treat employees like children and you often get childlike responses in return.

Quadrant 3 epitomizes the style of manager who, either through insecurity or a lack of motivation or both, refuses to take responsibility. Wishy-washy and overly submissive, this manager frequently abdicates the role of leadership to a person lower in seniority. Respect for the manager rapidly evaporates.

Quadrant 4 is truly the loser's position for any manager. Chaos abounds and the manager, lacking respect for his or her own abilities and for those of the subordinates, haphazardly frustrates everyone involved.[11]

Transaction analysis uses down-to-earth language that any supervisor or employee can relate to. Although no panacea, it is regarded as one of the greatest organizational behaviour tools to enter the world of work. The nature of transactions reflects the quality of working life in organizations, and if they are pleasant and productive then the organization and its employees should benefit. If, on the other hand, employees feel offended and defensive, productivity and morale suffer.

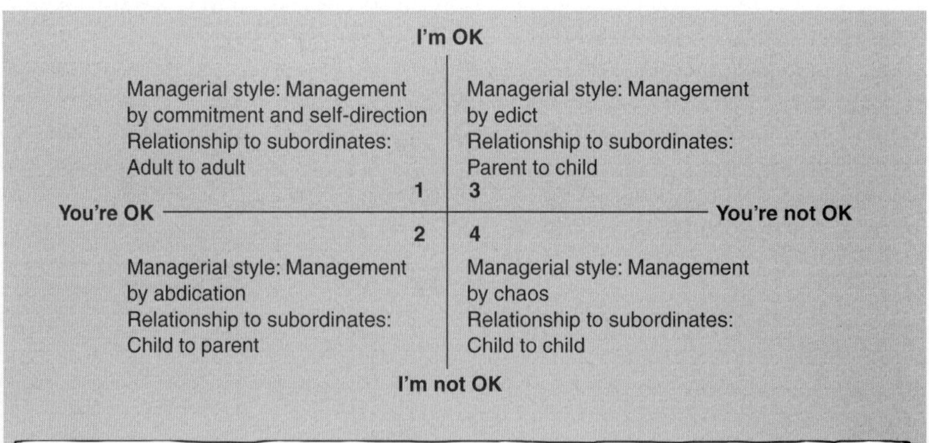

FIGURE 8.8 Management life position chart. Source: Villere, M.F., *Transactional Analysis at Work*, Prentice Hall, 1981.

Issues unique to the retailing of services

Retailers for whom much if not all of their activity and output is in the form of a service confront issues not readily experienced in the retailing of products. Such service retailers include banks, building societies, car rental and repair, hotels and restaurants, dry cleaning outlets, theatres, museums, beauty salons, hairdressers, health clubs, fitness centres, legal services and public services.

We need to remember that services possess four underlying characteristics: intangibility, inseparability, variability and perishability. From these particular issues arise others that will be of concern to service retailers.

Firstly, services are rendered and experienced. It is a process through which consumers go in interaction within the service provider. This has led to the development of the service blueprint which is basically a flowchart of the process[12] (Figure 8.9).

There are a number of essential steps in blueprinting a service.[13]

- Draw, in diagrammatic form, all the components and processes.
- Identify the fail points – where things might go wrong.
- Set executional standards – these are tolerances (band or range) set around each function and regarded as acceptable from a customer and cost viewpoint. Time to execute a particular task is a good example.
- Identify all the evidence that is available to the customer, e.g. telephone response time and manner, attitudes and appearance of employees, equipment, signs. Each of these represents an encounter point, in other words a 'moment of truth' for the customer.
- Analyze profitability – delays in service execution through errors or working too slowly affect profit.

Where to draw the line of visibility distinguishing the front office from the back office can be significant. The nature of the service and how it is delivered offers guidance: for example, a hairdresser's operation will be predominantly front office, while a credit card company operates a very large percentage of its service in the back office. Other services like a restaurant may feel ambivalent about where to draw the line. In making the distinction, a service organization needs to address the following questions:

- How much of the service does the customer need to witness/experience?
- Will greater involvement lead to more understanding and favourable impressions, i.e. improved effectiveness?
- What effect will there be on efficiency if the customer is allowed greater access to the service process?

A key factor in the debate over front versus back office dominance is customer contact. One view asserts that 'the potential efficiency of a service system is a function of the degree of customer content entailed in the creation of the service product'.[14] The formula arising from this states that:

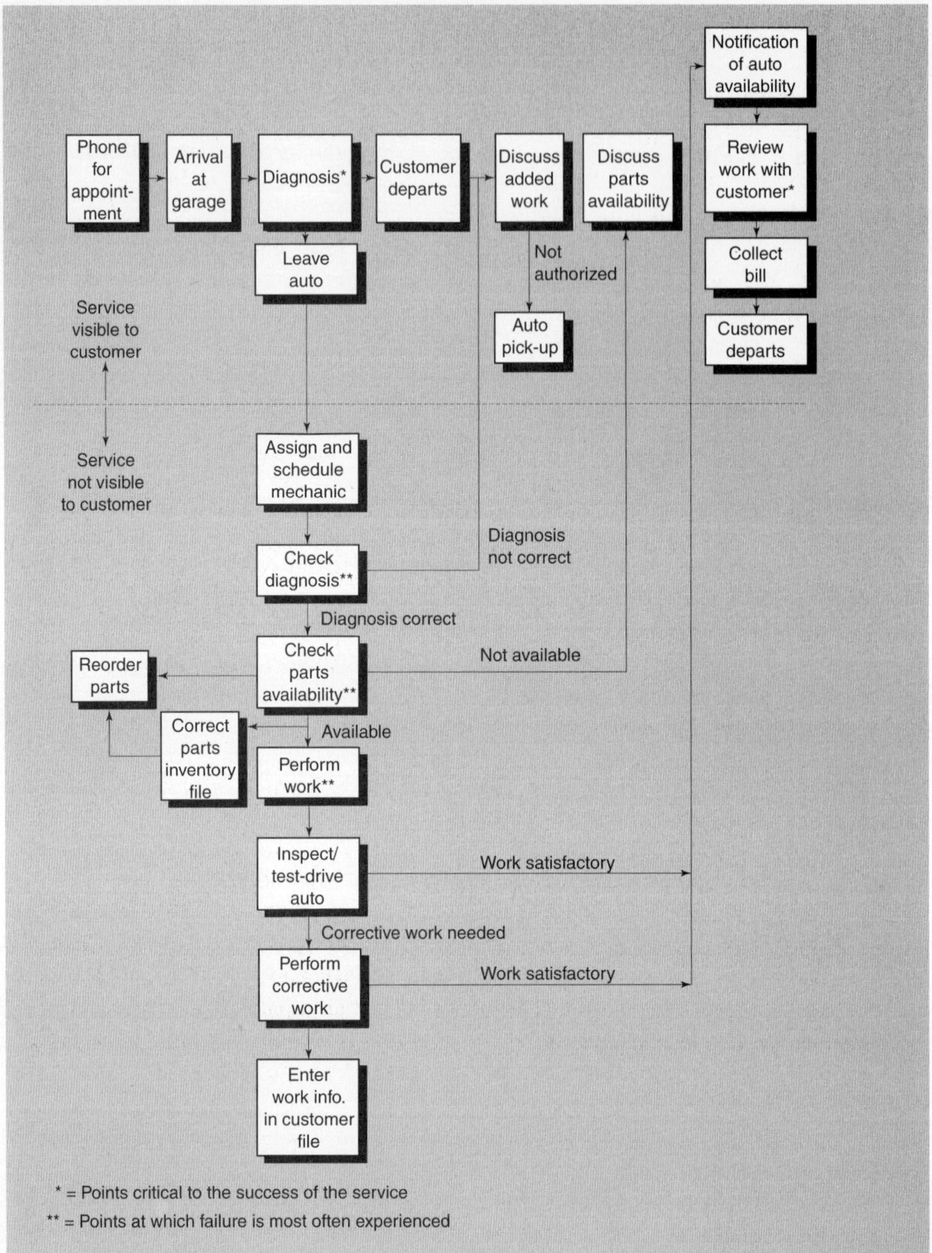

FIGURE 8.9 A process flow diagram for the auto repair business. Source: Heskett, J.L., Sasser, W.E. and Hart, C.W.L., *Service Breakthroughs: Changing the Rules of the Game*, Free Press, 1990.

$$\text{Potential facility efficiency} = f\left(1 - \frac{\text{Customer contact time}}{\text{Service creation time}}\right)$$

If we apply the formula hypothetically in two contrasting service situations – hotels (high customer contact) and financial services, e.g. an insurance claim (low customer contact) – the efficiency measure might be:

$$\text{For hotels:} 1 - \frac{2 \text{ hours}}{4 \text{ hours}} = 50\% \text{ efficiency}$$

$$\text{For insurance claims:} 1 - \frac{0.25 \text{ hours}}{2 \text{ hours}} = 87.5\% \text{ efficiency}$$

The ratio of customer contact time relative to service creation time is obviously much greater in the case of hotels, but does that mean that hotels are that much less efficient? Furthermore, if the hotel were to take an 'inefficient 8 hours' to create the service, the resulting efficiency index would be 75 per cent. The nature, as well as the amount of customer contact merits attention. Customer input to the hotel facility could be defined as rather passive, whereas a relatively low contact between insurance organization and claimant could degenerate into a protracted and acrimonious process. What all this means is that in the drive for operational efficiency and control (via back office supremacy) service organizations run the risk of neglecting (via front office impoverishment) customer expectations of what constitutes a satisfactory experience.

The author of the formula cited above (Chase) has subsequently reconsidered its value. The original view argued for shifting service activities to a remote back office in order to maximize efficiency. He now states:

> This, after all, seemed to work well for manufacturers because it kept outside influences, that is, customers, from disturbing the production process. If a technician is assembling a widget, you don't want the customer asking him what he's doing. Or if a clerk is processing forms, talking to the customer on the phone takes her away from her job. In retrospect, this closed system philosophy overlooked the fact that there are positive benefits to both the customer and the organization by having the customer closely linked to the server, even though the job is traditionally performed in the customer's absence. From an information exchange perspective, the greater the links between consumer and producer, the easier it is to understand and respond to the customer's needs.[15]

Satisfactory and dissatisfactory encounters

Service retailers, in particular, need to know what customers expect from the service experience. Specifically, they need to study what goes on during the encounter with service personnel to see if the service they provide lives up to customer expectations. A method suited to achieving that objective is the **critical incident technique**.[16] Firstly it can help identify employee behaviours that are regarded as either effective or ineffective in exchanges with customers. There are countless types of customer behaviour that may prove difficult to manage, for example unreasonable demands, demands against company policy, unacceptable treatment of employees, drunkenness.

Secondly, the critical incident technique can elicit the views of customers which may be invaluable for revealing the specific events that make for a satisfactory encounter. Critical incidents (events and behaviour) are uncovered by asking consumers the following:[17]

- Think of a time when, as a customer, you had a particularly satisfying/dissatisfying interaction with an employee of [service specified]?
- When did the incident happen?
- What specific circumstances led up to this situation?
- Exactly what did the employees say or do?
- What resulted that made you feel the interaction was satisfying/dissatisfying?

In addition to individual expression of satisfaction or dissatisfaction with a particular event or behaviour, customers may intimate their overall feelings, for example:

- Everything went right – 'a sincere and professional team effort, accommodating, polite but not pushy, warm atmosphere, courteous, efficient and professional, no waiting, best service ever received, everything was perfect'.
- Everything went wrong – 'inefficient, unprepared, slow, neither accommodating nor attentive, no assistance, unprofessional, bad decor/atmosphere.'

The script

To effect a satisfying experience, service retailers will usually resort to developing a script which has been defined as 'a predetermined, stereotyped sequence of actions that defines a well known situation'.[18] Scripts basically tell the customer what his role should be, the sequence of events and what other people are likely to do. Customer satisfaction will largely depend on whether the service received conforms to the script. The restaurant script is one to which most people can relate (Exhibit 8.3). It is perceived as a giant causal chain in which each action results in conditions that enable the next to occur. Any script will consist of a set of activities that has conventional roles, props, event sequences, standard entering conditions and standard outcomes. For each step in the process, performance can be monitored and set against organization specifications and customer expectations.

Yield management

A number of service retailers (hotels, airlines, railways) exhibit demand and operational characteristics in which:

- Capacity is relatively fixed
- The market can be fairly clearly segmented
- The services cannot be stored in any way (perishability)

Exhibit 8.3 Theoretical restaurant script

Name: Restaurant

Props: Tables, Menu, Food, Bill, Money, Tip

Roles: Customer, Waitress, Cook, Cashier, Owner

Entry conditions: Customer has money
Customer is hungry

Results: Customer has less money
Owner has more money
Customer is not hungry
Customer is satisfied/dissatisfied

Scene 1: Entering
- Customer enters restaurant
- Customer looks for table
- Customer decides where to sit
- Customer goes to table
- Customer sits down

Scene 2: Ordering
- Customer picks up menu
- Customer looks at menu
- Customer decides on food
- Customer signals waitress
- Waitress comes to table
- Customer orders food
- Waitress goes to cook
- Waitress gives food order to cook
- Cook prepares food

Scene 3: Eating
- Cook gives food to waitress
- Waitress brings food to customer
- Customer eats food

Scene 4: Exiting
- Waitress writes bill
- Waitress goes over to customer
- Waitress gives bill to customer
- Customer gives tip to waitress
- Customer goes to cashier
- Customer gives money to cashier
- Customer leaves restaurant

Source: Adapted from Schank, R.C. and Abelson, R.P., *Scripts, Plans, Goals and Understanding*, Erlbaum Associates, 1977.

- Services may be sold in advance
- The variable cost of making a sale is relatively low
- Demand can fluctuate substantially

As the capacity is largely fixed, along with the costs, the need to manage capacity as profitably as possible is evident. Yield management is a method which can help a company to sell the right unit of capacity to the right type of customer at the right time and for the right price. In effect, it is a question of how to allocate capacity – whether it is rooms in a hotel or seats on an airplane – to available demand in such a way as to maximize revenue or profit.

What is needed is a measure of the extent to which an organization's assets are achieving their full revenue-generating potential. This measure must take into account the relationship between the average price actually obtained per unit of service and the maximum price that might potentially have been charged for that same service unit – what is called the yield percentage or price efficiency. By multiplying the capacity utilization rate by the yield percentage, we can derive an **index of asset revenue-generating efficiency** (ARGE).[19] If we consider the hotel industry, the ARGE would be found from:

$$\frac{\text{Average rate of rooms sold}}{\text{Average rate potential}} \times \frac{\text{Rooms sold}}{\text{Rooms available for sale}}$$

For example, a hotel with 280 rooms sells in one night 140 rooms at £40 and a further 70 rooms at the maximum rack rate of £60. The ARGE would be:

$$\begin{aligned} \text{ARGE} &= \frac{140}{280} \times \frac{40}{60} + \frac{70}{280} \times \frac{60}{60} \\ &= 0.5 \times 0.666 + 0.25 \times 1 \\ &= 0.583 \text{ or } 58.3\%, \text{ which in revenue terms is £9794} \end{aligned}$$

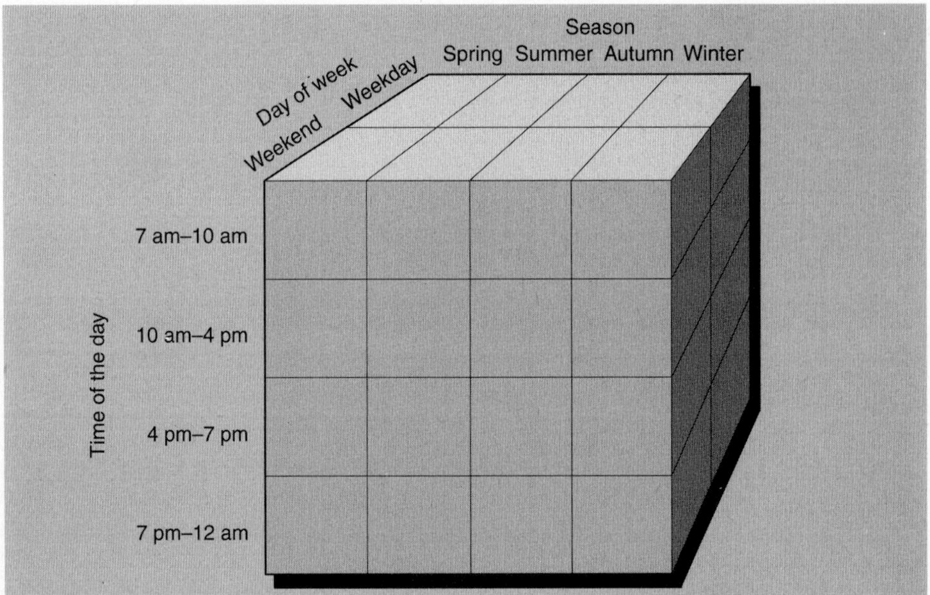

FIGURE 8.10 Variations in demand by time period.

The maximum possible revenues would be £16 800 (280 × 60).

In many situations ARGE is often a trade-off between the desire for high capacity utilization (or load factor) and the desire for selling capacity at the maximum price. The value of the ARGE approach is that it forces explicit recognition of the opportunity cost of accepting business from one segment when another might subsequently yield a higher rate. For example, should a car repair outlet process all jobs on a first come, first served basis, with a guaranteed completion time, or should it charge a premium rate for rush work, and tell customers with standard jobs to expect some variability in completion dates?

ARGE and demand patterns

To enable ARGE calculations and assessments to be made, service retailers need to classify demand periods and the variations between them. One possible classification can be seen in Figure 8.10.

In Figure 8.10, each of the 32 cells might have its own distinct demand level (at a particular price) and customer profiles. Analyses of this nature allow management to tailor capacity to meet variations in demand.

References

1. Wileman, A., 'Destination retailing', *International Journal of Retail and Distribution Management*, Vol. 21, no. 1, 1993.
2. Threlfall, K. quoted by Thornhill, J., 'Why location counts', *Financial Times*, 27 February 1992.
3. See Kneider, A.P., *Mathematics of Merchandising*, Prentice Hall, 1994.
4. Mason, J.B., Mayer, M.L. and Ezell, H.F., *Retailing*, Business Publications, 1988.
5. *Corporate Intelligence*, Research Publications Ltd, London, 1996.
6. Thompson, F., 'Keeping bosses up to the work', *Financial Times*, 10 February 1992.
7. Bernardin, H.J. and Beatty, R.W., 'Can subordinate appraisals enhance managerial productivity?', *Sloan Management Review*, Summer 1987, p. 68.
8. McGregor, D., *The Human Side of Enterprise*, McGraw-Hill, 1960.
9. Furnham, A., 'Are you an optimistic or pessimistic boss?', *Financial Times*, 1 September 1993.
10. Berne, E., *Games People Play: The Psychology of Human Relationships*, Grove Press, 1964.
11. Villere, M.F., *Transactional Analysis at Work*, Prentice Hall, 1981.
12. Heskett, J.L., Sasser, W.E. and Hart, C.W.L., *Service Breakthroughs: Changing the Rules of the Game*, Free Press, 1990, p. 107.
13. Shostack, G.L., 'Designing services that deliver', *Harvard Business Review*, January/February 1984.
14. Chase, R., 'The customer contact approach to services: theoretical bases and practical extensions', *Operations Research*, Vol. 29, no. 4, 1981.
15. Chase, R.B. and Hayes, R.H., 'Beefing up operations in service firms', *Sloan Management Review*, Fall 1991, p. 24.
16. Flanagan, J.C., 'The critical incident technique', *Psychological Bulletin*, Vol. 51, no. 4, 1954.
17. Bitner, M.J., Booms, B.H. and Terteault, M.S., 'The service encounter: diagnosing favourable and unfavourable incidents', *Journal of Marketing*, Vol. 54, January 1990.
18. Schank, R.C. and Abelson, R.P., *Scripts, Plans, Goals and Understanding*, Erlbaum Associates, 1977.
19. Lovelock, C., *Services Marketing*, Prentice Hall, 1991.

CHAPTER 9

Data presentation

WHAT IS IT ABOUT?

In marketing, as in most areas of business, the need to handle data will inevitably arise from time to time. The skilful presentation of data can be a vital tool to marketers, although a flawed data presentation can swiftly destroy credibility.

Vital as correct presentation is, before data can be presented at all, they need to be analyzed and interpreted by the presenter to determine the messages that they have to convey. Frequently, data do not arrive in a form that is convenient for analysis, and the presenter's first task is to organize the data into a manageable form.

This chapter takes the reader through the three skills of **data organization, data analysis** and **data presentation**. The various types of data are defined and appropriate methods of analysis and presentation described for each.

Statistical measures of analysis and spread are explained, and a brief reference is made to the size of possible errors when using sample data. Manual techniques are given, but reference is also made to statistical calculators and to computer spreadsheets. The data examples used are the responses to a travel agency questionnaire and a set of regional sales data.

Because, like any numerical skill, data analysis cannot be mastered merely by reading, the material in this chapter is interspersed with short activities for the reader to attempt and to learn from. These appear after each topic has been explained and should, preferably, be tried immediately. Solutions are given at the end of the chapter.

What are data?

In a dictionary, 'data' is classified as 'things known and from which inferences may be deduced'. The 'things known' will be about various features of interest. For instance, we may know the age, sex, hair colour and number of children of a group of customers. Each of these features (age, sex, hair colour and number of children) is called a variable (since they vary from person to person).

Variables can be classified in several ways (Figure 9.1). There are two main types: quantitative and qualitative variables. (The latter are also known as categorical or attitudinal variables.) The techniques one uses to analyze and display data depends to some extent on the classification, so we will look at these in some detail.

Quantitative variables are features which are measurable or countable, for example age and number of children. The values of the variable are genuine numbers and not just labels. Quantitative variables are further subclassified into discrete and continuous variables.

A **discrete** variable can assume only certain values, usually integer values. Since the number of children that you can have can only be a whole number, this is an example of a discrete variable. Similarly, the number of times someone has bought your product is a discrete variable.

A **continuous** variable can assume any value within a specified range. If the variable of interest was the time taken to read this chapter, then we could measure this variable to the nearest hour, minute or second, or even smaller divisions if we had the equipment. Someone's age, for instance, is an example of a continuous variable: we often only give it as a whole number of years, but you could quote your age to the nearest minute if you could be bothered to work it out. Money values are usually taken as a continuous variable: technically we cannot have values with fractions of a penny, but since we are usually working in pounds, penny divisions are quite continuous enough to warrant the name.

Qualitative variables refer to what category something falls into and are not naturally numerical. One's gender is a qualitative variable, and so is the colour of your hair. Sometimes qualitative variables will be coded as numbers (for instance, the colour

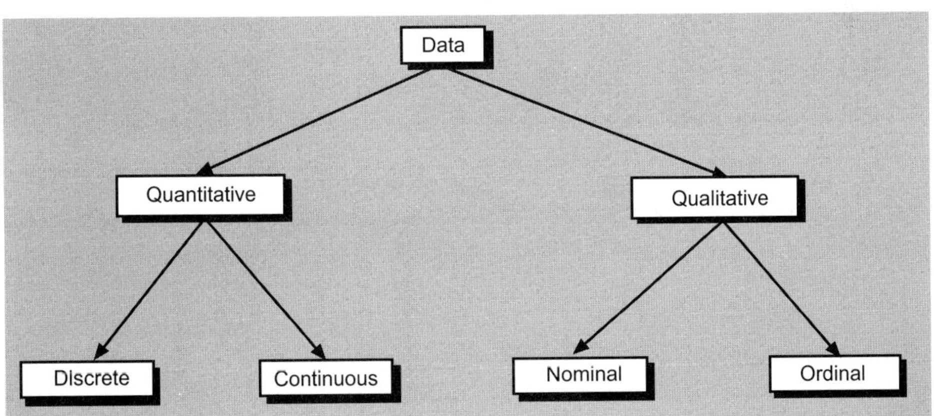

FIGURE 9.1 Classification of variables.

of shirt you buy may be coded 1 for red, 2 for white and 3 for blue), but these numbers are not a count or a measure of anything.

Qualitative variables are further subdivided into **ordinal** variables and **nominal** variables. The first type – ordinal – are variables for which the possible values have an underlying order; for example the shift you work (early, middle or late) or how you rate a chocolate bar (good, fair, poor, awful). The second type – nominal – are variables which are purely descriptive, for example sex, hair colour, country of origin, etc. In other words, the variable is merely a label.

ACTIVITY 1
Go through the questionnaire in Exhibit 9.1 and decide what type of variable each question will give.

Organizing your data

Imagine that you have been presented with a large set of data and what seems like a very short time to analyze it in. Where do you start? First you need to **organize** your data. They may have come to you as a large batch of completed questionnaires, or other type of record such as invoices or company reports. If so, the first step is to extract the relevant information and put it into a **spreadsheet**. If you can, use a computer spreadsheet package such as Excel, Lotus 1-2-3, Claris Works or Supercalc, but if one is not available then you can use a large sheet of paper ruled with rows and columns.

For a concrete example, we will suppose that your data are the responses from the questionnaire of Exhibit 9.1. The principle is much the same if the spreadsheet is to record any other form of data such as a set of invoices.

Setting up your spreadsheet

The rows

In spreadsheet terminology, rows are horizontal. You will need a heading row and then one row for each completed questionnaire. This row will record all the replies from that questionnaire.

The columns

Each column (the verticals) will contain values of one variable. The number of variables (columns) required to store the replies to a question will depend on the type of question. The first column should contain a reference number for the particular questionnaire: this will allow you to refer back to that record or to add extra information later. Question types are described as:

Exhibit 9.1 Questionnaire on travel agents

1. How much did you pay for your holiday package in total? £____

2. How many people was this for? ____ *people*

3. When choosing your holiday, how many travel agents, in total, did you visit before you made your holiday booking with one of them? *Please ring one answer.*

   One only **Two** **Three** **Four or more**

4. What was your *one most* important reason for choosing the travel agent where you (eventually) made your booking? *Please ring one answer only.*

   - **It offered the best prices**
   - **Nearest / most convenient travel agent**
   - **You had used it before**
   - **It had been recommended by someone else**
   - **It specialized in the type of holiday you wanted**
   - **Other reason (*please specify*: ______)**

5. How would you rate this travel agent for each of the following? *Please tick once on each line below.*

	Very good	Good	Fair	Poor	Very poor	No opinion/ Doesn't apply
Personal attention						
Range of holidays						
Efficiency						
Coping with problems						

6. Overall, how satisfied are you with this travel agent? *Please ring one.*

   Very satisfied **Fairly satisfied** **Not at all satisfied** **No opinion**

7. What types of holiday did you consider seriously before picking this holiday? *Please ring all that apply.*

   Activity holiday **Beach holiday** **Sightseeing from a fixed base**

   Coach tour **Camping holiday** **Self catering** **Cruise**

   Others (*please specify*: ______)

8. Which age group are you in? **Up to 24** **25–34** **35–44** **45–54** **55–64** **65+**

9. Are you male or female? **Male** **Female**

10. What other service would you have liked your travel agent to provide?

- **Single closed** questions (i.e. the ones where people had to pick one of a short list of possible responses) – these need one column only. Questions 3, 4, 6, 8 and 9 in our questionnaire are single closed. Question 5 is in effect four separate questions; it would need one column for the responses to 'Personal attention', another for the responses to 'Range of holidays', etc.

- **Multiple closed** questions (where people could pick more than one response from a given list) – these need one column for each possible response. Question 7 in our questionnaire is multiple closed; it needs eight columns, one for Activity holiday, one for Beach holiday, etc.

- **Open, quantitative questions** (where the response is a number) require just one column. Questions 1 and 2 in the questionnaire are open, quantitative.

- **Open, verbal questions** (where the response is a word or sentence, but not from a given list). Allow two or three columns for each of these questions, but they may be left unused. Question 10 is an open, verbal question.

Our questionnaire, then, would require the spreadsheet set out in Table 9.1.

Spreadsheet entries

The responses to each question need to be coded so that the information can be entered into the sheet. Code letters or numbers can be used.

Ordinal data

For ordinal data, it is better to use number codes, and numbers whose order corresponds to the natural ordering of the data. When the responses range from positive to negative, it is helpful to make the most positive response the highest number. This means that you can easily calculate an average response. Code 'No opinion' as 0 or leave it blank. (Questions 5 and 6 are ordinal data; see how they are coded below.)

'Other, please specify' responses

Allocate this response a code and enter this code normally in the spreadsheet. In addition, write the specified information on a separate sheet of paper with the respondent's reference number attached. After entering all the data, go through this list and spot any common responses (e.g. one that more than 10 per cent of the respondents gave). Each common response can be given a code of its own which can then be used to replace the 'Other' code against that respondent.

For example, for every person who chose 'Other' in question 4 you would initially enter 6 in the 'Reason' column. If you then made a list of the specified other reasons and found several people had written something about how friendly the staff were, you might take a new code of 7 for 'Friendly staff' and enter 7 against the people who had mentioned that.

TABLE 9.1 Spreadsheet created from the travel agent questionnaire

No.	Paid	No. for	Visited	Reason	Attention	Range	Efficiency	Problems	Satisfied	Activity	Beach	Fixed	Coach	Camping	Self cater	Cruise	Other	Age	Sex	Other services	
1	£900	2	1	2	4	5	3		2	1	1	1	0	0	0	1	1	4	0		
2	£250	1	3	1	2	3	3	4	2	0	1	0	1	0	1	0	0	2	0		
3	£125	1	4	6		2	3		2	0	0	0	0	1	1	0	1	1	1		
⋮	⋮	⋮	⋮	⋮	⋮	⋮	⋮	⋮	⋮	⋮	⋮	⋮	⋮	⋮	⋮	⋮	⋮	⋮	⋮	⋮	⋮

Sometimes you will be able to use one of the original codes if the written response was really covered by an answer you offered, e.g. if someone wrote 'Pass on way to work', you could allocate code 2.

Possible coding for the questionnaire

Question 3: Visited: 1 = One only, 2 = Two, 3 = Three, 4 = Four or more

Question 4: Reason: 1 = Prices, 2 = Convenient, 3 = Used before, 4 = Recommended, 5 = Specialized, 6 = Other

Question 5: Rating columns: Attention, Range, Efficiency, Problems
5 = Very good, 4 = Good, 3 = Fair, 2 = Poor, 1 = Very poor, Blank = No opinion

Question 6: Satisfied: 3 = Very satisfied, 2 = Fairly satisfied, 1 = Not at all satisfied, Blank = No opinion

Question 7: Type of holiday: One column for each type of holiday, entering 0 if not picked, 1 if picked.

Question 8: Age: 1 = Up to 24, 2 = 25–34, 3 = 35–44, 4 = 45–54, 5 = 55–64, 6 = 65+

Question 9: Sex: 0 = Male, 1 = Female

Entering the data into the columns

Work through the data, one questionnaire at a time, as follows:

- Single closed questions: enter the appropriate code.
- Multiple closed questions: enter 1 if people picked that response and 0 otherwise.
- Open, quantitative questions: enter the number given.
- Open, verbal questions: these have to be analyzed separately, making a list against the respondent's reference number in the same way as for 'Other, please specify' responses. Again, common responses can then be coded and entered into the columns reserved for this question.

See Table 9.1 as an example.

ACTIVITY 2
Set up spreadsheet columns and a coding system for the questionnaire in Exhibit 9.2.

Exhibit 9.2 Employee questionnaire

1. How long have you been in your present job? ☐ **years**

2. What is the level of your present job? (*Tick one box.*)

   Promoted post ☐ **Non-promoted post** ☐

3. Would you say you are happy in your present job?

   Yes, very ☐ **Yes, moderately** ☐ **Not very** ☐ **Not at all** ☐

4. Here are some of the things often thought important in a job. Which of these do you feel your present job offers? (*Tick all that apply.*)

   (a) Good pay ☐
   (b) Good holidays ☐
   (c) Security ☐
   (d) Pleasant atmosphere ☐
   (e) Interesting work ☐
   (f) Good staff relations ☐

5. From the above list, please choose the two things that you consider most important about a job and enter the appropriate letters, in order of importance to you, in the following boxes.

   First choice ☐ **Second choice** ☐

6. To what extent do you feel that your present job offers you these two things? (*Please indicate a position on the scale with a tick.*)

   Highly satisfactory ☐☐☐☐☐ **Highly unsatisfactory**

7. What would you like to see changed about your present job, if at all?

   ____

   ____

Other forms of data

Sometimes you will have just a single data variable to analyze. For example, the sales of your product (in £000) from various outlets might be:

74	52	93	57	69	79	61	55	84	88	65	63	72	50
74	64	67	77	102	82	54	61	68	50	66	72	82	94
50	60	71	81	92	53	61	70	89	91	54	61	73	87
58	69	72	64	78	68	53	75	81	90				

If you are using a computer spreadsheet for the analysis, you will still need to enter these data as a single (vertical) column before you can analyze them. Often, you will have other information you wish to bring into your analysis at some stage, such as which part of the country each outlet was located in and the population of its catchment area. These variables will form two extra columns on your spreadsheet (Table 9.2).

TABLE 9.2 Sales analysis by population and part of country

Sales (£000)	Catchment population (000)	Part of country
74	495	N
52	101	E
93	135	S
57	450	W
and so on		

Analyzing your data

Once your data are organized, you can begin analyzing them. Start by looking at each variable separately. Later you will look at them in pairs. The approach differs slightly for qualitative and quantitative variables.

The steps in a data analysis are:

1. Decide whether you wish to create any new variables. If so, create them.

2. Decide which variables you want to look at on their own. For each of these, produce:
   - tallies for qualitative or coded quantitative variables;
   - stem-and-leaf displays of short quantitative variables;
   - grouped frequency distributions and histograms of long quantitative variables;
   - measures of average and spread for quantitative variables.

3. Decide what your variables are telling you.

4. Decide which pairs of variables you want to look at. For each pair, produce:
   - tables for qualitative variables;
   - tables or scatter diagrams for quantitative or mixed pairs of variables;
   - measures of average and spread for each section of a quantitative variable.

5. Interpret your results.

We will now look at each of the skills that you need to do this analysis.

Creating new variables

Sometimes you will want to consider creating a new variable from your existing ones. For instance, a useful new variable from the travel agent questionnaire might be the 'amount spent per person' which we would create by dividing each answer to question 1 by the corresponding answer to question 2. For the sales data, we might want to find the 'sales per head of population' by dividing each entry in the sales column by the entry in the population column of Table 9.2.

Qualitative or coded quantitative variables

Tallies (frequency distributions)

Tallies are just counts of how often each category occurs (Table 9.3). A computer spreadsheet will do the counting for you (e.g. via the Pivot Table tool on Excel 5). Working by hand you can ease the task by using the 'five-bar gate' technique.

Method

- List the possible categories.
- Work through the column of data systematically, putting a stroke next to the appropriate category.
- Every fifth mark should go diagonally across the previous four, as on a gate, to make counting the marks at the end very easy (see Table 9.3).

TABLE 9.3 Frequency counts

Region	Tally	Count
N	𝍸 𝍸 𝍸 𝍸 II	22
S	𝍸 𝍸 I	11
E	𝍸 III	8
W	𝍸 𝍸	10
blank	I	1

Interpretation
Once you have your tally, look at it to see what it tells you. Consider:

- Whether the counts are what you expected.
- Which are the most frequently occurring categories.
- The **shape** of the distribution (see below), if the variable is ordinal or quantitative.
- Whether looking at percentages would be a good idea.

The tally in Table 9.3 would tell us how the outlets were distributed across the country. If we were using a sample, we would use this tally to tell us whether our sample represented the whole country correctly.

Tallies of question 8 (age) and 9 (sex) in our travel agent questionnaire would tell us whether we had achieved a representative sample. A tally of question 4 would tell us which were the most common reasons for choosing a travel agent, and tallies of questions 5 and 6 would tell us how satisfied the customers were.

Percentage tallies

You may find it helpful to work out percentages for some of your variables.

Method

- Each percentage is found from the following formula:

$$\text{Percentage} = \frac{\text{Count for that category}}{\text{Sum of the counts}} \times 100\%$$

- If you have some blank entries or non-responses in that column, it is up to you to decide if it is more meaningful to include the 'blank' category in the sum of the counts or not. Whichever you decide, note it down by your table – you will need to tell your reader what you have done when you present your information.
- It is usually best to record percentages to the nearest whole number: it makes their message easier to understand. Adjust your rounding if necessary, so that they add up to 100%. (In Table 9.4, straightforward rounding gives 43, 22, 16 and 20 which add up to 101. The 21.57 is closest to rounding down instead of up and so is the one to be adjusted.)

If you are tallying a question such as question 7 in the travel agent questionnaire where respondents can pick more than one answer, you may want to show what percentage of the respondents picked that answer (Table 9.5). In that case your percentages will total to more than 100. Make a note by the table to remind yourself (and others).

TABLE 9.4 Frequency counts as percentages

Region	Tally	Count	Percentage before rounding[a] %	Percentage after rounding %
N	𝍸 𝍸 𝍸 𝍸 II	22	43.14 (= 22/51 × 100)	43
S	𝍸 𝍸 I	11	21.57	21
E	𝍸 III	8	15.69	16
W	𝍸 𝍸	10	19.61	20
blank	I	1		

[a] Percentages have been calculated ignoring non-responses.

TABLE 9.5 Frequency counts as percentages under multiple response

Holidays considered	Count	Percentage of respondents[a] %
Activity holiday	55	35
Beach holiday	120	77
Fixed base	63	41
Coach tour	102	66
Camping	23	15
Self catering	89	57
Cruise	40	26
Other	39	25

[a] Percentages total to more than 100 owing to multiple response.

Combining tallies

When questions in a questionnaire share the same set of responses, it can be helpful to combine their tallies into a table (Table 9.6).

TABLE 9.6 Combining tallies of variables with the same set of responses (%)

	Very good	Good	Fair	Poor	Very poor	No opinion/ Doesn't apply
Personal attention	6	34	41	15	4	0
Range of holidays	10	59	26	3	0	2
Efficiency	3	29	42	24	2	0
Coping with problems	20	48	10	1	5	16

From Table 9.6 we would perhaps conclude that travel agents were rated best at 'Coping with problems'; however, it is difficult to decide which is best between that and 'Range of holidays'. 'Efficiency' is obviously the worst. Calculating an average rating can be helpful for ordinal variables, as we shall see later.

ACTIVITY 3

Produce a tally and percentages for the following coded responses to question 6 on the travel agent questionnaire. Interpret what the tally is telling you.

Coding:

3 = Very satisfied 2 = Fairly satisfied 1 = Not at all satisfied
Blank = No opinion

3, 3, 2, 1, 3, 2, blank, 3, 3, 1, 3, 2, 2, 1, 2, 3, 2, 1, 1, 3, 2, 3, 2, 2, 2, 2, 2, 1, blank, 3, 3, 3, 2, 2, 2, 1, 2, 2, 2, 3, 2, 2, 1, 2, 3, 2, 1, 2, 3, 3, 2, 2, 2, 1, blank, 2, 2, 1, 3, 3, 2, 1

Quantitative variables

Coded quantitative variables, such as questions 3 and 8 in Exhibit 9.1, can be tallied as for qualitative variables. Questions 1 and 2 on the questionnaire and the sales and population figures from the sales data (see above) will need one of the following two approaches.

Stem-and-leaf displays

If you have a fairly short data set with roughly fifty entries or less for your quantitative variable, then a stem-and-leaf display is the best way to analyze it.

A stem-and-leaf display is a method of seeing both the shape and actual ordered values of a variable. Construction follows the following steps. We will illustrate this with the sales data that we used previously, repeated here:

Sales (£000)

74	52	93	57	69	79	61	55	84	88	65	63	72	50
74	64	67	77	102	82	54	61	68	50	66	72	82	94
50	60	71	81	92	53	61	70	89	91	54	61	73	87
58	69	72	64	78	68	53	75	81	90				

Method

1. Identify the smallest and largest data values, here 50 and 102.
2. Arrange all the possible first digits, in ascending order, to the left of a vertical line. These are the **stems**.

5	
6	
7	
8	
9	
10	

3. To the right of the vertical line, record the second digit(s) for each data value on the appropriate line, working through the data list systematically to avoid missing any data. These are the **leaves**.

   The first sales value in the list above is 74: we write a 4 on the 7 line:

5	
6	
7	4
8	
9	
10	

The second value in the sales list is 52. We write a 2 on the 5 line:

5	2
6	
7	4
8	
9	
10	

After all the data have been entered in this way we have:

5	2 7 5 0 4 0 0 3 4 8 3
6	9 1 5 3 4 7 1 8 6 0 1 1 9 4 8
7	4 9 2 4 7 2 1 0 3 2 8 5
8	4 8 2 2 1 9 7 1
9	3 4 2 1 0
10	2

4. Order the digits on each horizontal line. (Take care to space the digits evenly and in vertical columns so that the stem length represents its frequency.)

5. Add a title and detail of the units of measurement.

5	0	0	0	2	3	3	4	4	5	8					
6	0	1	1	1	1	3	4	4	5	6	7	8	8	9	9
7	0	1	2	2	2	3	4	4	5	7	8	9			
8	1	1	2	2	2	4	7	8	9						
9	0	1	2	3	4										
10	2														

Stem-and-leaf display for the sales figures (£000)

This then, is the stem-and-leaf display for the sales data. Note how it gives a picture of the shape of the data values: we see that we have more sales towards the lower values with a tailing-off in the higher values.

If a straightforward stem-and-leaf appears to condense the data too much, then we can stretch it by using two or more stems for each starting digit, e.g. 5_L and 5_H for '5 Lower' and '5 Higher'. Here, numbers from 0 to 4 go on the Lower stem and numbers from 5 to 9 go on the Higher stem:

5_L	0	0	0	2	3	3	4	4
5_H	5	8						
6_L	0	1	1	1	1	3	4	4
6_H	5	6	7	8	8	9	9	
7_L	0	1	2	2	2	3	4	4
7_H	5	7	8	9				
8_L	1	1	2	2	2	4		
8_H	7	8	9					
9_L	0	1	2	3	4			
9_H								
10_L	2							

Here are two other stem-and-leaf examples. The first shows values ranging from 1565 to 2090, and the second values of 0.51, 0.88, 1.01, etc. up to 15.81.

15	65			
16	44	79		
17	33	66		
18	12	52	52	
19	12	54	67	88
20	08	44	90	

$0._H$	51	88		
$1._L$	01	10	31	
$1._H$	50	61	99	
$2._L$	00	49		+ one extreme value of 15.81
$2._H$	50			
$3._L$	04	31		

Notice how a value much larger or smaller than the other values has been dealt with. We call such values **outliers**. (You should always check that the value is not a transcription error.)

Sometimes you may want to round your data first to make the display clearer. A back-to-back stem-and-leaf plot can be useful for comparing two data sets:

Area A		Area B
	0	1 1 2 2 4 6 6
9 8 3	**1**	0 1 2 3 5 7
8 7 7 5 2	**2**	
6 5 4 1 1 0	**3**	2

Sales (rounded to the nearest £00)

Interpretation

When interpreting a stem-and-leaf display you should consider the following:

- The **shape** of the distribution. There is a terminology for the shape of distributions which we will look at next.
- The **actual values** – is there anything unusual about them?

For instance, the following is a stem-and-leaf plot of the hours that students said they spend on a project, ranging from 8 hours up to 30 hours (note how 8 and 9 are dealt with):

0_H	8 9
1_L	0 0 0 0
1_H	5 8
2_L	0 0 0 0 1
2_H	
3_L	0 0

In interpretation, we would notice how many 0s there are and conclude that most students probably did not time themselves and simply guessed a round answer.

The following diagrams illustrate some of the common terms used to describe the shape of a quantitative or ordinal variable. Usually the shape plotted will not correspond exactly to one of these shapes and you have to describe it as 'fairly normal' or 'fairly positively skewed'. Some distributions do not fit any of these terms.

Each of Figures 9.2 to 9.7 shows some typical shapes and the terms used to describe them. Each has a pair of shapes – the first is the shape you get from a stem-and-leaf where

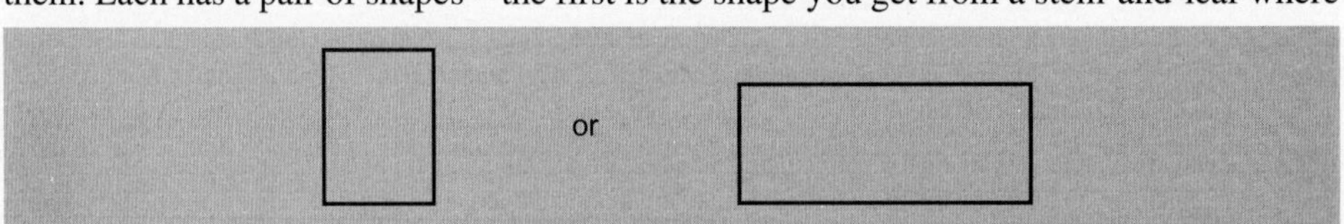

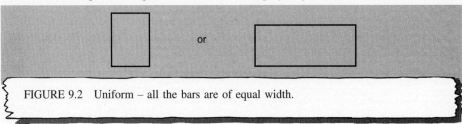

FIGURE 9.2 Uniform – all the bars are of equal width.

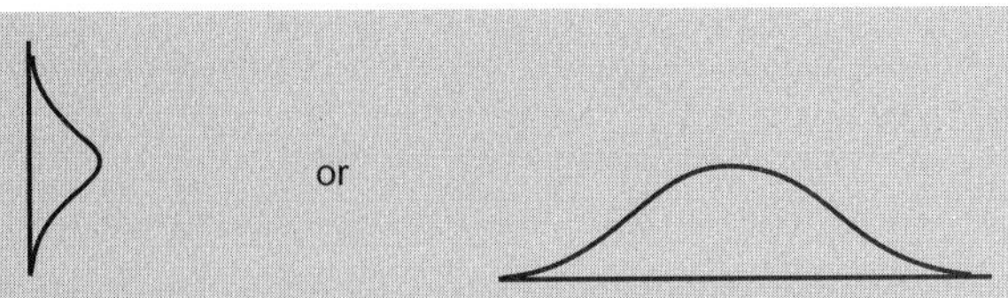

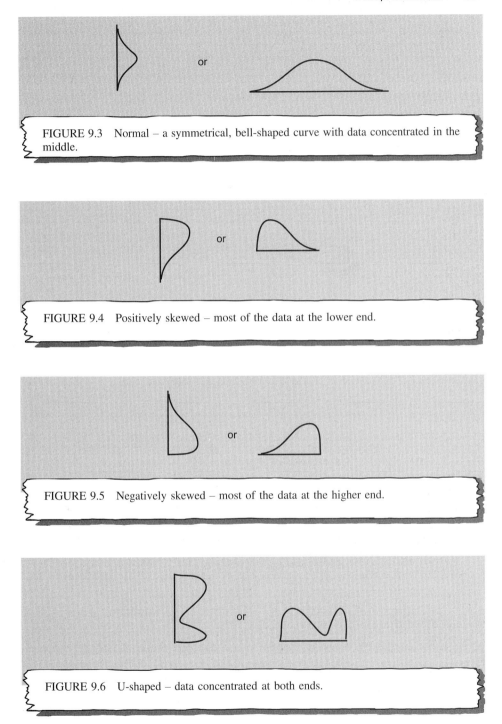

FIGURE 9.3 Normal – a symmetrical, bell-shaped curve with data concentrated in the middle.

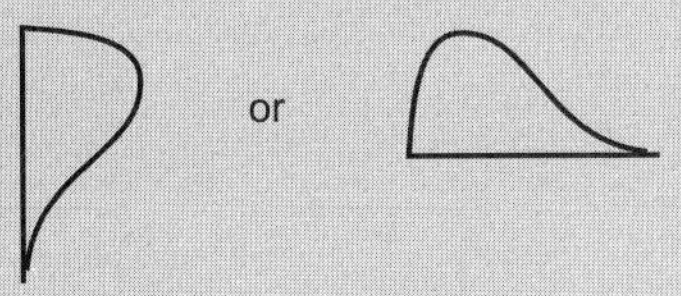

FIGURE 9.4 Positively skewed – most of the data at the lower end.

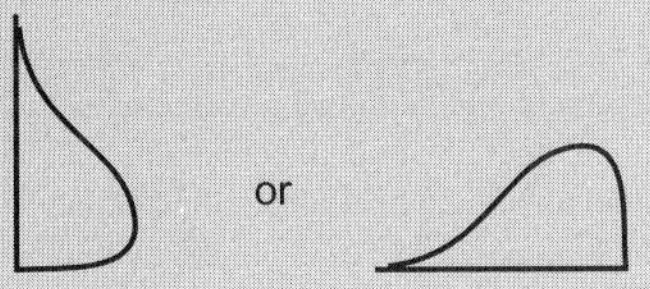

FIGURE 9.5 Negatively skewed – most of the data at the higher end.

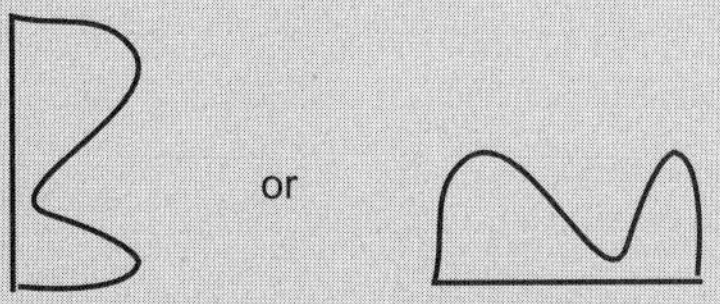

FIGURE 9.6 U-shaped – data concentrated at both ends.

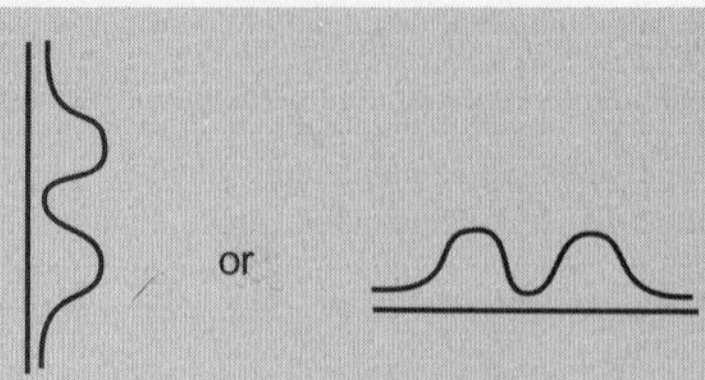

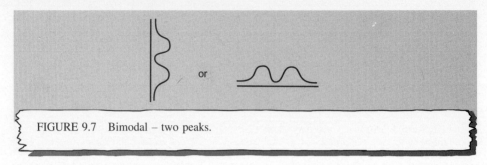

FIGURE 9.7 Bimodal – two peaks.

the axis is vertical. The second is the shape you would get from a 'histogram' of the same data. We will meet histograms later – they have horizontal axes.

If, like many people, you cannot remember the directions positively and negatively skewed, then say 'skewed with data concentrated on the lower values' (or 'higher values') instead.

ACTIVITY 4

1. **Draw stem-and-leaf plots of the population figures below for the North and South regions of the sales data in Table 9.2 (page 274).**

   North population figures (000):
   495, 101, 319, 286, 512, 419, 306, 109, 190, 236, 545, 234, 198, 423, 319, 98, 160, 418, 190, 200, 322, 467

   South population figures (000):
   135, 188, 516, 201, 167, 199, 189, 290, 148, 240, 301

   Interpret the displays using proper shape terminology.

2. **The price (in £) of an item in nineteen shops is:**

   0.99, 0.99, 1.49, 1.17, 1.49, 0.99, 1.35, 1.23, 1.49, 1.35, 1.52, 1.35, 1.49, 1.29, 0.99, 1.24, 1.13, 1.39, 1.00

   Examine the data by means of a stem-and-leaf display. Interpret what the display tells you.

Grouped frequency distributions

Quantitative variables in long data sets are too cumbersome to handle with stem-and-leaf displays. If the variable is discrete and there are only a few possible values (as in the answers to question 2 from Exhibit 9.1), a simple tally is usually possible (Table 9.7). Tallies for quantitative variables are almost always known as **frequency distributions** with the counts referred to as 'frequencies'.

TABLE 9.7 A simple frequency count

No. of people	Tally	Frequency
1	𝍸 𝍸 𝍸 II	17
2	𝍸 𝍸 𝍸 𝍸 𝍸 III	28
3	𝍸 𝍸 𝍸 𝍸 𝍸 𝍸	30
4	𝍸 𝍸 𝍸 𝍸 𝍸 𝍸 𝍸 𝍸 𝍸 IIII	49
5	𝍸 𝍸 𝍸 𝍸 III	23
6 or more	𝍸 III	8

Often, though, you will need to group the values first to make the resulting tally easy to interpret. For example, question 1 in the travel agent questionnaire will almost certainly require grouping.

Method

When choosing groups or classes, the following are good guidelines:

- Start by looking through your column and pick out the smallest and largest values.
- Make all the classes the same width, except perhaps for the ends where a wider class may help to avoid several empty classes.
- Use round figures for the class boundaries (to make understanding easy).
- Have at least 5 classes (so you keep enough detail).
- Have no more than 15 classes (or the result is hard to interpret).
- Avoid open classes such as 'more than 100'.

Example

Suppose that the smallest given figure for question 1 in the travel agent questionnaire was £525 and the largest was £5350. Classes all of width £1000 would give five classes, but most of the entries might be in the first class, '£0 but under £1000'. Classes of width £500 would require ten classes but spread the data out better. Whichever you choose, be prepared to redo the tally with different classes if the first attempt does not help you to understand the data well enough.

Table 9.8 is known as a **grouped frequency distribution**. Sometimes your data will come to you already grouped in this way, as does the age data from question 8 of the travel agent questionnaire (Exhibit 9.1).

Interpreting frequency distributions

When interpreting a quantitative frequency distribution, consider:

- The **shape** of the distribution.
- Its **average value** (and, preferably, its spread).

You may be able to pick out the shape of your distribution from the frequency distribution itself, but you will probably find it helpful to draw a **histogram**.

Histograms look rather like bar charts, but are subject to rather more rigid rules to prevent misinterpretation. Most especially, the height of each rectangle in a histogram

TABLE 9.8 Grouped frequency distribution

Amount paid	Tally	Frequency
£500 but under £1000	𝍸 𝍸 𝍸 𝍸 𝍸 ||	27
£1000 but under £1500	𝍸 𝍸 𝍸 𝍸 𝍸 𝍸 𝍸 𝍸 𝍸 𝍸 |	51
£1500 but under £2000	𝍸 𝍸 𝍸 𝍸 𝍸 𝍸 𝍸	35
£2000 but under £2500	𝍸 𝍸 𝍸 |||	18
£2500 but under £3000	𝍸 𝍸 𝍸	15
£3000 but under £3500	𝍸 ||	7
£3500 but under £4000		0
£4000 but under £4500	||||	4
£4500 but under £5000	||	2
£5000 but under £5500	|	1

illustrates the **frequency density** rather than the frequency itself. This is because one can change the frequencies in the classes simply by changing the size of the classes.

For example, in the distribution shown in Table 9.9, all the frequencies are 8 but the 8 people who are in the first class are spread over a range of 4 miles (0 to 4) whereas the 8 people who are in the class '4 and <6' are spread over a range of only 2 miles. It would thus be misleading to draw a histogram with all bars of height 8. We should, instead, show that the responses are more densely packed in some classes than in others.

TABLE 9.9

Miles from shop	Frequency
0 and <4	8
4 and <6	8
6 and <10	8
10 and <20	8

Method for drawing histograms

When all the classes are the same width (as in the grouped frequency distribution from question 1 of the questionnaire) the frequency density is equal to the frequency, and so the bars are drawn with height equal to the frequency (Figure 9.8).

We can interpret from Figure 9.8 that the spending is skewed, with most holidays costing under £2000 but a few costing up to £5500. (Notice the gap between £3500 and £4000, corresponding to the 0 frequency for this class.)

When you have a grouped distribution with unequal width classes, you must proceed as follows. (We will illustrate this by reference to the data in Table 9.9).

1. Set up an extra column called 'frequency density' which gives the frequency per standard unit range (Table 9.10).
2. Choose the standard unit range to be the smallest of the existing ranges. In our case we choose a width of 2 miles as the standard width.
3. Each entry in the frequency density column is the given frequency divided by the number of times that the class is bigger than the standard class.
4. The rectangles in the histogram are drawn with height equal to that of the frequency density.

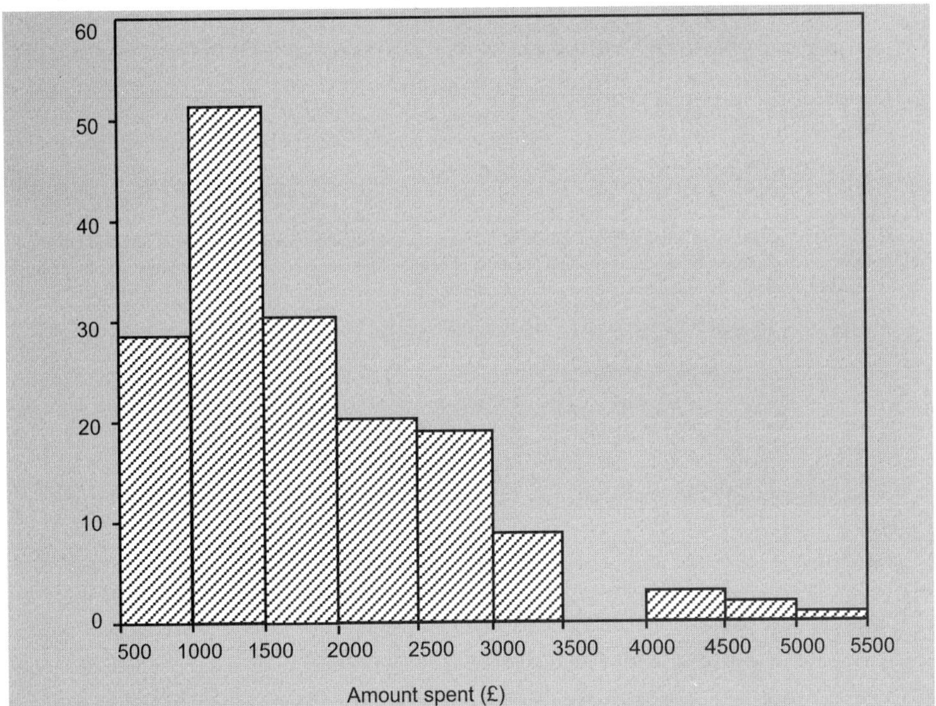

FIGURE 9.8 Histogram (question 1).

TABLE 9.10 Frequency density

Miles from shop	Frequency	Frequency density
0 and <4	8	4 = 8/2
4 and <6	8	8 = 8/1
6 and <10	8	4 = 8/2
10 and <20	8	1.6 = 8/5

5. The width of the bars will correspond to the width of the classes. In our data, the rectangle for '0 and <4' will be twice as wide as the rectangle for '4 and <6'. The easiest way to do this by hand is to label the horizontal axis like the axis of a graph as shown in Figure 9.9. The rectangle widths then arise naturally.

We can easily interpret from Figure 9.9 that the distances are slightly skewed, with most under 10 miles but a few between 10 and 20 miles. The most common distance is between 4 and 6 miles.

Other things to be aware of when drawing a histogram are:

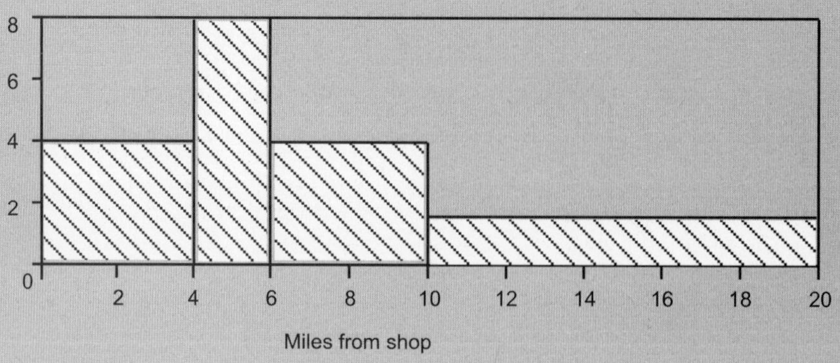

FIGURE 9.9 Histogram – classes are of unequal width.

- **No gaps.** In any histogram, take care not to leave gaps between the rectangles unless you have a genuinely empty class: otherwise you give the impression that there are gaps in the distribution which do not really exist. Computer spreadsheet packages often leave gaps by default, but these can be removed.

- **Open classes.** If you have an open class, such as 'Under 10' or '50 and over', the missing end of the class should be determined by looking at the original data, or by common sense if the data are not available. For instance, if the variable is the age of people buying chocolate bars, either 0 or 5 might be suitable lower limits for 'Under 10'.

ACTIVITY 5

1. Produce and interpret a histogram for the travel agent questionnaire age data given in Table 9.11.

TABLE 9.11

Age group	Frequency
Up to 24	24
25–34	24
35–44	26
45–54	26
55–64	27
65+	28

Activity 5 continued

Notes:

- Although the classes as given on the questionnaire are looking at ages as discrete, proceed as if the class 25–34 were '25 but less than 35', etc.
- Decide on your own sensible upper and lower bounds for the open classes.

2. **Produce a histogram from the data in Table 9.12 for the responses to question 2 of the questionnaire.**

TABLE 9.12 Frequency of responses to question 2 of the questionnaire

No. of people	Frequency
1	17
2	28
3	30
4	49
5	23
6 or more	8

The largest response was 10

Note: For discrete data, as in Table 9.12, treat each class as going from 0.5 below the number to 0.5 above the number, i.e. draw bars from 0.5 to 1.5, 1.5 to 2.5, etc., and the last bar from 5.5 to 10.5.

Other ways of looking at single quantitative variables

Percentages

Just as with qualitative tallies, it may help your understanding to work out percentages instead of frequencies.

Cumulative frequencies

It may help to know not 'how many people travelled between 4 and 6 miles' but how many people in total travelled less than 6 miles, or how many people in total travelled 6 or more miles. To help you answer these questions, you can set up **cumulative frequency distributions**, either 'less than cumulative frequencies' or 'more than cumulative frequencies'. 'Less than' are the more common form. Less than cumulative frequencies are found by accumulating all the frequencies from the start to that point. 'More than' ones are constructed from the end up, by accumulating all the frequencies from the end to that point. For instance, the following frequency distribution leads to the less than and more than distributions shown in Table 9.13:

No. of children	*Frequency*
1	4
2	6
3	2
4	9

Notice in Table 9.13 how the left-hand columns are labelled and how an extra row is added with 0 cumulative frequency. This extra row allows you to show the lowest and highest values.

Cumulative frequencies can be worked out as percentages as well, if desired. Table 9.14 is an example of a less than cumulative frequency distribution together with percentages.

TABLE 9.13 Less than and more than distributions

No. of children	Cumulative frequency	No. of children	Cumulative frequency
Less than 1	0 ↓	More than 0	21 (= 17 + 4)
Less than 2	4	More than 1	17 (= 11 + 6)
Less than 3	10 (= 4 + 6)	More than 2	11 (= 9 + 2)
Less than 4	12 (= 10 + 2)	More than 3	9
Less than 5	21 (= 12 + 9)	More than 4	0 ↑

TABLE 9.14 Cumulative frequency distribution

Annual sales (£000)	No. of shops (frequency)	Annual sales (£000)	Cumulative frequency	Cumulative percentage
0 and <4	8	Less than 0	0	0%
4 and <6	8	Less than 4	8	27% = $\frac{8}{30} \times 100\%$
6 and <10	8	Less than 6	16	53%
10 and <20	6	Less than 10	24	80%
		Less than 20	30	100%

Ogives

Cumulative frequencies may often be helpfully studied by drawing an 'ogive' or, more often, a percentage ogive (see Figure 9.10).

Method

- Set up proper scales on each axis: cumulative frequency or percentage on the vertical axis; class boundaries on the horizontal axis.
- Plot each cumulative frequency or percentage against the class boundary (e.g. in the example in Table 9.14, plot 0% against 0, 27% against 4, 53% against 6, etc.).
- Join the points with (ruled) straight lines.

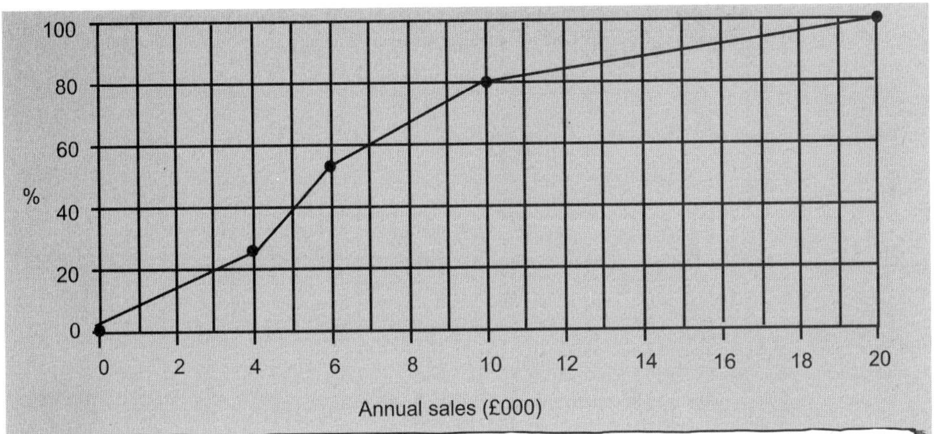

FIGURE 9.10 Less than percentage ogive.

Ogives are often used to find out **percentiles**, i.e. the percentage of a distribution under a certain level. To do this, draw a line across from the required percentage on the vertical axis and read off the horizontal position of the point where this line meets the graph. For example, to find the 'twenty percentile' of the above distribution, draw a line across at 20 per cent and read off the horizontal position of where it meets the graph: 3.0 here. Thus 20 per cent of the shops have annual sales of our product of less than £3000.

We will later discover that the fifty percentile is also known as the median, the twenty-five percentile as the first quartile and the seventy-five percentile as the third quartile.

Another common use for an ogive is to illustrate where the variable concentrates. A variable that was uniformly distributed across its range would have a straight ogive. Normally distributed variables have S-shaped ogives, and skewed variables have curved ogives. Sometimes the equivalent uniform distribution is superimposed on the ogive by joining the first and last points with a ruler. The result on a less than ogive is often known as a **Lorenz curve** (Figure 9.11) or a Pareto diagram (see chapter 3).

The fact that the ogive is all above the equi-distribution line in Figure 9.11 shows that the data are skewed towards the lower values.

Line graphs

Line graphs are only appropriate when the values of the quantitative variable have been recorded in a regular time order with, for example, the first value being for week 1, the second for week 2, etc. Figure 9.12 shows how the variable, here product sales, varies with time.

Method

- Time is always taken as increasing from left to right along the horizontal axis.

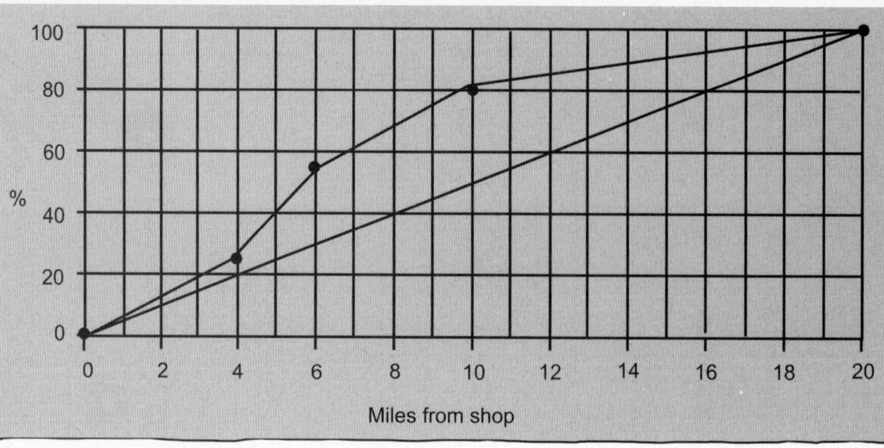

FIGURE 9.11 Lorenz curve.

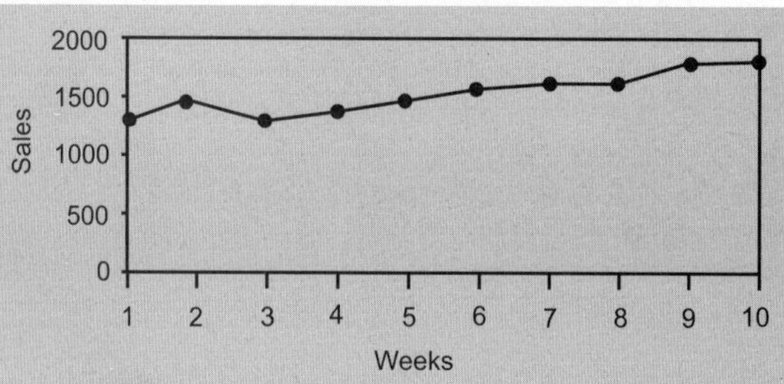

FIGURE 9.12 Line graph.

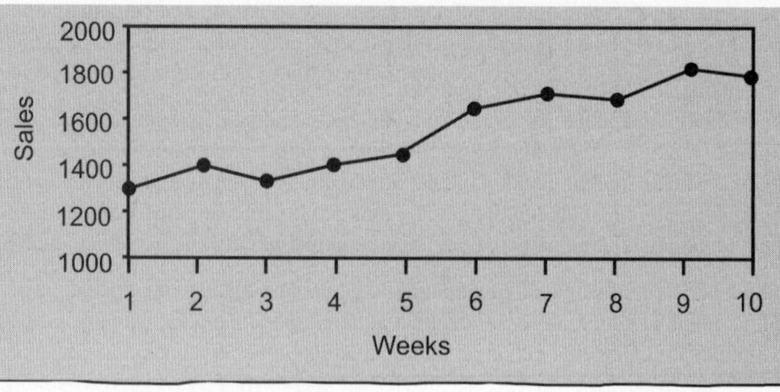

FIGURE 9.13 Detailed line graph.

  - Start the vertical axis at 0 if you just want to look at the general trend of the data.
  - Start it at a value just below the lowest value if you want to look at the data in more detail and spot any patterns (Figure 9.13).
- Above each time point, plot a point at a height corresponding to that time's value.
- Join the points (usually with straight lines).

ACTIVITY 6

1. **Produce a less than cumulative frequency distribution and an ogive for the grouped frequency distribution of question 1 of the travel agent questionnaire set out in Table 9.8 on page 284.**
2. **(a) Produce a less than percentage cumulative frequency distribution for the questionnaire age data given in Table 9.11 on page 286.**

   Notes:

   - Although the classes as given on the questionnaire are looking at ages as discrete, proceed as if the class 25–34 were '25 but less than 35', etc.
   - Decide on your own sensible upper and lower bounds for the open classes.

   (b) Produce an ogive of the data in Table 9.11.

Measures of average and spread

When analyzing a quantitative variable, as well as looking at the shape of the distribution it can be helpful to work out:

- What **size** the data are on average.
- How much the data **deviate** from that average.

Measures of size: averages

The three most common measures of size are the mean, the median and the mode.

The usual arithmetic average is called the **mean**. It is the best measure of average since it takes account of all the information. However, it is badly distorted by extreme values, so, in badly skewed variables use the **median** as the average instead. Government statistics often use the median since the distribution of the data is often skewed, e.g. incomes.

The **mode**, or most frequent value, is not helpful for continuous variables, though for discrete data it can be considered in addition to the mean or median to add extra information. However, it is never a very good measure of the average size of a variable.

The three measures are summarized in Table 9.15.

TABLE 9.15 Summary of the three measures of averages

Measure	Definition	When to use
Mean	$\frac{\text{Sum of entries}}{\text{No. of entries}}$	Always, unless the variable (or one it is being compared with) is badly skewed
Median	Half the data are less than this value	For badly skewed variables
Mode	Most frequent value	For discrete variables, as an extra

Finding the average value

Ungrouped data

- Mode – pick out from a tally or ordered list.
- Median – write out the data in an *ordered list* and pick out the middle item (or average the middle pair, if there is an even number of items).
- Mean – sum of entries (including repeats) divided by the number of entries.

Examples might be:

- *Data set A:* 7, 3, 1, 5, 5, 3, 5, 3, 5. Ordered: 1, 3, 3, 3, 5, 5, 5, 5, 7, giving:
  Mode = 5
  Median = 5

$$\text{Mean} = \frac{1+3+3+3+5+5+5+5+7}{9} = 4.1$$

- *Data set B:* 5, 3, 3, 1, 5, 3, 30, 3, 3, 5. Ordered: 1, 3, 3, 3, 3, 3, 5, 5, 5, 30, giving:
  Mode = 3
  Median = (3+3)/2 = 3

$$\text{Mean} = \frac{1+3+3+3+3+3+5+5+5+30}{10} = 6.1$$

Notice how the extreme value of 30 has distorted the mean to an unrepresentative value in data set B. This is why we use the median for such skewed data sets.

Grouped data

Note that it is generally better to work from the original, ungrouped data, if you have them.

In order to find the mean of a set of grouped data, the general rule is to take the midpoints of each class and add them together the correct number of times (given by the frequency). This can be written as:

$$\text{Mean} = \frac{\Sigma\ (\text{Class midpoint} \times \text{Frequency of that class})}{\Sigma\ (\text{Frequencies})}$$

where Σ means 'sum of'.

TABLE 9.16

Monthly rent (£)	Frequency
100 and <120	6
120 and <140	8
140 and <160	12
160 and <180	4

As an example we shall calculate the mean of the data in Table 9.16. The calculation will be:

$$\text{Mean} = \frac{(£110 \times 6) + (£130 \times 8) + (£150 \times 12) + (£170 \times 4)}{30} = £139.3$$

since there are 30 data values altogether: 6 between £100 and £120 (midpoint £110), 8 between £120 and £140 (midpoint £130), etc.

Turning to the median, the easiest way to find this for grouped data is to draw an ogive and use it to find the fifty-percentile. To do this:

- Set up a cumulative frequency distribution (less than is more usual – Table 9.17).
- Draw an ogive (Figure 9.14).
- Go half way up the vertical axis and then across to the graph.
- Read off the median as the horizontal axis value where the 50 per cent line meets the ogive.

The median from Figure 9.14 is just over £140, and from graph-paper could be read more accurately as £142.

Since this variable is not very skewed, we would quote its mean (£139) as a representative measure of the average size of the monthly rent or when comparing this average rent with others. (That is, unless one of the other rent variables we were comparing with was very skewed: then we would compare the medians for all the rents.)

TABLE 9.17 Cumulative frequency distribution

Monthly rent (£)	Frequency		Cumulative frequency	Cumulative percentage
100 and <120	6	Less than 100	0	0%
120 and <140	8	Less than 120	6	20%
140 and <160	12	Less than 140	14	47%
160 and <180	4	Less than 160	26	87%
		Less than 180	30	100%

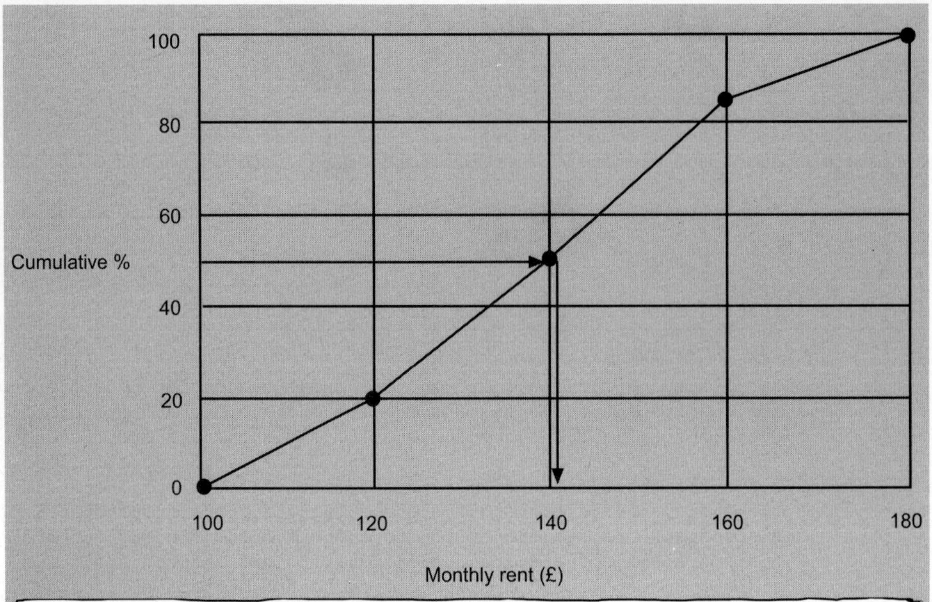

FIGURE 9.14 Ogive.

Averages for ordinal qualitative variables

It can sometimes be helpful to work out average values for ordinal variables, particularly when you wish to make comparisons amongst several ordinal variables with the same set of responses (Table 9.18).

By coding the responses from the worst up (ignoring the 'No response'), we can get average values (the mean is usually used, even if the data are skewed). Coding 'Very poor' as 1, up to 5 for 'Very good', we get an average for 'Personal attention' as follows:

$$5 \times 6\% + 4 \times 34\% + 3 \times 41\% + 2 \times 15\% + 1 \times 4\% = 3.23$$

These average ratings are set out in Table 9.19. The table shows 'Range of holidays' to be the most highly rated, with 'Efficiency' least highly rated. All, however, are rated on average between 3 (fair) and 4 (good).

TABLE 9.18 Several ordinal variables with the same set of responses

Rating:	Very good %	Good %	Fair %	Poor %	Very poor %	No opinion/ Doesn't apply %
Personal attention	6	34	41	15	4	0
Range of holidays	10	59	26	3	0	2
Efficiency	3	29	42	24	2	0
Coping with problems	20	48	10	1	5	16

TABLE 9.19 Average rating from ordinal variable responses

	Average rating
Personal attention	3.23
Range of holidays	3.70
Efficiency	3.07
Coping with problems	3.29

ACTIVITY 7

1. **Determine the means and medians of the population figures below for the North and South regions of the sales data in Table 9.2 (page 274).**

   North population figures (000):
   495, 101, 319, 286, 512, 419, 306, 109, 190, 236, 545, 234, 198, 423, 319, 98, 160, 418, 190, 200, 322, 467

   South population figures (000):
   135, 188, 516, 201, 167, 199, 189, 290, 148, 240, 301

2. **Find the mean and median of the responses to question 1 of the travel agent questionnaire from the grouped frequency distribution set out in Table 9.8 on page 284.**

Measures of spread (or dispersion)

Although quantitative variables vary in average size, they also vary in how much the individual values vary from this average value. This can be just as important a consideration as the average. Although a chart will give us an idea of the extent of this variation, it is handy to have a way of measuring this spread or dispersion, particularly when making comparisons.

Range

An easy-to-use measure of spread is the range, which simply states the lowest and highest values of the data set (e.g. 0 to 6). However, it tells *nothing* about how the data are spread within the range. We need a measure that will distinguish between data sets such as those whose histograms are shown in Figure 9.15.

Each of the variables in Figure 9.15 has the same average and the same range; the first two even have the same shape. However, the three obviously differ in their spread. There are two commonly used measures of spread:

- Semi-interquartile range (SIQR)
- Standard deviation, σ

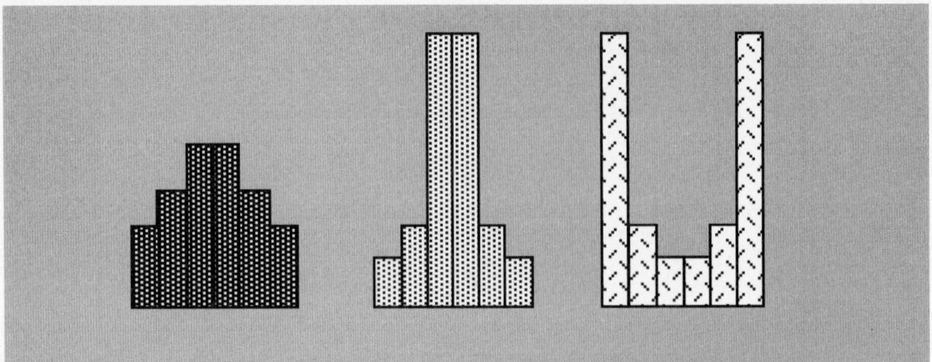

FIGURE 9.15 Three histograms – same average, same range, different spread.

The SIQR is used as a measure of spread when the median is being used as the average, and standard deviation is used with the mean.

Semi-interquartile range

The formula is:

$$\text{SIQR} = \text{Half the range of the central half of the data set}$$
$$= \tfrac{1}{2}(Q_3 - Q_1)$$

where Q_1 is the value that one-quarter of the data are less than, and Q_3 is the value that one-quarter of the data are more than.

There are several different ways of finding the quartiles of a data set, all giving slightly different results. None is more correct than any other. We will use the easiest of these methods, which simply takes the median of the lower half of the data set to give Q_1 and the median of the upper half to give Q_3. The procedure is as follows:

- Write the data out in order (or work from a stem-and-leaf display).
- Divide the ordered data into two halves, ignoring the middle value if there is one.
- Q_1 = median of lower half.
- Q_3 = median of upper half.

As an example, assume that our ordered data set is:

1 1 3 4 8 8 9 11   13 13 13 15 20 21 22 30

$$Q_1 = (4+8)/2 = 6 \qquad Q_3 = (15+20)/2 = 17.5$$

so SIQR = $\tfrac{1}{2}$(17.5–6) = 5.75.

An example using an odd number of data items might be:

22	31	40	52	61	78	85
	↓		ignore		↓	
	Q_1				Q_3	

so SIQR = $\frac{1}{2}(78-31) = 23.5$.

Note: The variables whose histograms are shown in Figure 9.15 have SIQRs of 1.5, 0.5 and 2.5 respectively. Thus the SIQR adequately compares how closely their data are bunched.

For grouped data, the quartiles are found by going one-quarter and three-quarters of the way up the ogive, across to the graph and then reading off the data value on the horizontal axis.

On the ogive in Figure 9.16 Q_1 can be read off by going across to the graph at a height of 25 per cent and Q_3 by going across at a height of 75 per cent. These meet the graph at horizontal readings of £124 and £154. Hence, the SIQR is: $\frac{1}{2}$(£154–£124) = £15.

Standard deviation

In one sense, the standard deviation (s.d.) averages the differences between the data values and the mean. However, since (a) some differences are positive and some negative

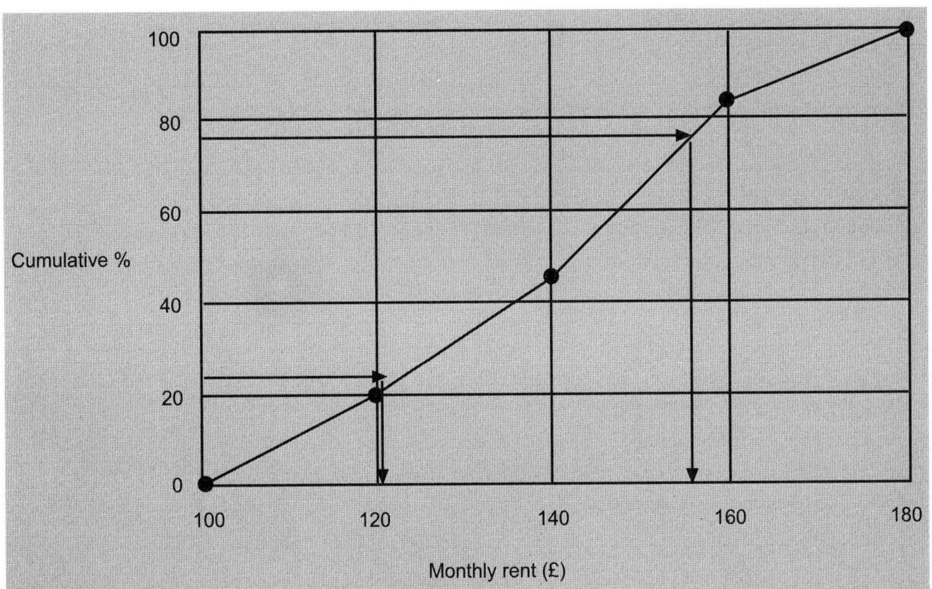

FIGURE 9.16 Ogive.

and so tend to cancel out, and (b) very small differences from the mean do not matter much, we square the differences *before* we average, thus giving all positive terms *and* making very small differences insignificant. To keep the units right, we must square root at the end.

The formula can be written as:

$$\text{Standard deviation} = \sqrt{\left\{\frac{\Sigma\,(\text{Entry} - \text{Mean})^2}{\text{No. of entries}}\right\}}$$

For example, for the data 1, 3, 3, 3, 5, 5, 5, 5, 7 where the mean is 4.1, the standard deviation is given by:

$$\text{s.d.} = \sqrt{\left\{\frac{(1-4.1)^2+(3-4.1)^2+(3-4.1)^2+(3-4.1)^2+(5-4.1)^2+(5-4.1)^2+(5-4.1)^2+(5-4.1)^2+(7-4.1)^2}{9}\right\}}$$

$$= \sqrt{\left\{\frac{(1-4.1)^2+(3-4.1)^2\times 3+(5-4.1)^2\times 4+(7-4.1)^2}{9}\right\}}$$

$$= 1.66$$

It is sometimes easier to rewrite this formula as:

$$\text{s.d.} = \sqrt{\{\text{Average value of } x^2 - (\text{Average value of } x)^2\}} \text{ where } x \text{ are the entries}$$

$$= \sqrt{\left\{\left(\frac{1^2+3^2+3^2+3^2+5^2+5^2+5^2+5^2+7^2}{9}\right) - (4.1)^2\right\}}$$

$$= \sqrt{\left\{\left(\frac{1^2+3^2\times 3+5^2\times 4+7^2}{9}\right) - (4.1)^2\right\}}$$

$$= 1.66$$

The calculations are most easily done by setting up a table as shown in Table 9.20. Hence:

$$\text{s.d.} = \sqrt{\left\{\frac{\Sigma(x^2\times f)}{\Sigma f} - (\text{Mean})^2\right\}} = \sqrt{\left\{\frac{177}{9} - (4.1)^2\right\}} = 1.66$$

When finding the standard deviation of grouped data, we use the class midpoints for x, just as when finding the mean (Table 9.21). Hence:

$$\text{s.d.} = \sqrt{\left\{\frac{593\,400}{30} - (139.3)^2\right\}} = 19.14$$

Note: The standard deviation of the data sets whose histograms were shown in Figure 9.15, are 1.6, 1.0, and 2.3, respectively. The standard deviation allows us to compare how closely the data are bunched around the mean value.

TABLE 9.20 Sum of entries squared

Values, x	Frequency, f	x^2	$x^2 \times f$
1	1	1	1
3	3	9	27
5	4	25	100
7	1	49	49
Sum (Σ)	9		177

TABLE 9.21 Sum of entries squared (grouped data)

Classes	Frequency	Midpoints, x	x^2	$x^2 \times f$
100 and <120	6	110	12 100	726 000
120 and <140	8	130	16 900	135 200
140 and <160	12	150	22 500	270 000
160 and <180	4	170	28 900	115 600
Sum (Σ)	30			593 400

'But, what does it mean?' is a question often asked. It is hard to get a feeling for the standard deviation, whereas the SIQR, as half the range of the middle half of the data, is much easier to understand. The standard deviation tells you how close to the mean the bulk of the data are, but is not terribly informative for single data sets. Do not worry about understanding it except when making comparisons.

As an example, the monthly rents data in Table 9.16 had a mean of £139.3 and a standard deviation of £19.14. If you knew that monthly rents in a different area had an average of £140.6 and a standard deviation of £39.91, you would know that the average rents did not differ very much in the two areas but that there was more than twice as much variation in the rents in the second area than in the first – there would be more rents much higher than £140.6 and more rents much lower than £140.6, whereas in the first area, rents would cluster more closely around £139.3.

Table 9.22 summarizes the measures of dispersion that we have discussed.

TABLE 9.22 Summary of three measures of dispersion

Measure	Definition	Advantage	Disadvantage	When to use
Range	Lowest to highest values	Simple	Ignores how data are distributed within the range	Rarely, except as extra information
SIQR	$\frac{1}{2}(Q_3 - Q_1)$	Cuts out extremes		When using the median, i.e. for badly skewed variables
Standard deviation, σ	Average of squared distances from the mean	Uses all the data	Distorted by skewed data	When using the mean, i.e. whenever data are not badly skewed

ACTIVITY 8

1. **Find and compare the standard deviation and SIQR for the North and South population data given in Activity 7 on page 295.**
2. **Find the standard deviation and SIQR for the questionnaire data set out in Table 9.8 on page 285. (Use your ogive from Activity 6.1.)**

Using a sample to estimate the standard deviation of a population

The standard deviation in the above form turns out *not* to be the best estimate of the standard deviation of the population that the sample was taken from, simply because a sample is always less varied than the population. To obtain the *best estimate* of the population standard deviation that the sample was taken from, one must divide by $n - 1$, i.e. the number of entries minus 1, when averaging the squared terms, instead of dividing by n. For example, if the data set 1, 3, 3, 3, 5, 5, 5, 5, 7 were *not* the whole population, but merely a sample from it ($n = 9$) we would use:

$$\text{s.d.} = \sqrt{\left\{\frac{1^2 + (3^2 \times 3) + (5^2 \times 4) + 7^2}{8} - (4.1)^2\right\}} = 1.76$$

as the best estimate for the standard deviation of the population.

Notes:

- The sample mean itself is the best estimate of the population mean – no adjustment is needed.
- Most spreadsheets assume that you are dealing with samples and use this $(n - 1)$ formula. Most calculators give both versions.

Calculators, symbols and terminology

Even using the tabular form, calculating the standard deviation is very tedious. Fortunately, many calculators will find standard deviations for you, as will all computer spreadsheet packages. Refer to the manual for instructions, but it will help you to be familiar with a few standard terms and symbols:

x	is used for the actual data values
f	is used for the frequencies
n	is used for the total number of data items.
$\bar{x}$ ('x bar')	is used for the mean of a sample
μ ('mu')	is used for the mean of a population
σ or σ_n or $x\sigma_n$	population standard deviation: where you are interested in the data for their own sake and not as a sample
s or σ_{n-1} or $x\sigma_{n-1}$	sample deviation: where data are a sample and you want the best estimate of the standard deviation of the population that the sample is from
σ^2	often called the variance, it is a little-used measure of spread

ACTIVITY 9
Repeat part 2 of Activity 7 (page 295) finding the standard deviation for the questionnaire data, but this time remember that the questionnaire data were based on a sample. (You should find that there is little difference for such a large data set.)

Margins of error

If your data come from a sample which you are using to estimate results for the whole population, you should be aware that there is bound to be some difference between the result from your sample and the true population result that you are trying to estimate. The theory behind this is known as **sampling distribution theory** and is beyond the scope of this book, but you should know the following results, which relate to samples of size 30 or more:

- The most that a sample mean is likely to be out when estimating a population mean, can be estimated from the formula:

$$2 \times \frac{\text{Standard deviation}}{\sqrt{\text{Sample size}}}$$

- The most that a sample percentage is likely to be out when estimating the corresponding percentage in a population, can be estimated from the formula:

$$2 \times \sqrt{\left\{\frac{\text{Sample \%} \times (100\% - \text{Sample \%})}{\text{Sample size}}\right\}}$$

Example

The mean amount spent on a holiday in our travel agent questionnaire was £1759.68 with a standard deviation (σ_{n-1}) of £919.61. This was based on a sample of 155 people, so the true average spending for the whole population (assuming that the sample was representative) will differ from £1759.68 by at most:

$$2 \times \frac{£919.61}{\sqrt{155}} = £147.73$$

The percentage of people in the sample who were either satisfied or very satisfied with their travel agent was 69 per cent. Provided that the sample was representative, the percentage of the whole population will differ from 69 per cent by at most:

$$2 \times \sqrt{\left\{\frac{69\% \times (100\% - 69\%)}{155}\right\}} = 7.4\%$$

ACTIVITY 10

1. **(a) Find the maximum error in using the mean of the monthly rent data from Table 9.16 to predict the mean of the population.**
   (b) What assumptions are you making here?

2. **(a) Of our sample of 155 people, 35 per cent had considered an activity holiday. How far out, at most, might this be as an estimate for the whole population?**
   (b) Can you be sure that more than 30 per cent of the population would consider an activity holiday?
   (c) Of our sample of 155 people, 15 per cent had considered a camping holiday. How far out, at most, might this be as an estimate for the whole population?

Note how the closer the sample percentage is to 50 per cent, the greater are the margins of error.

Two-way analysis

Once you have looked at each variable individually, you may well want to look at some variables in pairs. For instance, you might want to see how the two sexes differ in their satisfaction with their travel agent: are males easier to please, for instance? Or you might want to see how an outlet's sales depend on the size of the population it serves.

Before starting a two-way analysis, it is important to decide which pairings you really need to look at. For a data set with 10 variables, for instance, there are 45 different ways of pairing the variables: hopefully you need not analyze all 45.

For qualitative data, two-way tables are the best way to proceed. Scatterplots are also useful for quantitative data. You may also want to work out measures of average and spread for different sections of one quantitative variable, e.g. the average and spread of the sales for each geographical area.

Two-way tables

If we want to see how the two sexes differ in their satisfaction with their travel agent, we could set up a table as shown (Table 9.23).

- The Total row and column are both optional.
- When choosing which categories to go on the rows and which on the columns:
  - try to be consistent between tables, i.e. if you put the satisfaction levels as column headings here, do the same in the later tables;
  - check that it is easy to make the comparisons that you want to make: sometimes reversing the table will make a comparison easier.

TABLE 9.23 Two-way table

	Very satisfied	Fairly satisfied	Not at all satisfied	No opinion	Total
Male	6	48	9	2	65
Female	30	41	9	10	90
Total	36	89	18	12	155

- Computer spreadsheets will count the numbers in each cell for you (e.g. Pivot Table in Excel 5), or you can count by hand as with a tally, perhaps using five-bar gates.

Percentage tables

Tables, like tallies, may be more useful in a percentage form. Now there is a choice of which total you take the percentages out of: sometimes percentages of the column totals are the more useful (Table 9.24) and sometimes percentages of the row totals (Table 9.25).

In the case of percentages of columns, the formula is:

$$\text{Percentage} = \frac{\text{Count in that cell}}{\text{Column total}} \times 100\%$$

From Table 9.24 we can see that 17 per cent of the very satisfied customers were male and 83 per cent female; 54 per cent of the fairly satisfied were male and 46 per cent female, half of the not at all satisfied customers were male and half were female.

Actually, this is not very helpful here because there were far more women customers than men. It would be useful to consider what percentage of the males were highly satisfied, i.e. to work out the percentages as fractions of that sex or row.

For percentages of rows, the calculation is:

$$\text{Percentage} = \frac{\text{Count in that cell}}{\text{Row total}} \times 100\%$$

Now we see from Table 9.25 that, while the highest percentages for both sexes were fairly satisfied, a greater percentage of men than of women were not at all satisfied, whereas a much greater percentage of women were very satisfied. We can see also that a

TABLE 9.24 Two-way table: percentages of the column totals

	Very satisfied	Fairly satisfied	Not at all satisfied	No opinion	Total
Male	17% = 6/36 × 100%	54%	50%	17%	42%
Female	83%	46%	50%	83%	58%
Total	100%	100%	100%	100%	100%

TABLE 9.25 Two-way table: percentages of the row totals

	Very satisfied	Fairly satisfied	Not at all satisfied	No opinion	Total
Male	9% = 6/65 × 100%	74%	14%	3%	100%
Female	33%	46%	10%	11%	100%
Total	23%	57%	12%	7%	100%

TABLE 9.26 Representativeness of sample: frequency of each age group by sex

	Up to 24	25–34	35–44	45–54	55–64	65+
Male	10	10	11	11	11	12
Female	14	14	15	15	16	16

greater proportion of women had no opinion. Table 9.25 also shows the overall percentages for each degree of satisfaction.

There are no rules as to which percentages to take: you have to decide which is most sensible in a given situation.

Tables for discrete or grouped quantitative variables can be set up in the same way: e.g. we might use Table 9.26 to check that we had a representative sample of customers.

Scatterplots

If we want to see how two quantitative variables are related, a scatterplot may be more revealing and easier to produce than a table (Figure 9.17). It does not require us to group the data and so can represent the data values in more detail.

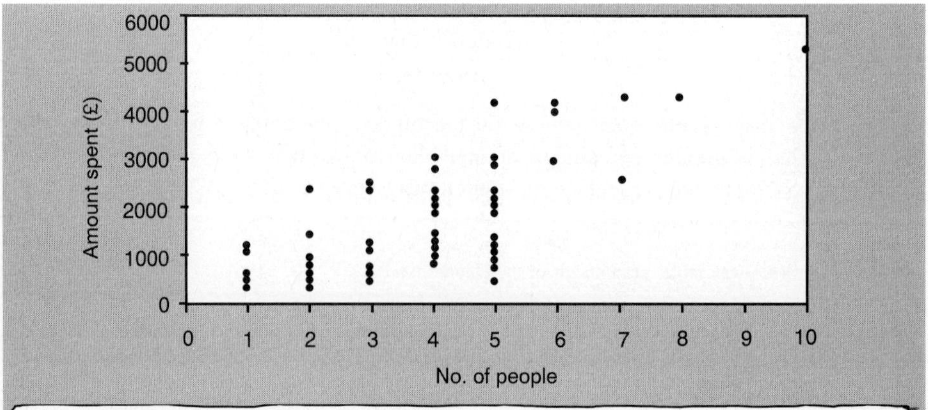

FIGURE 9.17 Scatterplot.

Drawing a scatterplot by hand

You should use graph or squared paper if at all possible.

- Choose one variable to go along the *x*-axis (horizontal) and one the *y*-axis (vertical). (If one of the variables depends on the other, it is usual to place the dependent variable on the *y*-axis, e.g. if we want to look at the amount spent on a holiday compared to the number of people involved, the amount spent will go on the *y*-axis.)
- Set up a scale along each axis that will allow you to show all the values of that variable. (It can facilitate the interpretation to start all vertical axes at 0, unless there is a strong reason to do otherwise.)
- For each record, mark the corresponding point with a cross or a neat dot.
- Do not join the points unless there is a logical order to them, e.g. one of the variables is time.

For example, to produce a scatterplot of amount spent on a holiday by number of people involved:

- Since the number of people ranges from 1 to 10, we may choose our *x*-axis to start at 1 and end at 10, using 1 cm steps for 1 person.
- Since the amount spent ranges from £525 to £5350, we may choose to start our *y*-axis at 0 and end at £6000, using 1 cm steps for £500.

We see from Figure 9.17 that, as expected, expenditure is higher when it covers more people. However, we also see that there are some low expenditures for 5 people: these are probably cheaper family holidays.

Drawing a scatterplot on a computer

Scatterplots on a computer may offer you the option of adding a 'trend line' (Figure 9.18). This shows the straight line (or curve) that best fits the set of data. Be careful,

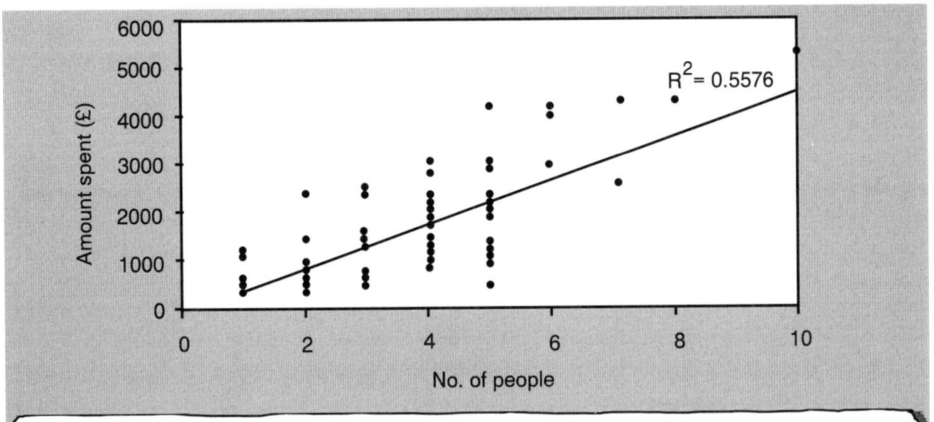

FIGURE 9.18 Scatterplot with trendline.

though – the package will produce the trendline you ask for, even when it is not a sensible thing to do. You should really study the topic of linear regression (on which these trendlines are based) before introducing them into your charts. If your package offers the option of displaying an r^2 (coefficient of determination) value for the trendline, choose it: r^2 should be fairly large (as a rule of thumb, 0.5 or more) before it is really meaningful to display the trendline. (Refer to Chapter 8, page 241, for an explanation of r^2.)

Comparing sections of a quantitative variable

It is often useful, for comparison purposes, to work out measures of average and spread for different sections of one quantitative variable, e.g. the average and spread of the sales for each geographical area from the data in Table 9.27.

Table 9.27 would be interpreted as showing that the average sales per outlet in the North and West were considerably higher than in the South and East. The sales per outlet in the East were very varied, however, whereas those elsewhere were more consistent.

TABLE 9.27

Area	Sales (£000)	
	Mean	s.d.
N	72	9
S	63	8
W	79	11
E	59	20

Five-point summaries

You will remember that the mean and standard deviation are distorted by very skewed data; in such circumstances you might want to produce what is known as a five-point summary for each section. This displays the minimum value, the first quartile, the median, the third quartile and the maximum value for each section. Table 9.28 sets out an example.

Boxplots

Five-point summaries can be illustrated by **boxplots** (Figure 9.19). To construct a boxplot:

- Draw a horizontal axis whose scale runs from below the minimum to above the maximum. For the data in Table 9.28 we could start at 50 and go up in steps of 10 to 110.
- For each section, using a new line for each:
  - draw a box from Q_1 to Q_3;
  - add a whisker from the left end of the box to the minimum;

TABLE 9.28 Five-point summary

Area	Sales (£000)				
	Minimum	Q_1	Median	Q_3	Maximum
N	61	66	72	78	93
S	54	58	65	72	82
W	61	63	74	76	88
E	50	53	61	73	102

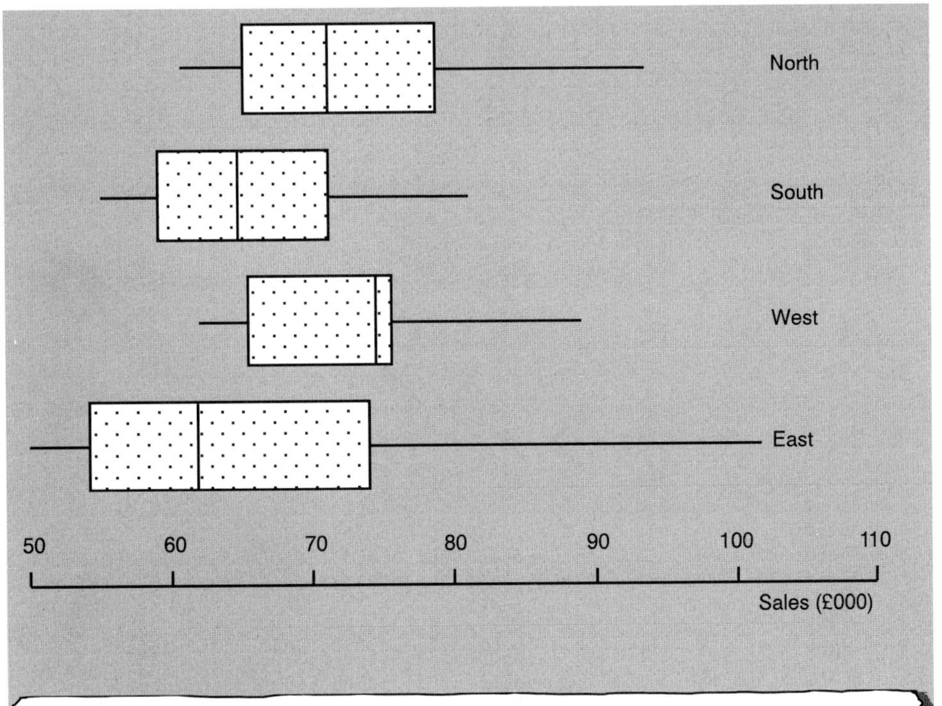

FIGURE 9.19 Boxplots showing sales by area.

  - add a whisker from the right end of the box to the maximum;
  - mark the median with a vertical line in the box.
- Label each boxplot.

The box marks the spread and position of the central half of the data, and the whiskers the top and bottom quarters.

- The longer the box, the greater the spread.
- The less central the box, the more skewed the data.

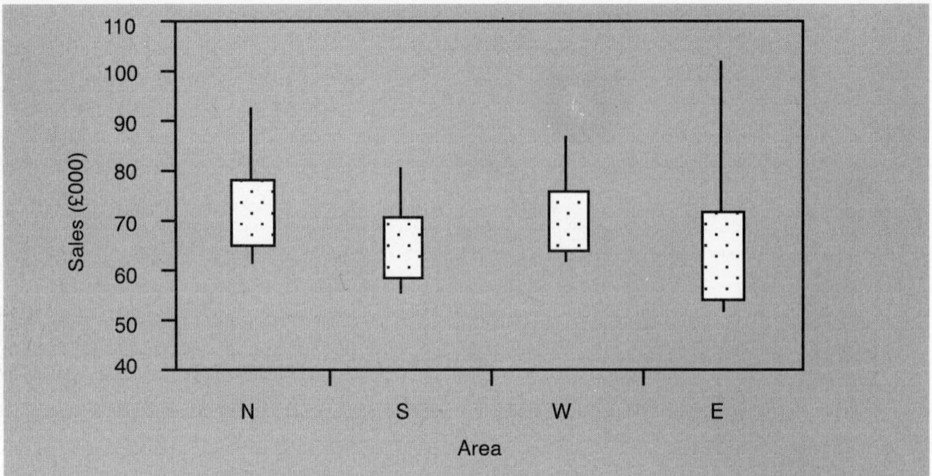

FIGURE 9.20 High–low plots.

From the display in Figure 9.19, we can see clearly that the sales in each area are quite skewed, with the bulk of the sales at the lower ends and longish tails at the higher ends. The East has the longest box, illustrating the greater variety of sales values in this area. The average sales in the North and West are still slightly higher than in the South and East.

Some spreadsheet packages produce plots similar to boxplots, but vertically. These are often known as high–low plots. An example is given in Figure 9.20.

ACTIVITY 11
Produce five-point summaries and draw a pair of boxplots to compare the North and South population data from part 1 of Activity 7 (page 295). Interpret what they tell you.

Presenting your data

Once you have analyzed your data and decided for yourself what it can tell you, you have to think about presenting it to others. The procedure to follow is set out below:

- **Decide what facts you want to get across.** You are likely only to have the time or space for a few facts so you must consider carefully what is essential.
- **Decide how best to get those facts across.** What is best will depend on the audience and method of presentation. The main aims are:

- to make it easy for the audience to take in the information;
- to keep the audience interested;
- to ensure that the audience will get the correct message.

- Once you have prepared your presentation or report, check that:
  - there is a suitable balance of text and diagrams;
  - there is sufficient variety in the diagrams not to be boring;
  - there are not so many different types of diagram that the report is hard to follow;
  - diagrams are consistent, in the colours used and in the ordering of the categories;
  - the diagrams are suitable for the intended audience, e.g. avoid lighthearted diagrams (such as pictograms) for a serious report, avoid 'academic' diagrams (such as boxplots or ogives) for a report to the general public;
  - you are not misleading your audience by misuse of scales or three-dimensional effects, etc.

We have already met several possible diagrams from tallies to boxplots. Do not despise the simple tally or table to convey your message, but consider breaking the monotony by replacing some with an alternative.

Points to watch in tallies and tables

Tallies

- Keep the order of categories logical:
  - use the natural order for quantitative and ordinal variables;
  - for nominal variables, consider ordering the categories in descending order of frequency.
- For percentages:
  - round to whole numbers;
  - ensure percentages add up to 100, except for questions where more than one answer could be ticked, in which case explain why they do not sum to 100.

Tables

The considerations for tallies above similarly apply to tables, but also:

- Consider which categories will form the rows and which the columns: swap if it improves the clarity, but be reasonably consistent. Many people find comparing down columns easier than comparing across rows.
- Consider highlighting a particular row or column to draw out your message.

Possible alternative diagrams to convey your message

If possible, use a computer spreadsheet package to draw your diagrams. You will need to type the tally or table you wish to illustrate into the spreadsheet first.

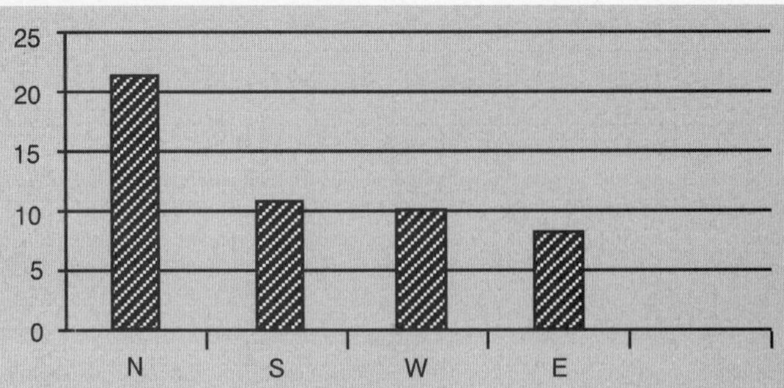

FIGURE 9.21 Bar chart.

One-variable diagrams

Bar chart

Advantages and disadvantages:

- Easy to draw.
- Familiar to all (Figure 9.21).
- Good for making comparisons.

Special points to watch:

- The order of categories should be logical and match any tallies of the same data.
- The bars should all be the same width.
- Start the vertical axis at 0, if possible.
- If you must start at other than 0 indicate this clearly by a break in each bar or in the vertical axis, with a zigzag or wavy stroke across each end of the break.

Stacked bar chart

Advantages and disadvantages:

- Difficult to compare heights of sections.
- Shows the total well. (Do not use a stacked chart if the total height has no meaning. In Figure 9.22 the height shows the total number of outlets.)

A stacked barchart would definitely *not* be suitable for illustrating the following data:

Applications received	69
Called for interview	12
Shortlisted	6

Here the 6 shortlisted are a *subset* of the 12 called for interview, who are a subset of the 69 applications. The total height of a stacked bar here would be meaningless.

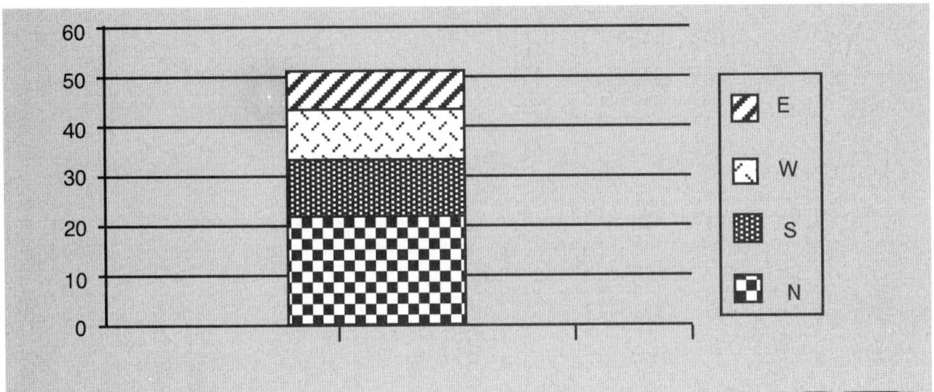

FIGURE 9.22 Stacked bar chart.

Line or area chart

Advantages and disadvantages:

- Use this only when there is a logical order to the points. In Figure 9.23 the order of N, S, W and E could be changed giving a completely different pattern to the graph so it is not a good chart for these data.

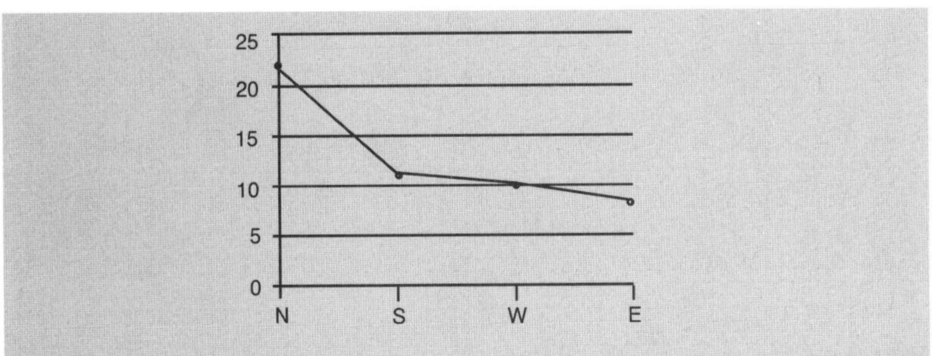

FIGURE 9.23 Line chart (not a sensible one!).

Pictograms

There are two types of pictogram: one where it is the number of pictures that represents the frequency and one where it is the height of the picture that represents the frequency.

- For the former, use a key to show how many items each picture represents (Figure 9.24).

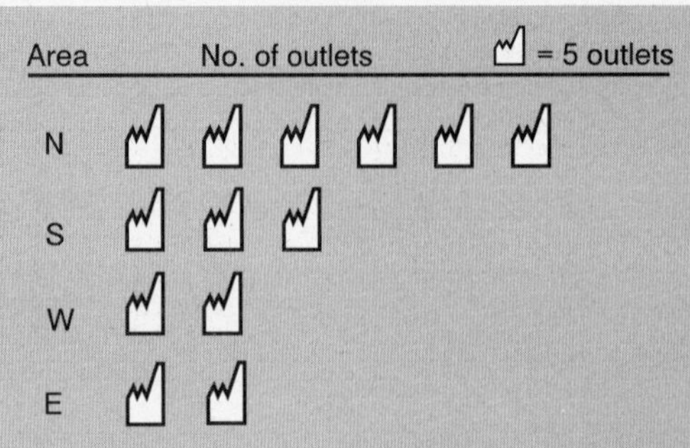

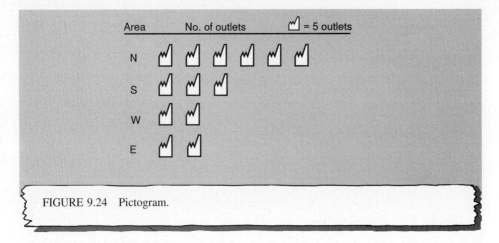

FIGURE 9.24 Pictogram.

- Use part-pictures if necessary.
- In the latter, take care that the width of the picture is the same for each picture and does not increase in proportion to its height: otherwise people will compare areas and so get false information. Better a distorted picture than distorted information (Figure 9.25).

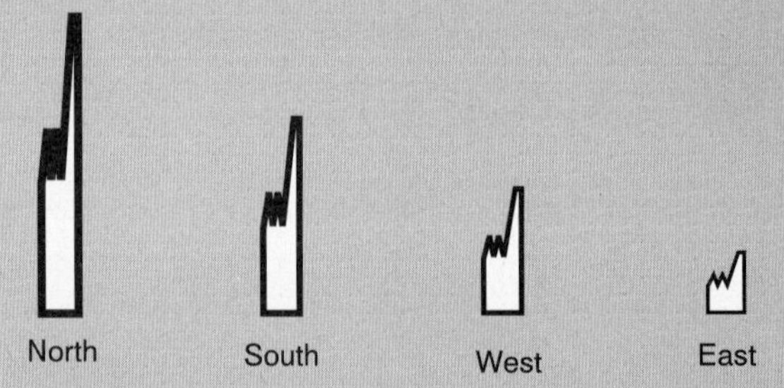

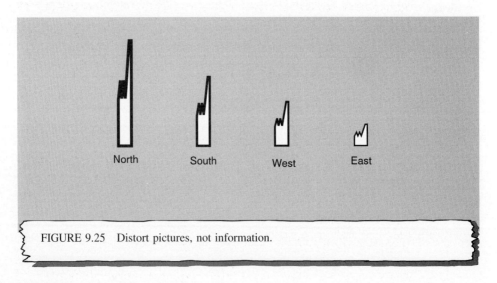

FIGURE 9.25 Distort pictures, not information.

Pie charts

Advantages and disadvantages

- Only shows relative, not actual, sizes (Figure 9.26).
- Difficult to compare sizes.
- It is not possible to show any categories that have 0 frequency.

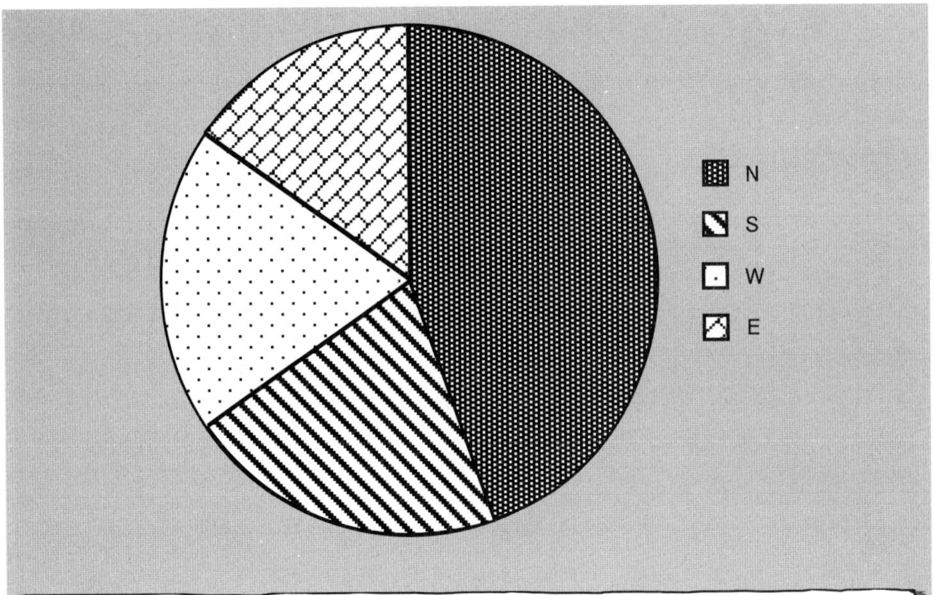

FIGURE 9.26 Pie chart.

To construct a pie chart:

- Using a protractor, draw each segment with angle calculated from the following formula:

$$\text{angle of segment} = \frac{\text{number in category}}{\text{total number}} \times 360°$$

- The order of categories should be logical and match any tallies of the same data.
- If there is one category of particular interest, consider 'exploding' its segment:

Two-variable diagrams

When illustrating tables, then stacked or multiple bar charts are ideal, but you must think carefully about the following points.

Firstly, which variable should be put on which axis (because it changes the message). Figure 9.27 illustrates the total number of each sex questioned, but this may not be what you want to show. Figure 9.28 illustrates more clearly the total number of people in each category. There is more logic in having the sexes on the horizontal axis for a *percentage* stacked bar chart (Figure 9.29) where the responses of the sexes are being compared.

Secondly, you need to consider whether to stack or use a multiple chart. Multiple

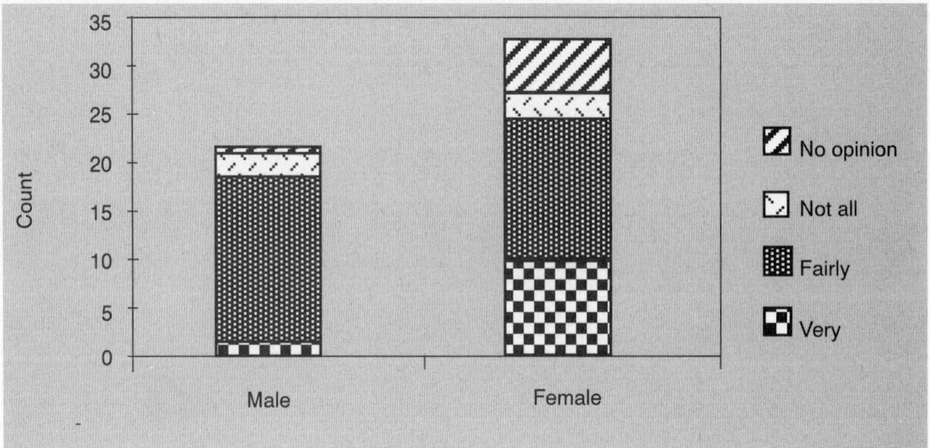

FIGURE 9.27 Poor use of stacked bar chart.

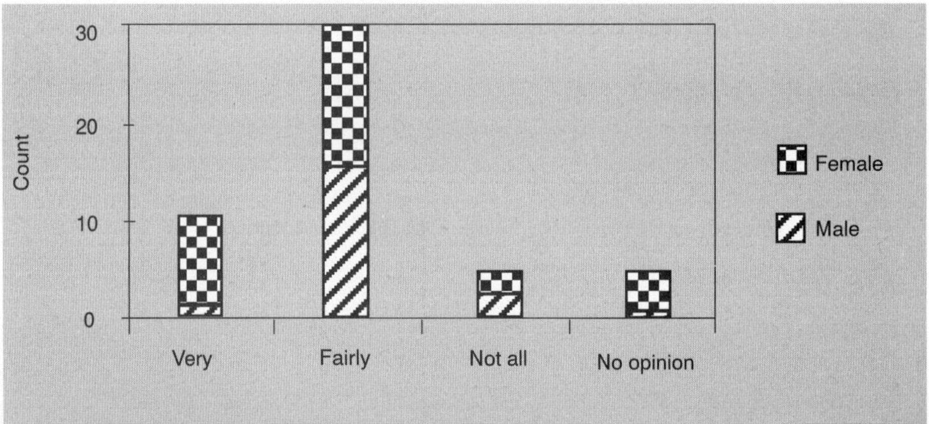

FIGURE 9.28 Good use of stacked bar chart.

charts are better if the totals in the stacked chart are not meaningful, and are also better for comparing heights of sections. Take care to insert gaps between the groups of bars so that the eye groups the bars together as it should (Figure 9.30).

Thirdly, consider whether the existence of a logical order to categories makes a line or area chart sensible (Figure 9.31). There is a logical order from 'Very' down to 'Not at all satisfied' (though the 'No opinion' category coming at the end makes the righthand end rather strange). Note how an area chart 'stacks' the data like a stacked chart and so indicates totals.

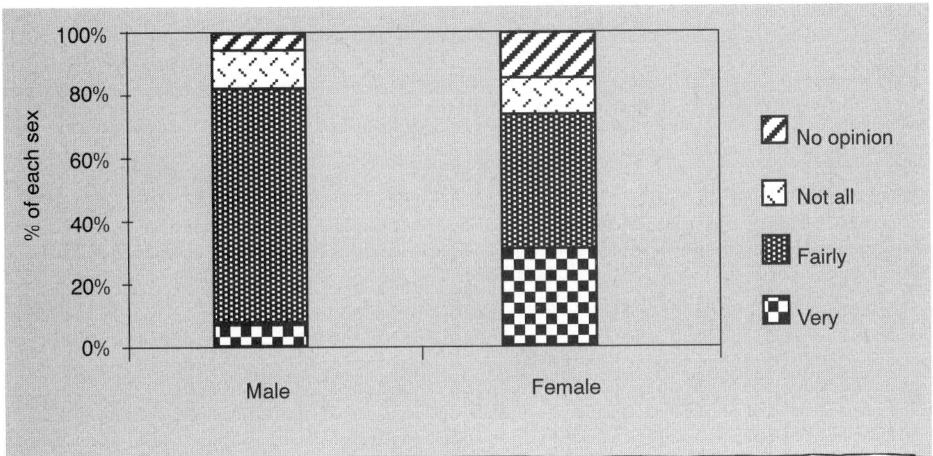

FIGURE 9.29 Percentage stacked bar chart.

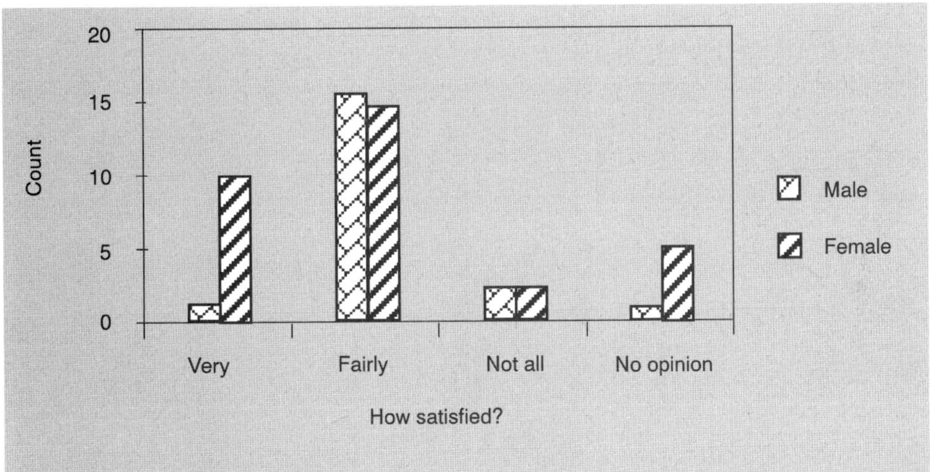

FIGURE 9.30 Multiple bar chart.

Quantitative illustrations

We have met histograms, ogives, stem-and-leaf displays, boxplots and scatterplots. Only the last of these is suitable for a report to non-specialists; the other diagrams, however, would be excellent to include in a report to anyone with statistical knowledge.

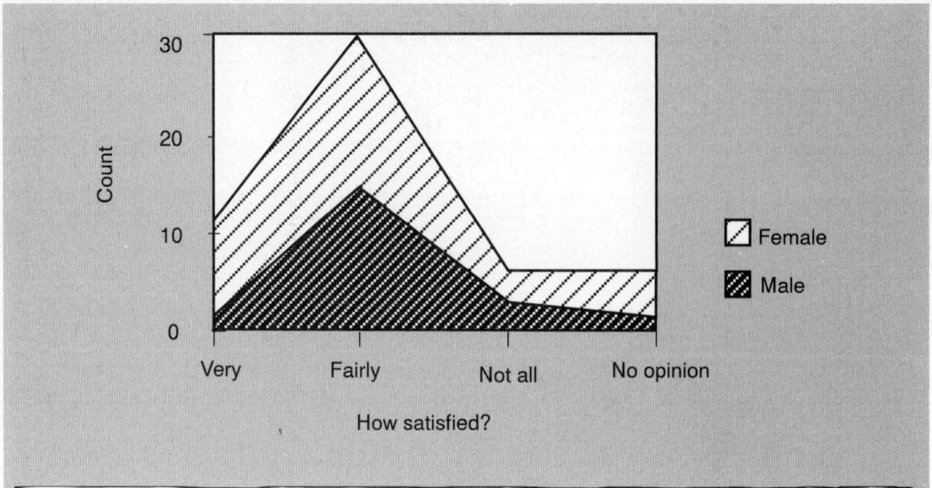

FIGURE 9.31 Area chart.

General points about charts

Include:

- Titles and units on axes, if appropriate
- Scales or labels on axes, as appropriate
- A key, if necessary
- Source of data if from outside your study
- Captions to the charts summarizing the main point of interest, e.g. 'Graph showing the skewed distribution of income'.

Sometimes two simple diagrams can communicate a message better than one complicated one.

If you show two different variables on the same chart, either:

- Use the same vertical scale for each; or
- Show the scale for one variable on the left axis and the scale for the other on the right axis (often called a **combination chart**, see Figure 9.32).

ACTIVITY 12
Each of Figures 9.33–9.38 and Table 9.29 either misled or confused its readers. For each, decide what was wrong with it and how the correct message could have been conveyed.

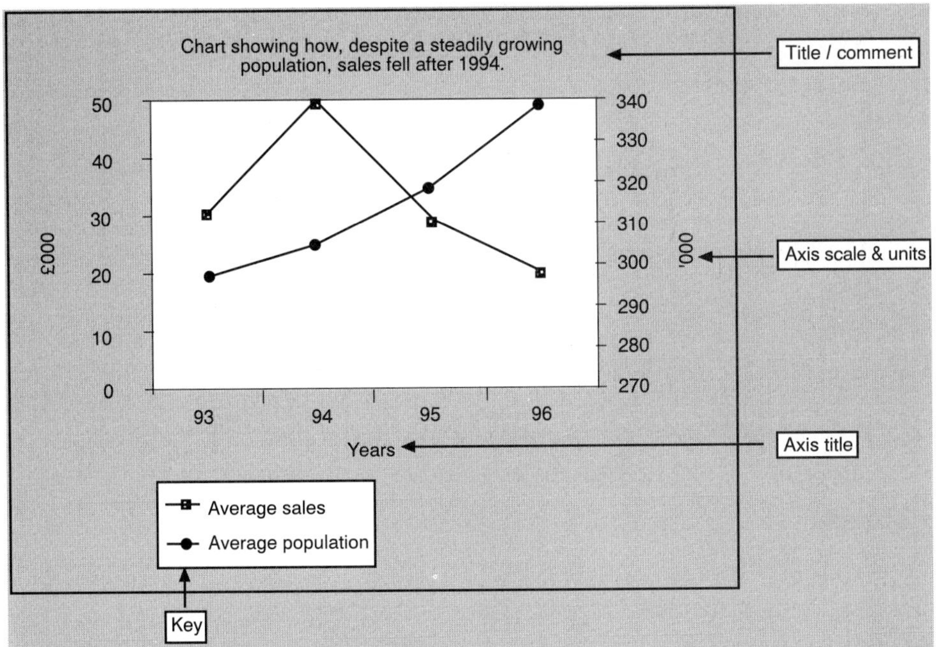

FIGURE 9.32 Example of a well presented chart.

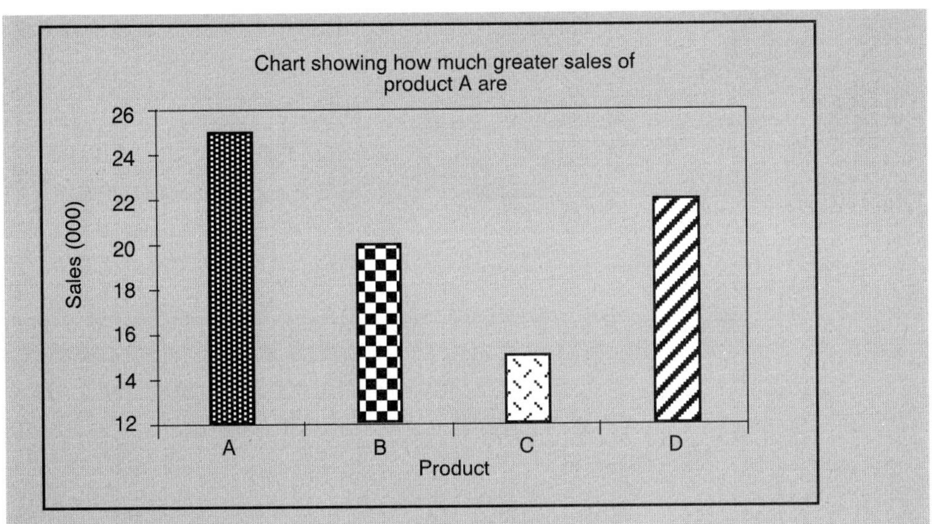

FIGURE 9.33

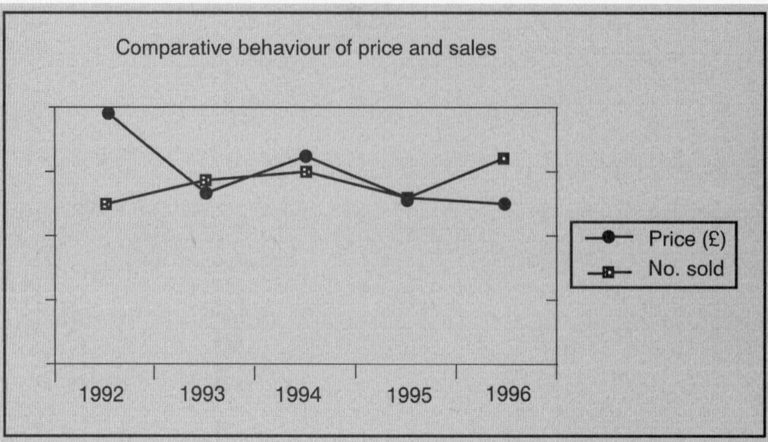

FIGURE 9.34

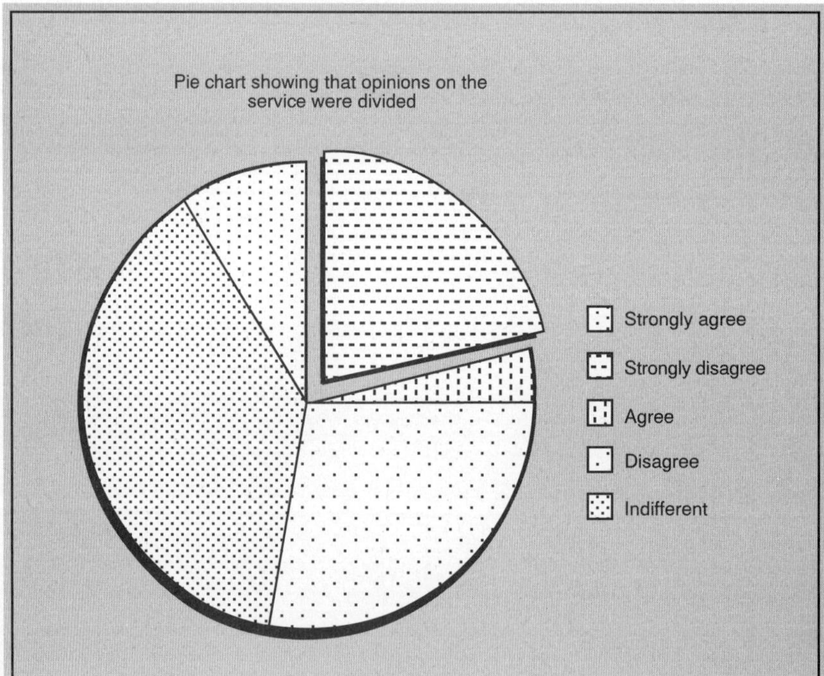

FIGURE 9.35

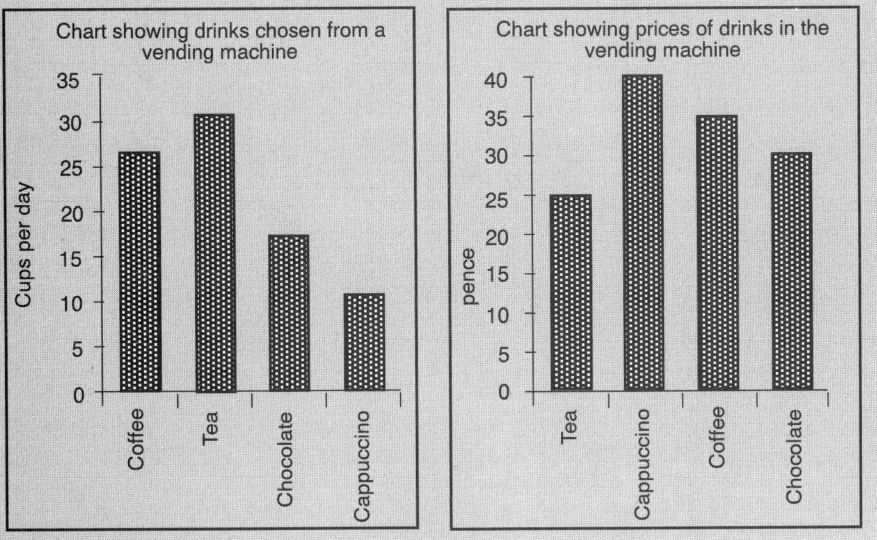

FIGURE 9.36

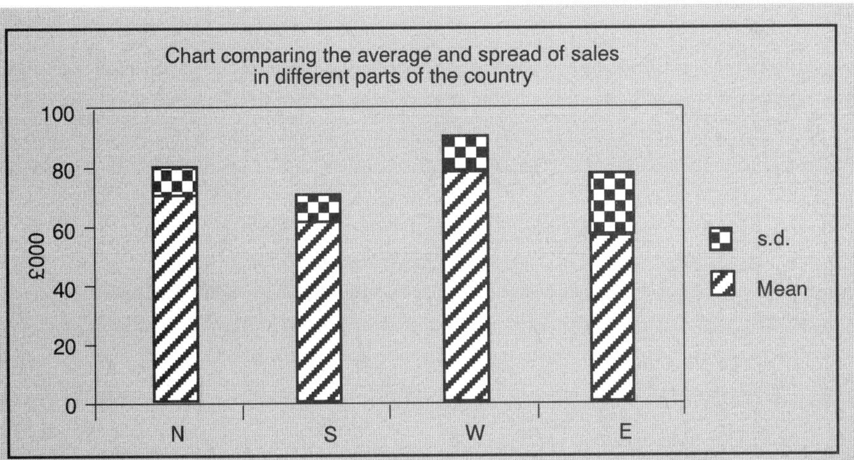

FIGURE 9.37

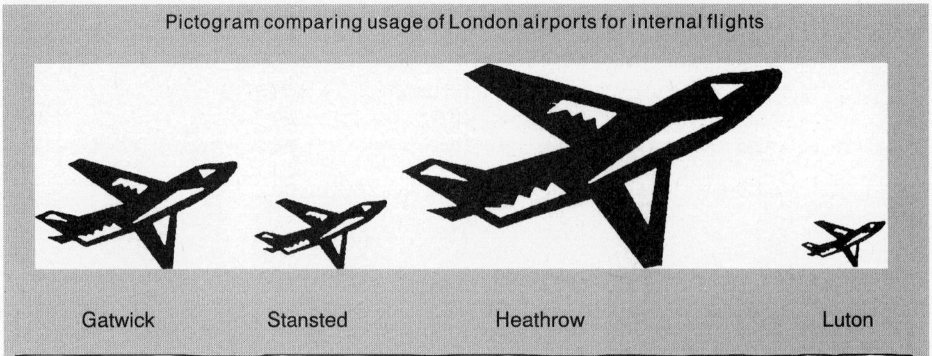

FIGURE 9.38

TABLE 9.29

	North	South	West	East
% of outlets with increased sales	21.978%	13.821%	33.549%	18.179%
% decrease in outlets over 1996	1.982	−2.175	5.210	10.569
% of outlets in this area	43	22	16	20

Suggested answers to Activities

Activity 1

Question 1: quantitative, continuous
Question 2: quantitative, discrete
Question 3: the underlying variable is quantitative, discrete but the responses will be qualitative, ordinal
Question 4: qualitative, nominal
Question 5: four qualitative, ordinal variables
Question 6: qualitative, ordinal
Question 7: qualitative, nominal
Question 8: the underlying variable is quantitative, continuous but the responses will be qualitative, ordinal
Question 9: qualitative, nominal
Question 10: open – text responses do not really fit into this classification

Activity 2

No.	Q1	Q2	Q3	Q4 a	Q4 b	Q4 c	Q4 d	Q4 e	Q4 f	Q5: 1st choice	Q5: 2nd choice	Q6	Changes 1	Changes 2

Coding: **Question 1:** no coding – enter number
Question 2: Promoted 2; Non-promoted 1
Question 3: Yes, very 4; Yes, moderately 3; Not very 2; Not at all 1
Question 4: for each: 1 if ticked, 0 if not ticked
Question 5: no coding – enter letter
Question 6: 5 for box nearest to 'Highly satisfactory' down to 1 for 'Highly unsatisfactory'

Coding for common responses to question 7 can be entered later.

Activity 3

Response	*Count*	*Percentage*
3 (Very satisfied)	18	31%
2 (Fairly satisfied)	29	49%
1 (Not at all satisfied)	12	20%

The above percentages are calculated ignoring non-responses. If you calculated your responses 'including non-responses', the percentages are: 3 – 29%, 2 – 47%, 1 – 19%, blank – 5%.

Activity 4

1. North — Population (in '000s)

0	98					
1	01	09	60	90	90	98
2	00	34	36	86		
3	06	19	19	22		
4	18	19	23	67	95	
5	12	45				

South

0						
1	35	48	67	88	89	99
2	01	40	90			
3	01					
4						
5	16					

A back-to-back stem-and-leaf would be even better.

Both sets of data range between about 100 000 and the mid 500 000s. The North data show a fairly normal shape, though they are also somewhat bimodal, peaking in the 100 000s and in the 400 000s. The South data are positively skewed, concentrating in the 100 000s.

2.

0.9	9	9	9	9
1.0	0			
1.1	3	7		
1.2	3	4	9	
1.3	5	5	5	9
1.4	9	9	9	9
1.5	2			

Note the large number of 9s, indicating that the item is often being priced just under a round figure. The data are bimodal with a peak at £0.99 and another at £1.49. There are no items priced under £0.99 and none above £1.52.

Activity 5

1. 15, 18 or 20 would be sensible lowest ages, and 85 or 95 sensible highest ages. Whichever is chosen determines the size of the lowest and highest bars. If 15 and 85 are chosen the histogram is as shown in Figure 9.39. (The class 65 but <85 has frequency density 14 (=28/2).)
2. The frequency density of the last class, 5.5 to 10.5, is 1.6 (=8/5). The histogram is shown in Figure 9.40.

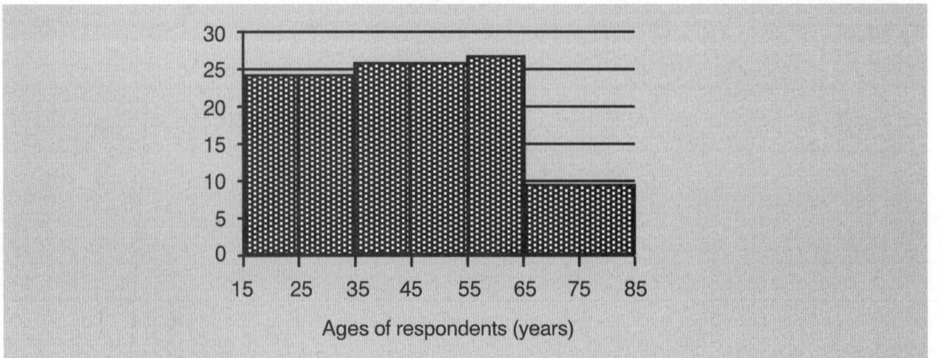

FIGURE 9.39

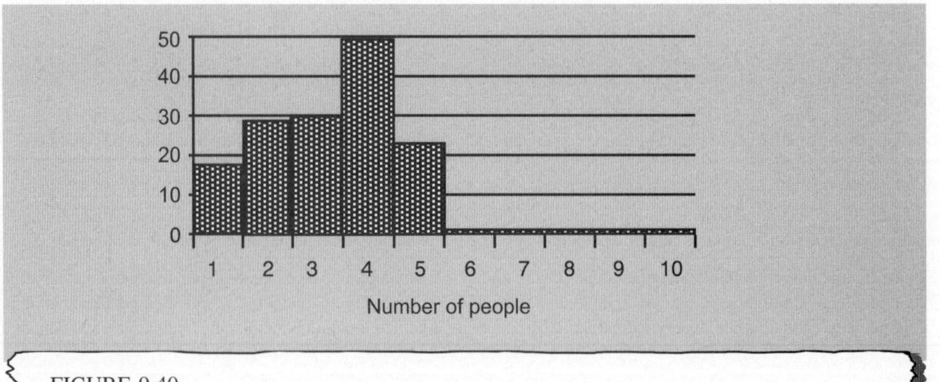

FIGURE 9.40

Activity 6

1. The cumulative frequency distribution is:

Amount spent (£)	*Cumulative frequency*
Less than 500	0
Less than 1000	27
Less than 1500	78
Less than 2000	108
Less than 2500	126
Less than 3000	141
Less than 3500	148
Less than 4000	148
Less than 4500	152
Less than 5000	154
Less than 5500	155

The ogive is shown in Figure 9.41.

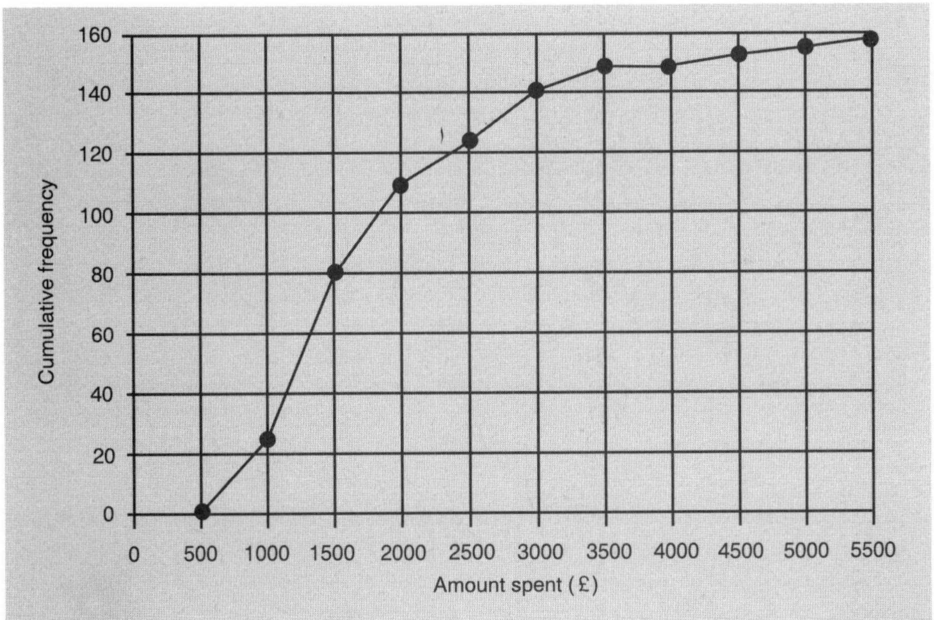

FIGURE 9.41 Ogive.

2. (a) Using the lower bound of 15 and upper bound of 85, the less than cumulative frequencies and percentages are:

Age (years)	*Cumulative frequency*	*Cumulative percentage*
Less than 15	0	0%
Less than 25	24	15%
Less than 35	48	31%
Less than 45	74	48%
Less than 55	100	65%
Less than 65	127	82%
Less than 85	155	100%

(b) The ogive is shown in Figure 9.42.

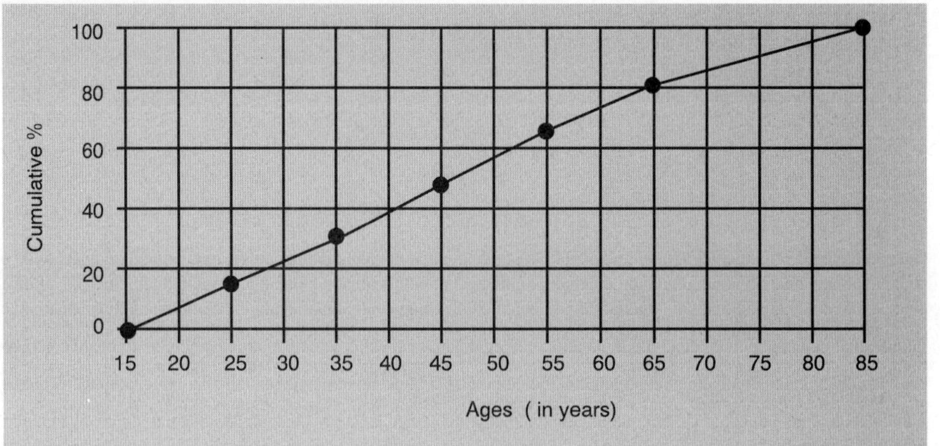

FIGURE 9.42 Percentage ogive.

Activity 7

1. North: mean 297.6; median 296; South: mean 234; median 199
2. Mean £1759.68; median (from the ogive drawn in Activity 6 part 1) £1495

Activity 8

1. North: standard deviation 135.7; SIQR = (419 − 190)/2 = 114.5
   South: standard deviation 102.4; SIQR = (290 − 167)/2 = 61.5
   There is a greater spread of population values in the North than in the South.
2. Standard deviation £916.64
   SIQR (Q_1 and Q_3 from ogive): £(2230 − 1115)/2 = £557.5

Activity 9

Sample standard deviation = £919.61

Activity 10

1. (a) Maximum error £7.11 (using, correctly, the standard deviation σ_{n-1} of £19.46. If you use the standard deviation σ_n instead, you get £6.99).
   (b) This assumes the sample was random.
2. (a) 7.7%
   (b) No. The percentage of the population might be as low as 27.3% (35%−7.7%).
   (c) 5.7%

Activity 11

The five-point summary is shown in Table 9.30 and the two boxplots in Figure 9.43.

The greater spread of the population figures in the North is apparent in the wider box. Also note the higher average and the less skewed shape of the northern data.

TABLE 9.30

Area	Population (000)				
	Minimum	Q_1	Median	Q_3	Maximum
South	135	167	199	290	516
North	98	190	296	419	545

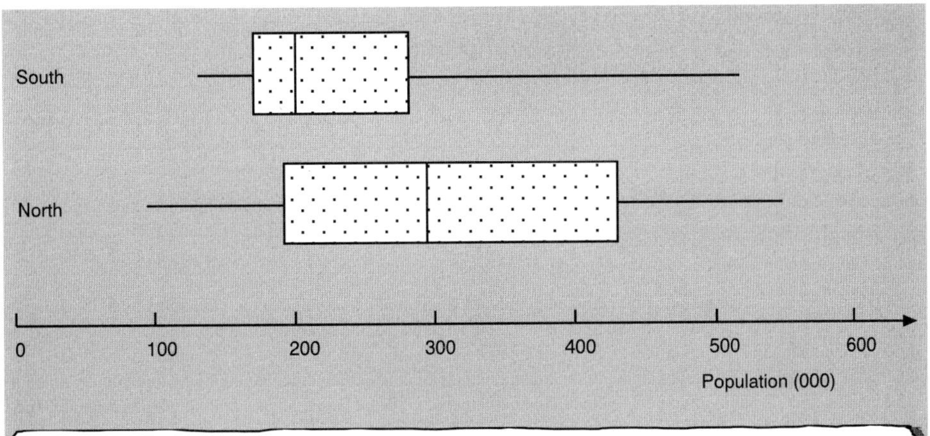

FIGURE 9.43

Activity 12

Figure 9.32: The vertical axis does not start at 0, hence A's sales appear to be about six times those of C, although they are really less than twice C's sales. This chart should have been drawn with the vertical axis starting at 0.

Figure 9.33: There is no scale shown on either vertical axis so it is impossible to tell whether the observed changes in price or in sales are negligible or significant. Scale for price should be shown on one axis and for sales on the other. The misspelling of comparative is also distracting (to those who can spell).

Figure 9.34: The shadings chosen make it impossible to work out which segment is which. The strange order of the categories also make it hard to take in the overall message of the data. Different patterns would be better, and also a logical order to the categories.

Figures 9.35 (a) and (b): The order of the drinks changes between the two charts; it should be the same on both. In particular, it would be helpful to put the drinks in descending order of demand in the first chart (tea, coffee, chocolate, cappuccino) and then keep the same order in the second chart (illustrating that the most popular drink is the cheapest and vice versa).

Figure 9.36: The total height of these bars is meaningless – it would be better to use a multiple bar chart here rather than a stacked one.

Figure 9.37: Is it the area of each plane we are meant to compare, or the length, or the height? The eye will naturally compare the area but that may not be the intention. It would be better, if a pictogram is desired, to keep each plane the same width and make the heights proportional to the airport usage. Alternatively, use the other form of pictogram, with the number of planes representing airport usage.

Table 9.29: Percentages are easier to take in if they are rounded. It is also confusing to have % signs on some figures and not the rest: they should be on all or on none. The last row figures should add up to 100%. Some readers will be confused by the minus sign, so it might be helpful to make a note by this figure. A better table is given in Table 9.31.

TABLE 9.31

	North	South	West	East
% of outlets with increased sales	22%	14%	34%	18%
% decrease in outlets over 1996	2%	–2%[a]	5%	11%
% of outlets in this area	42%	22%	16%	20%

[a] There was actually a 2% increase in the number of outlets in the South in 1996.

CHAPTER 10

Legal regulation

WHAT IS IT ABOUT?

An awareness of at least some of the law regulating marketing activity will help to prevent potentially expensive mistakes. This chapter explains that there are two main purposes for legal regulation of marketing activity. The government attempts, by legal regulation, to protect consumers from unfair practices and to protect commercial organizations from unfair competition.

The general regulatory framework is outlined and some of the procedures for regulating marketing activities are explained. The aspects of **contract law** which are most relevant to marketing – formation of contract, misrepresentation and unfair terms in contracts – are discussed briefly.

Thereafter there is a section on the **regulation of price**. Misleading indications as to price may amount to a contravention of the criminal law and the chapter explains the defences which are available to a person who is prosecuted. The provision of credit is extremely important to the modern consumer and it is an area where a great deal of protection is given to protect consumers from sharp practice. The system of consumer **credit licensing and regulation** is discussed.

Many disputes are caused by **misleading descriptions** of goods and services, and the chapter discusses criminal law penalties which may be incurred by a person using a misleading description to market goods or services and the role of civil law in providing redress for the consumer.

Criminal law also plays an important role in regulating the **safety of products**. There is also a possibility of liability for damages arising where an unsafe product causes loss or injury. Where the quality of products is unsatisfactory, the law provides remedies, such as the right to reject the goods and to claim damages.

Much of consumer law is based on legislation and therefore explanations are given of the **main provisions** of the legislation. **Leading cases** from which the law is derived are also discussed. These cases also serve as examples to aid understanding.

In order to clarify how these complex regulations apply to real life, some hypothetical examples are presented and discussed at the end of the chapter.

The chapter does not attempt to be an authoritative detailed exposition of all of the relevant law. It is intended as an indication as to some of the main aspects of legal regulation of marketing. It is intended to provide sufficient information for you to be able to recognize situations where legal consequences may arise from your activities.

Purposes of legal regulation

Many of the activities of commercial organizations are subject to legal regulation, and marketing is no exception. An awareness of the legal framework is essential so that businesses can avoid contravening regulations where the consequences could be expensive. Regulation may take the form of statutory legislation (Acts of Parliament and regulations), judicial precedent (cases decided by the courts) or codes of practice. In order to appreciate the need for regulation it is necessary to look behind the individual measures and to consider what is the exact purpose of that regulation. In the UK, laws are usually passed to prevent a 'mischief' in society and a better understanding of the law is achieved if we appreciate the harm which could occur in the absence of legal regulation.

Protection from aggressive competition

One of the purposes of regulation is to protect businesses from each other. The extent to which a government may wish to prevent unfair competition may vary according to the political mores of society from time to time, but it would be disastrous for the economy of any country if, by unfair and predatory practices, a few powerful organizations were able to obtain a stranglehold on certain markets. The probable consequence of permitting a monopoly to develop in any area would be rising prices and diminishing quality in the provision of goods or services. This would give rise to consumer dissatisfaction which could eventually cause the downfall of a government.

Protecting the consumer from unfair pressure

Another purpose of regulation is to protect the consumer from unfair pressure which may induce him to contract for goods and services which he does not really want and to protect the consumer from being duped by false or misleading information. Many people regard this as a paternalistic attitude on the part of government which is out of keeping with a sophisticated, educated society: but you need only study recent newspapers and watch consumer programmes on TV to see that there are many people who are gullible enough to be taken in by dishonest traders and who will be misled by advertising which seems perfectly unambiguous to its creators.

It is easy to appreciate that a consumer may need protecting against fraudulent or dangerous practices but it may be more difficult to perceive the need for protection when there has been no fraud by the producer or seller. The main justification is the inequality of bargaining power between the consumer, i.e. a private individual, and those selling goods or services or providing credit by way of business. In modern society the marketing of goods and services is conducted on an organized basis and by trained business executives. The untrained consumer is often not very capable of resisting persuasive selling techniques. In many types of consumer contract the terms and conditions are dictated entirely by the seller, who may use a standard-form contract. This leaves no scope for the individual consumer to negotiate on specific terms of the contract. Consumer law is constantly evolving to meet new needs and situations and, particularly over the past thirty years, there has been great expansion of consumer law in order to give consumers increased rights against businesses and a better deal when buying goods and services.

Methods of regulation

Consumer organizations

Consumers are, in the nature of things, isolated from each other when purchasing goods and services, and therefore may be ineffective as a pressure group promoting measures which will provide protection for consumers. Because of this, various groups have developed to assist the consumer to achieve some collective power of persuasion. These consumer organizations exist in various forms: as governmental bodies, government-sponsored bodies, non-governmental bodies and departments within local government.

Governmental bodies

Office of Fair Trading

The Office of Fair Trading (OFT) is the main governmental body responsible for consumer protection. It was set up following the creation of the office of the Director General of Fair Trading by the Fair Trading Act 1973. The parent department is the Department of Trade and Industry, which funds the OFT, most of whose staff are civil servants. The main functions of the OFT are:

- Overseeing the Monopolies and Mergers Commission.
- Control of restrictive practices.
- Provision of information to the public on consumer affairs.
- Taking action against traders who have engaged in practices which are unfair to consumers.
- Encouraging trade associations to prepare codes of practice for their members and to oversee their operation.
- Reporting annually to the Department of Trade and Industry.
- Administering a licensing system under the Consumer Credit Act 1974.
- Challenging unfair terms in consumer contracts.

Regulatory agencies

Regulatory agencies, for example the Office of Telecommunications (Oftel) and in relation to gas users, Ofgas, are statutory bodies set up to oversee the supply of services to consumers by nationalized or recently privatized industries such as gas, telecommunications and electricity. The regulatory agencies act as pressure groups in the interests of consumers. The agencies have been criticized for lacking 'teeth': there is no statutory requirement for British Telecom even to talk to Oftel let alone provide it with information about its activities. However, recently there have been signs of a growing confidence in the regulatory agencies: for example, reductions in the price of gas to consumers were achieved in 1992 as a result of pressure by Ofgas upon British Gas.

Government-sponsored bodies

Government-sponsored bodies include the National Consumer Council (NCC). This was set up by the Labour government in 1974 and receives a government grant but is independent of the government and preserves the right to be critical of government policy. Its chief function is to act as a pressure group representing the interests of consumers in negotiations with the government, to advise ministers on consumer affairs, and thus to influence policy, and to represent consumers on appropriate European bodies including the European Commission. Another government-sponsored body is the British Standards Institute (BSI). This organization came into existence in 1929 and received its present charter in 1992. It receives a grant from the government. Its principal functions are :

- To co-ordinate the standardization of materials, products and processes to eliminate wastage of effort.
- To establish standards for quality of goods and services, after consultation.
- To promote British standards (the 'kite mark' is the sign that a product has been tested by BSI – the mark can be withdrawn if the standard is not maintained).

There is a British standard relating to management and quality systems – BS 5750/ ISO 9000/EN29000 – and firms can display a British Standards logo if they have been tested and shown to comply with the standard.

Many of the British standards relate to safety, for example in relation to electrical goods and motorcycle helmets. Compliance with these standards is generally voluntary on the part of manufacturers, except where certain standards have been made compulsory by legislation.

Non-governmental bodies

Consumers' Association

Non-governmental bodies include the Consumers' Association. This is an organization which is self-financing and acts as a pressure group on behalf of consumers. It has been in operation since 1957 and publishes the magazine *Which?* which provides comparative information on competing products. The organization uses its membership to obtain feedback on the performance of products.

The Consumers' Association does not generally take up individual cases, although it operates a 'personal service' for members who subscribe to the service. Reports of its role in the resolution of these individual disputes are reported in *Which?* magazine as examples to other consumers.

The methods of the organization have been subjected to some criticism on the grounds that its membership comes from a fairly narrow sector of society, in the middle to higher socio-economic groups, and therefore its findings may reflect the interests of those groups only. The Association has close links with the NCC, the OFT and European consumer groups.

Citizens' Advice Bureaux

Citizens' Advice Bureaux are found in most towns across the country, and receive a grant from both central and local government. They give free advice to individuals on a wide range of topics, including consumer advice and legal advice. In recent years, much of this advice has related to debt problems rather than to problems associated with the purchase of goods and services.

Local authorities

Local councils play a large part in the enforcement of consumer protection. Councils operate trading standards departments, called by some authorities consumer protection departments or weights and measures departments, which administer the enforcement of the Consumer Credit Act 1974, Weights and Measures Act 1985, Trade Descriptions Act 1968, Consumer Protection Act 1987 and the Food Safety Act 1990, among others. Inspectors visit premises to weigh or measure goods, to check that measuring equipment such as petrol pumps are accurate, to make test purchases, or to check that food is fit for human consumption. Under various statutes, local authorities have power to enter premises, to seize goods, to close premises, and to initiate prosecutions. These powers vary according to the particular statute. Much of the legislation enforced by the local authorities is backed by criminal penalties.

Licensing of commercial activities

Another way in which the government controls certain commercial activities is by a system of licensing. Apart from controlling the activity in question, licensing ensures a minimum standard of quality.

In the field of marketing, the most important area where licensing is used is consumer credit. Under the Consumer Credit Act 1974, those wishing to provide services in consumer credit, consumer hire, credit brokerage, debt counselling, debt adjusting, debt collecting, or operating a credit reference agency have to be licensed by the Office of Fair Trading. Consumer credit business includes any business which provides goods or services on credit terms. With the increased use of credit cards as a method of payment this includes the majority of retail outlets as well as businesses dealing in expensive items such as motor vehicles and fitted kitchens. Licenses can be refused, suspended or revoked for bad practices. Licences run for fifteen years and are renewable. Trading without a licence is a criminal offence and can also lead to unenforceability of agreements.

Under the Fair Trading Act 1973, the Director General of Fair Trading can take action for the protection of consumers in relation to persistent conduct on the part of traders which is detrimental to the interests of consumers. He can seek a written assurance from such traders that they will refrain from such conduct. If the promise is broken, or if the trader will not give a promise, the Director General may bring proceedings before the Restrictive Practices Court, which can order the trader to desist from the conduct. The conduct referred to by the Act is conduct which contravenes criminal legislation, although it does not matter that the trader has not been convicted under the legislation. This provision is directed mainly at small businesses, but there are a number of multinational companies which have had to make an undertaking to the courts.

Codes of practice

There are voluntary codes of practice regulating particular industries, or areas of business. The Director General of Fair Trading has a duty under the Fair Trading Act 1973 to encourage trade associations to introduce codes. The Office of Fair Trading will endorse codes which meet its own guidelines.

The guidelines require that the trade association must have a significant influence on members, must make compliance with the code mandatory on its members and must impose penalties for non-compliance. The codes must improve upon the basic rights given by legislation, and must seek to remove undesirable practices. There must be an adequate machinery for handling complaints. There must be an annual report by the trade association. The codes must also provide for the provision of adequate information about products to customers.

Examples of codes of practice are the code published by ABTA (the Association of British Travel Agents) in 1975, the Code of the Credit Services Association published in 1991 and setting out guidelines for businesses which collect debts, and a Direct Marketing Code of Practice issued by the BDMA (the British Direct Marketing Association Ltd) in 1989.

One problem with self-regulatory codes is that different codes command different levels of obedience, depending on the power of the particular trade association in its own industry. ABTA has a great deal of power in the travel industry, and in 1990 imposed a fine of £105 000 on a tour operator after customers had been subjected to major changes in their holiday arrangements. Another problem is that in many industries, not all traders belong to the trade association, and those that do not belong can ignore the code.

Legislation

Much of the law regulating marketing activity derives its authority from Acts of Parliament. Statutes relating to consumer law generally apply throughout the UK, but there are some Acts which do not apply to Scotland. The Supply of Goods and Services Act 1982 is one such, although there are now provisions equivalent to Part 1 of that Act in the Sale and Supply of Goods and Services Act 1994. In another Act of fundamental importance – the Unfair Contract Terms Act 1977 – the sections relating to Scots law are contained in a separate part of the Act. The statutes which are most important in consumer law are:

Sales of Goods Act 1979
Sale and Supply of Goods Act 1994
Supply of Goods and Services Act 1982
Trade Descriptions Act 1968
Unfair Contract terms Act 1977
Consumer Credit Act 1974
Consumer Protection Act 1987

Not all legislation is embodied in the Acts of Parliament themselves: there is also delegated legislation which comprises rules, regulations and orders made under the authority of Acts of Parliament. Often, an Act of Parliament lays down the general principles of a reform of the law and leaves the detailed regulations to be made at a later stage by those with expert knowledge. Regulations are important as a source of consumer law as some modifications to the general principles laid down in an Act may be found in them.

All Acts of Parliament and regulations made under the authority of Acts of Parliament may be purchased through Her Majesty's Stationery Office (HMSO).

Decided cases

In the UK, not all principles of law are derived from legislation by, or under the authority of Parliament. Decisions reached by the courts in the settlement of disputes between individuals also serve to declare and develop the relevant legal principles. Even where there is comprehensive legislation covering a particular type of relationship, e.g. in consumer law, the courts have an important role to play in interpreting the Acts and regulations in individual cases. A decision reached by a court in an individual case is referred to as a **judicial precedent**. The principle of law embodied in the judgement of a case will be binding on all inferior courts in subsequent cases dealing with exactly the same point of law. The legal principle from the earlier case is referred to as the *ratio decidendi* (i.e. the reason for the decision) and this is the only part of the case which is binding. If the judge in a subsequent case wishes to depart from a precedent, he must distinguish the later case by demonstrating an important difference between the two.

It is essential that where legal principles are developed from decided cases there should be comprehensive documentation of the judgements. Cases in England and Wales may be found in reports such as the *All England Law Reports*, the *Law Reports*, the *Weekly Law Reports* and the *Times Law Reports*. In Scotland they are published in *Session Cases*, *Scottish Criminal Law Reports* and the *Scots Law Times*, and in Northern

Ireland in the *Northern Ireland Law Reports*. Cases of importance are also reported in the *Guardian* and the *Independent* newspapers. There are also databases which contain statutes and cases. The less expensive databases give summaries of current law and are useful for checking to see if the law has changed recently. There are also full text databases which contain comprehensive information on statutes and cases, but these are not widely available because of the high cost of subscriptions.

Civil and criminal law in relation to marketing

The marketing of goods and services is regulated partly by using criminal sanctions, partly by providing purchasers with remedies in the civil courts and partly by providing producers with rights of legal action to protect trademarks and to prevent the marketing of 'look-alike' products and illegal copies.

Criminal law

Criminal law is concerned with the relationship between the state and its citizens: it enforces law and order and suppresses conduct which is contrary to the standard of behaviour expected of citizens. A person who does not comply with the criminal law may be prosecuted in a criminal court and, if he is found guilty he will be punished, e.g. by a fine, a community service order or imprisonment. The aspects of marketing which are regulated by the criminal law include food labelling, food hygiene regulations and the use of trade descriptions. The main purpose of the criminal law is to deter people from committing offences and to punish them if they do. Payment of compensation to the victim may be part of the verdict in a criminal case but this is ancillary to the criminal prosecution. A person who is seeking redress would be better advised to negotiate with the seller on the basis of their rights under civil law and, if this fails, to resort to civil litigation.

Civil law

Civil law regulates relationships between citizens of the state. Civil law applies to a great variety of cases, e.g. disputes over land, recovery of debt, divorce, claims for damages. If a dispute cannot be settled by agreement, either party may seek a remedy in the civil courts. The courts do not intervene in a dispute unless one of the parties brings an action, and the majority of consumer disputes are settled without litigation (i.e. a case being heard in a civil court). Several areas of consumer relationships have developed arbitration schemes which provide an alternative method of dispute resolution and which avoid the costs and delays associated with litigation. Sometimes the same activity will be both a crime and the subject of a civil dispute, so, for example, if a retailer sells goods with a false trade description he commits a crime and the customer who buys such goods has a civil remedy for breach of contract.

Contract law

Consumer contracts

Some of the remedies available under civil law depend on the existence of a contract between the supplier and the customer. Sometimes the principles which apply between supplier and consumer would be the same as if the contract were between two businesses, but there are circumstances when additional protection is given to consumers. Consumer contacts are those contracts whereby a person acting in the course of a business sells goods to or provides services for a person acting in a private capacity (a consumer). Typical consumer contracts include selling goods in a shop, in an auction or by mail order, providing services such as repairing goods or decorating houses, contracts for hire of goods, public transport contracts, banking contracts, insurance contracts, provision of financial services and selling holidays.

The most essential feature of a contract is that it is an agreement. There must be at least two parties to a contract (therefore a person who is a member of an unincorporated organization cannot make a legally binding contract with that organization). The majority of consumer contracts involve an exchange. This may be goods exchanged for money (for example a sale), services exchanged for money (such as public transport) or goods exchanged for goods (barter). An agreement will only be regarded as a contract if it creates a legal obligation. Not all agreements are contracts, e.g. an agreement to meet for a social occasion is not a contract. If an agreement is a contract, the law will provide a remedy if one of the parties fails to fulfil its obligations.

In consumer law disputes it is often important to ascertain whether or not there has been a legally binding contract, whether the contract was valid and, if so, what the terms of the contract were. For example, if a shopkeeper has ordered goods which have not arrived, the supplier would be liable to compensate the shopkeeper for his losses if there was a binding contract. The supplier may claim that he thought that the alleged order was only an enquiry as to price and availability, in which case there may be no contract.

Contracts are formed by agreement between the parties. Agreement is usually evidenced by the existence of an offer by one party which has been accepted by the other. An offer is a proposal from one party in such definite terms that, if it is accepted, a legally binding contract will be formed. An offer must be distinguished from an invitation to treat which is merely an expression of willingness to negotiate.

Distinction between offer to sell and expression of willingness to negotiate

If goods are in a window with prices attached, this does not constitute an offer to sell those goods. The display of goods is an expression of willingness to negotiate. It is the customer who makes the offer to purchase at the suggested price and then the seller can choose whether or not to accept the offer.

In the case of *Fisher v. Bell* [1961] QB 394, a shopkeeper was prosecuted for illegally 'offering flick knives for sale'. The knives were displayed in his shop window with price labels attached. It was held that he had not 'offered them for sale'. Therefore it is clear that there is no legal obligation on a retailer to sell the goods on display in a shop window and the customer under the law of contract cannot insist on the goods being sold to him at the price indicated on a price label. There may be consequences under criminal law for giving a misleading indication as to price (under the Consumer Protection Act 1987), but this does not give the prospective customer any legal right to demand the goods at the displayed price.

The display of goods in self-service stores does not constitute an offer to sell the goods. It is merely an invitation to treat. The contract is concluded by an offer and acceptance at the cash desk and not by the customer taking goods from the shelves. Therefore the customer is entitled to put back the goods if he changes his mind and the store is entitled to withdraw the goods from sale at any time until the contract has been concluded at the cash desk.

This principle was established in the case of *Pharmaceutical Society of Great Britain v. Boots Cash Chemists* [1952] 2 QB 795. Boots changed one of their stores to a self-service shop. By law, the sale of certain medicines had to be supervised by a registered pharmacist. The Pharmaceutical Society claimed that if the customers were helping themselves then the sales were unsupervised. The court held that the contract of sale was formed by the customer offering to buy the goods at the checkout and by the sales assistant accepting. Since a pharmacist was present at the checkout, Boots were not contravening the law.

One exception to the rule that helping oneself to goods is not an offer to purchase is a contract for fuel at a self-service filling station. Since the goods cannot be put back in an unchanged form, putting fuel into the tank of a vehicle is an irrevocable offer.

Quotations

Quotations are usually regarded only as invitations to treat but, if they are expressed in sufficiently definite terms they may constitute an offer. In the case of *Philp v. Knoblauch* [1907] S.C. 994, Knoblauch wrote to Philp & Co.: 'I am offering today Plate linseed for January/February shipment and have pleasure in quoting you 100 tones at 41/3, usual Plate terms. I shall be glad to hear if you are buyers and await your esteemed reply.' The next day Philp & Co. replied by telegram. 'Accept 100 tons.' The telegram was followed by a letter of confirmation. Philp & Co. claimed that there was a binding contract as there had been an offer and an acceptance, but Knoblauch claimed that his letter had only been a quotation and therefore there was no contract. The court held that because of the very definite terms the original letter was an offer and it had been validly accepted by the telegram.

Advertisements

An advertisement is usually regarded only as an invitation to treat. The customer, having seen the advertisement, makes an offer to buy and the seller accepts, often simply by sending the goods. In the case of mail order catalogues, goods are often supplied on sale or return. In such circumstances the supply of the goods is an offer which the customer accepts by retaining the goods beyond the term of approval, adopting the transaction or by indicating acceptance of the offer. The transaction would be considered to be accepted if the customer used the goods or sold them to a third party. The indication of acceptance need not be a formal notice. The fact that payment was sent for the goods would be sufficient indication that the buyer had accepted the offer to sell the goods.

Occasionally an advertisement may be constituted in such definite terms that it does amount to an offer, as in the famous case of *Carlill v. Carbolic Smoke Ball Co.* [1893]1 QB 256. Mrs Carlill saw an advertisement in a newspaper which stated that the manufacturers of the carbolic smokeball were so confident of its curative and preventative properties that if anyone bought a smokeball, used it according to the instructions and still succumbed to the current epidemic of influenza, they would pay a 'reward' of £100. A sum of £1000 had been lodged with a joint stock bank to show their sincerity. Mrs Carlill bought a smokeball, used it for two weeks, caught influenza and claimed the £100 'reward'. The company refused to pay, claiming that the advert was not an offer. They argued that, even if it was an offer, it had not been addressed specifically to Mrs Carlill and even if there had been a valid offer, she had not notified the company of any acceptance and so there was no contract. The court held that the advert was expressed in such definite terms that it was an offer, that an offer can be made to the general public and it will be deemed to be an offer to whoever accepts it and that Mrs Carlill had accepted the offer in exactly the manner proscribed by the offer, i.e. by buying and using the smokeball. The offer did not require her to inform the company that she was accepting the offer.

Cases such as this, where an advert is deemed to be an offer will be unusual but it is important to bear in mind when devising advertisements that, if the advert is expressed in such a definite way that it could be construed as an offer then legal obligations could arise if someone purports to accept the 'offer', as once an offer is accepted there is a binding contract. It is also important to ensure that information provided to potential customers is accurate because a person who has entered into a contract on the basis of misleading information may have a remedy for misrepresentation.

Misrepresentation

A representation is a statement as to a fact made by one person to induce another to enter into a contract. A misrepresentation is a false statement as to a fact. Statements of intention, statements of opinion and exaggerative language used in advertising are not generally regarded as misrepresentation.

If one of the parties has relied on a misrepresentation and been induced to enter into a contract then the validity of the contract may be affected. There may also be a right to damages where the misrepresentation was made fraudulently or negligently. Negligence involves a breach of a duty, such as a duty to take care that one's statements are accurate. There are only a limited number of situations where a person is under a duty to take care that his statements are accurate. These do not include ordinary contracts by which goods are sold or services are provided but would include contracts for financial advice by experts, and the reports of surveyors on the physical condition of buildings.

Exclusion or restriction of liability clauses

The parties to a contract are free to include any terms that they wish, and often the stronger party will include clauses which restrict or even exclude his liability for breaches of contract. This is very common in brochures issued by travel companies. The company issuing the brochure may try to limit its liability for certain types of breach of contract by fixing the amount of compensation which will be paid to a customer. For example, the brochure may say, 'in the event of the accommodation which you have selected as your first choice being unavailable we will guarantee to pay you the sum of £50 per week.' The customer is not really given any choice over whether or not to accept such a term in the contract and therefore the law gives some protection to him, as the weaker party, via the Unfair Contract Terms Act 1977. This Act applies throughout the UK, and it applies to all contracts made in the course of business, including contracts transferring goods and contracts for services, but not insurance contracts.

The Act has the effect of rendering void any clause purporting to exclude or restrict liability for breach of duty in the course of any business if the clause relates to death or personal injury and of rendering it of no effect in any other case unless it can be proved that the clause was fair and reasonable when the contract was made. The term 'breach of duty' means:

- a breach of any obligation arising from the terms of a contract to take reasonable care or exercise reasonable skill in performing the contract;
- a breach of any common law duty to take reasonable care or to exercise reasonable skill;
- a breach of the duty of reasonable care imposed on occupiers of premises.

The party who wants to rely on the clause must prove that it was fair and reasonable.

The Act also states that a term in a consumer contract or standard form contract cannot exclude or restrict liability to the consumer or customer for breach of contract unless the term was fair and reasonable. A term in a consumer contract or standard form contract cannot allow a party to give no performance at all or performance substantially different from that which the customer expected unless the term was fair and reasonable. An example can be found in the case of *Elliot v. Sunshine Coast International Ltd* [1989] GWD 28–1252. A lady with a weak bladder had booked a coach holiday to Spain after she had been assured that the coach would contain a toilet. The coach did not have a toilet and she refused to board. When she sued for a refund of her money the tour operator sought to rely on a term in the booking form which allowed them to alter the form of transport. It was held that to supply a coach without a toilet mounted to performance substantially different from that which the customer reasonably expected and so she was entitled to her refund.

The Act also controls the extent to which the terms implied by statute into sale of goods and hire purchase contracts can be excluded. In a consumer contract, the terms which are implied into contracts by Acts such as the Sale of Goods Act 1979 cannot be excluded, and in a contract between businesses they can only be excluded if the exclusion was fair and reasonable.

In cases where the Unfair Contract Terms Act 1977 does not apply, e.g. contracts between businesses, any clause exempting a company from liability for breach of contract or limiting the amount of compensation which will be paid for a breach of contract, which is properly incorporated into a contract will be valid whether it is fair and reasonable or not. Consequently many disputes in this area hinge upon whether or not an exemption clause is part of the contract.

Unfair terms in standard contracts

One problem with the protection provided by the Unfair Contract Terms Act is that the Act depends on the consumer knowing that a term in a contract will have no legal effect and therefore challenging it. Many customers assume that because a contractual term is in a formal document such as a booking form then it must be legally valid. A recent development in the regulation of contractual terms, which is intended to improve the protection for the consumer, has been brought about by the Unfair Terms in Consumer Contracts Regulations 1994. These regulations were brought in to bring the UK law into line with the European Community Directive on Unfair Terms in Consumer Contracts 93/13/EEC, OJ No. 95/29.21.4.93.

The regulations apply to any term in a contract concluded between a seller or supplier and a consumer where the term has not been individually negotiated. Unlike the Unfair Contract Terms Act 1977, these regulations apply to insurance contracts. There is a basic requirement that written contracts must be in plain, intelligible language. A term which is unfair may be challenged. A term will be regarded as unfair if it causes a significant imbalance in the parties' rights and obligations arising under the contract, to the detriment of the consumer.

The matters to be considered include: the strength of the bargaining position of the parties, whether the consumer had an inducement to agree to the term, whether the goods or services were sold or supplied to the special order of the customer, and the extent to which the seller or supplier dealt fairly and equitably with the customer.

Challenging terms in standard contracts

Challenges can be made in two ways:

- A consumer may claim that a clause has been unfair to him and challenge its validity.
- The Director General of Fair Trading may take action against an allegedly unfair contract term drawn up for general use.

The Director General can seek undertakings from offending dealers and, if necessary, obtain an interdict or injunction to prevent the continued use of an unfair term. This is an important innovation: it gives the Director General a supervisory and preventative jurisdiction over unfair terms in contracts. The Consumers' Association is disappointed, however, that the Department of Trade and Industry has chosen to give this power only to the Office of Fair Trading when it could also have been given to other bodies representing consumers.

Complaints to the Director General

The Director General of Fair Trading can only take action once he has received a complaint. A complaint may be from anyone, including a consumer group. The Director General must consider every complaint unless it is 'frivolous and vexatious'. He then has a discretion as to whether to bring proceedings. He must give reasons for his decision to apply or not to apply for an injunction (in England and Wales) or an interdict (in Scotland). Action can be brought against any person appearing to the Director General to be using or recommending the use of unfair terms. Therefore action could be brought against not only sellers and suppliers but also manufacturers, franchisers and trade associations which recommend the use of unfair terms in standard forms. The interdict or injunction may, as well as prohibiting the use of a specific term in a particular contract, prohibit the use of a similar term in contracts produced or recommended by those involved. The court has a discretion to decide whether the interdict or injunction applies to an individual or to a whole industry.

The Unfair Terms in Consumer Contracts Regulations represent an important milestone in consumer law because they provide for protection of the consumer without depending on individual consumers either initiating litigation or relying on the unreasonableness of an exclusion clause as a defence in a legal action.

Regulation of indications as to price

There are specific regulations relating to certain aspects of commercial activity, and one of the most important is the regulation of prices. The price at which the retailer wishes to sell goods is information which is generally of crucial importance in the customer's decision whether to purchase. It would seem to be generally accepted by consumers, retailers manufacturers and wholesalers that price information is essential in the context of the types of transaction that take place daily.

Misleading indications as to price

Section 20 of the Consumer Protection Act 1987 (which replaced section 11 of the Trade Descriptions Act 1968) states that a person shall be guilty of an offence if, in the course of business, he gives (by any means whatever) to consumers an indication which is misleading as to the price at which any goods, services, accommodation or facilities are available in circumstances where some or all of those consumers might reasonably be expected to rely on the misleading indication and he fails to take reasonable steps to prevent the consumers relying on the indication.

It is immaterial whether that person is acting on his own behalf or for another or whether he is the person from whom the goods/services are available or even whether the indication only misleads some of the consumers. The Act lays down criminal penalties for those found guilty of a contravention. The penalties are, on summary conviction, a fine of up to £2000, and for more serious offences an unlimited fine and imprisonment for up to two years.

The Consumer Protection Act 1987 defines a consumer as any person who might wish to be supplied with goods for his own private consumption or to be provided with services or facilities (but not for the purposes of a business of his) or to occupy accommodation (but not for the purposes of a business of his). Price means the aggregate of sums required to be paid by a consumer or any method of determining that aggregate. The term 'misleading' includes such things as giving an indication that the price is less than it really is or that the price covers matters which it does not (section 21). Misleading indications include any of the following:

- That the price is less than in fact it is.
- That the applicability of the price does not depend on facts or circumstances on which its applicability does in fact depend.
- That the price covers matters in respect of which an additional charge is in fact made.
- That a person who in fact has no such expectation, either expects the price to be increased or reduced or expects the price to be maintained.
- That the facts or circumstances by reference to which the consumers might reasonably expect to judge the validity of any relevant comparison made or implied by the indication are not in fact what they are.

A misleading indication as to the method of calculating a price includes any of the following:

- That the method is not what in fact it is.
- That the applicability of the method does not depend on facts or circumstances on which it does depend.
- That the method takes into account matters in respect of which an additional charge will in fact be made.
- That a person who has no such expectation expects the price to be either altered or maintained.
- That the facts or circumstances by reference to which the consumers might reasonably be expected to judge the validity of any comparison made are not what in fact they are.

By these definitions a price display in a supermarket window which does not accord with the price printed on the goods on the shelves will amount to the commission of an offence and there is no need to consider whether the offer price or the shelf price is the price to be charged.

This part of the Consumer Protection Act only applies where one party is acting in the course of business and the other is a consumer. There is a code of practice drawn up according to section 25 of the Act which has no legal force but which should assist traders to avoid contraventions of the Act and which may be used as evidence.

Defences

There are defences which may be used against a charge under the Consumer Protection Act. The most important defence is a general defence that reasonable precautions were taken to avoid the commission of an offence and that due diligence was exercised (section 39).

Information which must be provided to the public

An important consideration when operating any marketing business is that care must be taken to comply with the regulations requiring that certain information is provided to the public. This is often in the form of statements which may be displayed as notices on retailing premises, or statements attached to goods. One example is the health warning which is required on tobacco products and tobacco advertising. There are also specific statements that are required in shop premises, e.g. if goods are described as 'reduced' but have not been offered at a higher price in the preceding six months then there must be a notice explaining this to the customers.

Certain statements are illegal. All business premises belonging to registered companies must, under the Companies Act 1985, display the name of the company outside each of its places of business, and on all its business stationery. The registered office address and registered number must also appear on the business stationery. If any business trades under a name other than the full names of its proprietors, it must, according to the Business Names Act 1985, state its registered name and an address at which documents can be served (in the case of a company), and the full names of the proprietors and an address at which documents can be served (in the case of unincorporated businesses) at every building to which the public has access, and on business stationery. This is to enable the public to establish the identity of the persons or company running the business, principally to enable them to raise legal proceedings against the persons or company. It is a criminal offence not to comply.

Under the Business Advertisements (Disclosure) Order 1977, a trader must make known to customers the fact that he or she is a trader. This is important to the consumer, since the implied terms on satisfactory quality and fitness for purpose in the Sale of Goods Act 1979 only apply to business sales.

Regulation of consumer credit businesses

The Consumer Credit Act 1974 introduced regulations on advertising and quotations in transactions involving credit. There are strict rules on the form and content of advertisements to ensure that they give adequate information. If a consumer submits a written request for credit information, he must be given a written quotation. A well known high street store was convicted of a breach of the Act by advertising goods with 'nothing to pay until September'. The advert contained no information on the interest rates which would be applied to this credit.

Another restriction applies to canvassing off trade premises. Canvassing involves making an unsolicited visit or telephone call to a person's home and making representations to anyone there. This need not necessarily be to the person who is the intended customer. It is a criminal offence to canvass unconnected loans (i.e. loans not linked to the supply of goods or services) off trade premises. The only defence is to prove that the visit was in response to a signed request made on a previous occasion. It is permissible to canvass the sale of goods or supply of services on credit.

It is a criminal offence to send any advertisement or information about credit or hire to persons under the age of 18, with a view to financial gain. It is a defence to prove that the sender had no reason to suspect that the person was a minor. It is also an offence to send a credit token, such as an account card for a store or a credit card, to a person who has not requested one.

Enforcement of the Consumer Credit Act

Enforcement of the Consumer Credit Act 1974 is under the control of the Office of Fair Trading and the trading standards departments of local authorities. They have the powers to enter premises and inspect records and to make test purchases anonymously to find out if offences are taking place.

Form and content of credit agreements

The Consumer Credit Act regulates credit agreements themselves by imposing regulations on the form and content of agreements to ensure that consumers are provided with all of the information necessary to make a decision on whether to accept credit from a credit company. The information must be in a legible form. The agreement cannot take effect until it has been signed by both parties. A copy of the agreement must be supplied to the customer within seven days of its taking effect. If these provisions are not complied with, there is a high probability that the agreement will not be enforceable by the creditor. (The only exception to this is if a court chooses to enforce the agreement on the basis that the customer is not prejudiced.)

Cancellation rights

Some agreements can be cancelled by the customer without his being in breach of contract. The cancellation rights are intended as a means of protecting customers from over-persuasive salespeople, particularly in the customer's own home. It was apparent that some vulnerable people were so oppressed by persistent salespeople who, once allowed into their homes, would not go away, that they would agree to sign contracts for goods or services which they did not want or which they could not afford. It would be very difficult to prevent such sales tactics by legal regulation. Giving the customers the right to cancel such agreements is a much more effective way of regulating sales techniques. It does, however depend on the customer being aware that they have a right to cancel and therefore the regulations require that information on the cancellation rights is provided in writing to the customer.

In order for the customer to have the right to cancel an agreement, the following conditions must be met.

- There must have been oral representations made in the presence of the customer by the creditor, the owner of the goods, or an agent or a dealer before the contract was made.
- The customer must have signed the agreement elsewhere than at the business premises of the creditor, the owner of the goods, a party to a linked transaction or a negotiator.

The customer has a right to cancel at any time up to the fifth day following the day on which he received his copy of the executed agreement. Cancellation is effected by written notice to the creditor, or to the owner of the goods or an agent of either.

The right to cancel gives valuable protection to the consumer and it became apparent that the same protection against over-zealous salespersons should be given where the contract did not involve the provision of credit. Therefore regulations have been passed to give a similar protection where the contract involves payment by cash – the Consumer Protection (Cancellation of Contracts Concluded away from Business Premises) Regulations 1987. In addition, the Timeshare Act 1992 has given cancellation rights in the case of contracts in the UK involving the use of property on a timeshare basis. This right extends to contracts concluded on the premises of the owner of the property.

Regulation under criminal law of misleading descriptions of goods and services

In order to protect the consumer from being induced by misleading descriptions relating to goods or services into entering contracts, the Trade Descriptions Act 1968 and the Consumer Protection Act 1987 provide for the legal regulation of descriptions used by businesses to attract customers. The use of criminal sanctions under these Acts to regulate business practices is in addition to the remedies available under civil law for misrepresentation or for a breach of the seller's duty to supply goods of the right quality.

Regulation by criminal sanctions has the advantage that it does not rely on the knowledge of the consumer as to his rights and his willingness to enforce those rights. Enforcement is by the local trading standards departments and the regulation has a deterrent effect on unscrupulous trade practices.

The activities described below are regulated by criminal law.

Applying a false trade description to goods

It is a criminal offence under section 1 of the Trade Descriptions Act 1968 for any person to apply a false trade description to goods in the course of a trade or business.

Section 1 states that:

> any person who, in the course of a trade or business, applies a false trade description to any goods; or supplies or offers to supply any goods to which a false trade description is applied shall, subject to the provisions of the Act, be guilty of an offence.

The term 'person' includes a limited company (section 20). Where an offence under this Act which has been committed by a body corporate is proved to have been committed with the consent and connivance of, or to be attributable to any neglect on the part of, any director, manager, secretary or other similar officer of the body corporate, he as well as the body corporate shall be guilty of an offence.

The word 'applies' is defined in section 4 of the Act which states that a person applies a description if he:

- attaches it to or incorporates it with the goods themselves or anything on or in or with which the goods are supplied, or
- places the goods in, on or with anything which has the trade description on or incorporated with it, or,
- uses the trade description in any manner likely to be taken as referring to the goods.

An oral statement may amount to the use of a trade description as well as statements on packaging or labelling or in advertisements.

Where the goods are described in response to a request in which a trade description was used and it is reasonable to infer that the goods were supplied as goods corresponding to that trade description, the person supplying the goods shall be deemed to have applied that trade description.

A false trade description is one which is false or misleading to a material degree as regards the matters specified in section 2 of the Act. According to section 2, a trade description is an indication, direct or indirect, and by whatever means given, of any of the following matters with respect to any goods or parts of goods:

(a) quantity, size or gauge;
(b) method of manufacture, production, processing or reconditions [e.g. hand-made];
(c) composition [e.g. real leather];
(d) fitness for purpose, strength, performance, behaviour or accuracy [e.g. waterproof];
(e) any other physical characteristics;
(f) testing by any other person and the results thereof [e.g. current MOT];
(g) approval by any person or conformity with a type approved by any person [e.g. conforms to British Standard];
(h) place or date of manufacture, production, processing or reconditioning [e.g. British-made];
(i) person by whom manufactured, produced, processed or reconditioned [e.g. painted by John Constable];
(j) other history, including previous ownership or use [e.g. the mileage of a car].

It is possible to disclaim a trade description in certain circumstances. The disclaimer must be as bold, compelling and precise as the trade description itself, e.g. the disclaimer of a car's mileage must be boldly placed on the cars odometer. The process of zeroing the odometer does not amount to a disclaimer, but is itself a false trade description contrary to the Trade Descriptions Act 1968.

Supplying goods to which a false trade description is applied

It is an offence under section 1 to supply or to offer to supply goods to which a false trade description is applied in the course of a trade or business. The application of the trade description is an offence only if it is associated with a supply of goods. Therefore a person with no interest in the subsequent transaction does not commit an offence where he makes a misleading statement about goods which the consumer subsequently purchases, since the statement is not associated with the supply of goods. A mechanic who refused to give an MOT certificate because he wrongly believed that the car was not roadworthy did not commit an offence.

Making false or misleading statements as to services

It is an offence under section 14 of the Trade Descriptions Act 1968 for any person acting in the course of a business to make a statement which he knows to be false or which is made recklessly, with disregard as to whether it is false as to any of the following matters:

- The provision in the course of a trade or business of any services, accommodation or facilities.
- The nature of any services, accommodation or facilities provided in the course of a business.
- The time at which, manner in which or persons by whom any services, accommodation or facilities are so provided.
- The examination, approval or evaluation by any person of any services, accommodation or facilities so provided.
- The location or amenities of any accommodation so provided.

In the case of services consisting of or including the application of any treatment or process or the carrying out of any repairs, the matters referred to in section 14 are taken to include the effect of the treatment, process or repair.

This section applies to statements made in advertisements, brochures and menus, and to information given orally or in writing. A typical case is that of *R. v. Sunair Holidays Ltd* [1970] 1 All ER 762, which involved a prosecution of a holiday company. Travel agents published a brochure in which they described a Spanish hotel as having a swimming pool, pushchairs for hire and special meals for children. When the customers got there, they found that there was no water in the pool, no pushchairs and no children's meals. The travel agents were convicted of an offence under the Trade Descriptions Act 1968, but were acquitted on appeal.

Another case involving a travel company was *Wings Ltd v. Ellis* [1985] AC 372. The tour operator had published a brochure which contained a false statement that a hotel in Sri Lanka had air conditioning. The mistake was discovered and steps were taken to mitigate the effect of the mistake. However, a customer booked a holiday from the unchanged brochure, even though at the time he did so the tour operator was aware that the statement was false. The court held, on appeal against prosecution under the Trade Descriptions Act, that Wings Ltd had committed an offence: 'the brochure was inaccurate, the respondent knew that it was inaccurate and the customer was misled'.

The case of *Smith v. Dixons Ltd* [1986] SCCR 1 was a prosecution of a well known high street retail establishment. Dixons was convicted for offering for sale a television set and a video recorder at an inclusive price with a 'free 5 year guarantee'. In fact the guarantee only applied to the television set although the advertisement did not say so. Dixons was convicted under section 14 of the Trade Descriptions Act 1968.

Enforcement of the Trade Descriptions Act

It is the responsibility of every local authority weights and measures department to enforce the Trade Descriptions Act within its area. Section 26 of the Act gives weights and measures departments the following powers in order to carry out their responsibilities, including the power to make test purchases and the power to enter premises and inspect and seize goods and documents.

Penalties

A person guilty of an offence under the Trade Descriptions Act is liable to the following penalties under section 18: on summary conviction to a fine not exceeding £2000 and, for more serious offences, unlimited fine or imprisonment for up to two years or both.

A compensation order may be made requiring monetary compensation to be paid to the victim.

Defences

There are defences under sections 24 and 25 which can be used in the event of a prosecution for an offence under the Act. In order to establish a defence a person is required to prove both of the following:

- That the commission of the offence was due to a mistake or to reliance on information supplied to him, or to the act or default of another person, or an accident or some other cause beyond his control.
- That he took all reasonable precautions and exercised all due diligence to avoid the commission of such an offence by himself or any person under his control.

The defence that the commission of the offence was due to the act or default of another may only be used if a written notice has been served on the prosecutor at least seven days before the hearing, identifying that other person. In proceedings for an offence of supplying or offering to supply goods to which a false trade description is applied, it is a defence for the person to prove that he did not know and could not with reasonable diligence have ascertained that the goods did not conform to the description or that the description had been applied to the goods (section 25).

It is also a defence for a person to prove that he is a person whose business is to publish or arrange for the publication of advertisements and that he received the advertisement for publication in the ordinary course of business and did not know and had no reason to suspect that its publication would amount to an offence under the Act.

Regulations relating to products

The legal regulations concerning products which are sold by way of business are mainly for two purposes:

- To ensure that products are safe.
- To ensure that the quality of a product matches the expectations engendered by the marketing of that product.

There are, of course, other regulations which need to be considered. Certain goods and services are provided only within a strictly regulated framework. The flow of some merchandise into the UK is prohibited by law, e.g. controlled drugs and pornographic materials. Other products are supplied under a licensing system which prevents sale to children, e.g. tobacco products, alcoholic beverages, fireworks, lottery tickets.

Regulations are of particular importance in relation to consumer safety where there are regulations dealing with the safety standards for different products. The Consumer Protection Act 1987 lays down general provisions on safety, and under the authority of this Act specific sets of regulations have been passed applying these provisions to specific products, including oil heaters, stands for carry-cots, electrical appliances, electric blankets, cooking utensils, toys, cosmetics, heating appliances, pencils, babies' dummies and perambulators.

Duty of sellers with regard to quality of goods

The Sale of Goods Act 1979 (as amended by the Sale and Supply of Goods Act 1994 and Sales of Goods (Amendment) Act 1994) imposes certain duties on sellers relating to the quality of the goods supplied. It does this by implying certain terms into contracts of sale. This means that these conditions are deemed to be present in all contracts to which the Act applies, regardless of the intentions of the parties. The conditions cannot be excluded from consumer contracts. There are three aspects to the duty to supply goods of the right quality, described below.

Implied condition that goods will correspond to their description

The first aspect is an implied condition that, where goods are sold by description, the goods will correspond with that description (section 13). A sale is a 'sale by description' if the purchaser has not seen the goods, e.g. if they are purchased by mail order from a catalogue or if the sale is of future or unascertained goods or if the goods are described as well as displayed, e.g. if they are in a package with a description or if there is a label on the goods or if the seller describes the goods. Future goods are goods which are not yet in existence or not yet acquired by the seller at the time of the contract. Unascertained goods may be goods to be manufactured or grown by the seller, purely generic goods, e.g. 100 kilograms of sugar, or an unidentified part of a specified whole, e.g. 100 boxes of paper from a warehouse containing 500 boxes.

The case of *Beale v. Taylor* [1967] 1 WLR 1193 concerned goods which did not correspond with their description. Taylor wished to sell his 1961 Triumph Herald motor car and advertised it in *Exchange and Mart* as a Herald Convertible, white 1961. Beale bought the car. On the rear of the car was a metal disc with 1200 on it. The vehicle proved to be unroadworthy and unsafe, being made of two halves welded together. Only the back half was made in 1961 and the engine was not 1200 cc. Taylor had not owned the vehicle for long and was ignorant of these facts so there was no fraud involved. It was held that Beale was entitled to damages because the vehicle did not correspond with its description.

Implied condition that goods will be of satisfactory quality

Where the seller sells goods in the course of a business there is an implied condition that the goods supplied under the contract are of satisfactory quality (section 14 as amended by section 1 Sale and Supply of Goods Act 1994). Goods are of satisfactory quality if they meet the standard that a reasonable person would regard as satisfactory, taking account of any description of the goods, the price (if relevant) and all the other relevant circumstances. The quality of goods includes their state and condition, including:

- fitness for the purpose for which goods of the kind in question are commonly supplied
- appearance and finish
- freedom from minor defects
- safety
- durability

It is hoped that the standard of satisfactory quality will prove to be easier to understand than the old law that goods should be of merchantable quality: there was often doubt about the exact meaning of 'merchantable quality'. The implied condition that goods must be of satisfactory quality applies whether or not the buyer has relied on the skill and judgement of the seller.

Implied condition that goods will be fit for their purpose

Where goods are sold in the course of a business and the buyer makes known any particular purpose for which the goods are bought, there is an implied condition that the goods must be reasonably fit for that particular purpose, whether or not it is a purpose for which goods of that kind are normally supplied (section 14(3) Sale of Goods Act 1979). The condition cannot be relied on if the seller can prove that the buyer did not rely on his skill and judgement. This condition requires only that the goods be reasonably fit for the purpose, not absolutely fit. In the case of *Bristol Tramways v. Fiat Motors Ltd* [1910] 2

KB 83, Bristol tramways bought vehicles from Fiat having made it clear that they were intended for the conveyance of passengers in heavy traffic in a hilly district. The vehicles supplied proved to be unsuitable for steep hills and it was held that the tram company was entitled to damages.

Sales by sample

In a sale by sample the goods must be free from any defect making their quality unsatisfactory which would not be apparent on a reasonable examination of the sample (section 15). A sale is a 'sale by sample' when there is an express or implied term to that effect. In a sale by sample the bulk must correspond with the sample and the buyer must be given a reasonable opportunity to compare the bulk with the sample.

These duties are owed by the seller of the goods. Any remedies exercised by the customer will be against the seller, not the manufacturer. The seller will, however, have a right to seek compensation from the person who supplied goods to him and he will have a right of redress against the person above him in the chain of supply. By section 20 of the Unfair Contract terms Act 1977, the implied undertakings as to quality cannot be excluded or restricted as against a person dealing 'as a consumer'. In other contracts, e.g. contracts between businesses, they can only be excluded if it is fair and reasonable to do so.

Unsafe goods

Perhaps the most important protection afforded to consumers is from the dangers of unsafe goods. Such goods are undesirable because they could lead not only to economic loss but also to injury or loss of life. At common law, persons who are injured by unsafe products, provided that they themselves bought the goods, may sue the seller of the goods in contract, using also the conditions implied by the Sale of Goods Act 1979 that goods must be of satisfactory quality and reasonably fit for their purpose. In addition, the injured party, whether or not they themselves bought the goods, may sue the manufacturer for negligence in tort (in England, Wales and Northern Ireland) or delict (in Scotland).

The leading case on the manufacturer's liability is the Scottish House of Lords case of *Donoghue v. Stevenson* [1932] AC 562. In this case, a manufacturer supplied a bottle of ginger beer in an opaque bottle to a café in Paisley. The product had not been opened since it left the factory. Unknown to all parties, the bottle contained the remains of a decomposed snail. A customer ordered an ice cream drink containing the ginger beer for her friend. After drinking most of the ginger beer, the friend discovered the remains of a snail in the bottom of the bottle. The friend became ill, and successfully sued the manufacturer for negligence. The case established for the first time that manufacturers owed a duty of care to the end-user, even where they had no knowledge of who that person would be. It was an important fact in this case that the café staff had had no opportunity to examine the contents of the bottle: if the retailer has a chance to examine the goods before supplying them to the customer, he too may find himself liable for damages for negligence.

Consumer safety

Legislators have been faced with a delicate problem which concerns the fact that sometimes it is not that the goods are inherently unsafe but that they may be unsafe, or potentially unsafe, in use if proper instructions have not been provided to prevent their unsafe use. Consequently, there are two main threads to the control of the safety of goods. These ensure that goods are safe in themselves and that sufficient information is provided with goods to prevent their being unsafe in use.

There is currently one main statute concerned with consumer safety: the Consumer Protection Act 1987. This Act repealed and consolidated all previous legislation relating to consumer safety and, in addition, contains controls over misleading prices. Specific regulations which deal with the safety of particular goods or classes of goods passed under previous legislation continue to be in force.

Parts I and II of the Consumer Protection Act 1987 both deal with unsafe goods. Part I implements the EC directive on product liability, and makes manufacturers strictly liable in tort/delict for defective products 'if the safety of the product is not such as persons generally are entitled to expect'. A product is defined as 'any goods or electricity'. Land and buildings are not products, but materials which will be used in the construction of buildings (cement, bricks and electrical cables) are included in the definition of goods. Agricultural produce is not classed as a product in the UK, although it is in other parts of the EU, therefore there would be no liability on the part of a producer who supplied potatoes containing a toxin, but there would be a liability on a processor who used some of those potatoes to make canned soup.

Where damage is caused by a defective product, every person who falls into the following categories shall be liable for the damage:

- Manufacturers.
- Abstracters of products (such as miners who extract minerals).
- Processors of products. This category includes any person or organization responsible for altering the essential characteristics of a product, e.g. a company which processes food products by cooking and packaging them.
- Own-branders, e.g. most supermarket chains.
- Importers to the EU.

A retailer, or a person who supplies goods in any other way (e.g. by hiring or giving as a promotional gift) may also be liable to pay compensation if he is unable to identify the manufacturer, own-brander or importer to the person who suffered the damage.

A product is classed as defective under the Act if its safety is not what persons generally are entitled to expect. The expectations of the individual customer are not relevant. The standard applied is an objective one and it takes into account such factors as the design of the product, the purpose for which it was marketed and the use of any warnings or instructions. No liability would arise, therefore, if a brand of wood preservative had been marked and clearly labelled as being for outdoor use only and a customer used it indoors and was rendered unconscious by breathing the fumes.

The Act states that there will be liability if damage is caused by a defective product. The Act defines this damage as covering death, personal injury or any loss or damage to any property. The loss or damage must be to private property, so damage to a private car may give rise to a claim but damage to a company van will not. No claim can be made under that Act if the loss or damage to property is less than £275. The producer is not liable under the Consumer Protection Act for loss of, or damage to the product itself. Any claim for compensation for damage to the product itself must be made under the Sale of Goods Act 1979. If the damage to the product is caused by a defect of a component which was supplied with the product then a claim cannot be made under the Consumer Protection Act 1987, but if the damage was caused by a component which was fitted later, a claim for the damage to the main product can be made under this Act. Therefore if a computer fails because of a faulty memory chip which was part or the computer when it was supplied, the value of the computer cannot be included in a claim under the Consumer Protection Act, but if the memory chip is purchased and fitted later and causes damage to the computer a claim under this Act can be made for the damage to the computer but not for the chip itself.

For liability to arise under the statute, it is necessary for the person who has suffered the damage to prove that he did suffer damage *caused by* the defective product. The fact that the burden of proof remains upon the person who has suffered the damage has been criticized because one aim of the directive was to reduce that burden for injured parties.

Defences

There are some statutory defences to liability. It is a defence to prove that the defect in the product is caused by compliance with a statutory provision. Another defence is that the goods were never supplied. This defence applies only to goods which were intended solely for the producer's own use or to goods which have been stolen.

It is not necessary for a claimant to show that he bought the goods, but claims cannot be made where damage has been caused in circumstances where the supply was not in the course of a business or for profit. Therefore no claim could be made if a product donated to a charity raffle caused damage.

Liability is only for defects which existed at the time of supply. A manufacturer may claim that a product has become unsafe only after excessive use or that goods have been tampered with. A supermarket would not be liable if poison had been injected into bottles of tonic water.

Another defence is the development risks defence which can be used where the state of scientific and technical knowledge in an industry is such that there was no way of knowing that goods were unsafe at the time they were supplied.

The liability of the producer may be reduced if he can show that the person who has suffered the loss, damage or injury has himself been negligent. This is known as contributory negligence and has the effect of reducing any award of damages according the percentage of blame attributable to the victim. A person may be deemed to have been contributorily negligent if he ignores a warning on the label of a product and uses it for a purpose for which it was not supplied. The defence of *volenti non fit injuria* applies where a person has voluntarily purchased and used a product which is inherently dangerous such as tobacco.

Criminal law regulation with regard to unsafe goods

Part II of the Consumer Protection Act consists of criminal provisions relating to consumer safety. This part of the statute provides for criminal penalties and allows the Secretary of State for Trade and Industry to make safety regulations for consumer goods in order to ensure that such goods are safe and that any unsafe goods do not reach consumers. He can make regulations in design of goods, contents, construction requirements, testing, on warnings to be provided with goods (e.g. in relation to precautions to be taken when using garden weedkiller or rat poison). The Secretary of State has a duty to consult relevant organizations such as trade associations before issuing regulations.

Regulations have been issued in relation to many products, including foam-filled furniture, fabrics, toys, gas cookers, children's pushchairs, and cosmetics. A breach of safety regulations can constitute a criminal offence.

Some hypothetical case studies

One of the difficulties that faces a consumer who has suffered injury or loss as a result of a breach of contract or from unsafe goods is knowing which are the legal grounds on which to base an argument for compensation. The following hypothetical situations illustrate some of the ways in which the legal rules may be applied.

Case study 1

Mrs Brown purchased a new television set and video recorder on 10 January 1995. She found exactly what she wanted in the local branch of Dixie's Ltd after seeing an advertisement in the local paper which said 'Buy now. Nothing to pay until September'. Mrs Brown asked how much the payments would be and she was told that, as the cash price of the goods was £650 she could pay at a rate of £50 a month starting in September. Mrs Brown paid a deposit of £50 and signed an agreement form which was entitled Budget Account. In September she started paying £50 per month. She was extremely surprised to receive a statement in January to the effect that she still owed £570. On examining the Budget Account form she found, in extremely small print on the back of the form the words APR 20%.

Remedy

In a situation such as this, the first resort would be to the trading standards or weights and measures department of the local authority. Other customers may also have been misled by the information provided and a criminal prosecution could be instigated against the company under the Consumer Credit Act 1974 for failing to comply with the strict rules on the form and content of advertisements to ensure that they give adequate information. The advertisement which stated 'nothing to pay until September' without giving an indication of the interest which would be charged contravenes the rules. It is possible that a compensation order for the company to pay damages to Mrs Brown could result from a conviction in a criminal court.

Whether Mrs Brown would have a right to cancel the contract is doubtful. It would depend on her being able to show that there had been misrepresentation. She would have to show that there had been a misleading statement as to a fact which induced her to enter into the contract and that the resulting error was sufficiently material to render the contract void. In the absence of fraud in the form of a misleading statement as to a fact made either without any belief in its truth, or recklessly with disregard as to whether it was true or false, she would be unable to claim damages. An additional consequence of these circumstances is that Dixie's Ltd could lose its licence to offer credit, although the probability of such a revocation is low.

Case study 2

John and Norma decided to book a family holiday on the Costa del Sol. They went to their local travel agent and consulted various brochures. They decided to book a two-week package holiday to the Eldorado hotel. The hotel was described in the Cheapo Charters brochure as having luxury rooms with en suite facilities and its own leisure club with a health club, golf course, tennis courts and heated swimming pool. The price of the holiday was shown in the brochure as £1500 which was stated to be '£100 per person less than the same holiday in Espana Travel's brochure'. The travel agent told John that there was a special offer price of £1200 if the holiday was booked by the end of January. John and Norma booked the holiday but when they arrived they found that they had been booked into the annexe of the hotel where the rooms had no en suite facilities. Residents in the annexe were not permitted to use any of the leisure club facilities unless they paid an additional fee of £150 per person. Their friends who had booked with Espana Travel at a price of £1600 had a room in the main hotel and full use of all the facilities without extra charge. Moreover their other friend who had booked with Cheapo Charters had been charged at the same rate as John and Norma even though he booked in February.

Remedy

A contract to provide a holiday is a contract for the provision of services, and section 14 of the Trade Descriptions Act 1968 will apply. The terms in the brochure advertising the holiday could be deemed to be misleading as regards the provision of services, accommodation and facilities. The brochure was incorrect with regard to the provision of en suite facilities. The offer of the holiday at the special price of £1200 if booked in January may not amount to a misleading indication of price, as the intention of the company at the time when John and Norma booked their holiday may well have been to discontinue the offer price at the end of January. Nevertheless, section 21 of the Consumer Protection Act 1987 states that an indication of price is misleading if it leads to the belief that the price covers matters in respect of which an additional charge is in fact made. The comparison with the price at which the holiday was offered by the other travel company may also be misleading. Cheapo Charters could be prosecuted for breaches of the Trade Descriptions Act and the Consumer Protection Act. The company could use as a defence that the misleading information was caused by reasonable reliance on another person and that they had exercised reasonable diligence to ensure that their brochure was accurate. A conviction may result in a compensation order to John and Norma. They could claim damages on the basis that they had entered into the contract on the basis of a misrepresentation that they would need to prove that there had been fraud. An alternative would be to sue for breach of contract as they had not received all of the services and facilities for which they had contracted.

Case study 3

Angus was enjoying a quiet drink in his local hostelry when he was approached by Fergus who explained that he was a travelling salesman selling watches and jewellery. He asked Angus if he would be interested in buying an Italian designer watch. He showed Angus an advertisement in *Vogue* magazine for watches of the same make and with the same serial number advertised for sale at a price of £475. He said that he was willing to sell a watch to Angus for £75 as he had been allocated a few additional watches in error by his company. Angus bought a watch in the belief that it was a great bargain. In the course of using the watch Angus discovered that it did not keep accurate time, and after one week it was forty minutes slow. The watch was not an Italian designer watch but had been mass produced in Japan; Angus had it valued by a professional valuer as being worth £25. The company selling the watches placed the advertisement in *Vogue* but has never actually sold any watches at the advertised prices. All of the company's salesmen had been instructed to use the sales technique employed by Fergus.

Remedy

There is no misleading indication as to the price of the goods in this case as it was made clear to Angus that the price was £75. The fact that the watch is poor value for the price paid does not give a right to any legal redress. Advertising the watches for sale at £475 does not amount to a contravention of law. It may be possible to argue that a false trade description has been applied to the goods in contravention of the Trade Descriptions Act 1968 but the term 'Italian designer watch' may in fact be a correct description: the watch, although of poor quality, may have been designed by an Italian. If, however, the term is taken to mean an Italian watch, there has been a contravention of the Trade Descriptions Act as the goods have been sold with a false trade description with regards to the country of manufacture. A criminal prosecution may be successful on such a interpretation. Angus should have a civil remedy under the Sale of Goods Act on the grounds that the watch is not of satisfactory quality as it is not reasonably fit for the normal purpose of keeping acceptably accurate time. As long as he acts within a reasonable time he should be entitled to return the watch and claim a refund of the price, assuming, of course, that he can trace the seller.

This case study typifies the difficulties which are faced in legislating to protect consumers. The law cannot protect consumers from making bad bargains, and regulation by criminal law will only be effective for controlling those activities specified in the legislation. The remedies under civil law are effective but they are contingent upon the consumer being knowledgeable about his rights and being in a position to assert those rights either through negotiation with the seller or by litigation.

Appendices

APPENDIX A Contribution to sales (C/S) ratio

Minimum volume increases required for price decreases

Price decrease %	0.10	0.15	0.20	0.25	0.30	0.35	0.40
1	11.11	7.14	5.26	4.17	3.45	2.94	2.56
2	25.00	15.38	11.11	8.70	7.14	6.06	5.26
3	42.90	25.00	17.65	13.60	11.11	9.38	8.11
4	66.67	36.36	25.00	19.05	15.38	12.90	11.11
5	100.00	50.00	33.33	25.00	20.00	16.67	14.29
6	150.00	66.67	42.86	31.58	25.00	20.69	17.65
7	233.33	87.50	53.85	38.89	30.43	25.00	21.21
8	400.00	114.29	66.67	47.06	36.36	29.63	25.00
9	900.00	150.00	81.82	56.25	42.86	34.62	29.03
10	∞	200.00	100.00	66.67	50.00	40.00	33.33
15		∞	300.00	150.00	100.00	75.00	60.00
20			∞	400.00	200.00	133.33	100.00
25				∞	500.00	250.00	166.67
30					∞	600.00	300.00
35						∞	700.00
40							∞

Maximum volume decreases permissible for price increases

Price increase %	0.10	0.15	0.20	0.25	0.30	0.35	0.40
1	9.09	6.25	4.76	3.85	3.23	2.77	2.44
2	16.67	11.76	9.09	7.41	6.25	5.41	4.76
3	23.08	16.67	13.04	10.71	9.09	7.89	6.98
4	28.57	21.05	16.67	13.79	11.76	10.26	9.09
5	33.33	25.00	20.00	16.67	14.29	12.50	11.11
6	37.50	28.57	23.08	19.35	16.67	14.63	13.04
7	41.18	31.82	25.93	21.88	18.92	16.67	14.89
8	44.44	34.78	28.57	24.24	21.05	18.60	16.67
9	47.34	37.50	31.03	26.47	23.08	20.45	18.37
10	50.00	40.00	33.33	28.57	25.00	22.22	20.00
15	60.00	50.00	42.86	37.50	33.33	30.00	27.27
20	66.67	57.14	50.00	44.44	40.00	36.36	33.33
25	71.43	62.50	55.56	50.00	45.45	41.67	38.46
30	75.00	66.67	60.00	54.55	50.00	46.15	42.86
35			63.64	58.33	53.85	50.00	46.67
40			66.67	61.54	57.14	53.33	50.00
45				64.29	60.00	56.25	52.94
50				66.67	62.50	58.82	55.56

0.45	0.50	0.55	0.60	0.65	0.70	0.75	0.80
2.27	2.04	1.85	1.69	1.56	1.45	1.35	1.27
4.65	4.17	3.77	3.45	3.17	2.94	2.74	2.56
7.14	6.38	5.77	5.26	4.84	4.48	4.17	3.90
9.76	8.70	7.84	7.14	6.56	6.06	5.63	5.26
12.50	11.11	10.00	9.09	8.33	7.69	7.14	6.67
15.38	13.64	12.24	11.11	10.17	9.38	8.70	8.11
18.42	16.28	14.58	13.21	12.07	11.11	10.29	9.59
21.62	19.05	17.02	15.38	14.04	12.90	11.94	11.11
25.00	21.95	19.57	17.65	16.07	14.75	13.64	12.68
28.57	25.00	22.22	20.00	18.18	16.67	15.38	12.50
50.00	42.86	37.50	33.33	30.00	27.27	25.00	23.08
80.00	66.67	57.14	50.00	44.44	40.00	36.36	33.33
125.00	100.00	83.33	71.43	62.50	55.56	50.00	45.45
200.00	150.00	120.00	100.00	85.71	75.00	66.67	60.00
350.00	233.33	175.00	140.00	116.67	100.00	87.50	77.77
800.00	400.00	266.67	200.00	160.00	133.33	114.29	100.00

0.45	0.50	0.55	0.60	0.65	0.70	0.75	0.80
2.17	1.96	1.79	1.64	1.52	1.41	1.32	1.23
4.26	3.85	3.51	3.23	2.99	2.78	2.60	2.44
6.25	5.66	5.17	4.76	4.41	4.11	3.85	3.61
8.16	7.41	6.78	6.25	5.80	5.41	5.06	4.76
10.00	9.09	8.33	7.69	7.14	6.67	6.25	5.88
11.76	10.71	9.84	9.09	8.45	7.89	7.41	6.98
13.46	12.28	11.29	10.45	9.72	9.09	8.54	8.05
15.09	13.79	12.70	11.76	10.96	10.26	9.64	9.09
16.67	15.25	14.06	13.04	12.16	11.39	10.71	10.11
18.18	16.67	15.38	14.29	13.33	12.50	11.76	11.11
25.00	23.08	21.43	20.00	18.75	17.65	16.67	15.79
30.77	28.57	26.67	25.00	23.53	22.22	21.05	20.00
35.71	33.33	31.25	29.41	27.78	26.32	25.00	23.81
40.00	37.50	35.29	33.33	31.58	30.00	28.57	27.27
43.75	41.18	38.89	36.84	35.00	33.33	31.82	30.43
47.06	44.44	42.11	40.00	38.10	36.36	34.78	33.33
50.00	47.37	45.00	42.86	40.91	39.13	37.50	36.00
52.63	50.00	47.62	45.45	43.48	41.67	40.00	38.46

APPENDIX B Present value of £1 due at the end of *n* periods

Period *n*	1%	2%	3%	4%	5%	6%	7%	8%	9%	10%	11%	Interest 12%
1	0.9901	0.9804	0.9709	0.9615	0.9524	0.9434	0.9346	0.9259	0.9174	0.9091	0.9009	0.8929
2	0.9803	0.9612	0.9426	0.9246	0.9070	0.8900	0.8734	0.8573	0.8417	0.8264	0.8116	0.7972
3	0.9706	0.9423	0.9151	0.8890	0.8638	0.8396	0.8163	0.7938	0.7722	0.7513	0.7312	0.7118
4	0.9610	0.9238	0.8885	0.8548	0.8227	0.7921	0.7629	0.7350	0.7084	0.6830	0.6587	0.6355
5	0.9515	0.9057	0.8626	0.8219	0.7835	0.7473	0.7130	0.6806	0.6499	0.6209	0.5935	0.5674
6	0.9420	0.8880	0.8375	0.7903	0.7462	0.7050	0.6663	0.6302	0.5963	0.5645	0.5346	0.5066
7	0.9327	0.8706	0.8131	0.7599	0.7107	0.6651	0.6227	0.5835	0.5470	0.5132	0.4817	0.4523
8	0.9235	0.8535	0.7894	0.7307	0.6768	0.6274	0.5820	0.5403	0.5019	0.4665	0.4339	0.4039
9	0.9143	0.8368	0.7664	0.7026	0.6446	0.5919	0.5439	0.5002	0.4604	0.4241	0.3909	0.3606
10	0.9053	0.8203	0.7441	0.6756	0.6139	0.5584	0.5083	0.4632	0.4224	0.3855	0.3522	0.3220
11	0.8963	0.8043	0.7224	0.6496	0.5847	0.5268	0.4751	0.4289	0.3875	0.3505	0.3173	0.2875
12	0.8874	0.7885	0.7014	0.6246	0.5568	0.4970	0.4440	0.3971	0.3555	0.3186	0.2858	0.2567
13	0.8787	0.7730	0.6810	0.6006	0.5303	0.4688	0.4150	0.3677	0.3262	0.2897	0.2575	0.2292
14	0.8700	0.7579	0.6611	0.5775	0.5051	0.4423	0.3878	0.3405	0.2992	0.2633	0.2320	0.2046
15	0.8613	0.7430	0.6419	0.5553	0.4810	0.4173	0.3624	0.3152	0.2745	0.2394	0.2090	0.1827
16	0.8528	0.7284	0.6232	0.5339	0.4581	0.3936	0.3387	0.2919	0.2519	0.2176	0.1883	0.1631
17	0.8444	0.7142	0.6050	0.5134	0.4363	0.3714	0.3166	0.2703	0.2311	0.1978	0.1696	0.1456
18	0.8360	0.7002	0.5874	0.4936	0.4155	0.3503	0.2959	0.2502	0.2120	0.1799	0.1528	0.1300
19	0.8277	0.6864	0.5703	0.4746	0.3957	0.3305	0.2765	0.2317	0.1945	0.1635	0.1377	0.1161
20	0.8195	0.6730	0.5537	0.4564	0.3769	0.3118	0.2584	0.2145	0.1784	0.1486	0.1240	0.1037
21	0.8114	0.6598	0.5375	0.4388	0.3589	0.2942	0.2415	0.1987	0.1637	0.1351	0.1117	0.0926
22	0.8034	0.6468	0.5219	0.4220	0.3418	0.2775	0.2257	0.1839	0.1502	0.1228	0.1007	0.0826
23	0.7954	0.6342	0.5067	0.4057	0.3256	0.2618	0.2109	0.1703	0.1378	0.1117	0.0907	0.0738
24	0.7876	0.6217	0.4919	0.3901	0.3101	0.2470	0.1971	0.1577	0.1264	0.1015	0.0817	0.0659
25	0.7798	0.6095	0.4776	0.3751	0.2953	0.2330	0.1842	0.1460	0.1160	0.0923	0.0736	0.0588
26	0.7720	0.5976	0.4637	0.3607	0.2812	0.2198	0.1722	0.1352	0.1064	0.0839	0.0663	0.0525
27	0.7644	0.5859	0.4502	0.3468	0.2678	0.2074	0.1609	0.1252	0.0976	0.0763	0.0597	0.0469
28	0.7568	0.5744	0.4371	0.3335	0.2551	0.1956	0.1504	0.1159	0.0895	0.0693	0.0538	0.0419
29	0.7493	0.5631	0.4243	0.3207	0.2429	0.1846	0.1406	0.1073	0.0822	0.0630	0.0485	0.0374
30	0.7419	0.5521	0.4120	0.3083	0.2314	0.1741	0.1314	0.0994	0.0754	0.0573	0.0437	0.0334
35	0.7059	0.5000	0.3554	0.2534	0.1813	0.1301	0.0937	0.0676	0.0490	0.0356	0.0259	0.0189
40	0.6717	0.4529	0.3066	0.2083	0.1420	0.0972	0.0668	0.0460	0.0318	0.0221	0.0154	0.0107
45	0.6391	0.4102	0.2644	0.1712	0.1113	0.0727	0.0476	0.0313	0.0207	0.0137	0.0091	0.0061
50	0.6080	0.3715	0.2281	0.1407	0.0872	0.0543	0.0339	0.0213	0.0134	0.0085	0.0054	0.0035

Using the above table to verify the figure of £172 on page 208, the figure 0.3186 is read from 12 periods at an interest rate of 10%. Simply multiply £542 by 0.3186 to obtain £172.

Rate 13%	14%	15%	16%	17%	18%	19%	20%	25%	30%	35%	40%	50%
0.8850	0.8772	0.8696	0.8621	0.8547	0.8475	0.8403	0.8333	0.8000	0.7692	0.7407	0.7143	0.6667
0.7831	0.7695	0.7561	0.7432	0.7305	0.7182	0.7062	0.6944	0.6400	0.5917	0.5487	0.5102	0.4444
0.6931	0.6750	0.6575	0.6407	0.6244	0.6086	0.5934	0.5787	0.5120	0.4552	0.4064	0.3644	0.2963
0.6133	0.5921	0.5718	0.5523	0.5337	0.5158	0.4987	0.4823	0.4096	0.3501	0.3011	0.2603	0.1975
0.5428	0.5194	0.4972	0.4761	0.4561	0.4371	0.4190	0.4019	0.3277	0.2693	0.2230	0.1859	0.1317
0.4803	0.4556	0.4323	0.4104	0.3898	0.3704	0.3521	0.3349	0.2621	0.2072	0.1652	0.1328	0.0878
0.4251	0.3996	0.3759	0.3538	0.3332	0.3139	0.2959	0.2791	0.2097	0.1594	0.1224	0.0949	0.0585
0.3762	0.3506	0.3269	0.3050	0.2848	0.2660	0.2487	0.2326	0.1678	0.1226	0.0906	0.0678	0.0390
0.3329	0.3075	0.2843	0.2630	0.2434	0.2255	0.2090	0.1938	0.1342	0.0943	0.0671	0.0484	0.0260
0.2946	0.2697	0.2472	0.2267	0.2080	0.1911	0.1756	0.1615	0.1074	0.0725	0.0497	0.0346	0.0173
0.2607	0.2366	0.2149	0.1954	0.1778	0.1619	0.1476	0.1346	0.0859	0.0558	0.0368	0.0247	0.0116
0.2307	0.2076	0.1869	0.1685	0.1520	0.1372	0.1240	0.1122	0.0687	0.0429	0.0273	0.0176	0.0077
0.2042	0.1821	0.1625	0.1452	0.1299	0.1163	0.1042	0.0935	0.0550	0.0330	0.0202	0.0126	0.0051
0.1807	0.1597	0.1413	0.1252	0.1110	0.0985	0.0876	0.0779	0.0440	0.0254	0.0150	0.0090	0.0034
0.1599	0.1401	0.1229	0.1079	0.0949	0.0835	0.0736	0.0649	0.0352	0.0195	0.0111	0.0064	0.0023
0.1415	0.1229	0.1069	0.0930	0.0811	0.0708	0.0618	0.0541	0.0281	0.0150	0.0082	0.0046	0.0015
0.1252	0.1078	0.0929	0.0802	0.0693	0.0600	0.0520	0.0451	0.0225	0.0116	0.0061	0.0033	0.0010
0.1108	0.0946	0.0808	0.0691	0.0592	0.0508	0.0437	0.0376	0.0180	0.0089	0.0045	0.0023	0.0007
0.0981	0.0829	0.0703	0.0596	0.0506	0.0431	0.0367	0.0313	0.0144	0.0068	0.0033	0.0017	0.0005
0.0868	0.0728	0.0611	0.0514	0.0443	0.0365	0.0308	0.0261	0.0115	0.0053	0.0025	0.0012	0.0003
0.0768	0.0638	0.0531	0.0443	0.0370	0.0309	0.0259	0.0217	0.0092	0.0040	0.0018	0.0009	0.0002
0.0680	0.0560	0.0462	0.0382	0.0316	0.0262	0.0218	0.0181	0.0074	0.0031	0.0014	0.0006	0.0001
0.0601	0.0491	0.0402	0.0329	0.0270	0.0222	0.0183	0.0151	0.0059	0.0024	0.0010	0.0004	0.0001
0.0532	0.0431	0.0349	0.0284	0.0231	0.0188	0.0154	0.0126	0.0047	0.0018	0.0007	0.0003	0.0001
0.0471	0.0378	0.0304	0.0245	0.0197	0.0160	0.0129	0.0105	0.0038	0.0014	0.0006	0.0002	0.0000
0.0417	0.0331	0.0264	0.0211	0.0169	0.0135	0.0109	0.0087	0.0030	0.0011	0.0004	0.0002	0.0000
0.0369	0.0291	0.0230	0.0182	0.0144	0.0115	0.0091	0.0073	0.0024	0.0008	0.0003	0.0001	0.0000
0.0326	0.0255	0.0200	0.0157	0.0123	0.0097	0.0077	0.0061	0.0019	0.0006	0.0002	0.0001	0.0000
0.0289	0.0224	0.0174	0.0135	0.0105	0.0082	0.0064	0.0051	0.0015	0.0005	0.0002	0.0001	0.0000
0.0256	0.0196	0.0151	0.0116	0.0090	0.0070	0.0054	0.0042	0.0012	0.0004	0.0001	0.0000	0.0000
0.0139	0.0102	0.0075	0.0055	0.0041	0.0030	0.0023	0.0017	0.0004	0.0001	0.0000	0.0000	0.0000
0.0075	0.0053	0.0037	0.0026	0.0019	0.0013	0.0010	0.0007	0.0001	0.0000	0.0000	0.0000	0.0000
0.0041	0.0027	0.0019	0.0013	0.0009	0.0006	0.0004	0.0003	0.0000	0.0000	0.0000	0.0000	0.0000
0.0022	0.0014	0.0009	0.0006	0.0004	0.0003	0.0002	0.0001	0.0000	0.0000	0.0000	0.0000	0.0000

APPENDIX C Standard normal distribution

The entries in this table are the probabilities that a random variable having the standard normal distribution assumes a value between 0 and Z; the probability is represented by the shaded area under the curve. Areas for negative values of Z are obtained by symmetry.

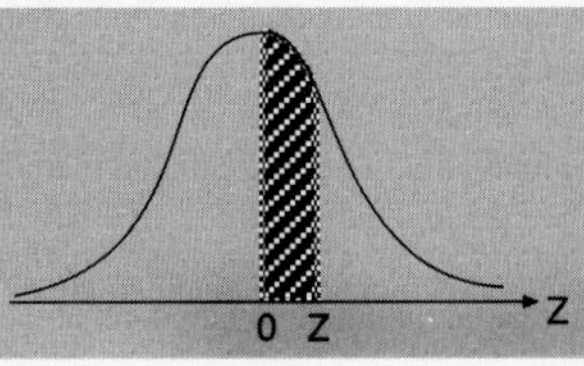

	Second decimal place in Z									
Z	0.00	0.01	0.02	0.03	0.04	0.05	0.06	0.07	0.08	0.09
0.0	0.0000	0.0040	0.0080	0.0120	0.0160	0.0199	0.0239	0.0279	0.0319	0.0359
0.1	0.0398	0.0438	0.0478	0.0517	0.0557	0.0596	0.0636	0.0675	0.0714	0.0753
0.2	0.0793	0.0832	0.0871	0.0910	0.0948	0.0987	0.1026	0.1064	0.1103	0.1141
0.3	0.1179	0.1217	0.1255	0.1293	0.1331	0.1368	0.1406	0.1443	0.1480	0.1517
0.4	0.1554	0.1591	0.1628	0.1664	0.1700	0.1736	0.1772	0.1808	0.1844	0.1879
0.5	0.1915	0.1950	0.1985	0.2019	0.2054	0.2088	0.2123	0.2157	0.2190	0.2224
0.6	0.2257	0.2291	0.2324	0.2357	0.2389	0.2422	0.2454	0.2486	0.2517	0.2549
0.7	0.2580	0.2611	0.2642	0.2673	0.2704	0.2734	0.2764	0.2794	0.2823	0.2852
0.8	0.2881	0.2910	0.2939	0.2967	0.2995	0.3023	0.3051	0.3078	0.3106	0.3133
0.9	0.3159	0.3186	0.3212	0.3238	0.3264	0.3289	0.3315	0.3340	0.3365	0.3389
1.0	0.3413	0.3438	0.3461	0.3485	0.3508	0.3531	0.3554	0.3577	0.3599	0.3621
1.1	0.3643	0.3665	0.3686	0.3708	0.3729	0.3749	0.3770	0.3790	0.3810	0.3830
1.2	0.3849	0.3869	0.3888	0.3907	0.3925	0.3944	0.3962	0.3980	0.3997	0.4015
1.3	0.4032	0.4049	0.4066	0.4082	0.4099	0.4115	0.4131	0.4147	0.4162	0.4177
1.4	0.4192	0.4207	0.4222	0.4236	0.4251	0.4265	0.4279	0.4292	0.4306	0.4319
1.5	0.4332	0.4345	0.4357	0.4370	0.4382	0.4394	0.4406	0.4418	0.4429	0.4441
1.6	0.4452	0.4463	0.4474	0.4484	0.4495	0.4505	0.4515	0.4525	0.4535	0.4545
1.7	0.4554	0.4564	0.4573	0.4582	0.4591	0.4599	0.4608	0.4616	0.4625	0.4633
1.8	0.4641	0.4649	0.4656	0.4664	0.4671	0.4678	0.4686	0.4693	0.4699	0.4706
1.9	0.4713	0.4719	0.4726	0.4732	0.4738	0.4744	0.4750	0.4756	0.4761	0.4767
2.0	0.4772	0.4778	0.4783	0.4788	0.4793	0.4796	0.4803	0.4808	0.4812	0.4817
2.1	0.4821	0.4826	0.4830	0.4834	0.4838	0.4842	0.4846	0.4850	0.4854	0.4857
2.2	0.4861	0.4864	0.4868	0.4871	0.4875	0.4878	0.4881	0.4884	0.4887	0.4890
2.3	0.4893	0.4896	0.4898	0.4901	0.4904	0.4906	0.4909	0.4911	0.4913	0.4916
2.4	0.4918	0.4920	0.4922	0.4925	0.4927	0.4929	0.4931	0.4932	0.4934	0.4936
2.5	0.4938	0.4940	0.4941	0.4943	0.4945	0.4946	0.4948	0.4949	0.4951	0.4952
2.6	0.4953	0.4955	0.4956	0.4957	0.4959	0.4960	0.4961	0.4962	0.4963	0.4964
2.7	0.4965	0.4966	0.4967	0.4968	0.4969	0.4970	0.4971	0.4972	0.4973	0.4974
2.8	0.4974	0.4975	0.4976	0.4977	0.4977	0.4978	0.4979	0.4979	0.4980	0.4981
2.9	0.4981	0.4982	0.4982	0.4983	0.4984	0.4984	0.4985	0.4985	0.4986	0.4986
3.0	0.4987	0.4987	0.4987	0.4988	0.4988	0.4989	0.4989	0.4989	0.4990	0.4990
3.1	0.4990	0.4991	0.4991	0.4991	0.4992	0.4992	0.4992	0.4992	0.4993	0.4993
3.2	0.4993	0.4993	0.4994	0.4994	0.4994	0.4994	0.4994	0.4995	0.4995	0.4995
3.3	0.4995	0.4995	0.4995	0.4996	0.4996	0.4996	0.4996	0.4996	0.4996	0.4997
3.4	0.4997	0.4997	0.4997	0.4997	0.4997	0.4997	0.4997	0.4997	0.4997	0.4998
3.5	0.4998									
4.0	0.49997									
4.5	0.499997									
5.0	0.4999997									

Index